Catholic Women
of Congo-Brazzaville

Catholic Women

of Congo-Brazzaville

Mothers and Sisters in Troubled Times

Phyllis M. Martin

Indiana University Press

Bloomington & Indianapolis

This book is a publication of

Indiana University Press
601 North Morton Street
Bloomington, IN 47404-3797 USA

http://iupress.indiana.edu

Telephone orders   800-842-6796
Fax orders   812-855-7931
Orders by e-mail   iuporder@indiana.edu

The paper used in this publication meets
the minimum requirements of American
National Standard for Information
Sciences—Permanence of Paper for Printed
Library Materials, ANSI Z39.48-1984.

Manufactured in the United States of America

Library of Congress
Cataloging-in-Publication Data

Martin, Phyllis.
  Catholic women of Congo-Brazzaville : mothers
and sisters in troubled times / Phyllis M. Martin.
    p. cm.
  Includes bibliographical references (p.   ) and
index.
  ISBN 978-0-253-35281-1 (cloth : alk. paper)
  —ISBN 978-0-253-22055-4 (pbk. : alk. paper)
  1. Catholic women—Congo (Brazzaville)—
History. 2. Catholic Church—Congo (Brazzaville)
—History. 3. Congo (Brazzaville)—Church
history. I. Title.
  BX1682.C59M37 2009
  282'.6724082—dc22
                                2008035753

1 2 3 4 5 14 13 12 11 10 09

For:
The Fraternity Women of Congo-Brazzaville
And the Sisters of Saint Joseph of Cluny

Contents

Preface and Acknowledgments

Just over twenty years ago, I found myself in Brazzaville, the capital of the Republic of Congo, looking for a place to stay while I carried out research on the social history of the city. Plans for accommodation had fallen through, my closest Congolese friends were away studying in the United States, and housing available for foreigners seemed in short supply or would take a bit of time to find. I was carrying a letter of introduction to the sister of a friend, and she suggested we go and consult Abbé Louis Badila, a well-known and highly respected figure in the Congolese church. Thus, through his intervention came my introduction to the Sisters of Saint Joseph of Cluny (Soeurs de Saint-Joseph de Cluny), who maintained a small guest house on their convent property in central Brazzaville, a site they had occupied since the arrival of sisters from their missionary congregation in the Malebo Pool region in 1892.

It was my introduction to an international group of religious women under Congolese leadership, primarily a teaching order but one whose orientation had been forced to change following the nationalization of church schools by a radical socialist government in 1965. When our paths crossed, the sisters were mostly engaged in social work, nursing, catechist teaching, and the mentoring of girls and women in the city's parishes. In the midst of their busy lives, the sisters were extraordinarily cordial to a stray American researcher who had taken up residence in their guest house, and when I was the only person there, they sometimes invited me to join them for Sunday lunch or to share in special celebrations such as All Saints' Day and Christmas Eve. As we became better acquainted and they learned of my interest in the history of the city, they occasionally took me along on their visits to different neighborhoods. They also patiently answered my many questions about their congregation, its history, and its work in Congo.

Through living at the sisters' guest house, my acquaintance with Catholic women widened when late one afternoon groups of women arrived and disappeared into the extensive gardens. Their singing and my curiosity drew me to investigate. I was warmly welcomed and invited to join in their meeting, where they were preparing for an anniversary celebration the following Sunday at the cathedral—to which I was invited. The church was packed to overflowing with some two thousand women, and others outside gathered around the doors and windows. They were members of women's associations referred to as *fraternités* (there is no female equivalent in French) or *mabundu* (Kilari/Kikongo, "communities," "family meeting"; sing. *dibundu*). Over the months that followed I attended other meetings and celebrations and came to know a great deal more about the origins, history, and purpose of the fraternity movement. These chance encounters were the starting point for this book.

No doubt, research projects may have unexpected beginnings even if they take a long time to come to fruition and must await the completion of other projects. A book so long in the making has involved a great many friends, colleagues, and family members. I cannot attempt to name them all, but they should know that my gratitude is no less strong because it is offered here collectively. To Jennifer, Philip, Ron, and Portia go a very special thanks.

I would like to acknowledge some of the individuals and agencies that have facilitated the completion of this work. Jean-Michel Delobeau, Scholastique Dianzinga, Abraham Ndingo-Mbo, and Jean-Pierre Ngole, members of the faculty at Université Marien Ngouabi, welcomed me, gave me practical advice on my arrival in Brazzaville, and have continued their support over the years. I am especially grateful to Professor Ndinga-Mbo, chair of the history department when I first met him and dean of the College of Letters and Human Sciences when he authorized this project. I must also acknowledge with gratitude the friendship and collegiality of Professor Dianzinga, whom I met on my first visit to Brazzaville when she was an instructor in the history department and with whom I have kept in touch ever since. At our early meetings we discussed the vacuum in the writing of Congolese women's history and decided to do something about it from our different perspectives. She later completed her doctoral dissertation in France and returned to be chair of the history department.

I am indebted for considerable financial support to the National Endowment for the Humanities, the Pew Charitable Trusts, the Overseas Ministries Study Center (New Haven), and Indiana University, which granted me research funds as Ruth N. Halls Professor of History.

For help with the bibliography and other research matters, my thanks go to J. Dubin, Jennifer Patton, Elizabeth Perrill, and Kate Schroeder. Comments from colleagues on the book proposal and all or part of the manuscript have been helpful and challenging, exactly what a writer faced with a mass of data demanding interpretation needs. In this connection, my thanks go especially to John Clark, Wendy Gamber, Jean Hay, Wyatt MacGaffey, Marissa Moorman, and the reader for Indiana University Press. The editorial skills of Dee Mortensen of Indiana University Press are becoming legendary due to the praises heaped on her by the many authors with whom she has worked on Africa-related books. I add my thanks to the chorus and also to her assistant, Laura MacLeod. I would also like to thank Scott Taylor of Indiana University Graphic Services, who created the maps.

To present and former missionaries and archivists in Congo, France, and Italy, I owe a large debt of gratitude for hospitality, willingness to engage in informative conversations, and access to archives. The Spiritan fathers in Brazzaville, Pointe-Noire, and Chevilly-Larue have shared their rich knowledge and long history in Congo with me. I particularly want to thank two archivists, the late Père Ghislaine de Banville and his successor, Père Gérard Vieira, for their help in locating sources and making them available to me. Also, my thanks go to Père Robert Gevaudan for assistance in Pointe-Noire and Père Guy Pannier and Père Pierre Wauters for sharing their knowledge of the Loango region.

I count myself particularly fortunate for the welcome I have received from missionary women in Europe and Africa, many of whom served for years in Congo before they retired, while others are still actively involved in the field. They have made arrangements for me to stay at their communities in Brazzaville, Pointe-Noire, Landana (Cabinda), Paris, Lyons, Ribeauvillé, and Rome and willingly shared their experience and knowledge. As the notes show, this work would not have been possible without the access I was granted to the archives of the four missionary congregations most active in Congo-Brazzaville during the period of this study. Each revealed the perspectives of the different congregations and the individual and collective experiences of missionary sisters: the Soeurs de Saint-Joseph de Cluny; the Soeurs Missionnaires du Saint-Esprit (Missionary Sisters of the Holy Spirit, or Spiritan sisters); the Franciscaines Missionnaires de Marie (Franciscan Missionaries of Mary); and the Soeurs de la Divine Providence de Ribeauvillé (Sisters of the Divine Providence of Ribeauvillé). Among the archivists, I owe most thanks to the late Sister Yves Le Goff (SSJC) who spent many long hours discussing the history and charism of her congregation and facilitating my understanding.

As the notes to this work demonstrate, Congolese fraternity women have been most generous with their time. I cannot thank them all by name but must acknowledge in particular for their assistance Firmine Malékat, president of the Brazzaville fraternities when I first met her in 1986, and Léontine Bissangou, president of the Pointe-Noire fraternities when I met her in 2000. It is to the fraternity women and the Sisters of Saint Joseph of Cluny that I owe the most, for without them the project would never have attracted my attention nor generated so much interest and enjoyment.

Abbreviations

BSRC	*Bulletin de la Société des Recherches Congolaises*
CAR	Central African Republic
CCAH	*Cahiers Congolais d'Anthropologie et d'Histoire*
CEA	*Cahiers d'Etudes Africaines*
CFCO	Chemin de Fer Congo-Océan
CJAS	*Canadian Journal of African Studies*
CREDIC	Centre de Recherches et d'Echanges sur la Diffusion et l'Inculturation du Christianisme, Lyons
DRC	Democratic Republic of Congo (formerly Zaire)
EHESS	Ècole des Hautes Études en Sciences Sociales, Paris
IJAHS	*International Journal of African Historical Studies*
IRD	Institut de Recherche pour le Développement (formerly ORSTOM)
JAH	*Journal of African History*
JMNR	Jeunesse du Mouvement National de la Révolution
JOAEF	*Journal Officiel de l'Afrique Equatoriale Française*
JSAS	*Journal of Southern African Studies*
MC	*Les missions catholiques*
ORSTOM	Organization de la Recherche Scientifique et Technique Outre-Mer, Paris
PF	Propagation de la Foi
URFC	Union Révolutionnaire des Femmes du Congo

Catholic Women
of Congo-Brazzaville

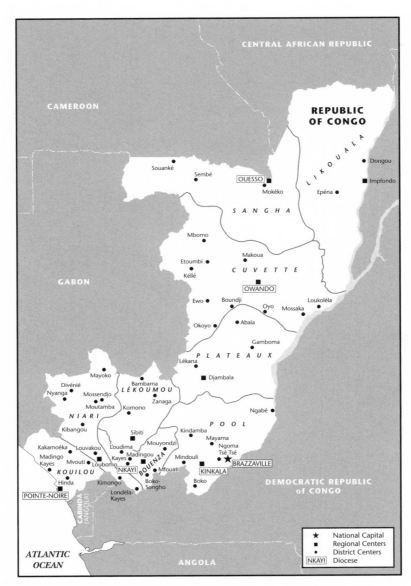

CENTRAL AFRICAN REPUBLIC

CAMEROON

REPUBLIC OF CONGO

Souanké
Sembé
OUESSO
Mokéko
Epéna
Dongou
Impfondo

L I K O U A L A

S A N G H A

Mbomo

Makoua
Etoumbi
Kéllé

GABON

C U V E T T E
OWANDO

Ewo
Boundji
Oyo
Mossaka
Loukoléla
Okoyo
Abala

Gamboma

P L A T E A U X
Lékana

Mayoko
Divénié
Djambala
Nyanga
Bambama
Mossendjo
L É K O U M O U
Moutamba
Zanaga
Komono

N I A R I
Kibangou

Ngabé

Sibiti
Kindamba
P O O L
Kakamoéka
Louvakou
Loudima
Mouyondzi
Mayama
Madingo
Madingou
Ngoma
Kayes
Mvouti
Kayes
Mindouli
Tsé Tsé
Loubomo
B O U E N Z A
Mfouati
BRAZZAVILLE
NKAYI
KINKALA

K O U I L O U
Hinda
Kimongo
Boko-
Songho
Boko

Londéla-
Kayes

POINTE-NOIRE

DEMOCRATIC REPUBLIC
of CONGO

CABINDA
(ANGOLA)

ATLANTIC
OCEAN

ANGOLA

★ National Capital
■ Regional Centers
● District Centers
NKAYI Diocese

Map 1. Republic of Congo, c. 1995.

Introduction

On 25 May 1998, tens of thousands of women walked through the streets of Brazzaville in a demonstration for peace. Sponsored by the church women's fraternities, the march started in various parishes throughout the city and converged at the old cathedral square, where the women were addressed by the archbishop of Brazzaville, three bishops, and a papal representative. Wearing their fraternity uniforms, the women walked mostly in silence, signaling the gravity of the circumstances. In Congo-Brazzaville, the previous ten years had seen economic disruption, social immiseration, unstable governments, and two civil wars that brought horrendous suffering, especially in the capital and the lower Congo. The event marked the opening of an international conference, *Colloque des Mamans Chrétiennes Catholiques de l'Afrique Centrale* (Conference of Christian Catholic Mothers of Central Africa) on the subject "God, Women, and Peace in Africa: Are These Words in Vain?" Some two thousand delegates attended, the great majority representing the fraternities of Congo-Brazzaville; two hundred from the *Mouvement des Mamans Catholiques de la République Démocratique du Congo* (Movement of Catholic Mothers in the Democratic Republic of Congo); and several from Equatorial Guinea and Cameroon. Among the conference's final resolutions was the establishment of a peace organization, *Mouvement pour la Paix des Mamans Chrétiennes Catholiques de l'Afrique Centrale* (MOPAX), focusing initially on the two Congos but having the goal of drawing in women from other Central African countries who had likewise suffered through violent years.[1] If the eight-day conference was a time of work and accomplishment, the meeting of the delegates with President Denis Sassou-Nguesso at the end of the proceedings was less than upbeat. There was the public recognition of being received by the nation's president, but his reaction to the conference findings was less than encouraging. He listened courteously as the various resolutions were read aloud, but his speech made it clear that in his view—shared by men in general, he claimed—Catholic mothers should be engaged in prayer, care of children, and the upkeep of neighborhoods, not involved in the political sphere to the detriment of their domestic responsibilities. He warned his listeners of the long struggle ahead if they persisted in trespassing in what were essentially male domains. Men would resist any such moves, although he "understood" the basis for women's actions and "encouraged" them in their efforts.[2]

It may seem odd to start a work of history with the end of the story, but the episode touches on the three interrelated themes that run through this book. The first considers the social and spiritual attractions of the Catholic church for Congolese women, how and why they came to the church after very hesitant beginnings more than a century ago, and how and why they have come to greatly outnumber men in the postcolonial church. At a mass celebrating the twenty-fifth anniversary of the women's fraternities in 1989, Hervé Itoua, bishop of Ouesso, acknowledged women's importance at the heart of parish life: "After a hundred years of evangelism, three-quarters of those in our Congolese church are women. They are more numerous and often the ones who give life to the church, spiritually as much as materially."[3] Taking a long historical view, this study looks at women's initiatives in creating for themselves a home and a basis for action in an institution so known for its male-dominated power structures.

A further strand in the story concerns women whose identity was closely attuned to their position as biological and social mothers. Clearly, individuals have multiple identities that emerge at different points in time, but the evidence from Congo suggests that the practice and priorities of mothering were often paramount for women and recognizable to others as a means of asserting social place. For women, marriage was a threshold to motherhood, not an end in itself, for marriage was unlikely to last without the children who were guarantors of social worth and long-term security. When women acted together as "sisters," they often did so out of mutual understanding of maternal demands and obligations. Yet history has also revealed motherhood as an unstable and malleable construct. If it can be a multi-faceted base from which to promote interests, it can also expose vulnerability and incite tensions. For the women who engaged in the 1998 peace march, motherhood was an expandable category, a basis for moral outrage and a platform for action, but for the president and other men like him motherhood was primarily about domesticity at home or in the service of the state. Thus, motherhood becomes contested and political at moments in time.

Thirdly, this study of church women goes beyond a single mission station or the missionary-African encounter. As the preface indicates, my starting point was an unexpected meeting with local church women and missionary sisters, and the first research proposal considered the relationships between these groups of women. Yet that scope seemed too narrow as the work progressed, and the study has arrived at an account of women's experience in a region of Africa little-known except as a byword for the neglect and violence of the colonial power—a conclusion that is not in dispute in this book, where women become a means of exploring the issues more closely. Nor did the situation improve much in postcolonial times, for as the study moves into the last decades of the twentieth century, women were living in a country split apart by economic and political instability instigated and exploited by ambitious leaders and their followers in conditions described by sociologist Patrice Yengo as marked by a "recourse to endemic violence."[4]

As the three themes in the narrative interplay, the major theme is joined: how and why women were gradually drawn to the Catholic church, where they formed social and spiritual communities through which to mediate their individual and collective priorities, often as mothers, in troubled times. The religious sisters, at first European and then African, who acted as "mothers" to children and mentors to women are an essential part of the story. That most hierarchical of institutions, the Catholic church, has, in fact, a long history of lay associations that have engaged in some degree of autonomous activity, female religious congregations that have followed their own charism under the weighty umbrella of the church, and adherents who have developed a popular Catholicism meaningful to them.

Mothers and Sisters

Throughout equatorial Africa, "wealth in people" has been the essential prerequisite for power, status, and economic worth. Control of individuals and the ability to command their dependence and loyalty has been a basic strategy of those called "big men" in the anthropological literature. "Things" such as iron and copper with high use and exchange value could be converted into wives, kin, and dependents; tribute might be paid through the transfer of people; and punishments might mean being condemned to servitude for others. Jan Vansina in his landmark study of equatorial African history has noted the persistence of goods as a means of transferring and adding "wealth in people" for, after centuries of trading, "wealth in goods was still converted into followers."[5] Likewise, reviewing the evidence for equatorial Africa, Jane Guyer found that the value οⅰ wealth in people was "a guiding and persistent principle of African social life, even when shifts in shape and content over time are clearly envisaged."[6] In this system, the value of women as workers, wives, daughters, sisters, and biological and social mothers has also been evident in the historical record: in the polygyny practiced by men of means, the two-to-one ratio of males to females sold into slavery in the trans-Atlantic trade, and the exchange of women to seal the negotiations of powerful men.[7] On the other hand, women could gain land, status, and security through successful alliances with men who had "people power."

Jane Guyer and S. M. Elo Bolinga have taken our understanding further through pointing out how accumulating people was also investing in critical knowledge: "social mobilization was in part based on the mobilization of different bodies of knowledge" and "leadership was the capacity to bring them together effectively."[8] Jan Vansina also highlighted the range of knowledge individuals and communities could put to use within changing environments, adding to their "cognitive inventory" far beyond what was needed for utilitarian purposes.[9] Gender complementarities were "part of compositional processes," for women and men had varying skills and social roles and a woman could enhance or undermine her husband's worth and bolster or endanger the health of the whole community. Women's "biological fecundity and agricultural fertility" were critical, as was their responsibility to "grow" others as they practiced and passed on their practical and esoteric knowledge to juniors, especially their biological and social "daughters."[10] The arrival of missionaries with their funds of new technical and spiritual knowledge has to be placed in this context. How might women be affected and what might be the responses to such opportunities, threats, and challenges in the long and short term? If women were critical for population growth and wealth, they were also essential repositories of knowledge.

Wendy James has used the term "matrifocality" to describe "the cluster of ideas surrounding the centrality of motherhood in a kinship system," and "a range of practices and institutions which seem to outsiders to indicate the strong pragmatic importance of mothers in family organization." Her findings led her to conclude that in a range of African societies there exists a "common cluster of ideas about the wider importance of women's child-bearing capacity, their creative role in bringing up the new generation, and even a recurring notion about the natural line of birth being handed on through women."[11] For those who organized their relations primarily along matrilineal lines, such as the Kongo-related peoples of the lower Congo, she found, as other writers have done, a particular emphasis on mothering in moral discourse and social life, writing that "the role of motherhood in particular is typically respected and honoured, and represented as a central social category from which other relationships take their bearing."[12] In lower Congo, for example, "mother" (*ngúdi*, Kikongo; colloquially, *mama, maama, mâ*) is used for a category of female kin including the biological mother, maternal aunts, and maternal aunts by affinity. In a society where age was highly valued and seniors accorded prerogatives, *mama* is also used more broadly by juniors as a sign of respect when addressing woman of their mother's age and older. Mothers enjoyed a particular status and prestige through giving children their social identity as members of a clan and lineage.[13] Simon Bockie in his autobiographical account of Kongo life tells in a section on "family relationships" that individuals are first defined by blood line and then in the distinction between senior and junior status. This, he says, is "most evident in the relationship between mother and child, the most important of all kinship categories." In Kongo culture, "mother" includes not only the biological mother but a "whole stratum of the family," as shown in the terms for maternal family members, where not only are the mother and aunts called *mama*, but others are positioned through their relationship to the mother (*ngúdi*), so that, for example, the maternal uncle is *ngúdi a nkàzi* ("the brother of the mother"), and the affinal maternal aunt as *nkênto ngúdi a nkàzi* ("the wife of the mother's brother").[14]

Matrilineal practices were deeply rooted in the history of the lower Congo.[15] Once studied as a contained social category, matriliny is again receiving attention not only from anthropologists but also from historians, who are turning attention to matriliny in a historical context and inserting gender into research and analysis. Pauline Peters, in an important review of approaches to the "matrilineal puzzle" (the purported tension between "father love" and "uncle rights," now called in question), discusses how older interpretations of matriliny as "bounded social structure" created "self-imposed puzzles" for social theorists.[16] Rather it is more useful and more within lived experience to consider matriliny as "clusters of characteristics" such as descent, marriage, and residence, and to understand that elements of "patriliny" were also present within predominantly matrilineal societies.[17] Indeed, the few historical studies that deal with Kongo family relationships before the twentieth century have shown flexibility in structural relationships.[18] This study of women within the Catholic church does not focus specifically on the "remaking of the family" nor can it attempt to historicize fully aspects of matriliny, for that would involve a different kind of project. Yet the persistence of women's ties to matrilineal kin in the face of missionary efforts to create a "stable," nuclear family on a European model indicates the endurance of deeply rooted social structures. Contrary to the view of nineteenth-century

Of course
men
want
Patriarchy

Europeans that matriliny was a backward stage on the road to a more progressive patriliny, aspects of matriliny such as inheritance and obligations to matrilineal kin did not necessarily fade away in Christian households but rather were integrated with practices taken over from Europe.

An article by Cherryl Walker that reviews the literature on motherhood in twentieth-century South Africa is especially useful for its conceptualization of the problem as practice, discourse, and social identity.[19] As the chapters that follow demonstrate, all were aspects of the construction and production of women's social roles in Congo-Brazzaville as women and men, Europeans and Africans, missionaries and white colonists, lived in a society under radical transformation. Fully apparent in the European historical record, discourse and practice relating to women were bounded by imperial anxieties and the gendered contours of contemporary French society. To this was added a missionary agenda, especially influential in Congo, where the colonial government did little about education or social programs until after the Second World War.[20]

this
was left
to
missionaries.

Yet, the historical record shows not only attempts at hegemony by outsiders but ordinary men and women on the ground who responded individually and collectively out of their own specific needs and experience.[21] Indeed, the literature on "domesticity" has revealed divergent outcomes as ideas and practices from Europe were appropriated and translated into local cultures selectively.[22] To cite an example from colonial Congo, the popularity of sewing in church schools and adult classes (up till the present) is worth examination given the skepticism of such activities by some foreign writers.[23] Nancy Hunt has cautioned against disregarding women's own understandings of change in their lives. Concerning choices that women might make in the colonial situation, she asks, "How can we so easily dismiss women's experience of positive change as false consciousness?"[24] Regarding motherhood, Cherryl Walker has advocated moving it from an explanatory category to "women's own understanding." Writing of the tendency to reduce motherhood to a patriarchal institution, she advocates more attention to "the multiple and complex meanings mothers themselves attach to their experience."[25]

This work about Catholic women is not only about motherhood, however, even if it was the basis for action and salient discourse at certain points in time. Women were drawn to the church by a range of priorities and aspirations, and together as "sisters" they engaged in a search for not only community but also spiritual communion through devotional meetings, Catholic action groups, and, in the later twentieth century, tightly organized associations. These may be located among the array of urban associations common in African cities, popular "networks of collaboration" for political, economic, social, and cultural purposes, but they were also deeply spiritual in their inspiration.[26] Beyond these immediate reasons, they can also be understood through the common practice of women with their deep roots in the past. In conversation with a woman from upper Congo, I commented on the popularity of women's associations, and it must be said that she looked at me with some surprise at such an obvious statement. She replied: "In our society the ideal of mutual help and assistance among women is fundamental," and went on to talk of the "sisters" in her home village, where at certain seasons farmers might have to walk twenty-five kilometers to their fields and stay several nights with their fellow workers and the children they may take along. "When something needs to get done, women join together," she added.[27] This may cover a range of "women's work"—not only farming but the birth and education of children, preparations for daughters' initiation, mortuary and mourning practices, fertility cults, dances and songs for special occasions, and household chores. Church associations grew out of such customary corporate action. As they evolved, they were similar to the *manyanos* in the Protestant churches of southern Africa, for the fraternities were likewise based on the synergy of religious devotion and social support.[28] Yet, whereas the South African church women's groups were started by missionaries in the early twentieth century to foster community and provide mutual support for mothers in a time of economic and social upheaval, the associations in Congo were the result of spontaneous actions by women in a postcolonial church in response to the street fighting and the persecution of priests. As they drew in popular support from urban neighborhoods, they slowly evolved into mutual aid associations to meet members' needs, and women's concerns came to pervade devotional, social, and political space.

Missionary Priests, Religious Sisters, and African Catholics

When in 1883, Pères Charles Duparquet and Hippolyte Carrie of the *Congrégation du Saint-Esprit* (Holy Ghost Fathers or Spiritans) arrived on the coast north of the Congo river to investigate possibilities of establishing a mission as a base for further expansion in the interior, they were not the first churchmen to visit the royal capital of Loango, a kingdom in severe decline by the time of the Spiritans' arrival.[29] While extensive missionary proselytizing in the Kongo kingdom from the late fifteenth century had resulted in the rooting of an indigenous Christianity south of the river (present-day Angola), two weak missions by Capuchin and French missionaries had no comparable impact in the region that was to become French Congo.[30] In 1663, Bernardino di Ungaro, working in the Kongo kingdom at the time, had become known to the Maloango (the ruler), who sent two sons for Christian instruction and baptism, and after the two young men returned home, he invited the missionary to visit his court. Ungaro, with the consent of his superior, traveled north, where he instructed and baptized the king and his wife and married them in a Christian ceremony. According to the account of Merolla, a fellow Capuchin writing some twenty years later, upward of 12,000 peoples were baptized before Ungaro fell sick and died a year after his arrival. The ruler sent to Luanda for replacements, but then he himself was overthrown by a rival hostile to Christianity, and a short time after, when another ruler requested missionaries, none were available. Belgian Franciscan missionaries attempted to revive the proselytization effort in 1673–74 but likewise were forced to leave through illness and lack of resources.[31]

About a hundred years later, French priests and lay brothers, again attempting to establish the church in the Loango region, found it "buried in idolatry" with no trace of previous proselytization efforts. Their mission continued sporadically over ten years (1766–76) and reported some good progress, but its members, too, fell victim to tropical disease and exhaustion and were forced to retreat definitively with their most lasting accomplishment a dictionary and grammar of the local variant of Kikongo.[32] When the Holy Ghost Fathers arrived over a century later, they searched for traces of tombs or inscriptions but found nothing, only one elderly man who said he had heard of these white men but his memories were "vague."[33]

The Spiritan mission was a different matter since by the late nineteenth century the means as well as the motives for European Christians to support a powerful overseas evangelical movement were much greater. In France, the most important money-raising organization in the hands of the laity was the Oeuvre de la Propagation de la Foi (Society for the Propagation of the Faith) founded in 1822. Through its publications, the *Annales de la Propagation de la Foi,* which reached a printing of 300,000 (of these, 178,000 in French) by the beginning of the twentieth century, and the popular, illustrated *Les Missions Catholiques,* the organization kept its supporters from poor parishioners to wealthy aristocrats well-informed on the achievements of missionaries in what were portrayed as exotic and "uncivilized" conditions. Another important organization, L'Oeuvre de la Sainte-Enfance, was founded in 1843 by diocesan clergy with the purpose of raising funds to support children and build schools and workshops. Missionaries in Congo drew heavily on both these funds.[34]

In Central Africa, the missionaries were also acting in concert—if not in camaraderie—with a wave of white men blazing their way into the interior, funded by home governments bent on keeping the region out of competitors' hands and empowered by capitalist enterprise and a technical knowledge (guns, drugs, communications) that were a considerable improvement over those available previously. Moving along the caravan trail from the Loango coast to Brazzaville, strategically situated at the commercial crossroads of Malebo Pool, they established mission posts and made the Pool the staging point for their progress northward along the Congo and its tributaries and to Ubangi-Shari (see map 2 in chapter 2). Over the next few decades, the Vatican divided the region administratively into two vicariates, that based at Loango in lower Congo and the other, in upper Congo, administered from Brazzaville.[35] The missionaries need some introduction here, for as Frederick Cooper and Ann Stoler have pointed out, the colonial situation evolved at a particular moment in time, and those doing the colonizing were part of the story.[36]

The congregations of the Holy Ghost Fathers and the Sisters of Saint Joseph of Cluny came from particular backgrounds within Catholic belief and practice. The Spiritans were guided by the ideas and teachings of Père François Libermann, who in 1848 had been appointed superior-general of the Holy Ghost Fathers, a new missionary congregation formed from the amalgamation of his own Congregation of the Holy Heart of Mary and the older Society of the Holy Ghost. The Spiritans thus fused the main goals of the two congregations: the first with its emphasis on conversion as a means of bringing about the "regeneration" and "moralization" of Africans caught in the net of slavery, and the second, the training of seminarians for the colonial clergy, for which it received government subsidies. Libermann's ideas were contained in his voluminous correspondence and writings. His basic belief was in the universal nature of Christianity; yet while he saw blacks as no less intelligent than Europeans, they were at a less advanced cultural state—in part due to the ravages of slavery—thus making it necessary for Europeans to play a strong role in the guidance of young Christians for a long time to come. He also warned of the dangers of removing an elite from their culture, but rather urged that the good in local culture must be retained where it was not in direct opposition to Christian teaching (read "superstition") and morality (especially the evils of polygyny). In his early writings, Libermann emphasized the education of an indigenous clergy to work under the oversight of missionaries, but in the long run teaching became the main Spiritan activity and their schools the principal means of evangelism. As for the missionaries themselves, Libermann wrote that they should adapt their lives as much as possible to local conditions while living within the bounds of Christian morality and they should strive to maintain good relations with civil authorities while making it clear to Africans that they were not government representatives.[37] Yet, as the following chapters will show, while superiors in Europe might develop policies on paper, realities on the ground greatly affected their implementation: the equatorial environment that caused high mortality rates; the personalities and predilections of individual missionaries; the anti-clerical bias of many administrators; and converts' propensity to embrace Christianity selectively in the light of beliefs and practices within their own cultures. My study emphasizes not only the local context in which proselytization took place but the intersection of the global, national, and local, something of a new departure for this region of Africa, where studies of the Catholic church have hardly gone beyond missionary accounts, which tend to be introspective, even if informative, and the older ones smacking of hagiography.[38]

While missionary priests might make inroads into the conversion of young men, their efforts with girls and women were more circumscribed for, to state the obvious, they had no female helpmates readily at hand as did Swedish Evangelical missionaries, their Protestant rivals in lower Congo. Early reports from priests generally included a section under the rubric "Work with Girls" that contained frequent and anxious reassurances to superiors that Christian morality and decorum were being preserved in relationships with females but that the help of Christian women was essential if the work was to advance.[39] The priests had, in fact, two options in searching out assistance.

One was to look to a first generation of Christian women as educators and "mothers" of girls and women who came to missions without sisters to prepare for baptism and marriage. As map 2 indicates, before 1940 there were many such missions in Congo, posing a problem for priests trying to establish Christian families but providing openings for local women to figure importantly in the "black advance" of the church while augmenting their place in new Christian communities.[40] Although there is now quite a large literature on the role of African women in the expansion of the Christian church, there has been an assumption, at least in Congo, that proselytization among women at Catholic missions would be difficult without the presence of missionary sisters. In work on early evangelism in the old Kongo kingdom, two historians have attributed early failures in attracting women to a lack of female missionaries "who alone could have reached Congolese women" and to "the absence of religious women who are rightly judged indispensable to the Christian formation of young black girls."[41] Spiritan sources from French Congo show, however, that while the post of catechist was mostly in male hands, the socialization of girls and young women in Christian communities was very much the responsibility of lay women, who also became models for the younger generation. It was a pattern of female involvement in socialization and evangelism that continued in a different guise over decades as women brought other women into the church.

A second strategy for the Catholic fathers was to request assistance from missionary sisters. In this respect, the Spiritans had many options, for the nineteenth century had seen what historians have called the "feminization" of the French church, brought about in part by a dramatic rise in the number of women graduating from novitiates. Between 1800 and 1880 nearly four hundred successful new female religious orders were established and some 200,000 women entered the religious life. In 1878 some 75 percent of religious orders and secular clergy were women, most of them *bonnes soeurs* ("good sisters") working as teachers, nurses, and social workers, who lived in scattered communities organized under mother-superiors responsible to the superior-general (or mother-general) at the mother house.[42] In spite of the anti-clerical biases of many French administrators and general public, the *bonnes soeurs* were mostly seen as useful, for they constituted a morally irreproachable and low-cost workforce at a time when services by the state were quite insufficient.[43]

Among the new, non-cloistered female congregations were many devoted entirely or in part to missionary work overseas. Thus, three years after they had established themselves at Loango, the Holy Ghost Fathers called on the Sisters of Saint Joseph of Cluny to send women to that mission, and then in 1892 they requested sisters for the work at Brazzaville.[44] The collaboration was already well established, for Libermann had identified in Anne-Marie Javouhey, the founder of the Saint Joseph's congregation, a kindred spirit who shared his belief in the universality of Christianity, a concern for the poor, and potential liberation from slavery not just through laws and humanitarian action but through the regenerative and moralizing power of Christianity. In 1844, he wrote to her, "your work is almost the same as ours," and appointed a priest from his congregation as the spiritual director of Mère Javouhey's congregation in Paris.[45]

Anne-Marie Javouhey's life and work is also worth some attention for her practical instructions, spiritual orientations, and strong presence as an ancestral figure that shaped the charism passed on to sisters in novitiates.[46] Indeed, she was the founder of one of the earliest missionary orders in France. Daughter of a prosperous Burgundian peasant, she entered the Order of the Sisters of Charity, one of the few non-contemplative female orders at the time. Following a vision of children of all colors appearing around her in her cell and hearing the voice of Saint Teresa of Avila telling her that this was her life's work, she established her own congregation in 1805. Her strong convictions were early displayed when she sought and was granted an audience with Napoleon, who authorized her congregation, and then received the blessing of the pope during his visit to France. In so doing, she was safeguarding the autonomy of her congregations against interventions from diocesan authority figures. Education was her main concern, and her novel pedagogy using a "mutual method" of teaching with more advanced students acting as monitors and instructors for younger ones brought her to the attention of the French government, who asked her to open schools and hospitals in the colonies. In 1817, she sent the first sisters to Bourbon (Réunion) in the Indian Ocean and then to Senegal in 1819. She herself worked in Senegal for two years, setting up schools for children who followed a strict daily schedule of farming, laundry, reading, writing, and catechism training. She was a woman of her times, and like Libermann, saw girls as future "mothers of families" who must continue to be rooted in their own culture as much as possible. She traveled to Gambia and Sierra Leone, where missions were later established, but her largest project and the one for which she became most famous was in French Guiana. There the colonial government gave her over five hundred freed slaves and a large tract of land, which she proceeded to establish as a quasi-autonomous territory, alienating not only the governor and male settlers but her ecclesiastical superiors. At her death in 1851, Anne-Marie Javouhey's congregation comprised 1,200 sisters scattered in 140 communities in five world regions.

Like the Spiritan fathers, the sisters also had constraints coming from the local situation. Letters from equatorial Africa show their vulnerability: subject to the sickness of equatorial zones; often isolated; under the patriarchal authority of the male clergy on whom they depended for subsidies, spiritual direction, and holy communion; working in a divided colonial society, and then in a postcolonial state that nationalized schools. Thus, this study looks at the educational and evangelical work of the European and Congolese sisters, but it also considers what their situation as Catholic women can tell us about a colonial society that was gendered and racist. While studies of Catholic missionary women have come some way since Elizabeth Isichei's summation in 1994 that "hundreds of missionary nuns worked in Africa but, as yet, this history has been little studied and their records little used," there is still much less work on Catholic missions than on Protestant ones, and the records of missionary sisters are as yet little exploited, especially for French-speaking Africa, where so many worked.[47] These letters and reports can reveal the sisters as they explored "latent avenues" for action, their position in "gendered missions," and the gradual integration of Congolese sisters into the order.[48]

The "feminization" of the nineteenth-century French church describes not only an increase in female congregations but an upsurge of popular piety among lay women who embraced a devotional life tied to the adoration of the Virgin Mary and a cult of saints, supernatural beings who could act as protectors and intercessors with the divine.[49] A series of Marian apparitions started in 1830 with the appearance of the Virgin Mary to the young novice Catherine Labouré, who received instructions for the striking of a "miraculous medal," a practice that, once authorized by church authorities, led to the mass production of these objects of piety for distribution and sale to common people, alongside other devotional artifacts such as rosaries and scapulars. Other apparitions followed throughout France, including the appearance of the Virgin to young shepherds at the village of La Salette (1846) and to the peasant girl Bernadette Soubirous at Lourdes (1858). Devotion to Mary and to saints was also marked in feast days, processions, and pilgrimages, accentuating the festive and communal elements in religious practice. Thus, it was not only the more formal elements of Catholicism such as confession, Mass, and attendance at Easter Communion that late-nineteenth- and early-twentieth-century missionaries carried with them to Congo but the popular practices especially known in rural France, which many Spiritan fathers and Sisters of Saint Joseph of Cluny called home. As will emerge in the chapters that follow, the popular Catholicism carried to equatorial Africa helped draw adherents who made sense of it within their own frame of reference. As Dorothy Hodgson has importantly pointed out in her study of women who joined the church in Maasailand, the religious response to Catholicism needs to be considered as much as the social advantages that have often been emphasized in studies of African church women.[50]

This book follows the history of African Catholic women into postcolonial times, situating their experience in a local and national context and taking account of the new directions of the church worldwide. As a recent study has suggested, the process of decolonization as it was worked out within and by the missionary church has received less attention from historians than has the church's part in the imposition of colonial rule.[51] In Congo, the later twentieth century saw the transfer of power to an African church hierarchy, the openings provided by the Second Vatican Council (1962–65), and an accelerated movement of women into the church so that it became predominantly a "church of women." While this phenomenon paralleled a similar trend in the church in Maasailand, the circumstances and the initiatives were quite different, thus making clear the importance of the local in what may seem largely explainable by global forces.[52] In the end, the agency of ordinary people—those who were engaged in the "complex process of selective ingestion of partial elements of Christian discourse and practice" and who found a place within the church that was socially advantageous and spiritually meaningful—is powerful.[53]

Locating the Study

This book deals primarily with the region of lower Congo that lies between Brazzaville and the Atlantic Ocean, although reference is also made to upper Congo (see maps 1 and 2). Difficulties of communication and subsistence in upper Congo, where the physical environment is dominated by marshy forests or sandy soils, mean that region is sparsely populated, and the great majority of the country's population live in the capital or lower Congo. According to a 1974 census, 70 percent were concentrated on 30 percent of the land in the southern part of the country, and the great majority of these were Kongo-related peoples.[54] It was also in the south that Catholic priests established most of their missions.[55] Before political independence in 1960 as the Republic of Congo (commonly Congo-Brazzaville), lower and upper Congo were part of Moyen-Congo, one of the four colonies of French Equatorial Africa (AEF)—along with Gabon, Ubangi-Shari (today Central African Republic), and Chad—with Brazzaville as its capital.[56] Brazzaville figures large in this study for the presence of an influential Catholic elite during the colonial period and as the center of the archdiocese in postcolonial times. Furthermore, any history that deals with the second half of the twentieth century can hardly avoid including the capital, for after the Second World War, Congo experienced a very high rate of urbanization, a trend that has continued until the present. By 1985, it was one of the most highly urbanized countries in Africa, with 61 percent of the total population living in towns and a third living in the capital, so that a special issue of *Politique africaine* (1988) took as its title: "Congo, a Suburb of Brazzaville."[57]

Three large forces impinged on the lives of the women who are at the center of this study. One relates to light population densities in the equatorial regions, a situation that has been variously attributed at different points in time to the environment, the Atlantic slave trade, and the ravages of a colonial rule that decimated villagers through conquest, forced labor exactions, and the spread of disease such as sleeping sickness. Anxieties relating to thin populations in France spilled over into colonial perceptions of Congo, where the situation did not improve in either reality or the imagination before the 1930s.[58] The value of women as farmers and bearers of children and the competition to control them by Europeans, chiefs, and other "big men" can well be understood in this context. Secondly, as summarized in an account of modern Africa, French Equatorial Africa was "a region first miserably exploited and then miserably neglected."[59] Compared to France's other colonies, Central Africa ranked at the bottom of imperial priorities; once the area was conquered and kept out of the hands of

European rivals, it was handed over to concessionary companies, who operated an "economy of pillage" for some thirty years.[60] It was not until after the Second World War that schools and infrastructure received a greater share of France's overseas investments. A third problem women had to face, since it affected their family life and their ability to raise children, was the rapid urbanization of the later twentieth century, which caused severe social and economic dislocation. Women's "coming together" in associations was a process too multi-dimensional to be explained simply in this context, but, as will be seen, it was part of their search for solutions.[61]

Historical research on African women is much less developed in France and Congo than in the anglophone world and some other African countries. In a special issue of the journal *Clio* on African women (1997), Catherine Coquery-Vidrovitch noted that the history of African women was "a subject almost un-recognized in French historiography," and that research was "very recent."[62] The editor of a book that grew out of a 2002 conference on colonialism, decoloniza-tion, postcolonialism, and gender also concluded that "if these themes are well-researched in the anglophone world, they are marginalized and isolated in the francophone world," although this volume as well as a recent work on gender in African history suggests that neglect is giving way to important new research.[63] Within Congo, a notable exception to lack of research on women's history has been the work of Scholastique Dianzinga, who in 1998 completed a French doc-toral dissertation on "Congolese Women from the Beginning of Colonization to 1960."[64] This general history of women during the colonial period has particular strengths in its discussion of the changing marriage code, women's economic activities, and the social ambitions of elite women in the late colonial period. To some extent, the study complements my own work, but my research also takes a quite different tack in considering a specific group of women and taking up issues such as motherhood, social identity, and women's church activities, and taking the discussion into postcolonial times.

For the Congolese church, the publications of Spiritan missionaries have already been noted. Work on syncretic cults and prophet-led churches has been more voluminous, while the publications by Swedish Protestant missionaries are useful as points of comparison with Catholic accounts.[65] The violence of recent times has seen an upsurge of publications mostly by political scientists and sociologists, who have analyzed the dramatic events of the 1990s and the mobilization of young men and militias around powerful individuals. The reli-gious dimensions of the conflict have been expressed in cults surrounding the political actors and an explosion of Pentecostalist and charismatic movements; yet here, too, gender seldom emerges as an issue.[66]

This book spans the "long" twentieth century from the arrival of the Holy Ghost Fathers and the Sisters of Saint Joseph of Cluny until the 1990s. It makes use of reports and correspondence from missionaries in the field to their superiors in Congo and Europe. Access to the archives of four female congregations has been critical in understanding the relationships of missionary sisters with girls and women and highlighting the structures African and European religious women had to navigate in the church and colonial world. "Reading between the lines," especially for the early period, is necessary in this kind of history, where the written documents privilege the missionary voice, and writers of women's history have to acknowledge the limitations of the sources. Government archives in France and Congo have also added some significant details. Other sources such as material objects, photographs, songs, and proverbs can sometimes be employed to give an immediacy to the past. Oral accounts have been invaluable in conveying women's own life experiences and opinions. These have been gathered as circumstances have allowed over the twenty years since my first meeting with fraternity women and European and Congolese sisters. Semi-structured interviews were carried out in 1986, 1989, and 2000 in Congo. While political insecurities made impossible a planned research trip in the late 1990s, some interviews with Congolese women in France proved very useful. On the whole, the lapse of time has been beneficial, for it has allowed the salient features of the project to emerge. As important as the interviews have been the hundreds of conversations that are not reported in the notes of this work: with Congolese laity, clergy, and sisters; with the small number of European Catholic missionaries still working in Congo today and retired missionaries in Europe; and with men and women outside the church. My attendance at many events with religious meanings has also been an essential part of my learning: small devotional gatherings, church services, burials, fraternity meetings, and anniversary celebrations. There have also been occasions attended by thousands such as Christmas Mass at the Bacongo parish church of Saint-Pierre Claver and *Toussaint* (All Saints' Day), when crowds exit the capital for cemeteries to visit the ancestors and tend their graves.

This book fuses a chronological and a thematic approach. The first four chapters deal with the period before 1940; the last two and the epilogue bring the story to the end of the twentieth century. The early chapters move between different centers of proselytization that become case studies for the ebb and flow of women into the church and their circumstances: first at Loango on the coast, then Linzolo in the Pool region, and then Brazzaville. The fourth chapter looks in greater depth at the experience of missionary nuns as sisters and mothers, their instruction and mentoring of girls and women, and the first African women to become sisters. Chapter 5 takes up the narrative after the Second World War and considers the growth of a popular Catholicism facilitated by the decrees of the Second Vatican Council and, paradoxically, under the Marxist-Leninist government. Chapter 6 considers the fraternities, a spontaneous popular movement established by church women themselves. The epilogue tells of the traumatic 1990s, when the country collapsed in civil war following failed attempts at democratization, and women organizing around a motherhood contested by political men.

The interweaving of women's experience as mothers and sisters, their movement into the church, and the evolving history of the region together provide alternative perspectives for a national history that has largely been constructed around the rise and fall of governments and the personalities and strategies of political and military leaders, while the history of common folk has remained much less known.

1. Mothers at Risk

Christianity arrived in the lower Congo in troubled times. Those living along the Loango coast and in its hinterland experienced the full impact of a colonial occupation that was violent and deeply disruptive. For many, daily life was full of risks, and it is within this context that the attraction—or lack thereof—of the arrival of Catholic missionaries needs to be addressed. Overall, the records suggest that although some came to the missions as "a place to dwell secure," they were in the great majority young men and boys.[1] The absence of young women of marriageable age and opposition of families to sending girls for Christian training are a constant refrain in the early reports of the Holy Ghost Fathers and the Sisters of Saint Joseph of Cluny who established communities at Loango in 1883 and 1886. Since Monseigneur Carrie, vicar apostolic of lower Congo, advocated the training of boys and girls and the establishment of Christian families as the "indispensable," "solid," and "enduring" base for the advance of the Congolese church, the problem of recruiting girls and young women threatened to undermine the evangelical project before it got off the ground.[2] This situation certainly bears investigation not only for an understanding of Catholic beginnings in Congo-Brazzaville but because it seems to differ from much of the experience of early Christians elsewhere in Africa, summed up by Adrian Hastings, the prominent historian of the African church, that "it is noticeable that the first converts were often women" and that this was the case "again and again in a mission history."[3]

One explanation would point to the importance of "people power" in equatorial Africa and the resistance of men who needed to control the human resources that women and girls represented. The missionary priests generally put this in the context of "polygamous old men." Certainly, the importance of women's labor and reproductive powers is not in dispute here, especially in view of the demographic crisis that existed in the early years of colonial occupation in a region already thinly populated.[4] Jan Vansina has estimated that by 1920 equatorial Africa had lost half of its population to the ravages of colonial conquest, with lower Congo one of the hardest hit areas.[5] Particularly destructive was the passage of large French expeditions that forced their way along the 580-kilometer trail from Loango to Brazzaville en route to Ubangi-Shari and Chad in the north. Chiefs competed with each other for tolls from passing caravans, and the requisitioning of food and supplies by Europeans and their militias could turn violent, with women seized as hostages, resisters shot as "rebels" and "bandits," and whole families fleeing into the bush to avoid the predations. Fights broke out between porters and guards and those living along the trail as they vied to maximize profits. Reports by colonial agents from the coast through the Mayombe to the Niari valley and to Brazzaville tell of pillaging, retaliations, and chaos (see map 2).[6] Writing of his experiences while attempting to force open a path for the Marchand expedition, Colonel Baratier, one of the few Europeans to address the reality of the colonial conquest, wrote of the "illusion that is called peaceful penetration . . . to refuse to admit the bloodshed behind the ideal is a beautiful but, unfortunately, unrealizable dream."[7]

Adding to the disruption throughout the lower Congo was the spread of disease. A series of droughts and famines induced by the exactions of expeditionary forces weakened villagers and made them susceptible to sickness. Smallpox, carried on ships from Luanda and São Tomé, affected coastal populations in the mid-1880s and again in the 1890s and spread along the caravan routes. Greater labor mobility took workers to new health ecologies. Most devastatingly, sleeping sickness, first reported at the end of the nineteenth century, brought high mortality rates.[8] Whole communities were wiped out, and those that lived struggled to produce the wherewithal to survive. At the Bouanza mission above the caravan route through the Niari valley, three-quarters of the population in the surrounding countryside died or left, and the mission was forced to close and relocate at Kimbenza in 1907.[9] Reports from the southern Mayombe graphically conveyed the awful conditions: "The people have not been able to look after their farms since they are so busy burying the victims." And, following a prolonged drought in a once well-populated region: "With the famine, sleeping sickness has struck the region in frightening proportions. In the interior, villages once densely populated are now abandoned. Corpses everywhere, dried, smoked and wrapped in cloth, are waiting to be buried."[10] Communities recovered gradually, but it was the 1920s before the colonial health service brought the epidemic under control and the 1930s before population levels began to recover from the early decades of colonial occupation.[11]

The assurance of adequate human resources was also less certain with competition for labor. The first three to four decades of missionary activity coincided with a time of economic uncertainty as male workers were drawn or forced into European enterprises and rivals scrambled to retain control of the labor and trade that was the essential basis of political power.[12] The slave trade did not stop with the end of the trans-Atlantic trade (c. 1870). Family heads and village chiefs now concentrated on turning their labor force to service the factories that stretched along the coast or mobilized slaves to work on the production of palm oil, palm kernels, and rubber, now the principal exports.[13] Competition from French recruiters for porters to man the caravans was intense. Writing of his experiences in the early 1890s, the administrator Jean Dybowski estimated that 7,000 porters were out on the trail each year.[14] Pierre Vennetier, reviewing official and unofficial sources, reckoned that on an average some fifty caravans and 1,160 porters per month made the journey from Loango to Brazzaville between 1890 and 1895.[15]

These aspects of colonial occupation might seem sufficient to explain the value of women's labor and the resistance to missionary demands for girls, but a closer look at the sources from women's perspective provides additional reasons. According to missionary nuns, women were their principal antagonists, and it becomes evident that the European sisters were challenging the very areas on which local women's position rested: the daily practice of mothering, girls' education, and ensuring of fertility. To send daughters to the sisters' mission was to alienate maternal responsibilities, endanger social health, and put future mothers at risk.

Women's Worth

Women's contribution to the household economy was richly documented by the German ethnographer and geographer Eduard Pechuël-Loesche, who lived several years on the Loango coast in the 1870s as a member of a German scientific expedition and then, again, in 1882–83. He was an acute observer and collector of oral traditions, and was familiar with the published literature.[16] Proverbs he collected testified to the importance of female labor: "the most beautiful girl is useless"; "an industrious woman is prosperity"; and "a slovenly woman is like a pot without a bottom."[17] Sources going back to the seventeenth century and continuing into the twentieth document women's work: cultivating basic food crops such as manioc, corn, and vegetables of all kinds; carrying water; cutting and hauling firewood; preparing food; cleaning and doing maintenance work around the compound; contributing to domestic economies by making pots and baskets; and collecting charcoal for blacksmiths. Such responsibilities likely fluctuated with historical conditions, but the basics were quite constant according to European observations and testimonies of present-day informants.[18] Men had essential and complementary tasks: hunting, fishing, clearing land, tending palm trees that produced wine and raffia materials, building houses, trading, providing porterage on long-distance routes, smithing, weaving, carving, and growing their own crops such as tobacco and sugar cane. Some work might be carried out cooperatively, with women helping men to set up nets to trap animals, and women fishing streams, ponds, and marshes while men concentrated on larger fishing projects in rivers, lakes, and the ocean. Men might also help with heavy work in the planting season. Other divisions of labor were ingrained in custom so that infringing boundaries might bring problems: for example, a mango or avocado tree climbed by a girl or woman was doomed to bear less-tasty fruit.[19]

Women's work was laborious, for during rest days and the dry season they still prepared manioc and carried water and firewood; on the other hand, they had clearly defined rights and could refuse if men asked them to do more. Women "are almost like the slaves of their husbands," wrote an eighteenth-century missionary observer, but the same account is contradictory in saying that "women usually have a house and fields and gardens and slaves themselves over which the husband has no right."[20] Wealth accumulated through their productive activities remained under their control. Pechuël-Loesche stated graphically: "Whatever she harvests above the meal requirements of her husband, whatever she gains from animal husbandry is hers. The spouse may not take a bulb from her basket, not an egg from her chicken coop. . . . It would be completely wrong to view the wife as the husband's beast of burden, as is customarily done." In the household, co-wives shared the cooking.[21] Similar themes emerge from descriptions of Mayombe settlements, where a European observer in 1913 noted, "a woman owns her cooking and farming utensils. The produce belongs to the woman who has worked or sowed the field. . . . Everything the woman acquires belongs to her."[22] Farming was a communal effort when women came together to maximize their production. In some regions of the lower Congo it was done in teams under a leader who negotiated disputes and instructed young women on the best techniques.[23] Such bonding together for women's work could transfer into managing relationships with men. Another Vili proverb said, "whoever strikes his wife strikes all women."[24]

While the essential productive activities of women started with the sustenance of their husband, children, and other household members, the expectations of good mothering went far beyond a woman's labor, potentially bringing her respect in the community beyond her own household and matrilineal kin. If proverbs from the 1870s were reminders of women's labor, they also conveyed the responsibilities of parents: "those who don't dry children's tears will cry themselves," and, "if you like the daughter, look at the mother." Proverbs collected more recently stress similar themes: on parenting, "the fruit grows because it remains attached to the stem" and "the woman is a blessing." The latter is explained by Mavoungou Pambou, a Vili scholar: "The woman is a blessing in the measure that she contributes to the prestige of the clan; she is a person without whom the survival of the clan cannot be certain." Tales of mothers saving children in great danger and a dead mother returning unseen to protect orphans and feed her baby were part of folklore.[25]

Even without the exigencies of the times, elders might hesitate to give up control of girls and young women, for their productive and reproductive activities were infused with specialized knowledge relating to essential customs, rituals, and prohibitions. Ignorance and disregard of these cultural practices could endanger the spiritual and social well-being of the whole society. Mothers had knowledge passed on by their own mothers, given to them by older, experienced, and respected women during the time of their initiation, and shared with each other in daily life experiences and special occasions. From their mothers, her co-wives, their grandmothers, and matrilineal relations, daughters picked up practical knowledge about household management, hygiene, and health care, about the education of their children, and about technical matters associated with everyday tasks from manioc bread preparation to farming techniques, and from basket weaving to knowledge of plants associated with medicinal care. Boys as well as girls stayed close to their mother until they were about five or six years old, when they would go to live with their maternal uncle and have relatively independent lives with their peers, going into the forest to catch birds and gather eggs and fruit, and by the age of fifteen learning house building, weaving, fishing, and other specialized activities.[26]

Girls continued to live in a woman's world, adding to their knowledge until the age of puberty and their preparation for marriage. Affairs relating to sexuality, such as withdrawal to a special house during menstruation, proper relations with a husband, advice relating to pregnancies, and other knowledge relating to adulthood were the subject of intensive education. For many of the northwestern Kongo this occurred during a girl's seclusion for weeks or months. Bodily fluids associated with sexual acts and biological reproduction were considered dangerous and unless properly dealt with could threaten the whole social body with contamination. From the onset of pregnancy, and long before if conception proved difficult, a woman would consult with a *nganga* (pl. *banganga*—priest, healer, diviner, magician) who specialized in gynecological matters and childbirth. Such individuals, both men and women, were skilled manipulators of the *nkisi* (pl. *minkisi*) associated with fertility.[27] According to Wyatt MacGaffey: "There is no good translation for the KiKongo word *nkisi* (pl. *minkisi*) because no corresponding institution exists in European culture. In Kongo thought a *nkisi* is a personalized force from the invisible world of the dead; this force has chosen, or been induced, to submit itself to some degree of human control effected through ritual performances."[28] One of the best known *nkisi* associated with fertility, tranquility, and justice was the *nkisi* Mabyala ma Ndembe, into which nails were driven (*nkisi nkondi*). Noted on the Loango coast in the 1880s, its representations, authority, and proscriptions had spread inland along the Niari valley to Malebo Pool by 1910.[29]

Women were also centrally involved in the most powerful therapeutic association in lower Congo. *Lemba* had developed in the face of declining royal power as an association of merchants, chiefs, and powerful men to regulate markets, structure trade, and give protection against witchcraft that might be activated by their prosperity. Recognized by the seventeenth century on the coast and in the Mayombe, its influence spread over the next two centuries as far as the Pool as its members consolidated their interests and alliances through intermarriage, rituals, insignia, and portable shrines. By the nineteenth and early twentieth centuries, with concerns for declining populations relating to the slave trade and the early colonial occupation, *lemba* specialists had broadened their therapeutic practices from a generalized medicine that included the fertility of the land and of women to a range of medicines and treatment for pregnancy and childbirth.[30]

Thus, expectant mothers, in consultation with appropriate *nganga,* followed special practices such as the avoidance of certain foods, the observance of certain rituals, or the wearing of special amulets: whatever experts recommended to undertake the perilous journey through pregnancy and to avoid miscarriages or the birth of children with physical and mental disabilities. Following childbirth, customs and proscriptions relating to all aspects of a child's life from the naming and first out-dooring ceremonies through the growing-up years to the transition to puberty had to be learned and respected, and passed on to the next generation of mothers. The whole process was "highly instructional" as "anxious mothers . . . drilled their offspring in essential knowledge."[31]

To be childless was a personal tragedy and a potential social disaster, with consequences for the matrilineage and clan. In such situations, "uneasiness and sorrow are felt and certain measures or practical steps must be taken." Couples might make many visits to a *nganga nkisi* to try to reverse their misfortune.[32] A childless marriage was grounds for a divorce, with infertility blamed on the woman. Those who had not borne children were a separate ritual category. In the Loango region, for example, the spirit of the ancestor, *nkisi nsi*, the first to occupy the land, was honored in a sacred grove where the image was tended by a *nganga*. Pilgrims arrived to perform rituals for fertility of the earth and body, but access was forbidden to certain categories of individuals including girls before puberty (those who had not yet been initiated and were in the category of children), virgins (more or less the same individuals since girls were married at puberty), and childless women.[33] Among the Beembe marriage was a "test" for women that could be "passed" only through having many children. Full payment of bridewealth was only made after the birth of the first child.[34] *Sita,* meaning "sterile," was a term of mockery for a childless woman.[35]

The sadness of a woman with no children was conveyed in a lullaby recorded by the ethnomusicologist Herbert Pepper at the village of Madingo-Kayes in 1954.[36] A mother tries to quiet the cries of her baby, Longa, by telling the infant that her pain is much less than that of friends who have no children and that of her father who is sick and trying to sleep. She also warns the child about making a foolish marriage:

(Kivili)

Yéyé yayé—niunguma kati bubu,	Yéyé yayé—cease your crying
Mi mbasi bakwèlé yayé	Think of the friends without children.
E-yi niunguma kwa bubu!	E-yi. Cease your crying, I implore you!
Eyé yayé yé—mabungu masiala	Eyé yayé—think of the friends without children
Bambasi bakwèlé Nzambi! E-yé yéya	Ah! my God! E-yé yéya.
Eyé yayé—ya Rémi tchinanu	Eyé yayé-ya. Think of brother Remi.
Bambasi bakwèlé yayé	Married but with no children. Yayé.
E-yé Longa, mi mwana ngama mamé	E-yé Longa, I also have a mother.
A! Vuéné ma vuéné!	Ah! Listen, dear. Listen!
Yé yé-yayé-ya Rémi tchinanu	Yé yé-yayé-ya. Think of brother Remi
Na mwana Bakamba é liélé!	Married to a Bakamba. What an idea!
Yé-yé Longa	Yé-Yé Longa.
Eyé yayé yé—tata mi kubéla	Eyé yayé yé—Think of your father who suffers

Inkota méné kwé. Yayé	And cannot sleep. Yayé.
E-yé Longà bambasi bakwèle!	E-yé Longa. To the friends without children!
E-yé yayé mwana lièlé E-yé Longa	E-yé yayé. Unreasonable child. E-yé Longa
Eyé tsialé! Yé-mabungu masiala Bambasi bakwèlé. Lièlé!	Eyé! What sadness! Yé- Think of the friends without children. Such misfortune!
E-Longa. Eyé tsiali! é-	E-Longa. Eyé—Such sadness! é-

No more graphic contemporary assertion of Bakongo concern for fertility, motherhood, and lineage continuity exists than the sculpted figures of mother and child known as *pfemba* (also, *phemba, mpemba*) that grace the show cases of western museums. Although maternity figures are common among different Kongo subgroups, the *pfemba* are remarkable for the number that exist in western collections and for questions unanswered concerning their function.[37] They originated mainly from the Mayombe region and were taken to Europe in the late nineteenth and early twentieth centuries. Raoul Lehuard, who has carried out the major study based on some 220 sculptures, notes that it would be possible to catalogue more than 600 known pieces.[38] While noting that outsiders have often categorized the female images that abound in African art simplistically as "fertility figures" and "ancestor figures," the art historian Mary Nooter Roberts describes the genre of *pfemba* figures as "one of the rare instances in African art where the female image is created specifically to assist with fertility."[39] Each sculpture has its own characteristics, and each doubtless is "the bearer of its own compelling stories."[40] Very little is known about the carvers, whether they represent a "school" or had their own workshops, or about the patrons, although they were almost certainly of high status.[41]

Small and intricately carved, the women are often seated cross-legged on a cushion or platform, or sometimes kneeling.[42] Their bodies are inscribed with marks that convey female beauty, high social status, and fertility: elaborate tattoos; filed teeth; high mitered hairstyles or prestige caps worn by authority figures in Kongo society; bracelets and anklets and necklaces of highly valued glass trade beads; and pectoral cords, possibly to ensure uplift of the breasts.[43] The wood is light and durable and has been anointed with layers of red *tukula* paste, a color that expresses transformation and movement between different worlds, as in initiation and childbirth.[44] In some cases, mirrors—materials that came into use in the lower Congo in the nineteenth century—have been inlaid

Figure 1.1. *Figure of Mother and Child (pfemba)*, front view. Yombe/Kongo. Brooklyn
Museum of Art. 22.1136. Museum Expedition 1922. Robert B. Woodward Memorial Fund.

Figure 1.2. *Figure of Mother and Child (pfemba)*, back view. Yombe/Kongo. Brooklyn Museum of Art. 22.1136. Museum Expedition 1922. Robert B. Woodward Memorial Fund.

as eyes to see something that is not there, that which is elsewhere in the other world.[45]

Although modern informants can say little about the function of the small statues, some clues remain in the written sources, especially the German sources from the 1860s and 1870s that tell of shrines with female *nganga* to treat problems of fertility, pregnancy, and childbirth.[46] Pechuël-Loesche gives a graphic description of a heavily guarded Loango treatment center with *pfemba* associations where only women and girls could enter. The *nkisi* was different from the later small Mayombe statues, but similarly named. Describing the place, the powerful *nkisi* housed there, and the number of clients who traveled long distances to seek out remedies, he wrote:

> Within it, the fetish used by women from Lubu resided, healed, and prophesied. She was portrayed in the form of a woman with bristling breasts held by the hands, and even at present continues in the innumerable small reproductions indispensable to the weaker sex. Mkissi Mpemba was a gynecologist whose consulting days were associated with the waxing moon. In the second half of the month, at the time of the waning moon, it rested and gathered new strength. During the couple of moonless days, it was inaccessible. Its residence remained closed.
>
> Mpemba's power was exceedingly great. Its fame reached to all territories. It had a large throng of women and girls who supposedly came to it even from the forest country [the Mayombe region] and even further in the interior. . . .
>
> Mpemba's robe played the main role in the gynecological treatment in the fetish hut, and besides that, a plank led down a slope through a hatch. . . . Whatever else happened inside the fetish remains a mystery. For only girls and women who wanted a good husband, who wanted to be free of sufferings, who yearned for the joys of motherhood, who wished happily to survive their moment of giving birth, were allowed inside.

The account goes on to describe how the "fetish" and its empowerment of women were seen as a threat by men, who were barred from entry. By the 1870s, the site lay in ruins and the "gynecologist" no longer practiced at the place, since men from Loangili had attacked the shrine and stolen, burned, or carried off *nkisi* Mpemba, or dropped it into a deep crevice during a moonless night. A slightly different version given by another informant noted that "the men of Lubu are said to have committed the bad deed because the profitable activity and the increased power of the village women had become alarming to them." The site had been abandoned, although "Lubu women still supposedly hold secret meetings." The *nkisi* Mpemba's "misfortune" had been a victory for another *nkisi*, Mbinda of Buluango, which also existed exclusively to address women's problems. Men, hair, tobacco smoke, liquor, and water were among the taboos for the women who attended the treatment center hidden in a palm grove. When its enemies captured it and threw it into the sea, its adherents rescued and refurbished it.[47]

While the success of women's therapeutic cults in the coastal regions some time before the 1870s is documented by such accounts, as is their spread far into the interior, the use of the small mother-and-child figures that proliferated in the Mayombe region from the 1880s to the 1920s remains unclear.[48] They may have had symbolic, commemorative meanings, relating to celebrated ancestors. Lehuard suggests that such high-status women may have been mothers celebrated for giving birth to many children.[49] Photographs have shown *pfemba* images on tombs, where they might have been protectors or companions of the deceased, and they appear on a post marking the door of a chief's house. Lehuard takes their association with household shrines and their presence on chiefs' insignia such as staffs, whistles, and fly whisks, and on musical instruments, as indications of the place of women in Yombe society.[50] The French anthropologist Albert Doutreloux confirmed the high respect in which women were held, the genealogical knowledge that they guarded, the magical powers for which some were feared, and the kind of pressures they could exert in village discussions, including leadership roles when men were absent. He concludes that "all aspects of women's worth culminate without doubt in motherhood. It is motherhood that finally consecrates and justifies the woman's place in society. On her depends the survival of the group, its expansion, and its essential wealth."[51] In the 1930s, Léo Bittremieux observed one of the *pfemba* in the hands of a male diviner in a ritual. He proposed that the word was derived from a Kiyombe word meaning to broadcast or eject, as in the seeds of potential children which may be planted in men or women. Thus, the statues may not represent particular women but be a general Yombe expression of nurturing women.[52] Even if the precise usage of the small maternal figures is not quite clear, it can be said that they well document the concerns for fertility, children, and motherhood at a time when societies were enduring the multiple stresses of colonial conquest and occupation.

Such specialized power vested in females did not translate by the late nineteenth and early twentieth centuries into the substantial economic and political power that would rival that of men, however. Individual women could access power beyond their households through their ability to speak eloquently in public assemblies, their position as *nganga nkisi,* and their marriage to wealthy men as with *lemba* wives. Overall, however, women's political power was in decline by the time of the missionaries' arrival, undercut by the slave trade that had seen the rise of a wealthy and powerful merchant class. In the area once dominated by the Loango kingdom (c. 14th–18th centuries), the declining authority of a royal official prominent in the structure of the kingdom, the Makunda, who was usually the mother or sister of the Maloango, seems to have paralleled the demise of the political kingdom and its structures. In the seventeenth century, she had great power, seeing to the interests of women, advising the ruler, and sometimes taking over the interests of the ruling clan during an interregnum.[53] Her main function, however, was "to represent all mothers, who were the propagators of the tribe, who bore all the burden and worriment of procreation."[54] Anyone could go to her court and ask for her justice, but she was particularly sought out by women and girls who had complaints against men. By the late nineteenth century, this power was gone, and the Maloango's position largely based on his residual spiritual authority. When Pechuël-Loesche, writing in the 1870s, describes the Makunda's position, he is leaning on seventeenth-century sources. In fact, he notes that "women would certainly have wanted this institution to continue up to the present time in its full power. But it, like so many old things has fallen into disuse and is only practiced on a small scale by princesses with land, as far as their power is recognized at all."[55]

Women were not powerless, for in household economies they shared essential, complementary roles with men, and their skills as religious specialists gave them access to important forms of authority.[56] Yet, in the lower Congo by the late nineteenth century, political power in the wider society involved generating wealth from trade, mobilizing households of dependents, and engaging in "restrictive" or "destructive" wars, often resulting from competition for scarce resources in unstable times.[57] The notebooks of Laman's informants (1912–19) reveal that "women in general take second place," even if some individual women were more influential than men.[58] One could not become wealthy through agriculture and local trade alone, the main generators of income for women, excepting perhaps those who could direct their produce to the markets of the traders and European workers in the Pool region and at coastal factories.[59] In the Mayombe region, individual women could have prestige, and mothers acting together could exert pressure on the group, but as in other regions, male activities such as trade and war were paramount in generating wealth, and, in comparison, women's productive labor in agriculture was "secondary" in terms of income.[60] Women as mothers and creators of bonds between kin had high social status, but matrilineality did not guarantee power for women, for it could be used to safeguard the political rights of men.[61] Motherhood continued to be venerated and recognized as the basis for social well-being and women had recognition in certain domains, but this did not translate into political authority. Missionaries and colonial agents contributed to the situation; coming from contemporary Europe, they talked with other men, and women, where they were noticed, were ignored or dismissed as backward and oppressed.

Kumbi: Knowledge for Womanhood

In 1888, Mère Saint-Charles, superior of the sisters' community at Loango, wrote to the superior of her congregation, telling of a visit the missionaries had made to the newly appointed Maloango at the royal town of Diosso. The goal was to head off an emerging crisis over three girls who had been sent to the mission as an act of diplomacy by the Maloango's predecessor. The missionaries were not well-received by the new ruler, and, as the sister wrote:

> He said that he would never agree as his uncle had done to the young girls be-
> ing with the Sisters. He thought it an abomination that they would not pass
> into the *case kicombe* [*kumbi* house] for three months when they were nubile,
> since this was the time when they were most exposed to losing their virtue.
> He said that he would never allow any girls from the Sisters to pass through
> this house. Concerning the girls with the Sisters, he said "I will see that they
> are fetched and I will make it known throughout my kingdom that children
> should not be sent to the mission. Since they do not go through the *case ki-
> combe*, they remain like monkeys."

Mère Saint-Charles went on to describe how the situation had been patched up when one of the priests returned to the capital and invited "the whole Loango court" to visit the sisters; after negotiations, the girls were allowed to stay at the convent. Two months later, after the mother-superior had sent a case of gin and paid a visit to the palace at Diosso, she reported that the Maloango had agreed the girls could stay with the sisters and the missionaries could arrange their marriage.[62]

Some twenty years later, the issue of *kumbi* continued to be identified by the missionaries as a major point of contention overshadowing the recruitment and education of girls. The monthly report on the affairs of the vicariate noted:

> We are at war against the institution of "Kikoumbi." Notably at Diosso, where
> a young Christian girl agreed to undergo this immoral practice, we closed the
> chapel and the teaching of the catechism was suspended. After two weeks of
> this regime, the guilty one came and presented herself to Monseigneur and
> asked for pardon. In the Mabindou area, the Mother-Superior goes in person
> to destroy these famous huts where young girls who submit to this ridiculous
> test live. We are hoping that in the end the practice will finally disappear, at

least in the neighborhood of the missions. Anyway, war has been declared against "Kikoumbi." and there will be no truce or mercy. Already punishments have been meted out to those who practice this deplorable institution.[63]

In 1914, a Loango sister again noted that for five years the missionary nuns had not been able to retain girls. "When they reach marriageable age, they run away or their parents take them from us to put them through the fetish ceremonies which are customary in this country."[64] Two years later, the French minister of colonies, finally waking up to the dire economic and demographic situation that colonial occupation had wrought in Congo, asked for opinions on the cause of the crisis. Père Le Scao, in reply to the question, "What is ruining the Congo?" listed the failure of the administration to prohibit gun powder, abuses by the militia, and excessive taxation, and, on the African side, "laziness," "poison ordeals," and "Kikoumbi." The latter he went on to describe as a "school of immorality. The effects are appalling: loss of physical strength, brain-washing, a horror of work, premature ageing . . . it is obviously a cause of depopulation." He suggested that the head tax on individuals might be lightened and that instead a tax might be levied on the special *kumbi* huts.[65] The quite different understandings of the ritual of *kumbi* were clear. For the Maloango, *kumbi*—a female ritual at puberty—had to do with social morality, a guard against pregnancies before marriage, and deeply rooted cultural practice. For missionaries, the institution was an overt celebration of sexuality, a flagrant display of immorality, an undermining of the physical and intellectual strength of young women, and a contaminant for Christians.

The institution, or some form of it, had long roots in the Kongo past. The practice varied over time and place in the details, but there were marked commonalities. Descriptions must also have varied with the observations and understanding of the observer. In the late nineteenth and early twentieth centuries the most elaborate forms were practiced in the Loango and Mayombe regions, but reports from other—but not all—Kongo regions show some form of girls' initiation.

An early reference can be found in a mid-seventeenth-century Dutch source: "With regard to marriage . . . usually mothers and fathers do not give their daughters until they have started menstruating"; "When young girls are leaving behind their virginity, they coat themselves with oil and redwood from Mayumba, and go to live in a small hidden house where, after a stay of a month, they choose a husband from among the young men who have served them best."[66] A century later, basing his account on the reports of French missionaries, Abbé Proyart wrote that a young man who wanted to be married must begin the process by taking gifts to the girl and her mother. Their acceptance was a sign that prenuptial proceedings could begin. As with the earlier Dutch description, a month had to pass before the marriage, and "during this time the girl appears in public, her body painted red, so that everyone knows that the man with whom she is seen is to be her husband. If this ceremony is not observed the marriage is illegal and sacrilegious and the parents of the girl would be justified in punishing her with death. The time prescribed by custom having passed, the red color is removed and the marriage is celebrated with dances and songs of the country."[67] Although other sources do not tell of such draconian punishments for violating pre-marriage laws, several cite beatings and ridicule for both individuals if a woman bore a child without passing through the *nzo kumbi* (house of *kumbi*), even if they were "promised" to each other. In the seventeenth century, Dapper wrote that in the Loango kingdom, if a man had sexual relations with a girl before puberty, and therefore before her initiation rituals, he had to go before the king and all the court to justify his actions, undertake special rituals, and receive a royal pardon. "There are some who imagine that if this pardon is not received, there will be a drought and the land will be infertile."[68] Like Proyart, later writers connected violation of the prescribed practices surrounding *kumbi* with beliefs that pregnancy before marriage would result in "a sickness to the whole social body that could lead to death."[69]

Several sources describe variants in the institution of *kumbi* for the late nineteenth and early twentieth centuries when the missionaries arrived.[70] There are also sources by Kongo scholars and informants from the twentieth century as well as field research by French anthropologists working in the 1960s. These confirm some of the contemporary accounts and offer other insights.[71] Particularly useful was my visit in 2000 to the small "Musée régional 'Ma Loango,'" housed in the royal residence at Diosso of the Maloango Poaty III, who died in 1975. Displayed there is paraphernalia donated by elderly women who wore the items as *tchikumbi* (Kivili, pl. *bikumbi*): glass beads, raffia skirts, armlets and leg rings, headbands with cowrie shells, and chunks of *tukula* redwood. The testimonies of these women also inform a pamphlet written for visitors by the curator.[72]

Unlike male initiation, the initiation of girls did not involve circumcision, but its mandatory rituals included a similar discipline and period of intensive education.[73] Whereas male initiation was often associated with withdrawal to a hidden place, *kumbi* rituals were more public. Although the girl herself was confined to the *nzo kumbi,* its location was known to her community, and certain individuals could stay with her and visit her. From the girl's perspective, the proceedings were not entirely unfamiliar, for she would have observed them in her growing-up years both in their public aspects, or more closely if she had been chosen to stay with a *tchikumbi*. Accompanying the initiate in the *nzo kumbi* were several junior girls, who helped her with essential tasks relating to hygiene and renewing the layers of *tukula*, doing small errands for her, carrying food from their homes, playing games, learning songs and dances, ridiculing unauthorized boys who came too close, and generally keeping her company.

At the onset of menstruation, the girl's parents would alert others in the community, and guns were fired to celebrate the onset of the child-bearing years. She would then be "seized" by a crowd of women, and the singing, joyous group would escort her to the *nzo kumbi*. Her supervision and teaching was in the hands of an older, experienced mother of children, whose duty it was to pass on beliefs, customs, and taboos concerning sexual relations with her future husband; the duties of a wife and mother that she might not already know; issues relating to pregnancy and childbirth; and other specialized knowledge needed by an adult woman. Most accounts tell of visitors coming and going, including her future "fiancé"—if he had already been identified—and young men and women of her age group who might bring her presents and stay to socialize with her, although she stayed in the doorway of the house.

The preparation of *tukula* paste from a mixture of crushed camwood (which yielded a reddish dye), palm-oil, and very fine sand, and the repeated application of multiple layers of this mixture over the *tchikumbi's* body, was a fundamental part of the initiation process.[74] The dramatic appearance of the initiate was a highly visible sign of the arrival of puberty and was remarked on by observers almost universally. Indeed, ethnographer Bastian called the place of confinement the *casa das tintas* (Portuguese, the "house of paint") and the trader Dennett, the "paint house." As anointed *pfemba* figures marked the passage to motherhood, so the smearing of the paste over the *tchikumbi's* body signaled the movement from girlhood to womanhood, a rebirth into a new life with all its potential.

While the initiation process was continuing, the *tchikumbi's* family would ideally be putting the final touches to the marriage contract, for at the end of the rituals the young woman would move out of her parent's home to the house of her husband. Indeed, the husband might have been identified when the girl was younger, and negotiations between families might already be concluded; but marriage had to wait until puberty. The young man might have been courting the girl and her mother with presents for some time. If the girl arrived at puberty without a prospective husband, the women in her family would broadcast the news in surrounding villages that their daughter was a *tchikumbi* so that a suitor might arrive. The main problem would emerge if no young man seemed interested, and this, together with protracted negotiations over the marriage contract, could prolong the stay in the *nzo kumbi* for months.

With the end of the training and the completion of negotiations, the *tchi-kumbi* could take the penultimate steps to married life escorted by women from the family and community. First, she was taken in procession to a river or the ocean, where the women would rub her body free of the *tukula* layers. She would then be washed and dressed in a raffia skirt, beads, copper or brass bracelets, and rings around her ankles and legs.[75] The celebrations could then begin. On the coast, Europeans wrote of seeing processions "promenading" the young woman. According to Voulgré: "When the marriage has been arranged, there exists a custom of parading the young girl, escorted by the women of the villages from house to house. Friends give her presents and, in the evening, the drums beat loudly." He observed an "exuberant procession."[76] Some of those who lived close to the French settlement at Loango added it to their itinerary. Dybowski wrote of the *tchikumbi* processions: "They go around in large groups to visit the surrounding villages, passing in turn before the houses of whites, and it is the custom to offer them some present."[77] In Castellani's description, following the end of seclusion, "the great day arrives, they are cleansed of their red coloring with which they are coated from head to waist, and adorned with the most beautiful jewelry. Thus decked out, they are hoisted on high and paraded in great pomp by the factories escorted by their companions, both younger and older, who follow shouting, beating drums, and playing flutes."[78]

The final events in the celebration before the young woman was escorted to the house of her husband involved feasting and dancing. She now had the chance to show off her beauty and her skills as a dancer. Women and the young girls who had been her assistants gathered in a circle to assist with the singing and clapping. One of their songs reassured the *tchikumbi*, "Don't cry any more today," and went on to say that even if she felt sad now that she was leaving her maternal home, she was not alone, for she had become a member of the community of women. The central figure then danced into the circle and performed intricate steps and positions, making her bracelets clatter together in a "language" those gathered understood.[79] Older people looked on, providing proverbs and their own observations. While the initiate was in the *nzo kumbi,* the families had been making preparations for this day. The men produced extra amounts of palm wine, fish, and meat, and the women put their effort into preparing manioc bread, sauces, and vegetables. At the end of all this, the young woman was escorted to the house of her new husband, and married life could begin. Presents from the husband's family, such as cooking utensils and other tools, awaited her.

Some overall impressions emerge from these accounts of *kumbi* rituals and celebrations. The care with which they were observed and their persistence over centuries shows them to be at the heart of a social order in which women's fertility and knowledge as a wife and mother had a primary place. They were, above all, a confirmation of a young person's sexuality and an authorization of marriage and the children that would follow. Congolese writers have commented that they reveal marriage as "a regulated and profoundly spiritualized contract," far beyond the exchange of wealth as it was perceived by Europeans and which it became in the twentieth century.[80] Women were at the center of the rituals. At certain junctures, men were part of the proceedings, such as negotiating the marriage contract and helping to provide food for guests. Yet, *kumbi* most affirmed women's place in society, and beyond that, it confirmed repetitively a hierarchy of women: from the small girls who aided and learned from the *tchikumbi,* now their senior, to the generation of the mother who supported the daughter and chose a woman to advise her in the *kumbi nzo,* to the grandmothers and older women who insisted on the good ordering of the process and participated in events such as washing away the *tukula* and dressing the young wife. The event was also about community for everyone participated at some point.[81]

After three decades of work in the Loango and Mayombe regions, the missionaries continued to find the practice of *kumbi* a significant hurdle in their goal of establishing Christian families. Père Marichelle, noting that some advances had been made in the work with women, wrote of *kumbi:* "Nevertheless, the old custom will prevail for a long time yet and keep women at a distance from us."[82]

Anxieties, Ambivalence, and Resistance

Women might have very specific reasons for shunning mission stations, but men were also slow to warm to missionary overtures even if the material advantages brought by Europeans were apparent. Thus, responses to the arrival of the Catholic fathers and sisters need also to be located in a broader context, namely, the potential advantages or dangers of the powerful new cult. Men and women shared a deep ambivalence concerning the missionaries, who, with their strange language, technical knowledge, and powers to manipulate holy objects, were clearly powerful *banganga* able to call on superior *minkisi.* Through their ritual control of charms, they might offer new ways of approaching the divine and combating the forces of misfortune but they might also be dangerous *ndoki* (witches) who could "eat" people (Kikongo, *dia bantu*)—that is, kill them by witchcraft— and send their souls across the water.[83] Several incidents in the sisters' early experience at Loango documented such fears. In one, for example, they reported that "the first time we went to the villages all the children hid. Someone had told them we would take them and eat them."[84] Also, at their school, "the children have fled to their mothers. An individual had convinced them that before baptism, someone would burn their hair and, after that, someone would be forced to eat the ashes and that person would eat them little by little."[85]

The inhabitants of the lower Congo found in Christianity both the familiar and the alien. *Nzambi mpungu,* or *nzambi,* was their high God, the creator, one whose sphere of action was universal. The missionaries accepted this being as the equivalent of the Christian God and called themselves *nganga nzambi,* yet there were distinctions, for unlike the Christian God, *Nzambi mpungu* was remote, unbounded by gender, location, or time, and too distant to be approached by mortals. Religious practice and veneration were thus turned to spirits or ancestors who could act as intermediaries. Spirits at the center of territorial cults were generally associated with natural phenomena and could be invoked for aid in matters such as rainmaking, fertility, and success in fishing, hunting, or agriculture. In the Loango region, Pedro Djimbel (or Peter Gimbel), chief of the village of Martinique (one of several villages established by freed slaves returned from the Americas) showed the newly arrived Père Carrie the gorge of Diosso, inhabited by a celebrated female spirit, Mboma, who took the form of a snake. He also pointed out other ravines, each with spirits who were the objects of local veneration and considered protectors of the Maloango.[86] Ancestors, members of the lineage or clan who had died and passed into the other world, might be recently deceased and remembered as persons, or they were more remote and known through others or imagined. Closer to God, they were essential as intercessors, mediators, or protectors, but they could also be demanding, exact great respect, and punish those who fell short. Familiarity with such intermediaries thus provided some common ground for those drawn to a Catholic piety that was centered on the Virgin Mary, saints, and great religious figures of the past. Yet there was room for misunderstandings, for whereas in Christian beliefs the dead passed on to heaven (or purgatory or hell) and were the object of prayers, Kongo ancestors lived in another world, but they might actively intervene for better or worse in human lives.

Richard Gray, in discussing the arrival of Christianity in the old Kongo kingdom, has written about "one of the deepest and enduring desires of all African societies: the anxiety to eliminate evil." He goes on: "Evil was experienced as that which destroyed life, health, strength, fertility and prosperity. Of course, Africans recognized the immediate causes of death, but for them the crucial task was to look behind these phenomena to discover the ultimate, determining causes. . . . At times of prolonged crisis, the burden of evil could become almost unbearable. . . . New religion was often seen as a fresh source of supernatural power."[87] As families grappled with all kinds of disruption, from the violence of colonial conquest to the crisis of sleeping sickness, Christianity was one of several emerging cults that claimed attention and required integration into Kongo cosmology. It was the practice of Christianity rather than beliefs that most attracted interest from those who interacted with the first *nganga nzambi* and saw them perform rituals and manipulate their holy objects just as *nganga nkisi* did.

Baptism, the first sacrament, which promised salvation from original sin and entry into the Catholic community, was at the heart of missionary evangelism but was a source of anxiety for those with whom they came in touch. It was recognized as a sign of acceptance into the new cult; Pedro Djimbel was willing to allow several of his sons to be baptized, but would not agree himself since it would undermine his authority in the village. That it might be an instrument of *ndoki* and lead to death was also a fear, encouraged by the fact that the priests and sisters rushed to baptize the moribund. In 1887, the mother-superior reported from Loango that three "big girls," whom the sisters were going to instruct in order to marry them to mission boys, had left, "saying that baptism would cause them to die."[88] Long after Christianity was firmly entrenched, the fear continued in some villages. In 1925, the sisters at Loango wrote of the need "to follow the sick who are hidden from us. . . . We need to make them understand that baptism does not bring death but creates a child of the good God and opens the sky." They also reported that a person on the brink of death had said, "Baptize me after I am dead."[89] In spite of such reversals, it was not long before such anxieties diminished in most places, and baptism was sought after as a powerful rite of purification and protection against *ndoki*. The short-lived mission to the Loango region in the late eighteenth century had similar experience, with the missionaries reporting baptism as a popular Christian ritual.[90]

In the holy objects of Catholicism and in the practice of worship, those in the lower Congo also found a potentially rich trove of charms, whether held by the priests or distributed to lay people on an individual basis. Liturgical vestments, holy water, medals, rosaries, crucifixes, statues, images, language, and writing could all be interpreted in a local idiom. Concerning the Bible, the Swedish Protestant missionary Efraim Andersson wrote that since it was believed that the missionaries were sorcerers who could "eat" people, their holy book was referred to as the "book of death." When the missionary opened it the audience was "gripped with fear."[91]

The mission station itself was a site for cultural confrontation. It symbolized ambivalence and contradiction, for if it was sacred space to the missionaries and their adherents, it was dangerous ground to those outside. It was a place where power and vulnerability and life and death coexisted side by side. The death rate among Europeans and Africans was high as endemic and epidemic disease took the lives of children, adults, and missionaries in the early decades. All this had to be understood not only in terms of physical loss but within people's systems of belief. On several occasions, as a new wave of sickness overcame the girls or the sisters died from tetanus, yellow fever, and other ailments described generally as "fevers," girls ran away and mothers showed up to remove their daughters. Given the close association of "evil" with the supernatural, this was more than just a physical response to tragedy; it was also the fear that missionaries were indeed practitioners of *ndoki*.[92]

The sisters also told of their visits to neighboring villages. Since celibacy was unknown, they were universally taken as the wives or women of the missionary fathers and were known as *mama nganga,* greeted with shouts of *"zi mèlées"* (the mothers).[93] Their medicine kits were *bilongo,* the term used for the medicines manipulated by *banganga* and added to *minkisi* to make them potent, and the sisters could not keep up with demands for portable sources of *nkisi*—medals, crucifixes, rosaries, and scapulars—although parishioners and patrons in Europe dispatched these objects of Christian piety to equatorial African by the tens of thousands. The sisters very consciously used the promise of distributing such holy objects to draw a crowd.[94] Indeed, the efforts of early missionaries to replace "fetishes" with items in their religious repertoire likely anchored more firmly the very beliefs that they were trying to eradicate, as recognized at the time by the English trader Dennett, who wrote, "Christianity worked hand in hand with Nkissism" and reiterated more recently by a missionary.[95] The local reinterpretation of Christianity in light of indigenous beliefs and practices was interpreted by the sisters as backsliding: "The Fiote, little energetic by nature, is not a Christian of granite like those in Brittany."[96]

If local people were engaged in selectively absorbing elements of Christianity into their practices, the missionaries believed they were at war with religious specialists in a "savage country." In 1890, Monseigneur Carrie decided against erecting a cross in the mission cemetery, since it would attract the attention of the "pagans," who would desecrate it.[97] In the same year, the missionaries claimed that two catechists and two graduates of their schools had been poisoned, and Carrie advised a young priest to "go slowly with attacks on fetishes: we do not want to turn the population against us."[98] Not surprisingly, given the importance of rituals such as *kumbi* in girls' education and widespread women's fertility cults, the sisters found their toughest competition came from mothers, aunts, grandmothers, and wrote that "the fetish priestesses are even more virulent than the men." In 1887, in the battle over competing charms the mother-superior reported that "a priestess has stolen the rosary of Soeur St. Justin." In 1899, two of the nuns set off for a village "resolved to launch an assault against the priestesses," but "in vain." A few months later, the mother-superior reported another confrontation, when a "very important fetish priestess" intervened to disrupt a meeting of women with a missionary.[99] In 1909, the mother-superior at Loango reported that "girls being the wealth of the country, mothers create a million obstacles to giving them to us." It was the girls' uncles who might bring them if "they thought it a good idea."[100]

Conclusion

Colonial conquest and occupation coincided with the arrival of missionaries, who were seen as bearers of a new cult full of rich opportunities and threatening dangers. During the first thirty years or so of their enterprise, the missionaries were challenged by the lack of women, whom they needed to establish their Christian communities on a long-term basis. No other phrase so dominates the letters of the priests in referring to women as "mothers of families." From local perspectives, Europeans could undermine the resources that women represented as wives and mothers, disrupt household economies, and endanger the education of girls, and thus the social and ritual health of lineage and clan. While individual women might have prominence and recognition through particular talents or achievements or associations with influential men, most women found that their political and economic domains were circumscribed in societies where historical circumstances had located power in the hands of the men who could mobilize sufficient economic assets to control kin and dependents. Men also monopolized the arms used in warfare against local competitors and invading colonial forces.

Yet women were powerful within certain domains where they had important rights and could assert their influence and press their demands. Motherhood was essential and fertility celebrated. A mother's work was not fixed in her household or "home," nor do notions of "public" and "private" spheres make much sense in analyzing the situation, for responsibilities and power were much more broad-based among extended kin and community in a kind of social motherhood. In this respect, the conveying of knowledge and the nurturing of "daughters" who numbered far more than biological children assumed great significance. Burgeoning fertility cults were also a source of female authority that women acting together jealously guarded against male encroachment. Such female associations were widespread not only in lower Congo but in neighboring regions of equatorial Africa. In Gabon, one French traveler reported an incident where "the women were spreading the word that their fetish was leaving its house to walk around the village. For three days no man dared to return to his house."[101] In another report connected to female initiation, the girls were cloistered to learn the "secrets" of married life. No one was allowed to see the rituals, or they would be attacked by women and die.[102] Paul de Chaillu also reported the consternation he caused when Bakalai members of a women's cult were performing secret rituals inside a house with no doors or windows. He dared to find a way of looking in and had to take to his heels when angry women chased him away. They demanded he pay them a heavy fine, and when he refused the women so menaced men in the community that they gathered together the means to pay.[103]

Given the difficulties of recruiting "free girls" in these early years, the missionaries turned to those who were not firmly rooted in kin groups and began to "ransom" slaves, a "liberation" strategy in line with the priorities of their congregations. Thus, many of the first generation of Catholic women started as girls in traumatic circumstances, passing through the hands of buyers until they were acquired by missionaries to be initiated into a different culture, but one in which motherhood continued to be central.

2. The First Generation

In 1910, the *Annales apostoliques,* a popular Spiritan magazine with letters, anecdotes, and reports from missionaries overseas, published an article by Monseigneur Derouet, vicar apostolic of lower Congo, entitled "Les lunettes de Mère Agnès" ("The Glasses of Mother Agnes").[1] It told of a women he had met on a visit to Linzolo while undertaking a tour of inspection in his ecclesiastical region, one he described as a "model of a faithful spouse, a devoted and hard-working mother," and a teacher of the catechism to girls and women. He did not indicate to his readers how far Agnès Mpolo had come from her troubled childhood: the first time she appeared in the historical record was as an entry in the Linzolo account book dated 21 January 1891, a girl of about nine years old sold to the missionaries at a cost of fifty-four francs.[2] Although this was clearly a particularly successful woman, her story was not uncommon, for many of the first generation of Catholic women came to mission stations in similar circumstances. Agnès was one of those known in the wider society as the "children of the fathers" or "the children of the mission."

At the other end of the caravan trail from Loango near Malebo Pool, Linzolo was an important distribution point for those whom the Catholic fathers bought out of slavery. About twenty-five kilometers from Brazzaville, it was to become a principal center of Congo Christianity and a major source of the elite who found their way to the AEF capital in search of wage labor. Unlike other early missions stations such as Loango and Brazzaville, there was no community of sisters before 1944, so that the priests were dependent on a generation of Catholic women such as Agnès Mpolo to mother and mentor girls and women. If there were some differences from developments at Loango, there were also similarities, for here too there was great resistance to handing over girls to missionaries for training. At Linzolo, as everywhere in the lower Congo, the resources that women represented were critical. Unlike those who lived toward the coast, there were no initiation rites such as *kumbi;* rather girls were contracted in marriage by family heads as early as six or seven years old, at which time they were usually transferred to the household of their spouse to be trained for adulthood by the women of that family. When they reached puberty, they could enter full marital relations either with the man who had concluded the contract or with a junior kinsman designated by him. This early age for marriage contracts may have arisen as a result of the foreign and domestic slave trade, as chiefs and family heads secured the resources that girls represented as soon as possible.[3]

Having put themselves in competition for children with other powerful men, the missionaries compounded their dilemmas by deciding that adults were too set in their ways to shed their uncivilized customs and be potential mission recruits. An early report from the Linzolo mission, echoed in others, noted: "We have no great hope with adults. Polygamy and fetishism hold them. We can occasionally convert them on their death beds."[4] And on the importance of recruiting girls: "That is the hope of the future. The truly Christian mother will more surely raise a good little Christian than all the efforts of missionaries."[5] Yet a lack of girls persisted. The gravity of the situation at Linzolo was described by the Duc d'Uzès, a leader of an expeditionary force and a devout Catholic, who stayed at the mission and wrote home that the missionaries had achieved "marvels": thirty-five hectares of land cleared and planted with fruits and vegetables by the sixty boys at the school. On the other hand: "They have been here nine years and have founded two embryonic Christian villages with thirteen households between them. In this respect the results are not very satisfactory."[6] In various letters to his superior at Loango, Père Kraft likewise reported the situation: "The big problem at Linzolo is to get women for our large children"; "Three of the boys have been out at night and had relations with women . . . another fled in the night and said he could not find a wife with the Fathers. They have been captured and beaten." A few months later, three of the "most trusted boys" originally brought by the missionaries from the Landana mission (Cabinda) had returned to the coast, "where they can more easily find a wife."[7]

Thus, many of the first generation of Catholic women started their lives in inauspicious circumstances, but they became critical as role models, leaders of church women, and mothers and grandmothers of large families. In so doing, they found for themselves status within the new communities.

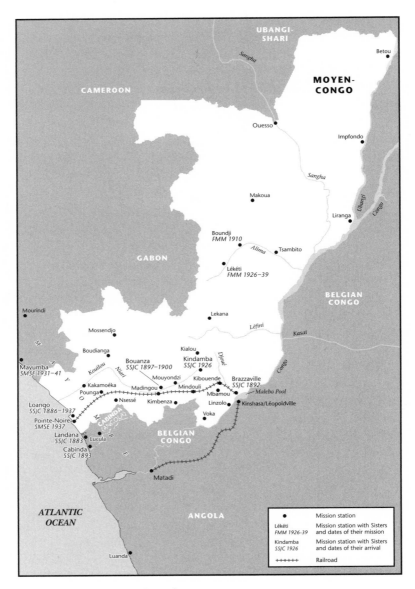

Map 2. Spiritan Missions in Congo by 1940.

Origins, Journeys, and Arrivals

The historiography of commodity trade in Central Africa that once divided the nineteenth-century trade neatly into a period of "the slave trade" and "legitimate trade" masked the composite nature of international commerce, where slaves continued to be part of the production of goods such as ivory, palm oil, and rubber well after abolition treaties and the departure of the last slave ships.[8] Throughout the Congo and Ubangi basins, slaves were used in a variety of essential roles from agricultural labor to porters and canoe operators and from militias to spouses. Nor did the inland trade cease when the Atlantic trade was phased out, for the trade in humans within the continent continued. Forms of servitude, collapsed in European accounts under the rubric "slavery," represented a complex range of dependencies and servility. Within matrilineal societies such as the Kongo, slave women were especially valuable to a powerful man, for their children belonged to his lineage rather than that of their mother. Slaves were a cornerstone of precolonial kingdoms such as Kongo, Loango, and Tio as well as smaller-scale societies. Furthermore, the commodification of humans in the Atlantic slave trade accentuated the crimes for which slavery was a penalty and encouraged the selling of war captives to slave dealers. The range of the institution within and between societies makes generalization difficult, and some individuals rose to receive high recognition in their communities, but in general to be a slave meant loss of freedom, vulnerability to abuse, and separation from kin, with accompanying rootlessness and loss of protection.[9]

Given insufficient girls and young women and the consequent flight of young men, the missionaries tapped into these domestic markets. Children also were "gifted" to them by traders, administrators, and riverboat captains, especially at Brazzaville and Linzolo. Anton Gresshof, the director of the Dutch trading company and at the center of a network that stretched upriver and to the Atlantic coast, was an important benefactor of the sisters at Brazzaville, bringing Mère Marie Dédié "gifts" of girls, food, cloth, and cash.[10] The administration also passed on unwanted women, as Père Bouleuc reported: "The government has sent female prisoners of war to Linzolo."[11] Conflicts in the Pool region also resulted in individuals falling into the hands of slave dealers. Among the northeastern Kongo, groups known today as the Nsundi, Beembe, and Lari were involved in a very gradual process of settlement that had been going on for two centuries and more. They displaced earlier Teke populations, whose traces remain in language, housing, and beliefs relating to land.[12] Among the Beembe, the settlement of the Mouyondzi plateau had taken place in the middle decades of the nineteenth century, but droughts and famines and contestations over control of markets continued in the period c. 1880–1910. According to the informants of Georges Dupré, a state of war was endemic at the time.[13] The expansion of Europeans intensified pre-existing conflicts along major trade routes, especially between the Niari and the Pool. Such happenings generated slaves whom dealers took to the Ubangi region, where they could be exchanged for ivory that was then transported to European markets. In the late nineteenth century, around the Pool and immediately upstream, slaves outnumbered free persons among the riverine populations.[14] In the 1880s and 1890s, traveling priests on the lookout for children returned to Brazzaville and the lower Congo with boys and girls from the Niari valley, the plateau to the north, and the Pool region. Accounts are peppered with such comments as "Père Giron has traveled twenty-five days into the interior ransoming boys and girls for the mission"; "A great good is realized in these missionary travels for we never return to the Mission without four, six, and as many as ten of these poor children who have the good fortune to be ransomed from slavery."[15]

Yet, children also arrived from points as far distant as eighteen hundred kilometers upriver from Brazzaville, where the Spiritan fathers founded missions at Bangui and Bessou on the Ubangi bend. Here raiders from the Sahara borderlands pushed people to the south while refugees and captives fleeing the punitive expeditions of the Congo Free State and concessionary company militias took sanctuary at the missions or were brought for sale by slave traders.[16] The launching in 1889 of a "floating mission," a boat on the Congo river, made the transport of individuals over long distances possible. From his base at Liranga at the confluence of the Congo and Ubangi rivers, Père Allaire sailed up and down the inland waterways "ransoming" children along the river banks.[17] In 1896, Monseigneur Carrie of lower Congo reported about eight hundred children bought from slavery, and three years later Monseigneur Augouard reported seven hundred children in the eleven schools of upper Congo; "most of them are ransomed inmates of our mission orphanages."[18]

Some sources offer glimpses of the children's experience. At Linzolo, Père Emile Zimmerman noted in 1901 that "at the most distant markets, there were opportunities to ransom some children (powder, cloth, etc. . . .). This was the prevailing system of exchange." By this time, numbers of boys were brought by their families for instruction: "It is only for the work with girls that we are obliged to search out the markets and villages some two or three days from the Mission."[19] Indispensable to the missionaries were assistants such as Jean Makitu, a specialist in recruiting porters and organizing caravans.[20] Describing one journey, Zimmerman wrote:

In these large markets some precautions have to be observed due to the tur-
bulence among the Sundis and Balalis, from Bula Tangu (north of the Niari).
We saw a tree that gave sufficient shade and traced out a circle; the men put
down their loads, and Jean Makitu warned the excited crowd that they should
be calm. Every corner of these large markets has a place reserved for sellers of
smoked meat, tobacco, food of all sorts, sellers of children, small girls, slaves,
etc. . . . If we were sufficiently stocked with powder and cloth, we could do
business. Generally, this negotiation was done in the village neighboring the
market. When everything was concluded, these fellows handed over two or
three children.

He went on to report:

Our porters, especially Jean Makitu, had previously inspected the state of
these poor youngsters, who seemed happy to be delivered from the yoke of
their savage owners. Night arrived and prevented all possibility of flight. Jean
carefully tied a strong line from a leg of each of these dark Gentiles to that of
a man in the caravan. The return to Linzolo took many different paths to con-
fuse the memories of the children being taken to the Mission.[21]

Other children experienced the journey downriver from Ubangi-Shari to Liranga. Charles Castellani noted an African woman who provided a vignette for
his book *Les femmes au Congo* (*Women of Congo*, 1898), and the children in her
care:

On board, descending the Congo, I found Mgr. Augouard who was taking back
a cargo of children of both sexes bought on the upper river: some of these little
unfortunate ones were *dying of hunger* during the voyage. The captain of the
vessel, M. Lindholm, a good man, took pity and gave them rice; otherwise all
the band would have died. These children were accompanied by a young and
pretty black woman who was doubtless serving as a governess; she was in good
shape. I suppose this fast would end when they disembarked at Liranga where
these good fathers have a mission.[22]

The weak state of the children, who "seem to arrive only to receive baptism and
take their flight into the sky" was a steady refrain in the monthly reports of the
mother-superior at the Brazzaville convent. An extract in the 1896 mission *Bulletin* read:

Usually these dear children arrive in groups of 10, 16, 20 and 30. How can one
describe the moving scenes that pass before our eyes? First, we hear the whistle
of the *Léon XIII*, the mission boat; we see it in the distance; our little group is
full of emotion. We run to the embarkation point on the Pool eight minutes
from the community. Cries of joy greet the vessel which edges into the tall
grasses along the banks and after a short time the good Père Allaire is in our

midst, bringing down the passengers. Then we watch, we quickly recognize them for each tribe has its tattoos and different markings. . . . At last, the older children take charge of the little ones and all this little crowd returns joyously.[23]

Arrival at a mission in the lower Congo did not mean that all the children remained there, however. With girls in short supply, they might be transferred between mission stations, although the priests competed fiercely for available recruits and insisted that the ones they had to send elsewhere be returned or replaced. Some of the older girls with a modicum of Christian education were sent with sisters to form the nucleus of a new community, while others were sent from missions without sisters to receive an education at a convent "orphanage."[24] Others were sent back to a mission in their own area, where they could help young sisters, whose language skills were generally very limited.[25] The experience of these journeys can be glimpsed in reports. Père Rémy, who took some girls along the caravan route from Loango to Brazzaville in twenty-one days, wrote: "We made a stop on the other side of the river for dinner. The little girls slowed down the march. They arrived tired out at camp"[26] In 1887, Monseigneur Augouard took with him four little girls of five or six years old in a caravan of fifty-five porters and two Senegalese guards from Linzolo to Loango with the purpose of handing them over to the sisters. En route, they were suddenly awakened in the night by "brigands" launching a surprise attack on the camp. A gunfight broke out, and "these poor little ones let out terrified shrieks and added to the turmoil."[27] And in 1897, Père Luec traveled from Loango to the interior and wrote: "I have arrived at Linzolo after a terrible journey: the donkey, cows, and girls made me lose many days."[28]

The ambiguities of a system where the missionaries claimed they were "ransoming" slaves while inserting themselves into markets alongside slave dealers were not lost on Central Africans. Missionaries appeared as foreign slave-holding chiefs as well as *nganga nzambi*. The missionaries might see themselves as offering physical freedom and salvation to those they "ransomed," but the idea of individual autonomy was alien to Kongo society. Everyone belonged in some way to a lineage and clan, and missionaries were behaving in much the same way as politically powerful men. The children had been acquired through an exchange of goods and initiated into a powerful new cult; they labored in the mission fields and were contracted in marriage by the white "big men," who received bridewealth for the girls and paid marriage money for the boys. The sisters were the "mothers" of their slave-dependents as well as the wives or women of the male missionaries.

In the account book of the Linzolo mission for the period 1889–1930 a close track was kept of the transactions as humans and goods changed hands.[29] The date and name of the individual is entered in the left-hand column next to the amount of "ransom" paid. A right-hand column gives the source of funding, showing the network that missionaries could tap: individuals such as the trader Gresshof or the administrator Dolisie, wealthy patrons and ordinary parishioners in France, and missionaries themselves. Other entries are more vague, such as an individual "brought by his master." The whole endeavor fitted easily into the "moralization" rhetoric of the French church, the teachings of the founders of the Holy Ghost Fathers and the Sisters of Saint Joseph of Cluny, and the moral and material *mission civilatrice* that supported French colonial expansion in late-nineteenth-century Africa.[30]

Growing opposition from church and secular authorities contributed to the phasing out of the experiment. In a letter to the minister of colonies, Savorgnan de Brazza, the administrator-general of French Congo, explaining his reluctance to subsidize the mission boat, wrote:

> The administration cannot concern itself with this work with its high-sounding appearance but where even the underlying principle is questionable. This buying of children by missionaries from their owners and their immediate removal cannot be likened to a liberation either in the eyes of the natives or the ransomed children. They only see a change from one master to another and not a change in their condition. . . . They see in these transactions a slave trade carried out under the patronage of French authorities.[31]

After 1905, when slavery was made illegal in French West Africa and Congo, attacks from anti-clerical administrators who considered the "ransoming" of slaves anachronistic and an affront to the ideals of the French Republic became more virulent.[32] Nor was Cardinal Ledochowski, the prefect of the Propaganda Fide, without ambivalence, for he told Monseigneur Carrie during a visit to Rome that "his ideas on ransoming slaves, without favoring the trade, indirectly gave a worth to this sort of merchandise."[33]

Problems on the ground also brought the project to an end. Those sold by slave dealers were often weak and unwanted by African buyers, causing high mortality rates, and competition for girls pushed up prices. Furthermore, although child labor was essential in its contribution to a mission's material well-being, there were some costs in providing support until the boys and girls reached a marriageable age, sometimes more than ten years after their arrival at the mission. By 1904, at a time when subsidies from Europe were being phased out, missionaries were also coming to the conclusion that "ransoming" slaves was no longer the most cost-effective way of finding recruits for baptism. Furthermore, they believed that the slave origins of the new Catholics kept some free persons away from the church.

Not least among their conclusions was that the "children of the mission" were more "troublesome" and "turbulent" than those who stayed with their families and attended catechism classes on a daily basis. Coming from such diverse origins, separated from kin, delivered to the mission after such turbulent experiences, and living in close proximity, this could as well be interpreted as the children engaging in an ongoing process of negotiation with each other rather than overt resistance to the authorities. Yet in learning their perceived rights, the children could also gang up to mount a resistance that played on European weaknesses and divisions. A children's revolt at Linzolo boiled over after simmering for several months. Sparked off by the transfer of a favorite priest to a mission upriver, resistance then targeted a plan to remove some girls to another mission. The remaining priest wrote to his colleague at Bouanza, where they were to be sent: "As for the little girls at Linzolo, I don't know when I will send them; that would be difficult given the bad state of the trails and the uproar among the children. One only hears of flights, flights of girls who do not want to go to Bouanza, flights of boys who are afraid that the girls are not coming back and as a result jeopardizing their chances of marriage. It is, therefore, prudent to wait. It is better to let things be for now."[34] He wrote much the same in a report to Monseigneur Carrie, reminding him that "girls are rare and expensive."[35] Four months later, the children had indeed fled, some going to Brazzaville. Père Bouleuc wrote to his superior: "Now they are at the post bringing shame on us. They have gone so far as to burn their rosaries and scapulars and others have sent back these holy objects to the mission not wanting, they say, to hear of that Religion which has caused them so much suffering."[36]

At Loango, Monseigneur Carrie shortly before his death in 1904 wrote: "We have furthermore remarked that free children are the best auxiliaries for missionaries; for us, the future is not the work with slaves."[37] The decision to phase out this work was not least influenced by the numbers of African families beginning to see the advantages of a missionary education and bringing not only boys but girls to missionaries.[38] Still, as their boat plied the Ubangi river, the Catholic fathers continued to buy children and bring them to the Pool during the regional conflicts of the First World War.[39]

Women without Sisters

Throughout their early years in Congo, the Sisters of Saint Joseph of Cluny struggled for survival due to high mortality rates and the inability of the home congregation to send adequate reinforcements. Sickness and death were constant companions as they succumbed to the diseases that felled Europeans and Africans in the early years of colonial occupation. Of the twenty-one European sisters who arrived at Loango between 1886 and 1900, eleven died, eight were evacuated home sick, and two were left when the decision was made to close the convent in 1900. It reopened seven years later but never with more than two or three sisters. After just over two years in existence, the convent at Bouanza closed when an African novice and one of the two European sisters died. From Linzolo, families who wanted their girls to be trained by missionary sisters had to send their daughters to the large convent in Brazzaville, where high mortality rates were also experienced by the nuns in the early years: three Europeans dead in the first eight years and two African sisters not long after.[40] The Holy Ghost Fathers were also weakened by disease, but reinforcements allowed them to maintain a much stronger presence. Within thirty years of their arrival, they had established twelve stations in the Vicariate of French Congo.[41]

In the absence of sisters and without wives, the priests turned to lay women for assistance. Priests who reported to bishops, and bishops who reported to Paris or Rome, sought to reassure their superiors that at missions without sisters boundaries between males and females were observed and that they themselves were setting a good example for African Christians, whose moral fiber was suspect. While it was accepted that men should instruct women and girls for baptism, hear confession, and administer the sacraments, distance had to be maintained. Following the closure of the sisters' convents at Loango and Bouanza, the problem and its solution was summed up by Monseigneur Carrie: "The two convents have closed and their charges entrusted to some young Christian women under the supervision of the missionaries. . . . We will do what we can to raise the girls with the aid of Christian women. It is a critical situation for us and perhaps unique on the coast of Africa."[42] In the priests' monthly progress reports, a standard rubric was "the work with girls." These accounts and the yearly reports of the work with children reveal the indispensable work of Catholic women as caregivers, wet nurses, mentors, guardians, and teachers, and their emergence as anchors of new communities. The records of the Linzolo mission give a sense of the life experiences of this first generation of Catholic women and the girls in their charge.

Initially, the girls were boarded with Catholic families in conditions laid down by the mission and tailored to allay European fears of predatory male household members. Monseigneur Carrie's report read: "Because of the lack of Sisters to raise the young girls, the missionaries are going to try and entrust three to a Christian family, with separate rooms, special regimes, active surveillance, and as careful religious instruction as possible."[43] By 1890, with seventy-five boys and fourteen girls in their charge, the priests decided on an additional strategy. While they and their male assistants organized the boys' school, they had found "an excellent mother of a family" to be responsible for the work with girls under missionary supervision.[44] A dormitory, known locally as *ndi,* or the "marriage-village," was built near the Christian village of Saint Isidore and placed under the patronage of Saint Anne.[45] The system was new at Linzolo since girls were not confined for instruction at puberty, but for others it would make sense. In the Mayombe region, for example, girls at puberty were not confined to individual huts as they were at Loango but housed together in a dormitory, a *nzo kumbi,* for instruction before marriage.

Appointed as supervisor of the girls was Hélène Sanda, who had received instruction from the sisters either at Loango or a few miles down the coast at Landana.[46] Under her supervision, the girls learned the routines of their new life and their expected conduct. Each morning, she sent a girl to the mission store-rooms where rations were issued, mostly the product of the girls' own labor since they cultivated and prepared their own food. In mid-morning, they took a break from housework and fieldwork when a monitor arrived to take their catechism class. Since this individual was male, the fathers assured their superiors that they could keep an eye on the work from their window. In the afternoon, while the boys went to school, the girls returned to the fields or prepared food such as manioc bread for the wider mission community. After an evening meal, Hélène Sanda shepherded the girls back to their dormitory and locked them in for the night. For the success of the work, the missionaries gave credit to the director. In 1890, the girls produced "an excellent peanut harvest, also maize and manioc. All this, of course, involves a great surveillance but it works well at little cost."[47] Two months later, a reassuring letter reached Loango: "The work is going marvelously and I defy anyone to make a single, serious, and well-substantiated reproach of the Director and her children. . . . It is difficult to find a woman like Madame Sanda. She would tear out the eyes of anyone who dares to enter her cradle. At fixed hours and according to the rules she is at work and, as far as we can tell, she carries out the supervision well."[48]

Two other aspects of this dormitory system, one relating to religious practice and the other to social relations, suggest what girls might learn out-side of their work schedule and their catechism classes. In naming the house after Saint Anne, the missionaries were introducing into the religious life of the girls a patron saint, a life full of meaning that made concrete the human ancestors at the heart of Catholicism. The choice of the patron saint at Lin-zolo was instrumental in itself, for in church history Anne was the mother of Mary, the grandmother of Jesus, and the patron saint of many causes including childless individuals (since she and her husband were married twenty years before God's intervention allowed her to conceive), pregnancies, women in labor, mothers, and grandmothers. Saints and the very human figures around Jesus were also made concrete through their images on medals and in small pictures distributed by missionaries, the charms of the new religion. What all this meant to the dormitory girls cannot be ascertained, but this orientation of Catholic teaching is mentioned here because the saints were fully embraced in the spirituality of Catholic women later in the century, when a cult of saints became central in their religious practice and their corporate identity as church women.

Into the location and regulations of the girls' dormitory were also injected lessons of sexuality and Catholic morality. The whole system was designed to distance males and females and exact severe corporal punishment for breaking the rules. As Mary Malone has written for nineteenth-century Ireland, "part of the civilizing project was about control of the body and girls and women were the main target for this venture," a situation that seems to have pertained at missions in Congo also.[49] There was also the problem that conceiving a child out of wedlock meant the parents could not be married in the church and their potential value as founders of solid Christian families was prejudiced. As noted in the previous chapter, in the lower Congo, conceiving a child before the conclusion of a marriage contract likewise incurred sanctions from the elders, for it potentially endangered the health of the lineage and meant that the child carried the stigma of an abnormal birth. Yet sexual play among young people was tolerated and accepted. Indeed, in some areas of the Mayombe region boys were allowed to gather at the hut of the *tchikumbi* in the evenings for songs and dancing, to socialize around the girls' dormitory. According to one account: "The kikumbi is a meeting place for young people; they play and laugh with the young girls, bring them palm wine and presents. They leave them completely covered with red powder. However, the fiancé is not received; he gives his presents at the entrance and goes off followed by the mocking laughter of the girls."[50] It was a different matter on the Catholic mission station, where the physical configuration of the buildings and the rules of conduct emphasized a more rigid code of conduct in the interactions of young people.

Hélène Sanda became something of a model for other missions in lower Congo, where a first generation of African women supervised the mission girls either in their homes or in a dormitory. When the sisters were forced to leave Bouanza and Loango, the girls in their charge were handed over to lay women for supervision. At Linzolo itself the number of women involved in training girls and young women increased, although the dormitory system continued. Young men brought their "fiancées" to live with a family for several months, and the young women provided help to the women of the household in return for their upkeep and instruction.[51] In 1910, 115 young women and 60 little girls were receiving training at different levels, all but 30 living with Catholic families. Concerning the "fiancées," Père Doppler wrote: "The arrangement costs us nothing. These young women are boarders with Christian families where they work, eat, sleep, and chat with our mothers who are very glad to have help in their households and in their fields."[52] In 1922, the priest reported that for girls "the form our work takes has not changed. During the day, the catechist students live in the homes of Christian families with widows or even in surrounding villages. They spend the night in cubicles made for them." He noted the double advantage: that it cost the mission budget nothing and "it liberates us from concerns that are of little interest."[53] Clearly, the women were key figures in the formation of future wives and mothers, complementing the work of the missionaries, catechists, and teachers.

One of those who began her Catholic socialization in Hélène Sanda's care was Agnès Mpolo, with whom we began this chapter. Her name suggests that she came from the surrounding region where the Lari predominated, although this is not certain since names of children were sometimes confused or changed. On arrival at the mission, she lived in the girl's dormitory and was given a simple dress or cloth according to the "Rules for the children of the mission."[54] Six months after arriving at Linzolo, Agnès was again on the road. Together with fourteen others she was selected by Carrie as strong and old enough to make the arduous journey along the caravan trail to the sisters' mission at Loango "for a more complete education." Some fifteen others thought too small and frail to make the journey were left behind in the care of Hélène Sanda. According to the Loango news bulletin, the sisters were "thrilled" with their new recruits, who had received some training from "an excellent mother of a Christian family."[55]

At Loango began a more intense education directed by the sisters, and a whole new world opened up for the girl, one in which Catholic material objects and European notions of physical, social, and spiritual time and space were fine-tuned to turn out a young woman with the discipline and virtues expected of a Catholic wife and mother. Under the tutelage of the sisters, girls such as Agnès Mpolo experienced a more varied curriculum and acquired more specialized knowledge than was possible at Linzolo. Working in the fields and carrying water continued to be central in the daily schedule, as were catechism lessons, but other knowledge that marked a woman who had passed through the care of the sisters was also transmitted: deportment in a European manner, singing to European music, washing and ironing in the European style, and simple French. Adoration of holy objects in the sisters' chapel and yard was learned and experienced: a large cross, statues of *mama nzambi* ("the Mother of God") and Saint Joseph (the sisters' patron saint), and the Stations of the Cross. A portrait of Anne-Marie Javouhey, the great ancestor of the sisters to whom prayers were said every day, hung on the chapel wall. Rosaries, medals, and scapulars were the reward for progress in piety and good behavior. For the sisters, such objects of piety were important teaching tools in conveying basic ideas of the "good God" to the girls and young women in their charge, those they referred to as their "poor" or "wild" children.[56]

The priests kept track of the girls sent from their stations to Loango, since they were such an essential resource. A note by Carrie in 1894 listed the names and fortunes of the fifteen girls who had arrived from Linzolo three years earlier: one was a postulant, four (including Agnès Mpolo) were continuing their training at Loango, three had returned to Linzolo, three had gone to Brazzaville, and four had died in an epidemic.[57] In January 1897, now about fourteen or fifteen years old and of a marriageable age according to canonical law as well as local practice, Agnès was returned to Linzolo, where she was married, probably to a catechist or a mission worker. At Loango, she had come under pressure to become a postulant, but according to the priest at Linzolo: "Jeanne and Agnès Mpolo say to whoever wants to hear that they do not want to be nuns."[58]

Agnès Mpolo helped start the tradition of strong women leaders at Linzolo who are still remembered today.[59] Her fame rests on several achievements. She had many children, three by the time she was twenty and seven by 1910, when she was not quite thirty. She was one of the first Linzolo women to learn to read. She had specialized household skills learned from the sisters and not yet common among church women. She had been to the coast, an experience that drew the same kind of awe as travel to Europe at a later date, and she had the approval of the priests, who found her indispensable in teaching the basics of the Catholic faith to future wives and mothers. Or, as the head of the mission wrote in 1904: "For a long time, the missionaries complained about the impossibility of getting girls to come to catechism classes. Those who were opposed to the idea were won over by the appointment of two female catechists."[60]

Less is known about the other woman catechist, Marie Mbousi, who was about the same age as Agnès, also sent to Loango in 1891 and returned to Linzolo. Together, they appear in the priests' reports as the backbone of the women's work well into the 1920s. In the morning and evening they conducted catechism classes with the mission girls and the young women preparing for baptism and marriage. Once a week, a priest fluent in Kilari would go over the recitations with class members and explain their meaning further. They also taught singing to groups of women and advanced catechism classes to their most promising students.[61]

Returning to Monseigneur Derouet's account of Mère Agnès, she was portrayed not only as a model wife and mother but as a pious, modest, dignified, and soft-spoken churchwoman in whose life two motherhoods converged. She was a mother of a large family and she was "a sort of religious teacher, let us say at once, a Mother Superior, and the community she directs is not ordinary." The twenty or so girls whom he had observed her teaching during his visit to Linzolo were "her work, her community, her second family."[62] The vicar warmed to his ideal of blended motherhood in the service of the church as he described his subject, "liberated from protocol" and conducting her class with her youngest child, Basile, in her arms or crawling around at her feet. When he realized Mère Agnès's eyesight was failing, he decided to reward her by sending to Loango for a pair of glasses, news that "caused a public sensation" at the thought of the teacher with "two mirrors in front of her eyes."[63] The writer assumed the reaction to be a gauge of modernity since "glasses like shoes are the product of civilization, and these at present are prohibitively expensive in Congo."[64] Yet there were likely multiple meanings for observers who considered books and writing as powerful spiritual paraphernalia and glass and reflecting mirrors in the eyes of fertility and *nkisi* figures an entry into the occult.

Expanding Horizons and Emerging Communities

Like colonial administrators and ethnographers, missionaries engaged in a reorientation of space, developing their own maps with boundaries of vicariates and symbols for principal Catholic centers. Plans of the main stations located the social, technical, and spiritual knowledge of the new religion: church, presbytery, schools, dispensary, print shop, dormitories, Christian villages, cemeteries, farms, and uncultivated land. Such physical changes were powerful reminders of the new cult for neighboring societies whose experience of physical space was more shifting and porous and buildings less permanent, although they knew bounded areas of spiritual and social protection. Around mission property processions paused at the statues, crosses, and cemeteries that marked contours of piety and adoration.[65] In the surrounding countryside, chapels, schools, and crosses contested older social and ritual markers such as *kumbi* huts and *lemba* shrines. Services and saints' days helped routinize new temporal rhythms that jostled but did not necessarily replace the customary notions of work and rest that co-existed with them.[66] It was in this context that the making of Catholic communities took place. As they grew to maturity, the first generation of Catholic women transmitted ideas and practices that helped anchor such emerging communities.

Settling newly married couples in Christian villages on mission property was a standard feature of missionary strategy throughout Africa in the early decades of evangelization. In lower Congo, there were seventeen such communities with 117 families by 1907. At Brazzaville, there were five with about 200 households in 1910.[67] The ordering of these settlements demonstrated European intentions: grouping Christians together, maintaining discipline, and creating showplaces to impress potential converts and European observers. At Brazzaville, a missionary reported: "In the villages, we wage war against the laziness common in our good Blacks and all the inhabitants must justify their means of existence or they will be expelled."[68] Administrators so admired the "perfectly aligned streets" of the Christian villages as well as the ease of inspections for order and hygiene that it influenced their design for the African *quartiers* of Brazzaville.[69] Yet, turning this discussion around from themes of mission goals and local resistance, there is the question of why new Catholics stayed and what their relations were not only with the Europeans but with each other.

The answer seems to lie in the relative freedom of action that inhabitants of these constructed communities retained in spite of appearances to the contrary (for example, in postcards published by missionaries to demonstrate the progress of their work), and in the degree of convergence between missionary intentions and the religious life and social ambitions of African Christians. On a most basic level, missionaries offered some protection to those who chose to remain under their aegis, against not only a predatory colonial state engaged in conquest and occupation but also the upsurge of witchcraft and poison ordeals that the disruptions brought.

Bernard Mambeke-Boucher, who arrived in Brazzaville as a child in 1919, shared his perceptions of what happened:

> So, for most of the time, the missionaries defended Congolese Christians
> when they had problems or were arrested. It was always the priest who would
> go and protest about the situation to the police superintendent. That caught
> the attention of the administration and also attracted the attention of the
> Congolese who would say, well, all the same, you do have moral support there.
> That would give encouragement for those who were thinking of joining the
> church.

Figure 2.1. Christian family, Catholic mission, Brazzaville, c. 1905. From a mission postcard.

There was also room for independent action that did not fit the missionary model, for at any given time the two or three Europeans at a station could be felled by recurrent sickness, sent home for leave, or absent while inspecting catechists at their outlying posts. Mambeke-Boucher pointed out that the inhabitants could always leave for whatever reasons, economic, social, or religious. He himself never converted to Catholicism, for the demands were just too complicated and troublesome:

> It was not easy then. If you didn't go to confession, you could be refused communion. If you weren't married in the church you couldn't go to communion. Next, if you wanted to be baptized, you had to attend catechism class, know God's commandments, and the seven sacraments, etc, etc. If you were baptized, another cycle started before the first communion. Then another cycle of catechism for the solemn communion etc.... And still more. If you die and you don't have the Last Rites, your body cannot be taken to the church for the Mass. After all that some people said, "it is too much."[70]

Richard Gray suggested that turning attention away from the travails of the missionary church, as portrayed in their reports, to an African perspective would lead to a better understanding of the "process of interaction in which Africans found help in their specific needs and concerns."[71] This seems to have been the case for the early generations of Catholics, who remained at the Christian villages, where they found a measure of protection, community, and a sense of identity in a society under duress. These were also communities where many were drawn together in religious practice as they attended Mass, celebrated saints' days, and attended family celebrations such as post-baptismal parties and end-of-mourning festivities. Feast days and special events with their extravagance drew in the wider community. Such was the occasion at the Loango mission for the installation of the statue of Our Lady of Lourdes, a landmark occasion around a symbol that fused healing and prayer in a place where sickness was omnipresent. A description of the dedication relates the spectacle:

> On 5 December, on the holiday of the Immaculate Conception towards five in the afternoon, the Fathers in their robes, the Brothers, the Children of the Mission, and the girls of the Sisters walked in procession to the foot of the statue of Our Lady of Lourdes, carrying banners and torches and singing litanies for the Holy Virgin. The broad avenue of banana trees and the area around the statue had been decorated with care. Two lines of colored Venetian lanterns lit up the decorations. In the middle of this illuminated space was the beautiful, cast-iron statue of Our Lady of Lourdes, 1.70 meters high, that had been tastefully painted by Père Le Louet. It appeared more beautiful and majestic than ever on its pedestal. After the Magnificat, that was performed in two parts, Père Sauner gave a short and moving address on the splendor and power of the Immaculate Virgin. Then Monseigneur in his pontifical robes assisted by Père Giron as deacon and with Père Levadon as sub-deacon solemnly blessed the statue. After the ceremony, we returned in procession with flaming torches to the church and chanting Ave Maria.[72]

The graves of these founders of the Congolese church can still be visited in the cemeteries at the old mission stations at Linzolo and Loango. An exhibition at Loango in 2000 displayed photographs of the earliest buildings and some of their inhabitants.[73] One showed Suzanne Tchibassa outside her house in the Christian village of Saint Benoît. Like Agnès Mpolo, she had started with nothing and rose to be a model of a good Catholic wife and mother. She is buried alongside her husband in a family plot in the shade of the mango trees that line the path from the central mission to the beach at Loango Bay. About the same age as Agnès Mpolo and Marie Mbousi, whom she must have known well, she was raised at the sisters' school. For a brief period she was a postulant and novice, but she never took her vows. In 1897, when she was about fourteen, Suzanne Tchibassa married Polycarpe Kiassinda, a young man from the Congo estuary who had been raised by the Holy Ghost Fathers and brought by Carrie to help found the Loango mission. According to their granddaughter, "the

Fathers and the Sisters helped them with their marriage and setting up their household at Saint Benoît." By the time of the marriage, Polycarpe Kiassinda had risen to be head of the mission printing shop and one of the fathers' most trusted assistants. He had additional status, for he worked the bellows of the church organ. Anne-Marie Kambissi, who lived with her grandparents at Saint Benoît when she was a child, remembered that her grandfather had built the house from wooden planks, remarkable at the time. She also noted that the couple had nine children and that her grandmother was a devout Christian and a rock in the local Catholic community. Her testimony both recalls the life and conveys how Suzanne Tchibassa is remembered by her granddaughter as a "good" Catholic mother for her religious practice, her work, and her support of family and community:

> I was about seven years old when grandmother taught me to pray. She used to like especially the invocation to Jesus, Mary, Joseph, and all the others it was necessary to recite. There was a little altar in the house with a cross, a statue of the Virgin Mary, and another of the Sacred Heart. We prayed in front of the altar morning, noon and night. We also recited the Angelus together. Also, grandmother went to mass at the church every morning. She sent me to the mission to learn the catechism from Félicien Goma.

About her grandmother's devotion to the mission, she added:

> Grandmother liked farming. When she was old, the Mission gave her a piece of land near Tchilassy. I used to go with her to her farm. Before she began her work, she said a personal prayer such as, "Thank you, Lord. You have brought me to this place, now bless my work." When the Angelus sounded she stopped working to recite that prayer. Grandmother grew potatoes and manioc, in particular. She was very generous and would take whole loads to the boarders at the mission: potatoes, manioc, yams, and taros. Her many children often brought her some money and it was then her joy to request masses for the dead.

Suzanne Tchibassa's husband, who was considerably older than his wife, died in 1932. In her old age, she moved to stay with her daughters in Pointe-Noire, where she lived until her death at around eighty-eight years. Her granddaughter remembered the requiem Mass said for her grandmother at the Sacre-Coeur parish church of Loango and her burial in the old Christian cemetery. She concluded: "Suzanne and Polycarpe were a very united couple, very faithful. They got along well in spite of Polycarpe's tendency to drink too much from time to time. Suzanne also thought her husband not firm enough with the children. She, on the other hand, was good but stern."[74]

By the first decade of the twentieth century, missionaries increasingly recognized that expanding their work through training small children bought out
of servitude had severe limitations and did not constitute a solid base for the future church. Rather, the main work of proselytization lay with African catechists
working in villages supervised through occasional visits by itinerant priests.
Thus, after some two or three decades of trial and error, the mission stations
themselves became specialized institutions with schools, novitiates, seminaries,
and dispensaries, while the task of reproducing the faith more broadly was put
in the hands of catechists at "chapel-schools" or "rural-schools." African clergy,
who traveled around the villages within reach of the mission stations to pros-
elytize, baptize, visit the sick, and administer the sacrament, were also critical
in this work since they understood the language and the culture, but there were
very few. Fifty years after the arrival of the first Spiritan missionaries there were
only eight African priests in the colony of Moyen-Congo.[75] As the initial contact
point with catechumens, catechist posts became the key proselytizing institution and contributed to a growth in the numbers of those baptized.[76]

Catechist posts radiated out into the countryside. Modeled after the mission
station, their extent depended on the energy and commitment of the catechist
and his wife, the level of support from the Christian community in the making,
and visits from missionaries who could be appealed to in conflicts with government agents. While the catechist had the full skills of a ritual expert passed on to
him by his master, the *nganga nzambi,* his wife also had status, for she generally
knew how to read and write and was responsible in part for teaching women and
girls the catechism, telling their rosary beads, reciting Hail Marys, handing out
medals, and leading new songs. Like her husband, with intercessory prayers she
might comfort the sick and those who thought themselves in danger from evil
powers. She could also give her husband advice on suitable girls to send to the
mission for further training. Pairing catechists with women who could teach the
catechism was mission policy, for as stated by Monseigneur Carrie: "It seems
more natural that women teach the catechism to women and girls rather than
the catechists themselves. That is the reason that the catechists should be married as far as possible to individuals capable of teaching the catechism to girls."[77]
Also, when catechists were married to literate women, "this allows us to pair the
education of boys and girls."[78]

One such woman considered to be the ideal wife to complement her husband in his work was Marie-Antoinette, who attended the sisters' school at the
Loango mission around the same time as Agnès Mpolo, Marie Mbousi, and
Suzanne Tchibassa. She married Antoine Mpadi, one of the top students at the
fathers' school, who had gone on to train as a catechist.[79] In 1894, the couple was

Figure 2.2. Catechist post/rural school, c. 1898, near Loango. Reproduced from *Les Missions Catholiques*, 1898.

chosen to establish a catechist post at Sainte-Marie du Kouilou (near present-day Madingo-Kayes) north of Loango, a difficult assignment since it was known for "the strong devotion" of women to a "fetish" and a female *nganga* whom "everyone feared."[80] Subject to labor migration like most of the surrounding communities, the area had, nevertheless, a stable and quite prosperous population, with men specializing in ocean and river fishing and the women farming and processing fish. In spite of deaths from sleeping sickness and other disease and the alleged poisoning of some Christians by the local *nganga,* there was a nucleus of 150 individuals baptized or attending catechism classes by 1914.[81]

Like the wives of other catechists, Marie-Antoinette had important responsibilities that fell to her as the social mother and a leader of women in the nascent Catholic community. She was admired as someone with innovative practical knowledge and as a minor religious specialist in her own right. Such women helped organize teams of women in farming and church-related construction projects, thus bonding the new community together in familiar work environments.[82] At Notre Dame de Victoire, an outpost of the Linzolo mission, the catechist Joseph Bemba had organized the building of a chapel, a house for the visiting priest, and huts for the school children. There was also a large cross where the community gathered for prayers. It was the women of the church who provided much of the basic labor, cleared the land for the broad paths that converged at the post, and produced food for the workers. The celebrations for the opening of the chapel found in attendance not only villagers from the surrounding areas but several chiefs.[83] This was a strong community with a dynamic catechist, and to be married to a man like Joseph Bemba was to be married to a "big man," with the concomitant status and benefits for his wife and her children. The catechist, given his position under the aegis of the white missionary, was free from the forced labor and humiliating punishments that other men suffered under the co-lonial regime, and his skills might be called on by other important men who were illiterate and did not know much French, unlike a catechist after two or more years training at the mission station.[84] At Kindamba, when the administration was grouping together villages in new units for administrative purposes, chiefs competed for catechists to read their mail.[85] In 1932, the lieutenant-governor of Moyen-Congo complained that groups living under a catechist "have a tendency to constitute a State within a State," for they paid taxes and performed labor services but did not contribute to the economic development of the colony, and the catechist drew his authority from the church rather than through adminis-trative structures.[86]

The catechist and his family also had material possessions that lifted them above the average villager. Since he was usually paid less than he could earn if he worked for other white employers and had to be given benefits to encour-age him to stay in the employment of the church, missionaries augmented fam-ily resources with gifts such as chickens, goats, pigs, and cloth. The quality of his house was sometimes augmented with materials brought from the mission station, thus elevating it above those in the neighborhood. Appearances were important for a catechist and his family as they were for others.[87] Those under the authority of the Linzolo station had to maintain a strict dress code. In the chapel and on visits to local chiefs or colonial authorities, the catechist had to wear a "very clean" uniform consisting of a cloth, a jacket or waistcoat, and the special crucifix issued to one in his position. On Sundays, his wife was expected to wear a cloth and head-scarf and the children to be neatly dressed. They might also have access to more prestigious and mysterious items, such as the eyeglasses of Agnès Mpolo. Félix Nkaoua, who had come from the coast and was chief of a Christian village before becoming a catechist, carried an umbrella when he traveled, just like the Loango elites.[88]

The community centered on the chapel-school was integrated into the wider Catholic network through the travels of the catechist and missionaries and the comings and goings of schoolchildren and others to and from the mis-sion station. On Sundays and holy days such as Christmas, Easter, and Corpus Christi, men, women, and children would make the trek, led by the catechist and his wife. Such journeys under missionary protection could mitigate the controls and abuse that villagers might otherwise suffer from colonial militias and allow them to cross circumscription boundaries to meet up with friends and family. In inscribing alternative contours of allegiance, they were thus exploiting for their benefit the tensions of church and state, invoking the patronage of the church to contest limits imposed by secular authorities.[89] The exuberance of these treks that echoed the festive and communal side of Catholicism so common in France at the time was encouraged by missionaries as a sign of the vitality of the faith and a means of "taking hold of the land" through spiritual and physical pathways.[90] Although the destination was not the shrine of a saint but rather the mission church with its large congregation, resplendent rituals, statues, and images, the events were akin to pilgrimages elsewhere but with a particular local cachet.[91] This was given by the catechist and the "pilgrims" under his leadership converging at the mission station in a display of popular Catholicism. A report from Linzolo described such celebrations:

> From Saturday afternoon at 4 PM until 8 AM on Sunday morning, people flow along the roads that lead to the station. From far away when they see the clock of their church—for Linzolo has a true church—they let out the loud cries that are part of their culture, and, echoing through the hills, they alert the missionaries to their arrival. Soon, a long file of more than 800 Balalis and Batekes appears, carrying on their heads firewood that they will use to light the fires through the night, and under their arms, rolled up in banana leaves, their manioc.

As darkness fell, torches lit up the hillside paths leading to the mission station. At Sunday Mass, the diverse crowd gathered at the mission church:

> The mission clock strikes 8 AM. The sixty Christian families come to join the crowd who arrived yesterday; and from the other side of the yard comes Père Zimmerman with his seventy school children. But where will they put all this crowd? The church seems to have space for 600 people but there are more than a thousand at the door.... Gradually everyone finds a place. Certainly, there are neither benches nor chairs. In the nave, all are mixed together, small and large, young and old, men and women, slaves and masters. But at the front on the raised platform are the region's aristocracy; these are the heads of the sixty Christian families of Linzolo. It is from among them that the cantors have been chosen.... The young men in the choir who support and embellish different parts of the ceremony are dressed in black cassocks and white surplices.[92]

Such communities were at the heart of early church expansion in regions beyond the mission stations. Many catechists' posts became important centers, but with others progress was quite erratic as they were subject to all the disruptions of lower Congo at the time; survival was predicated on the availability of missionaries to provide material support, help counter attacks by indigenous religious specialists, and stand behind the catechist. Opposition from chiefs, healers, *nganga nkisi,* and anti-clerical colonial officials could make it difficult for catechists to persevere if visits from the missionary were not visible on a regular basis. In some cases, they and their wives were not well-respected because they were young or strangers or of slave origins. Although missionary accounts tell of success stories, there are also reports of abandoned chapel-schools, buildings sinking into disrepair, and catechists leaving their posts and taking their families to the towns in search of more remunerative employment. It was all part of the new and complex world that was being constructed in the midst of the disruptive colonial occupation.

Conclusion

The experience of the women whose record survives suggests that they made themselves indispensable for the growth and maintenance of the church and the attraction and nurturing of following generations of Catholic women. They worked in the shadow of a patriarchal institution, but like the missionary sisters they were engaged in creating space in which to pursue their perceived social roles. They shared with local women who had not been drawn into the missionary orbit similar understandings of women's work: generating resources for support of the family, its reproduction, and religious life. This did not much change even if the meaning and context might. Yet the domain of Catholic women was in danger of shrinking as the church and the colonial world impinged on their lives. Many were disadvantaged in relation to men, who through their education acquired the means of securing wage-earning jobs. Although the education of daughters at home continued, as exemplified in the life of Suzanne Tchibassa and in the memory of her granddaughter, girls gradually started to go elsewhere to be trained for Christian marriage and motherhood; this trend accelerated over the following decades as new knowledge at home and work was in demand. Grandmothers, aunts, and mothers might resist the dilution of practices such as *kumbi* and the knowledge learned through the institution, but that was becoming less relevant, not least in the minds of young women themselves.

The openings for religious specialists also narrowed as the church hierarchy edged women out of positions as catechists. Even the status of Mère Agnès seems to have been a matter of ambivalence in the mind of Monseigneur Derouet, who refers to her as a "sort of religious teacher" and "a Mother Superior" rather than as a catechist. Unlike the male catechists, she worked unpaid, her services apparently flowing from her position as a maternal figure in the community, "her second family." His article did, however, end with a strong appeal for funding so that her position and that of Marie Mbousi might be upgraded to that of men. It is not clear that this happened.[93] Only a few female catechists are mentioned in the official church statistics in later years. For the Vicariate of Lower Congo, with its seat first at Loango and later at Pointe-Noire, the statistics for catechists show only two years when women were employed (one in 1926 and six in 1927), perhaps associated with an exodus in these years of fifteen men to better-paying jobs on the railroad, in commerce, and the administration. Otherwise, the numbers of male catechists rose from 58 in 1920 to a peak of 518 in 1939.[94] In the Vicariate of Upper Congo centered on Brazzaville, there was one year (1927) when 8 out of 220 catechists were women, but otherwise there were never more than 5 women catechists in the years between 1924 and 1936, whereas in the same period the number of male catechists rose from 208 to 464.[95] This state of affairs may have been linked not only to the orientations of European men of the church but to the training of catechists, which became more rigorous and involved long stays at the mission for training and refresher courses, a requirement that became necessary as the Catholic missions upgraded their standards to compete for adherents with the Swedish Evangelical Mission. Women were deemed unable to leave their domestic responsibilities, although even those like Mère Agnès who were part of a mission community also seem to have been edged out. As language skills were upgraded few women had the necessary proficiency in French, at least before the 1930s.

Yet, as they worked together in projects at the catechists' posts or in the urban church and met in prayer groups, women formed alternative communities and found means of asserting their individual and collective interests. They shared with the European missionaries a common ground on the importance of their identity as mothers, whether biological or social, for that was their principal base in local society, while the missionaries also saw women primarily as mothers of families. Yet, as will be seen in the following chapter, the meaning, substance, and responsibilities of marriage and motherhood remained a matter for diverse interpretations and arenas for ongoing negotiation, both among African Catholics and with their missionary teachers.

3. Means of Transition

By the second decade of the twentieth century, there was a marked increase in the number of girls and young women enrolling in preparatory classes for baptism and marriage. From Loango, Mère Jerôme reported that "the era of Christian families is now on a sound footing and all the young people want to have a Christian marriage and are not against it as they were previously."[1] At Linzolo in 1911, an official visitor noted that only one hundred marriages had been recorded in the church register during the previous twenty years.[2] By 1917, "there's like a movement favoring Christian marriage."[3] In 1916, the mission account book no longer showed the "ransoming" of slave children as a significant expense; instead donations were being directed to a "dowry fund" to provide bridewealth payments for mission-trained young men.[4] At Mbamou in the Pool region, a priest wrote that "the work with fiancées so difficult at the start is progressing." Two hundred fourteen young women were enrolled in catechism classes with a view to Christian marriage.[5] At Brazzaville, more than one hundred marriages were taking place annually in the 1920s, and for 1929–33, the sisters reported 1,057 Christian marriages, with 700 girls waiting for admission to their schools. They could not keep up with the demand and pleaded for the Mother House to send reinforcements.[6]

The process of "marrying well," becoming mothers of Catholic families, and joining with others in church communities claimed the attention of the women who are the focus of this chapter.[7] They searched for the means, sometimes in concert with the men in their lives and sometimes independently, and engaged in ongoing negotiations with male missionaries, who, however "godlike" they might appear, could never suspend dialogue as women were essential in their shaping of the mission church.[8] Other women within the church and missionary sisters were important resources for the transmission of social knowledge, daily life support, and advice in practical Christianity. In the three decades before the Second World War, Catholic women undertook significant transitions as they engaged in shifting "landscapes of power," a notion borrowed here from Richard Roberts's study of women and their use of colonial courts in the French Soudan. Traversing such landscapes, as he suggests, involved both "intentionality and action."[9]

Conditions stemming from the impact of colonial occupation provided the backdrop and impetus for social change. While male policymakers in church and state tended to reduce their discourse on the control of women to questions of polygyny, women themselves were dealing with a range of issues, one of which might be to do with their husbands. In rural areas, women and men were often faced with rapacious colonial agents commandeering their labor as porters, farmers, and road-construction workers, all activities in which they were forcibly enlisted. After 1916, the colonial administration started the reorganization of districts under appointed chiefs, who, with little alternative infrastructure, employed militias to collect mandatory taxes and fulfill quotas. In this situation, women were often subject to threats and violence.[10] Also, in much of the lower Congo the construction of the railroad, the Chemin de Fer Congo-Océan (CFCO), between 1921 and 1934 with its demands for workers and food drained the vitality of villages already decimated by sleeping sickness. During the years of construction, 127,250 workers were employed and living in camps, more than half from the Pool and lower Congo region.[11] The administration reorganized village production so that women had to produce specified amounts from their individual plots and from the "fields of the *commandant*" that they farmed collectively. If quotas were not met corporal punishment, fines, and imprisonment resulted.[12] In a letter to Monseigneur Guichard, one official put his case:

> Concerning work in the fields, that is women's work in this country. This work is obligatory and in anticipation of this problem, the Governor-General has issued a decree authorizing corporal punishment for the offender. The need to prevent the famine that devastates some regions of the Colony and the demand for food by the many workmen employed in projects that benefit the public means that we must squarely implement a policy of zero intolerance against slackers.[13]

In such conditions, mission stations offered a measure of security.

Shifting landscapes of power were also increasingly experienced in urban environments. Pointe-Noire, the Atlantic terminal of the CFCO, developed into Congo's second largest town. Such reorientations of space forced the Holy Ghost Fathers to close some of their mission posts and open others near new population centers: Pounga and Mindouli along the railroad and Madingou on the Pointe-Noire–Brazzaville road, for example. The emigration of workers turned the Loango region into a backwater while Pointe-Noire rose in importance, becoming the episcopal seat after the Second World War.[14] Moyen-Congo was only experiencing the early throes of the urban growth that transformed the country and the church in the later twentieth century, however. The population of Brazzaville was around forty thousand in 1940; that of Pointe-Noire just under ten thousand in the mid-1930s.[15] Still, even if their numbers were small, male workers who were mostly graduates of Catholic schools wielded influence well beyond their numbers, for they were purveyors of modernity, displaying their material success and the creativity of their "style" most persuasively.

Negotiating Marriage

Marriage was an important and strategic pathway to social advancement and motherhood in the emerging new society as it had been in the old. In some cases, the families of those seeking a church marriage might be involved, but in others the origins of the prospective spouses might be more problematic for the priest, given the social disruptions of the times. Either way, in order to proceed with a church marriage, he had to ascertain the status of the couple and ensure that the union was acceptable under canon law. In many cases, this was not possible without a special application to the higher authorities, for the clergy found themselves asked to process "irregular unions," sometimes relating to Kongo marriage practices or to previous marriages where women claimed they had been "abandoned" by the father of their children. There was also the problem of what the church called "mixed marriages," that is, marriage between a Christian and "pagan." One early appeal for clarification by the priest to his episcopal superior read: "I do not know what the church and Your Grace thinks of mixed marriages. I would be happy to receive different advice. . . . Is it necessary that we forbid Marriage? The Church it seems to me should not be so severe. I am appealing to Your Grace for a categorical reply. . . . Are you authorizing me to conduct mixed Marriages, if the case presents itself? Can I also if the case occurs unite a man and a woman who are both pagans?"[16]

The very complications for the church created openings for the plaintiffs who with the assistance of a priest carried their petitions to the church courts. At a time when the basis for African marriage was a customary law contested by men as they sought to control women, marriage sanctioned by canon law and supported by a European missionary helped secure the position of a woman in her chosen community. In many cases, and especially in the town, it could also mean marriage to a mission-trained man with a wage-earning job and some social standing. Applications for marriage dispensations between 1918 and 1936 carrying the stamped approval of the vicar apostolic in Brazzaville show how men and women took initiatives to have their marriage authorized under the care of the church.[17] The applications were written by the priest in the official church format, and some were likely framed to make them acceptable to higher authorities, but the documents come across as appeals negotiated by the petitioners and their missionary sponsor.

"Customary" marriage practices created one set of dilemmas for European priests, and a great deal of time had to be spent sorting out the relationships and age of the petitioners so that they could be presented to the episcopal court in a satisfactory manner. Men "ransomed" as boys and raised at a mission station might happily take a wife with a similar foreign background where relationships were not an issue, but those of free origins showed a marked preference for marriage to a woman they knew and to whom they were related. Working out the precise nature of the relationships was often difficult for the priest, for there was no distinction in the language between a biological relation and a classificatory one. For example, as already noted one's biological mother and her classificatory sisters were all referred to as *ngúdi*. For the church, consanguinity in a direct line or in the collateral line to the third degree were impediments to marriage.[18] In presenting each case, the priest drew family trees to locate the petitioners' relationship to each other but also supported his case by pointing out the moral danger of "sinful" relationships. Jean Baptiste Nkondia and Rosalie Ndembo, for example, appealed for a dispensation relating to level of consanguinity, with the priest recommending approval on the grounds of "the cessation of public concubinage."[19] For Silvestre Nkodi and Françoise Nzombe, there was the additional reason "that their alliance has existed for a long time."[20] For "the faithful Prosper Mounkala and Martine Thérèse Oumba," the relationship should be approved because of the "small number of unmarried Catholic women in the region where they live."[21] All these cases were granted a dispensation. Clearly the couple had strengths in such negotiations given the urgency of establishing Christian families for the priests.

Age at marriage was also a common issue. In 1918, the Vatican promulgated a new Marriage Code that for the first time set a definite minimum age for marriage: fourteen for women and sixteen for men. Previously, twelve or the age of puberty had been considered permissible for the young woman and the timing of marriage left to the discretion of the priest.[22] For example, when Marie Mbousi returned to Linzolo from her training at the Loango convent in 1898, the priest wrote to his superior that he had been able to establish only three families "due to the lack of marriageable young women," adding that he had a young man ready to marry her, but "I think at thirteen and a half Marie Mbusi is still too young, I am waiting."[23] Setting the age at fourteen increased the number of appeals to the courts since the concept of precise age was quite alien in the Kongo marriage process, where puberty was what counted. The plaintiffs often seem to have had the upper hand since ascertaining the sexual development of the girl presented difficulties for the priest, who in most cases had to guess, take the word of the petitioners, or try to locate the girl's family. The case of Binatori and Marcienne Bikindou involved a correspondence between two priests: one had married them, but when the couple arrived at Linzolo a second priest declared the girl was only twelve and too young. The answer from the episcopal authority in Brazzaville was that the priests needed to sort things out as best they could, and the marriage does not appear to have been annulled.[24] Cases concerning age of marriage continued well into the 1930s as those seeking church marriage raised issues relating to traditional practices or, as the missionary wrote concerning the young age of marriage for girls, "the struggle against this pernicious custom of the Balali is ongoing: the fight is hard but necessary."[25]

Many cases arose where women wanted to remarry and came to the church courts to plead their case. Preferential treatment was usually given to widows since the church abhorred the practice of levirate. Thérèse Matala, for example, having been claimed on the death of her husband by his brother, had come to the mission station, where she met Jean Souamounou, a Christian. Together, they applied to the church court for a dispensation for their marriage, which was granted.[26] In other cases, women claimed a dispensation since their husbands had left to find work and had not returned. For example:

> The faithful Marguerite Nkassa, desirous of contracting a Christian marriage begs Your Grace to waive the appearance [in court] of her first and unfaithful spouse. The reason is the impossibility of making him appear since he is resident in Belgian Congo. The messenger sent to him reported that this particular witness refused the summons to resume cohabitation.[27]

Another read:

> The faithful Henriette Nlolo, desirous of contracting a Christian marriage, humbly requests from Your Grace the dispensation of summons to her unfaithful husband, Mbemba. The reason for the request is the difficulty of locating Mbemba who is in the Upper Congo. He has besides already received the reimbursement of the bridewealth.[28]

In January 1925, the Brazzaville court granted a request to "the faithful Catherine," who pleaded the impossibility of locating her first husband who "may be deceased."[29] Another case concerned Martha Louvoudou, who had been separated "for a long time" from her first husband, by whom she had two children. She had remarried a "pagan" and had two children by him, one of whom was deceased. She had then enrolled in catechism classes at Linzolo and was newly baptized. Her husband had also been a catechumen for a year. The priest, wanting to "regularize this union," had sent two catechists to find Martha's first husband, Mafia, but he was not in his village since he had gone to Brazzaville. On his return, he told a third catechist that he had two other wives and that he no longer wanted to be married to Martha. He also said that he would not convert and that he would not give up his two wives. Martha asked that since her first husband lived far from Brazzaville and refused to come to a hearing of the case, a dispensation be granted so that she and her second husband could be united in a Christian marriage. Her request was granted.[30]

Faced with a number of such requests, Monseigneur Guichard, who had succeeded Monseigneur Augouard as vicar apostolic, prepared guidelines for conditions under which matrimonial dispensations might be granted. This was within his jurisdiction since the Vatican promulgated marriage codes but delegated powers of dispensation to bishops, vicars apostolic, and others having pastoral care over souls. According to retired missionaries, there was usually more flexibility in the colonies, given the "newness" of so many Christians.[31] Based on cases that had come before the court and emerging from the realities of the local situation, the document is chiefly remarkable for its accommodation of those seeking a church marriage.[32] Application for a dispensation was justified when the situation of the petitioners was "more serious than the obstacle to the marriage" under the usual application of canon law. In other words, the purported danger of individuals living in sin if the right to marry was denied was the prime consideration. Of the sixteen conditions under which a dispensation request could be submitted, several show how men and women could through the courts obtain approval for their marriage even if it was "irregular" in the eyes of the church. These included, "a widow with children to support exposed to vice because of her poverty"; "the age of the woman when she is twenty-four and has not yet found a partner"; "lack of sufficient bridewealth, preventing the woman from finding a partner outside her family"; "a too great familiarity and habitation under the same roof, giving rise to suspicion and exposure to danger"; "preventing dishonor to a mother and child when conception has taken place through illicit trafficking"; "the danger of incestuous relations"; and "bringing to an end public concubinage."

Thus, women arrived at mission stations for a range of reasons, but church and state continued a dialogue over polygyny that seems in part to have been "camouflage" over their need to control women's movement and choices, with the state in denial over the conditions it had created and desperate for women's labor and the priests bent on finding wives and mothers for Christian families.[33] It was exactly this uneven landscape that women might exploit to their advantage. The standoff continued over several decades. In 1910, the governor-general of AEF decreed that "native tribunals must apply local customs in all cases if they do not contravene the principles of French civilization."[34] This followed a similar ruling in French West Africa, where administrators opposed any attempt to codify "custom" that would interfere with its "natural evolution" under French rule.[35] The position was reiterated in the influential survey of AEF by Georges Bruel in 1935.[36] Interpreting the decree with its ambiguities, Governor-General Antonetti in a circular letter of August 1932 continued to defend the authority of the local courts and their prohibition on women leaving polygynous marriages.[37] A system of *justice indigène* gave jurisdiction in "minor matters," including those that would involve women's relationships with their husbands and kin, to village chiefs, whose economic position and status was heavily dependent on large households and several wives. It also appointed African assistants to the European *circonscription* and subdivision administrators who presided over courts at these levels of government.[38] Thus, colonial administrators fined and imprisoned catechists for "kidnapping" women while the church appealed to the governor-general to intervene for their release.[39] In his annual report of 1932, the chief administrator of Moyen-Congo wrote: "In the Lower Congo, incidents relating to the taking of women, married according to native custom, and claiming they want to convert and leave their former husbands to marry Christians are on the rise. The Christian villages are too often refuge places for natives who want to escape the authority of the chiefs who are recognized by the Administration."[40] In 1934, the state instituted for certain categories of subjects a civil status, part of which required that a civil marriage had to precede a church marriage. According to Scholastique Dianzinga this was a move to reduce the prestige and authority of the missionaries among the educated men who were mostly affected. Also, according to her assessment, the 1939 Mandel decree that guaranteed the free consent of women in marriage and freedom for widows to decide their status was a move to resolve differences between church, state, and local interests.[41]

Where the state saw the maintenance of "custom" as essential to the imposition of "order," the church was engaged in its "mission to moralize," including freeing women from the "wretchedness" of their everyday lives and offering the European vision of basic human rights.[42] Priests continued to teach their model of liberated women in well-ordered, monogamous, stable, Catholic households. For Père Pedron, not only was polygyny morally wrong in the eyes of the church, monogamy meant redemption for women trapped in exploitative marriages even if they did not know it. In one sermon, he told his listeners: "The family! Christian women, never in this debased world will you be able to appreciate the good fortune brought to you by the Gospel message. . . . The birds in the air and the fish in the water do not understand their good fortune. Put a line around the foot of a bird, take the fish from the water and, suddenly, in the face of misfortune they understand the extent of their loss." Père Marichelle told how he preached the advantages of monogamy when he visited the catechist post of Sainte-Marie du Kouilou: "I would insinuate the idea patiently and whenever I could. Then, I would use the great power of ridicule, showing how in pagan and polygamous marriages there were many disputes and often few and sometimes no children."[43]

Yet marriage arrangements continued to be fluid, for as Barbara Cooper has shown in her study of marriage in Niger, the institution is not fixed but responds to the demands of circumstances such as the changing economy, urbanization, and Christianity.[44] In Moyen-Congo, by the 1930s, a range of marriage arrangements was the norm among Catholics. Assessments of the colonial impact in general and of the church in particular acknowledge the integration of different marriage practices and highlight their flexibility, although these are generally stated by European administrators or churchmen as unfortunate residue of backward societies in the face of progress.[45] Historical studies of Kongo society have shown flexibility in kinships strategies over time as in the co-existence of matrilineal and patrilineal traits.[46] Thus, European cultural norms, including those preached by missionaries, were adopted selectively according to individual circumstances in concrete situations.

Missionaries raged against "polygamy, concubinage and free unions"—the latter common in the 1930s with the unemployment causes by the Depression and young men unable to make marriage payments—but they also found women's continuing ties to their matrikin a stumbling block to their vision of a stable family life. In Brazzaville, the residence of husbands and wives under the same roof for a continuous span of time was interrupted when women left to visit their families, an absence that could last for weeks or months. One report described it as "an ebb and flow which joins the city and village from which they are never separated," and "woman and babies are absent with the agreement of their husbands for lengthy periods."[47] Annual reports from the Linzolo mission echoed the problem, saying that "Christian women are passing long months in the village of their families outside married life with or without the consent of their husband," and explained the situation: "a woman is still always regarded as being on loan" and "customary practices still too often govern unions."[48] Modern informants also referred to continuing ties with the village of their maternal family although not as strong as before. Anne Ngondjo said: "When Brazzaville was Mfoa, girls and their mother often went to visit their mother or grandmother. They took presents and stayed for a time. But it's more difficult now. It takes money to raise children and transportation is difficult and more people have their family in the town and visit them on Sundays."[49] Antoine Boudzoumou explained that, "women belonged to their families much more than now."[50] Yet economic issues were also a factor in women's mobility as they started to lose the plots of land within the town limits on which they could grow staple crops such as corn, peanuts, manioc, and beans. Already by the 1930s prime land was increasingly being taken over by European planners bent on urban "improvements," a situation contested by women who were forced to walk miles to their fields outside the town.[51] Inherited and allocated family land became critical, and groups of women, especially those born outside the city in the accessible Pool region, continued to travel to their home villages, necessitating absences from their urban families.

Knowledge for Marriage and Motherhood

The centrality of the mission church in training girls and young women can easily be understood given the appalling record of the colonial state in matters of education. At the bottom of France's overseas priorities, AEF received few public monies for social projects.[52] As late as the early 1930s less than 1 percent of the annual budget went on education, specifically earmarked for teaching the French language and culture and training a small group of male auxiliaries. Fearful of anti-colonial tendencies, the colonial state discouraged the emergence of an African educated class and predicated primary school admissions on the anticipated number of available jobs. Or, as one assessment of colonial policy in AEF has put it: "The French believed that education for Africans was a dangerous drug which should be dispensed in minute quantities to avoid untoward side-effects."[53] Apart from a small government trade school established in 1906 and an underfunded urban school in Brazzaville started in 1912, the first government primary schools were opened in Moyen-Congo in the mid-1920s, with few places for girls.[54] Indeed, an official review of education in AEF in 1931 noted that there were no public schools or classes for girls and that only "a few little girls" attended the boys' schools.[55] Around the same time, a government inspector wrote that "the administration by its own admission has still done little for African education" and "has to rely on the private schools."[56] It was only after the completion of the Congo-Océan railroad, whose construction had consumed the lion's share of the colony's resources, that the reformist Governor-General Reste allocated more funds to education and enrollment in public primary schools increased. On coming to office, he noted that "there is in this colony not a single trained teacher, a single doctor, a single veterinarian, a single forestry agent, a single agent in the agriculture department or public works, who is a native."[57] In response to the situation, the colonial government established the Ecole Edouard Rénard (1935), the first public school to offer a one-to-three-year post-primary education for teachers and government employees. In 1939, only about three hundred Africans in the four colonies of AEF had the primary school certificate.[58]

In lieu of funds and a willingness to invest in schooling directly, the French government early contracted with the Holy Ghost Fathers to take responsibility for education in AEF. Such a gesture was a minimal acknowledgment of the *mission civilatrice* and allowed the training of some literate employees for the administration and private enterprise. In 1884, the minister of colonies granted the first subsidies to the Catholic mission to establish primary schools, especially to teach French language and culture. Anti-clerical elements in France and Brazzaville made the subsidies erratic, but they did supplement funds that the Catholic mission received from benefactors and church organizations in Europe.[59] Church education was limited in its scope, however, by both resources and design. In a report to the minister of colonies concerning the state of church schools in 1919, Monseigneur Augouard, nearing the end of his long tenure in Brazzaville, reported that catechist "chapel-schools," where teaching was in the vernacular and the content largely religious, constituted the basic education. From these schools, the brightest students were sent to the mission stations, but retention was a major problem, with most leaving to take up wage-earning jobs after two or three years. Altogether, Congo was not as "advanced" as Senegal, he wrote, "not ready for secondary schools. . . . I am guarding against raising them to a European level which is bad for them and for society.... We need a few elites but higher instruction is generally for the future." He made an exception for a technical education that turned out carpenters, stonemasons, and other craftsmen.[60] Upward mobility was thus as limited in the church schools as it was through the public schools, even for boys. The few that went on to post-primary education attended a seminary or went abroad, for example, to the William Ponty school in Dakar or to France.

The leaders of Congolese urban society were, therefore, products of mission schools, with those from the lower Congo predominating. In 1934, two-thirds of the students at the Catholic schools were categorized by the administration as "Kongo."[61] Their restricted and retarded access to schooling meant that they occupied low-level jobs in the economy, most favoring positions as clerks or messengers. Higher level administrative positions were in the hands of better-educated foreigners, such as those from the French West Indies, favored by the colonial government, and West Africans, heavily recruited by commercial companies.[62] Some Catholic school graduates also worked independently as artisans. Income from trade was limited since the colonial occupation had cut out many who had previously dominated commerce at the Pool and on the coast; important stores and market stalls were generally in Portuguese, Greek, or West African hands. This was a very different situation from some other colonies. In her study of the elite in early colonial Lagos, its very size and diversity caused Kristin Mann to focus her work on professionals such as doctors, lawyers, and engineers, those "at the top of the growing population."[63]

On the other hand, those in Moyen-Congo did constitute a new African social category with aspirations. Their models tended to be the black foreigners who lived beside them in the Bacongo and Poto-Poto neighborhoods of Brazzaville. According to Elikia M'Bokolo, they were neither a *petit bourgeoisie* nor a *classe dirigeante* with political aspirations, for that development came to AEF after the Second World War. Rather these men called themselves *évolués* (and here we call them elites), those whose identity and status derived from their material culture and intellectual life. They were mostly defined by their life styles and their creative appropriation of foreign symbols, a practice that was nothing new in the lower Congo, where people had been borrowing from each other and the Atlantic world for centuries, injecting imported forms with meanings that resonated with local practices and values: in clothing, furnishings, architecture, music, and religious symbols, for example.[64]

In this context, what qualities might an aspiring member of the African elite look for in a wife and the future mother of his children? Paul Bouanga, who had just celebrated his eightieth birthday when I met him at his home in

Pointe-Noire in 2000, told me something of his expectations as a young man. Born at the royal town of Diosso near the Loango mission, he had gone to Brazzaville after the death of his father to live with an older brother and a cousin who were tailors. There, he attended primary school, was in the first class to enter the Ecole Rénard, became an employee of the administration, and returned to Pointe-Noire in 1950 when the government of Moyen-Congo was transferred there. His views were those of an educated man of his times. He and his peers, he said, were looking for a woman from a good family, one who would be faithful and attentive to her husband's needs and a good mother of their children. His answers were stated in very practical terms. She must have some education and be "cultured" and know how to maintain a household correctly: "The house was not just a cooking pot in the corner." To have possessions and have a wife who was ignorant about their uses was troublesome for her husband, who could be teased by his friends. When visitors arrived, they would be entertained in the parlor, unlike the old days "where everyone would sit around in the yard and talk." A girl trained by the sisters knew how to sweep the house; wash dishes—"it was not just everyone eating out of the same wooden bowl"; use cutlery, and "drink from a glass without making a mess." She would know how to wash and iron and repair shirts, dress well, and sew clothes for herself and her children. She would also pass on her knowledge of household matters to her daughters so that they in turn could make an advantageous marriage. Women received money from their husbands for certain items in the household budget, but they also worked. As he said, "even if trained by the Sisters, a Congolese woman would farm, trade, sew, and earn an income." When I met Paul and Augustine Bouanga, who was quite a bit younger, they had been married forty-two years, had several adult children and grandchildren, and lived in a large, airy house with a yard planted with fruit trees, flowering bushes, and all kinds of vegetables. Augustine Bouanga was also born near Loango, where both her father and mother had been educated at the mission school. Her mother died in childbirth and she was taken into the family of her aunt, whose husband was a school teacher. When he was transferred, she went with them to Djambala in the north and then returned to Pointe-Noire to attend the middle school of the Spiritan sisters before marrying her husband.[65]

Most young men went to the town and worked for several years before they returned to the home village to find a wife.[66] Jean-Claude Ganga's father had followed the example of many young men of his generation, working first in Brazzaville for several years before marriage and drawing on help from women of his maternal family to identify a spouse. According to Ganga's account of his childhood:

When I was born my father had already risen on the social ladder to a remarkable degree. He was a messenger in the Governor-General's office. That may not seem to say much but for a former porter at the *Port de la Briqueterie*, it was an achievement and a promotion of great importance. Especially if one considers the path he took to arrive there. . . . He was first hired by a captain in the French army who one day noticed he could speak some French and hired him as a gardener. Then, finding that the young man was intelligent he made him messenger in his office. After his departure, Edouard Ganga benefitted from a warm recommendation from his old boss and was hired in the office of the Governor-General of French Equatorial Africa.[67]

About his mother, he wrote:

Where and when did he meet Mâ Soueneta, our mother, his only wife? He often told us that it was his aunt Maleka who found for him his fiancée at Douka-ba-Koutala [the family's home village]. . . . When the marriage contract was concluded, Père Bonnefont called "Maboni" came to fetch the young girl and sent her to the convent of Mère Marie [in Brazzaville] to prepare for baptism and marriage. The stay lasted two years. The fiancé did not have the right to go and visit his fiancée. My mother was baptized by Père Augouard, the first bishop of Congo. The bells of the Brazzaville pealed to celebrate their union before God and men on 29 December 1923. Did they love each other much? Our mother said little on the subject. It was like that with us. We did not show our feelings much to each other, even those close to us, things that touched on intimate subjects, of love. It was not a taboo, but one was discreet on this matter.[68]

Not only demands from young men but also those of family elders who wanted to conclude advantageous marriages for their daughters brought pressures on the sisters to reconsider the curriculum of convent schools. Over the years, the curriculum was influenced by three factors: the nuns' own education in church schools in France and in the novitiate, the resources available in Congo, and the policies and level of support of their male superiors.[69] By the 1920s, there was clearly a large area of agreement among the missionaries and between them and family elders concerning the future of girls as wives and mothers and the kind of preparation this necessitated. It was a convergence of views that legitimized the education nuns offered, shaped the nature of the curriculum in the 1920s and 1930s, and ensured a continual flow of enrollments at the convent schools.[70]

A program called "the work with fiancées" was initiated. According to a Spiritan sister who helped run a program for fiancées in Pointe-Noire, "the stay of the fiancées fluctuated from a few weeks to two to three years—longer if they did not study the catechism sufficiently, behaved badly, but especially if the payment of their dowry was late."[71] In other words, the enclosure of the young women was akin to that experienced by the *tchikumbi* in the Loango region and was, at least in part, approved by parents because of the strictness of the discipline and the control of the young woman until her marriage was ensured. As Sister Christiane Masseguin put it: "The work is a bit like being enclosed in a sort of penitentiary."[72] The curriculum included basic catechism classes, housework and gardening, lessons in hygiene and childcare, laundry, sewing, and nutrition.

At the same time, enrollments of girls in regular classes increased. Fieldwork remained a basic part of the training, for the community had to support itself, and the schools now shared with mothers the training of girls for their future lives. At Brazzaville, Joséphine Peka remembered: "My mother took me to the Sisters when my older sister no longer wanted to look after me. She went dancing. The house was called 'Mère Joseph.' All who went there are now in the fraternité Saint-Joseph. I returned to my parents when I was fifteen. If a man was interested he had to bring drinks to the girl's parents three times. The dowry usually was 500 francs but a girls who had lived with the Sisters could get 1000 francs."

Anne Ngondjo, who enrolled in the Brazzaville convent school in around 1930, also recalled her experiences: "For a long time schools were not known to us. To go to school at Javouhey was a burden. It started from 7 AM till around noon and then from 2 to 5 PM. Manual work was compulsory. One had to be strong and the teachers gave special treatment to the more gifted children."[73] Catechism classes and lessons in singing, sewing, and laundry skills also filled up the day. By the 1930s and in response to the demands from families who saw the increased bridewealth paid for girls with superior skills, a more varied curriculum was introduced.[74] Reporting on the work with ninety girls in the Spiritan school at Pointe-Noire, the sister wrote that "they work in the fields in the morning and evening; in the late morning, they learn to read and write and count in French; they also have catechism and singing classes for one and a half hours" and "parents hand over girls with the only goal of seeing them read and write in French which adds to their value at the time of marriage."[75] The Sisters of Saint Joseph of Cluny presented the first girls for the primary school certificate in 1937.[76]

Among the skills taught by the sisters, sewing was popular in the school curriculum and in adult classes.[77] Once treated by Western feminist scholars as a trivial kind of activity that filled schoolgirls' time while boys learned more academic subjects that would lead to an income-generating occupation, the activity seems worth revisiting given its popularity at the time and even today. While

14. - CONGO FRANÇAIS

Leçon de couture, par une Sœur de Saint-Joseph de Cluny - Brazzaville

Figure 3.1. An early sewing lesson, Sisters of Saint Joseph of Cluny, Brazzaville, c. 1905. From a mission postcard.

boys did indeed have the advantage in their ability to obtain wage-earning jobs, sewing and other household skills made sense to parents and daughters and were seen as movement in a positive direction. In that sense, their response was similar to that observed for women and classes on maternal care in the Gold Coast: they selected what was important to them from the skills offered by white women.[78] For many of the girls and women who attended the sisters' classes, working with cloth was aesthetically and practically pleasing and potentially an income-generating activity. Furthermore, investment in family was critical and might ameliorate the advantages of men in other domains.[79]

The fabrication and embroidery of cloth and its symbolic importance in bodily adornment dated back into the Congolese past, and in this context the expertise offered by the sisters can be better understood. Dress signified power and wealth, and cloth was essential in transitional events such as negotiating marriage contracts, naming babies, and preparing corpses for burial. When bridewealth was monetized, cloth was still included in the presents a man gave his future mother-in-law even in the later twentieth century.[80] In upper Congo, where European imports were slower to penetrate and the internal slave-trade and colonial violence disrupted the flow of goods, the weaving and embroidery of raffia cloth remained important in the early twentieth century. Along the Alima River, the Franciscan sisters, who introduced their own brand of simple, practical Christianity, found in weaving and needlework a means of communicating with women who brought their knowledge of working raffia to the novel techniques introduced from European convents. One sister, talking of the early work at an important but isolated mission, said, "At Lékéti, sewing was about the only thing that worked." It was the daily-life cement that held the place together and, apart from their evangelical work, the achievement of which the sisters were most proud: "Classes didn't work, fieldwork was unpopular; this was not an add-on activity, it was central." As the women from the region taught the sisters to work raffia cloth—necessary since supplies of cotton thread from downriver often did not arrive—and the sisters introduced their skills in working imported textiles, they together produced mats, cushion covers, tablecloths, handbags, and furnishings. Their workshops were famous among Europeans in the colony, and the sisters sent their products on consignment to tourist outlets in Léopoldville, Brazzaville, and Paris, and paid the women a small wage.[81] In lower Congo, while men had been responsible for the production of high-quality palm-cloth, women produced woven household objects as well as baskets and pottery, and this also provided an entree into the particular techniques introduced by the Sisters of Saint Joseph of Cluny from their Catholic schools in France.[82]

Missionaries had great potential as a source of clothing that brought status to an individual and the family. Indeed, the distribution of items of dress was a prime attraction of the mission stations. In 1890, Monseigneur Carrie warned the director of the Catholic schools against handing out clothes to children "too soon, for they will take them and leave."[83] An old photograph of parents and two children shows the mother wearing a cloth, her husband dressed in what may have been a catechist's uniform, and her baby and little girl wearing dresses. Mothers had particular responsibilities for maintaining the family's wardrobe. On special occasions, it was noticed when she had made the layettes and baptismal dresses for babies and the special clothes for Sunday wear, weddings, funerals, and *matanga* (end-of-mourning celebrations). Even if a family's wardrobe was sparse, she had to ensure that the members were dressed correctly in public since it was part of a new style in respectability.

By the 1920s, sewing was well established in the sisters' schools in the education of girls and fiancées. Cloth, needles, thread, and scissors were given out as prizes. The youngest girls started by sewing their own dresses; those with some dexterity helped the sisters repair church linen. Once sewing machines arrived from France they were used by older girls, and by the 1920s when a Sister of Saint Joseph with fine skills in lacework and openwork embroidery arrived, these arts were introduced at the Brazzaville workshop.[84] Knowing how to use a sewing machine was the mark of a convent-trained girl. Martin Balossa, when asked, "Why did girls go to school?" replied: "They learned to sew clothes, use sewing machines, knit, and crochet. They used Singer sewing machines. Because the girls were trained at the Mission, they brought in a larger bridewealth. Also, they could sew for a living."[85] By 1932, groups of women came every day to the mission or met in the African neighborhoods for two hours of catechism followed by "a sewing lesson which is very popular and attracts many to the mission."[86]

Even Andrée Blouin, who wrote an otherwise bitter and scathing account of her unhappy fourteen years at the sisters' "orphanage," wrote positively about sewing. It was "the one skill in which we excelled. . . . The older girls did the most refined embroidery: sheets, pillow cases, table cloths, and napkins. These were sold at religious fairs in Africa and Europe by the mother house of Saint Joseph of Cluny. I became an expert in making my own dresses when I was quite young." When her father showed up with a doll that she was allowed to keep, "I began to design and cut out dresses, sewing and fitting them."[87] At seventeen she climbed over the convent wall and ran away to live in Poto-Poto, where her dressmaking skills allowed her to build up a clientele among white women whom she visited in their homes in the European Plateau district. For the next few years as she moved around from Bangui to Belgian Congo and back to Brazzaville, work as a seamstress allowed her to support herself and her children.[88] In statistical reports of mission work, it was no accident that sewing and embroidery classes were listed under the rubric "workshops," alongside carpentry, mechanics, shoemaking, and bookbinding.[89] The main problem for female seamstresses was competition from male tailors. Blouin's clientele was scattered, and she had to walk long distances, whereas the men could set up their machines outside the Portuguese cloth stores and have the item ready to wear in a matter of hours.[90]

The wedding ceremonies staged at the Loango mission church and at the Brazzaville cathedral were like a school graduation, the culmination of an education by the sisters and a public expression of the convergence of missionary and local interests. For the church they demonstrated the expectations of a monogamous marriage and the promise of a Christian family. For the couple it marked adulthood and their emerging elite status. Wedding ceremonies on this scale were novel in Moyen-Congo, where initiation and the negotiation of marriage contracts were the main events.[91]

At the Brazzaville cathedral, weddings attracted a large crowd of onlookers, especially in the 1920s when the mother-superior staged multiple ceremonies, a centuries-old custom transplanted and reinvented from her home town in Brittany.[92] As many as sixty couples were married in a ceremony that took place four or five times a year. It was a brilliant piece of Christian propaganda. According to one account in a popular magazine published by the sisters:

> From before dawn the fiancés were there in the square in front of the church with witnesses and the families of the wedding couple. . . . All were chattering excitedly. From time to time they stole a glance down the road to the Sisters' residence looking for the procession and their loved ones. . . . Finally, there below, emerging from the clump of bamboos came the throng of women joyfully climbing the slope led by the "Mother."

The bells of the cathedral pealed as the couples came together and lined up to enter the church. After the marriage ceremony, the festivities continued:

> In the square comes the first outburst of joy amidst the warm congratulations of family and friends. The wedding clothes that show off the fortunes of each are inspected: one can see jackets of an impeccable cut, pretentious ties, polished shoes and different styles of hats. The young women with circles of beads around their ankles in lieu of shoes display an infinite variety of cloths and blouses in printed cotton. Their friends bustle around tying multicolored scarves that serve as their headdress from now on.[93]

Photographs of the couples lined up after the ceremony confirm the scene. They are a statement of the symbolic power of dress for the missionary patrons

Figure 3.2. Multiple weddings at the Brazzaville cathedral, c. 1925. Archives, Sisters of Saint Joseph of Cluny. All Rights Reserved.

and the newly married couples, and many years later they convey the gendered nature of the colonial world.[94] When shown the photographs and asked to comment on the clothes, informants said that the men wore European clothes because they earned cash and that was how office workers dressed at the time. One added that if the man was a domestic servant he would not be allowed to wear shoes to work. About the women's dress, they said Congolese women were comfortable in cloth, and only a few "young girls" took over Western dress. Certainly, they would wear cloth for important occasions. They also said that women could not afford shoes nor could the sisters, who might have helped them with presents of cloth for their wedding day.[95]

For Mère Marie, the mother-superior, such events were the culmination of almost four decades in Congo. As she wrote to the Mother House in 1929: "this year I have married 224 girls: There are not many mothers in France who have done as much."[96] She added that "Christian marriage is now fashionable." We cannot know precisely what she meant by that adjective, and perhaps she was only referring to the popularity of the wedding ceremony itself. Yet beyond that, and given the efforts she had made to develop such a successful program, Mère Marie likely knew that she had been instrumental in giving the young women the knowledge they needed to make a good marriage, maintain a household in the manner of the new elite, and as Catholic mothers educate their children.

The image of family elders and fiancés bringing girls and young women to the mission schools hardly tells the whole story, however. Such profound changes provoked a lingering ambivalence and resistance by those who continued to questioned the utility of the knowledge girls received and the loss of family labor. Even Catholic mothers who were willing to release their girls for catechism classes might baulk at further schooling. Even as girls' education became more popular, such realities continued to impinge on school enrollments and attendance. Informants remembered parental opposition and tensions between parents. One recalled that her father, who was educated at a Protestant mission, approved her school enrollment but that on several occasions her mother refused to cook for her since she had not helped produce the food.[97] Another said, "My father told me to go and hide when the nuns came to look for me. He said a girl can't go to school. I stayed at home and cooked fish so that when my mother came from the fields she could eat. We also gathered firewood."[98] Another gave a fuller account of her childhood:

> When I was born, I grew up and as I was growing up, the Mother came and proposed that I go with her in order to attend school. *Mama* refused and said I was a girl. . . . So she taught me how to work in the fields. I grew maize and banana. We would work in the morning, both of us would work and work. Then she would start collecting firewood and I would gather manioc leaves. Then *mama* would tie the firewood into a bundle and would make me a small one. She would take the manioc leaves and we would come back home. Then I would pound the manioc leaves when *mama* got tired, then go and fetch water, and come back with it, sit down, and watch *mama* cooking. When the cooking finished we would eat. Sometimes a friend called me to play. Well, since *mama* had decided against my attending school, I went to the fields until the priest came and I decided to go to the catechism class. By that time I was a bit older. . . . I carried on until I was baptized. At the time there were no black teachers. Just these Mothers.[99]

A sister who arrived in Congo in 1923 remembered her forays into the Bacongo neighborhood in search of missing students, especially during peak farming seasons, when the attendance of girls was erratic. The end of the long vacation in October coincided with some short rains, and many of those enrolled the previous academic year would not show up.[100] Mothers also arrived to reclaim their daughters who were boarders at the Loango mission, saying that they were needed for farm work.[101]

Contesting Boundaries

Two incidents in Brazzaville from the 1930s seem worth relating, for they illustrate how church women might contest pressures from men when these seemed
to intrude too heavily in their legitimate domains. In both cases, religious practice, Catholic morality, and what constituted a good wife and mother were at
stake. The ensuing altercations, on the one hand with spouses and on the other
with a priest, ended by claiming the attention of the mayor's office and stirred
up church-state rivalries to the women's advantage. The incidents also show the
networks and bonds that Catholic women were constructing with each other as
they moved to the towns.

The first dispute erupted over women's prolonged absence from home as
they participated in prayer groups, vigils, and retreats. The women who came
to Catholic missions were seeking both protection from the disruptive forces of
colonial occupation and access to a religious power that could counter witchcraft
accusations, sickness, and misfortune. In some ways, such coming together in
devotional groups was an extension of familiar religious practice, whether in
cults of healing and fertility, vigils for the dying, or mandatory mourning rituals.[102] In their practice of Catholicism, women not only joined with others at
Mass and the great festivals of the church over which men presided but carried
on an intense devotional life that gave them a degree of autonomy. Centered on
meditation and the repetitive saying of the Rosary, women might meet in small
groups or larger retreats, for short periods of time or several days. Rituals of
supplication such as novena—nine days of prayer to invoke the help of Mary or
a favorite saint in times of distress—and retreats for meditation and study were
central in their religiosity.

Women's collective prayer life seems to have intensified amidst the social
upheavals of the early 1930s. In Bacongo, where many of those from the Pool
and lower Congo lived, the Depression had thrown many out of work, forced
others to return to their villages, put beggars into the streets and women into
prostitution. The situation was made more volatile by the administration's persecution of André Matswa and his followers. Matswa was by no stretch of the
imagination a nationalist agitator, but while living in Paris in 1926 he had started
an association advocating greater participation for Africans within the colonial
structures. Continuing his campaign on his return to Brazzaville, he attracted
to his movement many among the Kongo elite who staged demonstrations demanding political reform. This was met with a crackdown by the government
and the trial and exile of Matswa, who eventually died in prison. In 1930, angry

supporters who had gathered at the Brazzaville town hall were fired on by the police, leaving several dead and many wounded. Many left the church, saying the priests were collaborators with the other whites and refusing to attend the fiftieth anniversary celebrations of the mission at Linzolo. Such was the context for a rise in retreats and prayer meetings.[103]

In May 1934, some five hundred women who were attending a retreat at the chapel in Bacongo left home around six in the morning and returned after dark. This happened for several days in a row. Tensions ran high as men complained of trouble in their households since women were gone during the hours when the public fountains were open and their families had run short of water. Food was also a problem. Some claimed that their wives had not cooked for several days and that other women who had been asked to bring the evening meal had shown up late. Whereas co-wives or kin might fill in for absent women in polygynous households, those in monogamous marriages and without village support networks had more difficulty in finding help. The men claimed that the women had been impervious to their complaints and had continued going to the retreat, leaving their husbands and children to suffer.

At this point, the men decided to ask the priest to order the women home, but the missionary only made matters worse, for he sided with the women and their right to attend to their religious devotions. He further heightened tempers by saying that the problem was not serious and that the men were being stirred up by a group of Matswa supporters who were bent on making trouble for the church. The men then decided to take matters into their own hands by attempting to block the passage of the women, threatening them in the streets, and scrawling graffiti on the walls of the chapel. Although some women had been turned back, most had been able to break free and make their way to the church.

When the altercation reached the level of a public disturbance, it was reported to the mayor's office. He dispatched a representative to gather evidence from three township chiefs. According to the ensuing report, the trouble had nothing to do with Matswa agitators and everything to do with domestic disputes caused by women's liking for long retreats and their purported neglect of their wifely and maternal duties. The mayor informed the administrator of Moyen-Congo, who had also heard of the incidents, but the administrator declined to act, although he blamed the church for its excessive demands on the women. He warned that the matter was not to be taken lightly, for women were planning their next extended retreat in July and there would be other incidents.[104] The situation was not unique, for neglect of family was a charge also leveled against fraternity women later in the century; according to David Blackbourn, in spite of frequent admonitions to obey their husbands, women in the European church would on occasion play off the priest against their husbands or fathers to their advantage.[105]

In another incident some two months later, Catholic women showed they were also prepared to challenge male clerical authority by contesting a priest's definition of Catholic motherhood. They likewise exploited church-state tensions to their advantage. In this case, the problem at issue was women's participation in dance groups. In the town, the neighborhood of Poto-Poto, with its great mix of peoples from different parts of Moyen-Congo, was famous for its dance associations. These were a major source of entertainment for the crowds that gathered on Sunday afternoons in the Grande Place, where regional groups performed accompanied by drummers.[106] The culmination of the performances came during the Fourteenth of July celebrations, the largest annual public holiday in AEF, when work was suspended for several days, all kinds of official and non-official events organized, and regulations on drinking, drumming, and curfews unenforced.[107] In the streets, a carnival-like atmosphere prevailed for days and nights. Dance competitions were especially popular, with groups practicing new music and dance steps for months in advance. The celebrations were also marked by people buying new cloths and traders noticing an upsurge in sales.[108] According to Adèle Nsongolo: "On the French holiday, your husband bought you two lengths of cloth. You wore one in the morning and one in the afternoon."[109] While the Protestant church banned dancing and disciplined members for participating, Catholic policy allowed single-sex dancing but found regional dancing that involved women and men and the new craze for "modern" partnered dancing immoral and "obscene."[110]

In the days before the Fourteenth of July celebrations in 1934, members of a women's dance group went to the market to buy cloth for matching outfits. During Mass four days before the big event, Père Moysan addressed the women in his homily, telling them that he did not want them to form dance clubs or participate in dances that were "scandalous," "immoral," "unfit for Christian mothers," and a bad influence on children and other women. The competitions held at the fairground during the Fourteenth of July celebrations were especially inappropriate because many children wandered about among the exhibition booths and might see mothers performing.

According to the account of Augustine Mbonga that was later recorded at the mayor's office: "Père Moysan has been trying for two years to stop us without success but this time he said if we persisted the Pope himself would come."[111] The women further told how the priest had arrived to inspect their homes. According to Emilie, he had arrived when she was absent, and when her mother protested that there were no hidden cloths, "he searched everywhere in the house, and found nothing."[112] The women decided to defy the priest and go to the dance grounds since they had practiced their dances and had spent money buying their cloths. According to the deposition of Antoinette Akolombi, when the women were leaving Poto-Poto at 2 PM on 14 July on their way to the fairgrounds they encountered the father at the Hausa market, barring their way. He was sufficiently threatening on the consequences of disobeying the authority of the church that some of the women turned back.[113]

Their anger at the priest for searching their homes and attempting to stop them from performing in the annual celebrations caused the women to take their complaints to the mayor's office, where an official took down their depositions. Since the administration sponsored the dance competitions, the women likely realized that the European officials would be on their side. The mayor judged the priest's action unwarranted interference in the officially sanctioned events marking the national holiday. He also agreed that women had the right to participate in dance groups that he judged "harmless." In fact, he wrote, they gave the celebrations "a particular attraction" and were good for the retail cloth trade.[114] The incident did not end there, for it was reported in a local newspaper as evidence of the overbearing pretensions of the church. In a memorandum to the governor-general's office, a Moyen-Congo administrator accused the Catholic mission of launching "a propaganda effort" to counter anti-clerical attacks and requested the governor-general to take up the matter with the bishop of Brazzaville.[115] The resolution of the issue does not appear in the sources, but the incident demonstrated both the authority of a priest and its limitations as women acting together challenged his definition of Catholic motherhood and asserted their multiple identities in the wider society.

Conclusion

As the colonial world closed in around them, women struggled to deal with adverse conditions and traverse uneven terrains of power. Reluctant at first to enter the missionary orbit, some were drawn by the protection the church offered as the realities of colonial occupation became apparent. Joining a Catholic community did not necessarily improve women's economic situation, for their previous inability to gain access to economic resources on a par with men was compounded by the education for wage-labor that boys received. Women's interests most converged with missionary goals through their role as mothers of families and the investment of their resources to that end. From church schools—the only ones available—girls could acquire knowledge that made them popular with elite men, bring in an elevated bridewealth, and give their mothers the promise of future security.[116] To become a Christian was not only a social project, however, for it brought women into a spiritual community where they could join with others in a distinctive devotional life.

Yet many women continued to be unwilling to release their daughters, for they needed their labor and considered school subjects knowledge without utility. Older men who acquired girls through early marriage contracts still wanted to safeguard their investment, and families wanted to retain control of girls' education, for to do otherwise might compromise their daughters' chances of a good marriage and endanger the health of children, lineage, and clan. This is best documented in the case of *kumbi* because of the public nature of the practice. Contemporary European accounts attributed a decline in the institution to missionary agency, for example, in the southern Mayombe region, where a Belgian administrator remarked on the priests and sisters who destroyed the *tchikumbi* huts.[117] On the other hand, young people themselves were being distanced from the practice through the mobility of their families, their attendance at school, and their milieu. Augustine Bouanga said that she would not have become a *tchikumbi,* even if she had stayed in the Loango region and not traveled to the north with her aunt and uncle, for her family were Catholic; also, for those who left the region, it was impractical and inessential.[118] Paul Bouanga said of himself and his peers: "We didn't really understand the missionary beliefs and so we couldn't understand their opposition." In the context of the youth of the present, he thought some of the old customs had advantages, for they helped discipline the young, but they were not part of his experience.[119] Resistance from girls who went to school and lived in towns brought pressure on mothers and grandmothers. By 1935, the girls were enlisting missionary intervention. In one case, when three of them told the nuns at Loango their parents wanted them to go through the *kumbi* rituals, the sisters had the father-superior "threaten the families."[120] The passing of girls' education from the hands of women at home to teachers in school—in many cases boarding school—helped blur the boundaries of maternal authority, especially for mothers with a traditional education. Ephraim Andersson, for many years a missionary of the Swedish Evangelical church in the lower Congo, summed up the situation: "The collectively administered upbringing has taken on a foreign cast."[121]

The experience of missionaries in these decades suggests that they were both powerful and vulnerable. As *nganga nzambi* they could control unknown forces and call on mysterious other-world figures, such as the pope, to punish the wicked. Yet, especially in the early decades of their work in Congo, priests were thin on the ground. They could not control all areas of their congregation's lives, and continued references to polygyny, absent wives, beliefs in *ndoki*, "immoral" dancing, and *tchikumbi* show the limitations of their authority. Furthermore, African clergy were few, and although many catechists successfully carried out the critical work of evangelism beyond the mission station, their influence varied greatly. At the same time, the Sisters of Saint Joseph of Cluny were usually understaffed, and in 1935 there were no African nuns, a subject to which we shall now turn.

4. Religious Sisters
and Mothers

There were few communities of missionary nuns in the first fifty years or so of the Catholic presence in Congo, yet in their mothering of generations of girls and women, their education of a female elite that provided leadership within the church and society, and the teaching of their religiosity, the European sisters had an influence greater than their numbers might suggest.[1] Women educated by the sisters, especially the last generation before the nationalization of schools in 1965, became advocates of women's causes in the postcolonial years, created their own networks, and founded the fraternity movement.

Within the female religious congregations in Congo, African sisters today constitute the great majority as European women have retired or died and not been replaced, but in the early decades the missionary effort to recruit local women was almost entirely a failed enterprise. If resistance to giving up girls for baptism and church marriage was strong, the loss of a young woman to a religious vocation was unthinkable: the vow of celibacy unnatural and a denial of social obligations, the vow of poverty incomprehensible, and the vow of obedience an irreparable loss. Joan Burke, in her study of the Sisters of Notre Dame de Namur in lower Congo (Zaire/DRC), tells how the mistress of novices struggled to create equivalent words in Kikongo for celibacy and to state the condition of poverty in a positive sense.[2] In Congo-Brazzaville, stories of family resistance to girls' entering the novitiate were "folkloriques" in their prevalence, repetition, and embellishment.[3] In Europe, former nuns have written at length on how radical separation from their families was one of the toughest lessons they had to learn as postulants and novices, even as they entered the new family of their religious congregation. Physical enclosure was most intensely practiced by contemplative orders, but separation from kin was also part of a religious vocation in a non-cloistered congregation, starting in the novitiate and rigorously enforced in the past, although less so in the period of reform following the Second Vatican Council.[4]

Letters from mothers-superior in the lower Congo to the superior-general of the Sisters of Saint Joseph of Cluny in Paris give an "insider's" perspective on the experiences of missionary nuns and the broader communities they forged with the girls and women who lived alongside them. These monthly reports richly document the experience of the missionary women. As a source, the hierarchical context in which the letters were framed needs to be recognized as well as the individual author, her character and priorities. Those written by Mère Marie-Michelle Dédié, who worked for forty-nine years in Africa (ten in Senegal, 1882–92, and thirty-nine as the superior of the Brazzaville convent, 1892–1931) are particularly remarkable. Almost three hundred are extant in her congregation's archives.[5] Addressed to "Dear Very Reverend Mother," the letters generally start with a confession of the writer's failings and move on to the tenor of community life; the young sisters in her charge— their emotional and spiritual state and their prowess as missionary nuns; relations with male ecclesiastical authorities; material and financial issues; the convent schools and workshops; evangelical sorties to nearby villages; and relations with outsiders such as colonial authorities and visitors. Over time the language changes. In the late nineteenth century, the girls are referred to as "*les pauvres petites*" and, occasionally, "*les petites sauvages*" (translatable as "wild" or "uncivilized" beings). By the 1920s, Mère Marie refers to her charges as *les filles* or *les fiancées*. Early letters tend to give space to faith and the challenges of life on an African frontier; later ones convey the writer's spiritual state but are more practical concerning the preparation of women for Christian marriage.[6]

Pervading these letters is a maternal ideology, that of the mother-general in Paris to the sisters in Africa, of the local mother-superior to the sisters and women and children in her charge, and between the older and younger schoolgirls. Within the convent compounds, the reality and imagery of Christian motherhood was conveyed to children and aspirants through the constructed environment, the human interactions, and the teaching. For the sisters, the ongoing inspiration had been handed down over decades in a maternal hierarchy

Figure 4.1. Centenary cloth, Sisters of Saint Joseph of Cluny, 1986. Photograph by Phyllis M. Martin.

that dated back to the founder of their congregation, Anne-Marie Javouhey. She was the most important ancestor and the model for a life lived in accordance with "God's Will," made familiar to the convent girls through lessons, images, and prayers as well as a constant presence in the reading and devotions of the sisters.[7]

The missionary sisters and the African women who graduated from the novitiates and joined the congregation were part of the story of Catholic women in Congo-Brazzaville, but it is by no means for that reason alone that a chapter is devoted to them here. They were first and foremost religious women following the charism of their founder and engaged in the work of missionary evangelism. They also lived primarily in a world of ecclesiastical patriarchy, subject to the dictates of male clergy yet creating communities stamped by their own priorities. Yet while their habit, habitation, and rules might accentuate their apartness in the eyes of others, the sisters were also an integral part of the colonial society with its power relations and hierarchies, and they themselves were instrumental in the process of constructing social categories such as gender and race that were indispensable to colonial order. Thus, their lives have something to tell us about the peculiar world of religious women, but they are also a commentary on the colonial project itself.

Creating Community

Location, planning, daily routines, and human interactions helped shape religious communities that had their own specific challenges in late-nineteenth-century equatorial Africa. While being a member of the same religious tradition helped hold members together, it could not always obviate obstacles such as insufficient resources, a debilitating environment, conflicting personalities, and local resistance. All these could affect the missionaries and have ramifications for those who lived alongside them. The word "convent," commonly used by outsiders to designate a place where nuns are located, seldom appears in sisters' letters, which rather speak of the "community" with its meaning of a dynamic group of women living together. The emphasis on the persons rather than the location has entered popular usage, for in Brazzaville individuals will still say they are going "chez les Soeurs" or "chez Javouhey" or "chez Saint-Joseph," and call the convent "Mère Marie."[8]

Early reports from mothers-superior described the physical layout of the buildings, designed and constructed by the Holy Ghost Fathers with African workmen and located at a distance from the male establishment to safeguard ecclesiastical propriety and keep interaction of boys and girls to a minimum. Only on Sundays and important religious festivals such as Easter and Corpus Christi did the girls walk with the sisters to join the male community at the mission church. Apart from priests who arrived to say Mass and hear confessions, a few employees, and occasional visitors, life was self-contained at the nuns' community. The buildings were positioned to allow the sisters to maintain the privacy of their own quarters, with their own rooms and devotional space, and adjacent buildings to accommodate the girls and women with whom they lived and worked. At Loango, the convent buildings were on a hill overlooking Loango Bay, about a kilometer from the fathers' mission. Thought to be advantageous because of sea breezes, shade trees, and a water supply, the site proved to be unhealthy with a marshy environment and poor soils. In Brazzaville, the convent was located at the foot of the mission hill some ten minutes' walk from the fathers' compound. In both instances, the buildings were visible guides to the sisters' work, symbols of a functional, well-ordered space. Their plan gives an indication of the inner circle of the sisters and the wider one that included girls and women, and their interaction. At Loango, for example, the plan took the form of a rectangle. On one side were the sisters' living quarters and an office; opposite were the children's dormitory, a school, and a sickroom. The chapel and a parlor for receiving important visitors occupied another side of the rectangular space, and opposite these, a storeroom, separate kitchens for preparing the children's and sisters' food, the children's dining room, a laundry room, and an ironing room. A chicken coop and pen for small animals occupied one corner of the compound; close by were fields where the girls cultivated much of their own food. A "hospital" (sickroom) for African women was projected for the future.[9]

The constructed physical environment was transformed into spiritual space as it was filled with the artifacts of material Catholicism sanctified by priests and animated through the prayers of supplicants.[10] The Sisters of Saint Joseph of Cluny were largely recruited from conservative, rural France, where popular piety was expressed through devotion to images: the crucified Jesus, Mary the Mother of Jesus, and the saints. Wayside shrines in country lanes and large crucifixes in church yards were common.[11] The feminization of the French church had encouraged the centrality of Marian devotions in women's spirituality. The vision of Bernadette Soubirous in the grotto at Lourdes happened only three decades before the first sisters set foot in lower Congo, and major devotions centered on the Rosary, the Sacred Heart, and the Stations of the Cross.[12] It was an orientation shared by the Spiritan priests. In 1908, the superior-general of the congregation asked that all mission stations place a statue of the Virgin Mary on their property.[13]

Thus, the statues, scapulars, medals, rosaries, crucifixes, and picture cards requested and received from European benefactors were an important part of the sisters' spirituality and easy for girls and women to assimilate as power objects or charms. Mary and the saints could be interpreted as ancestral figures who could be asked to intervene benevolently to address human problems. Since in Kongo cosmology those who had passed to the other world of the dead were white, these great religious ancestors made sense.[14] In their communications of paths to the divine, the Catholic women and local women had much in common, even as their interaction created a dynamic African Catholicism that from the European perspective was often based on "misunderstandings" or a "dialogue of the deaf."[15] Furthermore, at a time when African women could not read or were at the beginning stages of literacy, the power of the Object likely surpassed the power of the Word, a situation that may well have been prolonged in the experience of girls and women since their access to literacy and to learning French was so limited. For their part, the sisters were slower to learn local dialects than their male colleagues, not because they lacked facility but because they lacked experience and opportunity. Their education in parochial schools was dominated by prayers, the catechism, bible history, and the life of saints. The novitiate training concentrated on turning out sisters worthy of their particular congregation, with a more restricted curriculum than in seminaries, where missionary priests were urged to learn African languages.[16] For most sisters and their students, language acquisition was to be a very gradual process picked up from each other rather than learned formally. The situation was put by a young sister a few months after her arrival: "They do not understand me and I do not understand them which makes the task more difficult. All I can do is repeat the same words one hundred times and return to them every day, but when I see them on their knees singing or reciting a prayer, which unfortunately they do not understand, it seems to me that the Good Lord is pleased all the same and that consoles me."[17]

Medals and other portable objects were handed out in the tens of thousands as friendly gestures to children who thronged around when the sisters visited villages, rewards for good behavior, prizes for achievement, and presents on special occasions.[18] The sisters carefully recorded the arrival and installation of the most precious religious artifacts: statues of the Sacré Coeur, Notre Dame de Lourdes, Notre Dame de Victoire, Notre Dame de Perpetuel Secour, Notre Dame de France; Saint-Joseph, and Sainte-Thérèse; pictures of the Stations of the Cross; and pictures and busts of Mère Javouhey, to name a few.[19] Saint-Joseph, the sisters' patron saint, had great significance, with special devotions such as novenas during March (his month in the religious calendar), and celebrations on March 19, his feast day. Such information was taught to the girls in lessons about saints and marked in the community calendar. Instruction on the proper approach to Mary, the Mother of Jesus, and the saints was part of the 1894 Loango catechism. Lesson 16 read: "Saints can help us through prayer, they are God's friends. We must especially pray to Mary, the Mother of God, through the Salutation Angé-lique" (Hail Mary or Ave Maria). Lesson 17 taught that "images, statues and relics remind us of the person of the saint. It is a matter of adoration not worship."[20] The sisters had no doubt in the efficacy of holy objects in teaching children the path to the "good God":

> We are waiting for the two statues to arrive so that we can better bring to life in our little fiotes a love of Jesus and Mary.... Our children are beginning to love Saint Joseph and during March they gladly followed all the exercises. On the 19th, especially, they happily sang the songs in his honor, asking him to cure their comrade who is sick with anemia.... She is recovering and all the little fiotes think it is Saint Joseph who has cured her.[21]

The following month, Mère Saint-Charles noted that "the statues have arrived in good condition and the children did not know how to express their pleasure. They chanted '*Zambi* and *Maman Zambi* are very beautiful.'"[22] Mère Marie paralleled her religious instruction with the visual aids in the chapel and gardens. She further engaged the children in learning through hands-on experience:

Each year we look forward to celebrating the birthday of our Very Reverend Dear Mother. The evening before we made preparations for a long walk on 14 June. After the sung mass, we took the road, or more exactly the path, to the Stanley Falls. The Congo hurtles down a steep incline, the waters crash into large boulders in their path and are thrown into the air before falling again in a white foam. There we happily passed the whole day.

On the return journey each child and each of us carried back to the house a rock for the future Grotto of Lourdes which will be built in a copse of trees at the end of an alley of avocados. With will and determination, which is not lacking in our little girls when we have to do something for heaven, we ended with enough rocks; but the statue is missing. . . . We are hoping the Immaculate Virgin will provide.

Continuing her description of the spiritual adornment of the landscape:

Our good Father Saint Joseph is now enthroned on a nice pedestal in the middle of the yard surrounded by orange, mandarin, and coffee trees, and shaded by acacias which stretch out their branches in the form of a parasol. The statue was brought over the caravan route and took three years to arrive. The inauguration was 15 August 1897. On the same day, as a birthday gift for our good Mother, our generous benefactor M. Greshoff, gave us the necessary sum to buy and transport a statue of Saint Antony of Padua, his patron; it is now installed in our chapel.[23]

In 1927, a priest at Linzolo organized the building of a grotto of Lourdes at the foot of a hill where there was a spring.[24] Sixty years later, women could still be seen toiling up the steep slope carrying containers with holy water.[25]

If creating appropriate space signaled mission order, so did the structuring of time. Temporal discipline was not only a necessary means of control but a tool of instruction. Understanding local conceptions and ordering of time was well beyond the comprehension of the sisters, for like other Europeans they brought to Africa their notions of time, work, and leisure, forged in the "civilized" capitalist, industrial world.[26] Two months after their arrival in Brazzaville, Mère Marie and two other sisters reported that on their first evangelical journey to a village, they had found men and women "abandoning themselves to appalling laziness and vice, doing nothing more from morning to evening than eating, sleeping, and smoking pipes two meters long that are lit by their slaves."[27] A daily timetable reassured the Mother House that life was proceeding according to the Rule of the congregation, at least in theory. The sisters observed the Offices starting at 5:15 AM with various prayers, mass at 6 AM, individual devotions in mid-morning, Vespers and Compline in the early afternoon, and various litanies and Lauds before supper at 7 PM, followed by evening prayers.[28] In this scenario, those who lived in the sisters' compound were never far from the sounds of the chanting, prayers, and bells that punctuated the day. For the girls, fieldwork, prayers, laundry, and catechism lessons dominated the curriculum.

The church calendar marked by Sundays and special holy days was also learned by the girls through having something extra added to their diet (when that was possible), wearing their best dress (they were issued two), and, not least, going to attend Mass at the fathers' mission. Monseigneur Augouard was known among his peers for his liking of pomp and ceremony and displaying the majesty of the church. The Corpus Christi procession was a high point for the Brazzaville crowd at a time when the small town offered little in the way of organized public entertainment. Hundreds, and by some estimates thousands, would line the route to watch the procession with the Host pass by: the clergy in full ceremonial robes, the choir in their surplices, and the boys' club band dressed in military-style uniforms. The mission girls were much involved, too. Mère Marie reported:

> Every year, Corpus Christi celebrations become more grand in their solemnity. For eight days our children work on the portable altar with an enthusiasm we can only encourage. Some go to find green branches in the forest, others make garlands and prepare flowers.[29]

Mère Emilie, who lived in Poto-Poto, remembered the excitement when she was a day-girl at the sisters' school in the 1930s and the thrill of being chosen to participate:

> In the procession, we would follow the bishop with flowers. The sisters would dress us well with a veil like a woman being married. We enjoyed ourselves. Afterwards, the bishop would give us presents—avocados, oranges, and coconuts. Some of us were chosen to stay overnight at the convent. I have thrown a silk handkerchief at Corpus Christi.[30]

Women also remembered the quieter moments of their convent experience with the sisters in sewing classes or in the corner of the schoolyard. In some instances, mothers who had passed through the sisters' schools had named their own daughters after a favorite sister, and several had nuns as godmothers.[31] They also recalled the tough disciplinarians, the "mothers" who were especially severe.[32] In the early days, life at the sisters' community was likely more intimate than in later years. One catches a glimpse in a letter from Mère Marie: "The children gather around the stove of Soeur Césarina. They like the fire and while she is cooking she teaches them small, interesting things to pray and to sing. They help her do housework and carry water."[33] While the sisters in their celibacy and single-sex communities could not live out the qualities of a model family

life as could Protestant missionary couples, they passed on their version of social motherhood especially to those who arrived in their care as small children,
stayed throughout their childhood as boarders, and went on to live their own
interpretation of Christian marriage and motherhood. For the girls, it was not
only religious and practical knowledge that they could pick up but notions of
"correct" behavior. Photographs are telling, for they show not only the dress of
the girls but the poses that convey the required demeanor that the sisters taught.
An encounter between a young Frenchman and the sisters and their charges in
Brazzaville about 1912 gives a glimpse of what constituted orderly conduct:

> This morning I met the Sisters from the Catholic Mission taking for a walk
> their young pupils, about a hundred black girls dressed in matching-cloths
> and blouses. They were walking in line two by two as in France and the Sisters
> were supervising them closely, displaying their authority. They were carrying
> their lunch for a picnic just as at home in France. It was a very amusing sight.[34]

For the priests who wanted to define girls' education narrowly in terms of baptism and marriage, this sight was potentially dangerous, for they feared a "root-
less" society where women might harbor aspirations beyond their life as farmers
and reproducers of family. "We do not need *grandes dames*," Carrie and Augouard both proclaimed in their letters to the mother-general. The Loango vicar
complained about the quality of the sisters whom the Sisters of Saint Joseph of
Cluny were sending to Congo, for they raised girls who "want to live like ladies,
eat well, dress well, and do nothing." He added, "Fortunately, we do not have the
same difficulties with the girls entrusted to the care of Christian women at other
mission stations."[35] Yet in the towns, elite men were soon bringing their future
wives to the sisters for a training that went beyond mere practical skills. As for
the women, they could selectively appropriate what they had picked up from
their teachers and each other and integrate it into what became local style.

The Burden of Mothering

Order on paper can be tested and fall apart in the realities of daily life. Missionary nuns faced challenges to some extent similar to those at home but accentuated in Brazzaville and the lower Congo. Some arose from the harsh physical environment, lack of adequate resources, and African resistance. Some came from
living in a gendered European society dominated by men who had expectations
of the services *bonnes soeurs* would provide. Others stemmed from the position
of nuns in the ecclesiastical hierarchy and from tensions within the community,
made worse by isolation and distance from advisors at home. Although the con-

gregation sent superiors to the mission field who already had overseas experience, many young sisters were freshly graduated from the novitiate and full of an idealism that was difficult to sustain in equatorial Africa. Three large problems overshadowed their work in the early years: sickness and insufficient personnel, the burden of "domesticity," and ecclesiastical patriarchy.

The hostile environment that took such a tragic toll on African populations also drained the resources of the missionaries, who, unlike other Europeans, were expected to remain at their posts for lengthy periods. Mère Marie, who returned to France only three times in her thirty-nine years in Congo, was administered the Last Rites several times. Tetanus, dysentery, yellow fever, malaria, and other "fevers" ended the careers of several sisters in the initial decades of their work. Conditions were more stable by the second decade of the twentieth century, although the sisters were frequently sick. In 1918, Monseigneur Girod at Loango reported six male missionaries dead in the previous year; he himself died a year later, after only five years in his position.[36] Within colonial society, it was not until the 1920s that medical knowledge was sufficiently advanced for European men to take their families to Moyen-Congo, and, as already noted, it was well into the 1930s before the African population showed an upturn after the ravages of the colonial occupation. Sickness and malnutrition undermined the health of children, especially those "ransomed" by the priests, who were often in poor condition given their origins. Thus, the small communities of sisters, women, and children were joined in sickness and death as in other aspects of daily life. In 1894, a report concerning Mère Marie said: "Our mother fell gravely ill and her condition was absolutely desperate. For two months she was between life and death. We prayed to Notre Dame de Lourdes, Saint Joseph, and our Venerable Mother each in turn; novena succeeded novena; our little girls multiplied their sacrifices and prayers never ceased at the mission."[37]

While the sisters might resign themselves to personal tragedy as a glorious sacrifice and have the consolation of making it to Paradise, those left behind faced serious problems compounded by the inability of the Mother House to send sufficient reinforcements.[38] At Loango, the position was especially difficult since after its reopening in 1907, and for the next thirty years of its existence the community never had more than three sisters. At Brazzaville, an expanding mission, the situation was not so dire, but there were multiple demands on the community. Thus, at Loango: "Two Sisters are in bed and another is looking after them. The older girls are working well without supervision. All the fathers are sick"; "The community is turned into a hospital with four out of six in bed"; and "The Sisters have been sick and more than a month has passed since we visited the villages."[39] From Brazzaville, letters arrived: "We are understaffed . . . the

Sisters are tired and weak," and "We ought to go often to the villages but that
has been impossible for some time. We have too much work and Soeur Anne
has been sick since the beginning of the year."[40] It was hardly surprising that in
those circumstances the mother-superior had to spend a considerable amount
of time defusing tensions within the community. One young sister wrote that
there was "no exercise of the Rule" and she was trying to keep up with her own
devotions. Another wrote from Loango that days had passed without the community praying together, that she was depressed, and Mère Saint-Charles asked
for instructions on how the Rule could be kept "when we are sick."[41]

The sisters' work was additionally compromised through the demands of
the male clergy, whose perceptions and agendas were set by preordained gender
roles. Whereas, following the example of Mère Javouhey, Cluny sisters were oriented to teaching and evangelism, churchmen saw them primarily as "sisters"
who were useful auxiliaries to male proselytizers. Indeed, the Spiritan fathers
called themselves "missionaries," but the women religious were "sisters." The
fathers' collection of buildings that included the church or cathedral was the
"Mission" but the sisters resided at their "community." At Loango, Monseigneur
Carrie's publication, *Oeuvre des Soeurs de Saint-Joseph de Cluny dans la Mission
du Congo Français* (1897, "Work of the Sisters of Saint Joseph of Cluny in French
Congo"), governed the sisters' lives. A section on "Condition of the European
nuns in the Mission" made clear the lines of authority. While article one acknowledged the sisters' right to administer their religious and daily life according to the Rule of their congregation unless dictated otherwise in canonical law,
article two stated: "As for the direction and administration of the work allocated
to them they must be entirely submissive to the Chief of the Mission and follow
the line of conduct designated for them." Article three went on: "The work of the
Sisters being in its nature secondary to the Mission and dependent on the ecclesiastical Superior, he will have the right to judge any difference that can arise
between the Sisters and the Missionaries, and in the case where agreement is not
possible and too difficult, the nun will change her Community and be recalled
to France." Financially, the mission would provide lodgings and furnishings and
give an allowance for daily life in Congo; the sisters could keep any income from
their work (for example, the sale of sewing or the wages of teachers and nurses),
but they were not allowed to send money back to the Mother House or "divert
from the Mission any other income."[42]

Such arrangements may have been quite normal and expected in the context of the Catholic church, but in Congo the problem for the sisters was that the
"work allocated" to them was so heavily oriented to the side of domesticity. In
France, lay women and lay sisters might do most of the physical work, but in the

missionary situation lay sisters were not so common, and it took time to train African women in specialized work such as maintaining the church linen.[43] It was the combined task of reproducing the display of the church and doing domestic chores for the male missionaries that exacted so much time and energy from the sisters, leaving little for their own mission to teach and evangelize. The rationale that their relationships with the priests were complementary—the sisters washing, repairing, sewing, and ironing the church linen while the priests sent a chaplain to preside over Mass, confessions, and retreats—might sound reasonable, but the "beauty" that Monseigneur Carrie demanded in religious rituals and Monseigneur Augouard's insistence on pomp and ceremony came at a price. Beyond that, the sisters were expected to fill the role of wives (or mothers): for example, from Mère Marie: "Gave S. Césarina more sewing and S. Maxima is to repair the linen of the community and the socks of the Fathers. Each week they bring us 7–8 pairs with holes that need repair. Monseigneur sends his laundry on Monday and Wednesday afternoons; Tuesday we do our own laundry and wash the cassocks and linen for the services at the Mission."[44] They were also called on to create special foods such as pralines and caramels for the men and their important visitors. In 1889, the Mother House received a request for a mold for desserts to serve visiting dignitaries from Loango town.[45] The sisters were also called on as nurses. In January 1902, Mère Marie reported she had gone to "look after Monseigneur every day for a month," and in January 1909, the sisters nursed Augouard through his illness "day and night."[46] Letters show that while the sisters, given their situation, training, and vocation, were usually willing to accommodate such requests, some aspects of the priests' demands tried even Mère Marie's patience and sense of duty. In one letter, addressing a tentative project of Monseigneur Augouard that involved moving their community from Brazzaville to the Alima River (upper Congo) since he was "afraid that our children will give themselves to white men as they do on the coast," she added that her male superior had said the sisters were necessary "for *cooking!*, caring for the sick Fathers and doing the Cathedral laundry."[47]

Colonial men also made demands on the missionary sisters, for even to most republicans and members of the anti-clerical lobby, they were acceptable as *bonnes soeurs*, women who at home would provide health care and perform charitable works.[48] Furthermore, the exigencies of the situation in French Congo, where health care was almost non-existent, muted men's views of the religious women who brought them soups and mothered them through illness. It was a role that Mère Marie was willing for her sisters to undertake, for as she wrote: "In a country where there are no white wives, it is natural that the men turn to us for food at such times, especially since we are nuns."[49] But the demands for womanly care did not stop there. In 1893, the sisters were asked to make twenty large republican flags and ninety-six napkins for the Fourteenth of July celebrations; in 1902, the new lieutenant-governor asked the sisters to make curtains for his residence. To the latter request, Mère Marie permitted a rare show of exasperation: "We are not happy but we cannot refuse"; and "Monsieur Gentil seems to think it quite natural that we have made six pairs of large curtains for his residence. He had one of his office employees thank us, that is all."[50]

It cannot be said with any certainty that the Brazzaville mother-superior performed the role of a *bonne soeur* as part of a conscious strategy to enlarge her options in a difficult situation. She did suggest to her superiors that relations with colonial men were a matter of reciprocity, but overall the sources lead one to believe that her actions suited her temperament and sense of vocation.[51] Unlike Anne-Marie Javouhey, she was not one to use confrontational tactics, nor was she a feminist pushing back boundaries like some of her contemporaries in Europe. Rather she worked within the system, maximizing it to achieve her own goals. She was undoubtedly part of the process of "domesticating the empire," a woman portrayed by religious and secular men as a shining example of devotion, heroism, and self-sacrifice, the gentle and courageous face of the imperial mission and a living witness to the maternalism of the French republic.[52] Largely due to Monseigneur Augouard's brother, who was a priest in Poitiers and a principal fund-raiser for the Brazzaville mission, tales of her life found their way into magazines and books at a time when the reading public in France was voracious in its demand for stories and images of empire. She is also mentioned in accounts by men who were part of the expeditionary forces of occupation. Colonel Albert Baratier, for example, passed some time in Brazzaville while waiting for a boat to continue his passage upriver. After his meeting with Mère Marie, he wrote: "On seeing her so weak, so pale, almost white with a complexion robbed by anemia, I admire the contrast she offered with her surroundings. . . . Here everyone acknowledges her and the Sisters, voluntary exiles, whose enemies cannot deny the sacrifice. . . . Their presence gives a charm of smiling sweetness and kindness to the French occupation. . . . The Sister is the link between Africa and France."[53] For her own part, Mère Marie used her reputation and connections to good effect on behalf of her impoverished mission and in the face of an imperious vicar apostolic and European clergy who were highly ambivalent about the role of the sisters in the process of church expansion. For practical needs, one strategy was to turn to benefactors, a common practice in the church and difficult to dispute. For several years, a major supporter of the Brazzaville sisters' community was Mère Marie's good friend Anton Gresshof, director of the Dutch trading company. Although not a Catholic himself, he answered appeals in desperate situations and sent unsolicited help for the girls. In January 1899, when Mère Marie was seriously ill and called back to France on leave, Gresshof paid her train fare to the coast and upgraded to first-class her ticket from Bordeaux to Paris.[54] There were also staunch Catholics in the white community who offered support, and once families arrived parents brought their daughters to the convent school, thus allowing Mère Marie an entrée into the wider European community. In the 1920s, some French women started a branch of the Red Cross and did volunteer work at the sisters' "hospital."[55]

Another strategy was to approach the administration directly for assistance. Mère Marie wrote that her small requests were "never refused."[56] An official report that railed against the "virulent" and "aggressive" behavior of Monseigneur Augouard noted, "On the other hand, the best relations have always existed between the administration and the nuns of Saint Joseph of Cluny."[57] Crossing boundaries determined by the vicar apostolic was fraught with problems and could risk incurring his wrath. Letters give glimpses of the situation as Mère Marie shared her dilemmas with the mother-general. On one occasion, when she needed funds to take a sick sister to the coast and appealed to the administration—having been turned down by the vicar, who said she needed to find the means herself—she wrote of Augouard's displeasure and how she had to go "on her knees like a child" to beg his forgiveness. Two years later, while Augouard was on a trip upriver, she accepted land from the administration to enlarge the convent property. On his return, she reported, he was incensed that such action had been taken without his consent, that the land had been put in the name of the Sisters of Saint Joseph of Cluny, and that the administration seemed to grant the nuns' requests but not his. Although the land was necessary, given the expansion of her work, she felt compelled to return it, another dilemma since it was a public display of division within the mission. A few years later, the mission director relented and the land was acquired. At times, when he was somehow disturbed by the sisters' actions, he showed his displeasure by staying away from their compound, thus creating more anxieties among the vulnerable community of religious women.[58] Everywhere one sees centuries-old ecclesiastical patriarchy transported to the missions of equatorial Africa.[59]

Yet the Brazzaville mission survived the early years, and the vicar apostolic and the mother-superior arrived at a *modus vivendi* in their eighteen-year collaboration. By the time Mère Marie was called home to retirement (strongly against her will), her community and its work was described by one European observer as "flourishing."[60] If the mother-superior needed vindication it was seen in the demands for girls' education, the training of fiancées, and the growing number of women in the church.

The situation at Loango was quite another matter, for several factors had brought the community to its final demise and exposed the vulnerability of the sisters: emigration, local resistance from those who defended *tchikumbi* seclusion and polygyny, traditional religious practices, lack of reinforcements from the Mother House, and male ecclesiastical authorities who wanted to close the convent and open a new mission at Pointe-Noire. In 1927, an official visitor was sent by the mother-general to assess the situation of the three sisters and the children. Her report was not encouraging:

> The Rules are not much observed and the religious communal life non-existent. They are attached to their vocations but the Mother-Superior is tired. There are no contacts with the Mission Director.... The Sisters are totally dependent on the Mission for their support and the children, too. By misplaced zeal, they are expected to cost the Mission as little as possible. As a result, they lack food and especially clothing.... The girls are pitifully dressed beside the well-dressed boys.

She recommended sending out a new superior, who might be able to find more support from the priests and repair the troubled situation.[61] Arriving to take over a few weeks later, Mère Alphonse further elaborated on the situation with the girls:

> They go to Mass at the Mission twice a week in the morning, some of them half-naked and the rest in a dirty shirt. They run after each other to see who can go the fastest, and on the return journey they run away and stay the rest of the day in the villages.... In the evening in the dormitory they carry in their own cooking pots and baskets and eat into the middle of the night. During the day, they go to the villages when they feel like it and sometimes stay there two or three days. To obey is not something they know. The bell sounds, one calls them, and they do not budge.[62]

The senior students had addressed food shortages as they knew best, for the sister further wrote that "the older girls work in the fields each on their own piece of land and only return to the Mission when they want to."[63]

Although the arrival of the new superior did inject some "order" into community life, lack of support from the fathers and the population shift to the rising port city and CFCO terminal at Pointe-Noire were insurmountable problems. The mission was closed ten years later and the work relocated in Pointe-Noire under the care of the newly arrived Spiritan missionary sisters. In 1986, when the Sisters of Saint Joseph of Cluny marked their centenary in Congo with a pilgrimage to the site of their first community at Loango they found only a few rusty pipes.

Authority and Hierarchy

Inequality, discrimination, and hierarchy were ingrained in the church and colonial society. The sisters could not escape the gendered structures that were brought from Europe and perpetuated in equatorial Africa. At times, they were able to work through these constraints, but at other times they reinforced them through a tacit if not passive acceptance. In colonial Congo-Brazzaville, race was another social category in process of being enacted, and the sisters were also agents in its construction, although the policies they helped implement were generally designed by their male ecclesiastical superiors. In their own lives, although drawn together in a shared sisterhood, they lived under a system of layered matriarchy.

Under the patriarchy of the church, female religious orders were governed through a hierarchical system. Mothers-superior were under the authority of the mother-general and the governing body of their congregation in Europe, and they themselves were at the head of a community of sisters for whom they interpreted the Rule of the congregation in case of doubt or disputes in the community. Reports from the mothers-superior contained news of the other sisters: those who were having difficulty adjusting to local conditions; those who were "good nuns" and "true vocations"; those who needed to be transferred or return home for sickness or personal reasons; recommendations for those who asked to renew temporary vows or requested permanent profession. The Sisters of Saint Joseph of Cluny, like many orders with deep historical roots, were divided into choir sisters and lay sisters, who took the same vows but had different responsibilities. Traditionally, the choir sisters were upper class and well educated by the standards of the times, and their families gave "dowries" to the religious order when their daughters entered the novitiate. They were responsible for leading community recitations of the Divine Office, teaching, and fine handwork. The lay sisters were generally from more humble backgrounds with less education; they did the cooking, cleaning, and other heavy work, although they might also teach sewing or the catechism. All this was evident in the operations of an African mission and visible through gradations in dress. In theory, there was little distinction in the standing of the sisters, but, according to older women who joined the congregation before the Second Vatican Council (when such distinctions were abolished), choir sisters could mete out rough treatment to lay sisters, and a great deal depended on personal relations and a judicious mother-superior.[64]

In such communities, the first African postulants and novices received training and sisters took their vows. Not only did they have to deal with the built-in hierarchy of the European congregation, they also experienced the gross discrimination of the clerical hierarchy, premised on their perceptions that these young women came from backward cultures and were low in moral fiber. Shortly after the arrival of the female missionaries in Congo, the position of African sisters was clearly set out in two documents, one by Monseigneur Carrie for lower Congo and the other by Père Rémy, vicar-general for the Oubangui province (upper Congo).[65] The Loango vicar apostolic had already laid down policies for the training of African clergy and "all the native apostolic personnel," where the importance of retaining "simplicity of customs" was his basic premise. "We think that to place them on the same material footing as European clergy would be a real misfortune for them and the country."[66] According to Côme Kinata, race discrimination practiced by teachers in the seminary rather than lack of vocations was a factor in keeping the numbers of African clergy so low in the early decades.[67] Carrie's instructions on "Native Sisters" decreed that their training would be in the hands of European sisters supervised by "the Missionaries" and that they would not be part of the sisters' congregation but separate or "affiliated" in their own order, the Congregation of Saint-Pierre Claver. Article 22 laid down that "the native Sisters can never be on the same footing as Europeans in regard to clothing, food, and lodging. They will not wear shoes or stockings, they will be content to wear simple sandals." Furthermore, "the costume will be simpler while being very modest and sufficient to distinguish them from secular persons. . . . They will eat the food of the region and therefore will have a kitchen and table separate from the white Sisters. Their lodging will be that of the country, a little improved for ease and hygiene." The Brazzaville document was very similar. In this case a Third Order was established for African sisters, also separate from the Sisters of Saint Joseph of Cluny. A section on "Relations with the White Sisters" stated: "The native Sisters are received into the service of God in a Third Order to help the European Sisters in their apostolic work, given that the climate is too severe for them." The African sisters must always be "respectful" and, given their "inferior education," must not harbor any feelings of envy. "They will always be ready and happy to be of service to the white Sisters."[68]

At Loango, the novitiate was opened in 1892 following the arrival of the small girls sent from Linzolo by Augouard to receive training from the sisters. Several began their education as postulants. Two years later, three were deemed ready to become novices, don the habit, and take religious names: Soeur Marie Saint-Antoine (Angèle Tchibinda), who died shortly after at age seventeen; Soeur Marie Saint-Jean (identified as Adelaide) who also died; and Soeur Marie (identified as Martha), one of the daughters of the Maloango, who had been left with the sisters as a diplomatic gesture.[69] According to one of her peers interviewed in 1929 by the current mother-superior, "she is still alive but she turned out badly."[70] Of two other novices in this first generation of African sisters, Suzanne Tchibassa left to be married, and Soeur Saint Marie-Joseph Mpolo, one of the Linzolo girls, took her vows and was sent with two European sisters to establish the mission at Bouanza, where she died of sleeping sickness when she was about twenty. Of the other postulants, some, like Agnès Mpolo, declared they wanted to be married, and several were judged unfit for a vocation. Such was the fate of three who ran away in the night to live with European men in Loango town, only to be rounded up by the priests and returned to the sisters, where they were "demoted." The fragile state of the whole endeavor was also tested by the sickness and death of the white sisters. In 1898 when the mother-superior died and the other nuns were ill, "all the postulants fled."[71] When the convent closed in 1900, "the remaining postulants were left to their own devices," according to one who had later married and was the mother of a large family.[72] Thus, the experiment with indigenous sisters came to an end at Loango. In 1923, Mother Jerôme who had been superior since the community was reestablished in 1907, wrote that there were "still no vocations for the life of a nun."[73]

The history of the first generation of African sisters at Brazzaville differed very little. The novitiate was inaugurated in 1897 with two beginners: Madeleine-Charlotte Kalouka, a Linzolo girl who had been sent back from Loango, and a second, Bathilde Liré, the mother of a child of mixed race. The two were photographed by Castellani for his book *Les femmes au Congo,* together with a ten-year-old girl, Marie-Thérèse Elongo, who had been in the first group of "ransomed" children brought by Augouard from upriver. She had achieved the distinction of being selected by Mère Marie as the godchild of the mother-general, an honor reserved for those who were model children to be held up as an example for others. The three were photographed standing in front of the sisters' building with a bust of Mère Javouhey on a pedestal between them and behind the group a statue of Saint Joseph holding the infant Jesus.[74]

Several others became postulants and novices, but they died or left for a variety of reasons. Two graduated from the novitiate and became the first African sisters in Brazzaville. Kalouka, called Sister Anne-Marie after the founder of the congregation, took her first vows in 1901. Another sister, whose name appeared as Angèle-Louise Zoungoula in the baptismal record of the Saint-Paul des Rapides (Bangui) mission in 1894, had been brought down the river to Brazzaville and admitted as a postulant in 1899. She took her first vows with the name Saint-Pierre Claver three years later.[75] Both young women gave the European nuns essential support working in the laundry, helping with the children, acting as interpreters, and assisting at the mission hospital, especially in the lazaret for

Figure 4.2. Bathilde Liré, Marie-Thérèse Elongo, and Madeleine-Charlotte Kalouka, Brazzaville, 1898. Reproduced from Castellani, *Les femmes au Congo*.

sleeping sickness patients. They themselves died of sleeping sickness, Zoungoula in 1905 and Kalouka four years later.[76]

Like Mère Marie, these Brazzaville sisters became known beyond the Congo mission, for their stories found their way into French publications that highlighted qualities of courage, suffering, and piety, all paths to eternal salvation. Colonies were not only "a physical but an imagined space," and stories of Zoungoula and Kalouka in religious journals helped to fill in this space for the faithful.[77] The story of Zoungoula, entitled "Une fleur noire," was first told by Père Rémy in *La semaine religieuse de Poitiers*, a religious weekly, and then, as "Une fleur Congolaise" in the Spiritan journal, *Annales apostoliques*. Other versions of the story were subsequently published by Monseigneur Augouard and his brother and appeared in the popular *Les missions catholiques*, and in volumes of Augouard's letters.[78] Such publications together with Augouard's frequent trips home were highly significant in raising funds.[79] The title of the articles, "A black flower" and "A Congolese flower," and their story of suffering and simple piety would not have been lost on readers, for they evoked the life of their contemporary, Thérèse of Lisieux, who died in 1897 at age twenty-four and became "one of the most popular saints of the twentieth century." In an oft-quoted statement, she said she considered herself of little account, a "Little Flower." Mary Malone has suggested that Saint-Thérèse's practice of a "spirituality of hiddenness and the devotion to the small ordinary tasks of everyday life" were "perfectly suited to the church's agenda" to "harness the talent and energies" of women.[80] The stories of Zoungoula and Kalouka continued to be told, for example, in a biography of Augouard published shortly after his death, by which time Zoungoula was referred to as "Une sainte noire," her life an example of what might be achieved in "savage" equatorial regions in spite of "obstacles put in the way" by anti-clerical administrators.[81]

Thirty years were to pass before other African sisters graduated from the novitiate of the Sisters of Saint Joseph of Cluny and took their vows as religious women. If the first generation were drawn from the most vulnerable members of society—those "ransomed" by the missionary priests—several members of the second generation were likewise brought to the sisters as girls with no family ties to encumber their progression into the novitiate, for they had grown up in the Orphelinat Augouard, a boarding school for *métisses* opened by the missionaries in 1924.[82]

In the colonial world, distinctions in the making were as much social and cultural as they were physical, for "skin shade was too ambiguous."[83] In Congo, missionaries had a particular role because of their virtual monopoly of education and the divisions they could implement. In one of his many publications making explicit mission policy, Monseigneur Carrie early set the parameters for children who fell through the cracks in his vision of "white" and "native." In his directions for the "Work with Children," he argued that children from different backgrounds and levels of "civilization" demanded different schooling and treatment. He left little to chance, or as Jean-Loup Amselle has put it, "cultural traits are not distributed haphazardly"; rather, "for culture to be 'set' it must constitute a symbolic schema that can be recognized and can trigger feelings of emotion in a subject."[84] Carrie's policies affected the visible details of daily life: "two dishes" instead of one because of the "delicate" health of those with mixed parentage; wearing hats and shoes on Sunday and on outings from the mission if their parents provided them; manual work in the mission gardens instead of heavy labor in the fields.[85] In his directives to the sisters, the most intelligent African girls and all the girls with a European parent were to be taught in "advanced classes" with writing, grammar, math, and singing.[86]

Children had been left by their fathers and mothers at the missions since missionaries first arrived in Congo, but for both the secular and ecclesiastical authorities, the "problem" of *métis* became more pressing after the First World War as French soldiers returning to Europe left behind children they had fathered with African women.[87] Discussion of their future was a matter of some debate not only in Congo but in other parts of the empire, full of anxieties about sexual promiscuity, threats to white prestige, displays of European degeneration, and moral decay. In France itself there were similar debates linked to postwar disorder, population decline, qualifications for citizenship, and bourgeois respectability.[88] In Moyen-Congo, the sexual and moral anxieties of the church overlapped with the administration's interest in controlling the middle ground at a time when European women were arriving in greater numbers and whites were withdrawing into segregated communities.[89] Or, as stated by Andrée Blouin, she and her comrades were "aberrations of the species" with "their potential for disrupting things."[90]

In 1919, Monseigneur Augouard, using the same language of "abandonment" and "innocence" that had appeared in the Indo-China context twenty years earlier, appealed to the minister of colonies for a subsidy, stressing patriotic duty and moral responsibility: "It behooves France to take care of these poor children who will return to a wild state . . . abandoned without remorse by their fathers. . . . They are perhaps worse off than the small blacks and it is a truly sad sight to see these half-whites wandering about without care and often without clothes. These children are not, however, responsible for the faults of their parents and it is necessary to come to their aid."[91] In a follow-up letter he added: "It is truly a matter of the honor of France. In this population of color, one category particularly deserves our pity. It is the little girls who without us will be fatally doomed to prostitution."[92] Five years later, the Orphelinat Augouard was opened in a building alongside but separate from the premises for other girls. Twenty-four children between the ages of five and nineteen were enrolled, some destitute and others brought by their father or mother, who paid fees depending on their means. The girls were forbidden to speak any language but French, instruction was in French at all levels, and classes prepared the girls to take the primary-school certificate. Gardening was part of the daily schedule, while the early evening was reserved for sewing, with the older girls taking care of the altar cloths and clergy's vestments, a task mandated for them by Monseigneur Guichard.[93] By 1939, enrollment had risen to eighty-five. A significant number came from outside Moyen-Congo, for the school was very popular with parents throughout the region.[94] In 1938, a third of the girls came from the Belgian Congo side of the river.[95] Word was passed around not only between Europeans but among African mission elites who corresponded with the priests and sisters in Brazzaville. Regarding the Orphelinat Augouard as something of a "finishing school," young *métis* sought out girls who as future spouses would be allies in situating the couple in colonial society through their skills: speaking good French, using the correct body language, maintaining a house with European-style furnishings, and dressing appropriately for their social position. A network of priests and sisters seems to have acted as some kind of marriage service, facilitating contacts between suitable young men and women. In 1936, a chaplain at the Kilo Moto mines in the Ituri region of northeastern Belgian Congo wrote to the Brazzaville mission concerning Pius Biye, "a well-behaved and intelligent young man" who announced his intentions to marry. He had been to Brazzaville and seen some girls from the Orphelinat Augouard "who pleased him." The priest was now writing to the Brazzaville mission director, asking if he might intercede with the sisters to find a suitable bride. A year later, the mission director received a letter from a contact in Kinshasa, saying that there were "quite a few mulatto men who want to marry a girl from the Brazzaville Sisters." Around the same time, the mother-superior received a letter from Albert Mbuy, president of the Association des mulâtres de Léopoldville: "Allow me, Very Reverend Mother-Superior, to inform you with a full heart, that the orphanage you and your congregation took the happy initiative to establish in Brazzaville is the only and the best that we have in our region up till now."[96]

Many of the girls who passed through the orphanage did marry those chosen for them by the missionaries and established Catholic families. Andrée Blouin was one of the rebels. She was particularly scathing about the priests' attempt to create the village of Saint-Firmin for *métis* couples, designed to keep them separate from the Bacongo and Poto-Poto neighborhoods on the one hand and the European community on the other. For her the village was part of "a diabolical plan to keep the couples of mixed blood under the surveillance of the Catholic mission forever." Taken to visit Saint-Firmin by the sisters when she was ten years old, she found it "repellent" and rejected a "made to order marriage" in favor of making her own way in Poto-Poto.[97] With their training, graduates of the Orphelinat Augouard were able to fill positions not open to African girls. Some were sent for further education to the Franciscan sisters in Kinshasa to train as nurses, and others became monitors.

There were also those who claimed a religious vocation and helped revive the sisters' novitiate, now moved away from proximity of the town to Kindamba. They thus established a second generation of African sisters.[98] The first two sisters, both *métisses*, took their vows in 1938 and in so doing reestablished the affiliated order of Congolese nuns on a firm footing.[99] By 1950, when the African sisters were fully integrated into the congregation, there were fourteen Congolese sisters, several of them graduates of the Orphelinat Augouard.[100] The regional origins of these sisters were broad, showing the growing reputation of the sisters' schools: four from upper Congo, four from Belgian Congo, one from Gabon, and five from lower Congo.[101]

Conclusion

The Catholic sisters who worked in Congo before the Second World War were women of their times. They took to their overseas postings their own experience, education, and perspectives, often from rural France. By the 1930s, a few were licensed nurses or teachers, but many had gone straight from their convent school to the novitiate and mostly learned their skills on the job. They thus transmitted to girls and women their limited education, their social values, and their practice of the Catholic faith. From their place in the hierarchy of the male ecclesiastical and colonial world, they had to navigate the system. In the early days and before lay women were trained to take over some of the domestic chores, they spent a great deal of time providing services for the male missionaries, and this impinged on their ability to do evangelical work, a source of frustration that showed in their letters home. As white women in colonial times, they were not just located in particular social roles that they could not much control, but also they actively contributed to the shaping of colonial society.

To many of the girls who were raised in their communities and attended their schools, the sisters were practitioners of a social maternity. Many of their students later married and brought the next generation of children for education in convent schools, others rebelled and were never seen again, and for some the sisters remain a "thread" in a network of contacts. In June 1997, one of the periodic gatherings of former "Javouhey" students was held at the Mother House of the Sisters of Saint Joseph of Cluny in Paris. Those present had attended the schools in Congo before their nationalization in 1965. Later, a former student talked of the Orphelinat Augouard, where she was taken by her father, a French medical doctor working in the colonial service. While she was enrolled, she experienced the integration of the sisters' schools in 1950 and attended the College Anne-Marie Javouhey. She did not paint an over-rosy picture of life in the *métisse* boarding school but said, nevertheless, that the sisters were the only mothers she had known, her peers were like siblings, and some remained among her close friends. "In the boarding school, the big girls looked after the middle-sized girls and they looked after the little ones. That was our organization, the older ones did the little ones' hair and helped with their laundry." Referring to the reception we had attended, she said: "Look at last Saturday. All these women were in school with me as girls. If one has a problem, we telephone and the others come. It has kept us going. It is why there are associations in Congo—to meet, to reminisce, to sing, to pray."[102]

5. Toward a Church of Women

The approach to the convent of the Sisters of Saint Joseph of Cluny in central Brazzaville lies along a narrow paved road lined with lofty royal palms planted in the days of the first Mère Marie. On the left side of the road are some low buildings once part of the Orphelinat Augouard, and in 1986, on my first visit, a child-care center. To the right, a large building towers over the road. It is part of a secondary school and, on further exploration, turns out to be one of three wings built around an extensive yard. It was established in the 1950s as the Collège Anne-Marie Javouhey. I knew it as Lycée Lumumba, for its name had been changed after the socialist revolutions of the 1960s, the nationalization of education by the one-party government (1965), and the seizure of church property. Such powerfully symbolic name changes occurred elsewhere: the school of the Sisters of the Divine Providence of Ribeauvillé in Ouenze, the northeast extension of Brazzaville, changed from Lycée de l'Immaculée Conception to Ecole Paul Loudé, after a young revolutionary hero killed in the street fighting. In Pointe-Noire, the secondary school of the Spiritan sisters was closed and the girls and boys joined in a mixed school: the Lycée Monseigneur Carrie was renamed Lycée Trois Glorieuses, after the three days of uprisings in August 1963 when the first president of the Republic of Congo, Abbé Fulbert Youlou, was forced to resign and his place was taken by Alphonse Massamba-Débat, supported by trade unionists, left-wing intellectuals, and radical youth inspired by "scientific socialism."[1]

The time span from the period of decolonization (c. 1945–60) through the postcolonial years to the calling of a national democratization conference in 1991 saw major political transformations punctuated by outbreaks of violence that sent families scrambling for shelter, refugees fleeing, and combatants fighting in the streets. Imprisonment and death at the hands of rival factions occurred sporadically in circumstances often little understood. There was also a rapid expansion in the Catholic church, especially among women, something of a paradox since for much of the time the country was ruled by a radical socialist, one-party state.

In the decolonization struggle, the church was a polarizing presence. Conditions in the colonies and wartime France caused General de Gaulle and the governors of the French African colonies to meet at the Brazzaville conference (1944) to draw up recommendations for the future. Several key reforms removed the worst abuses. The colonies were to remain in a new imperial framework, becoming France *outre-mer* ("France overseas"), and have some representation in the French National Assembly. Other measures included a new penal code, the abolition of forced labor, and investment in education and infrastructure.[2] The ending of colonial rule in Congo was once explained as the result of an agreement between elite men and colonial officials that involved little popular participation. As Florence Bernault has shown, however, many were involved in electoral campaigns, forcing amendments to political agendas, creating cults that spread ideas about the magical powers of leaders, and ultimately substantially influencing the outcomes of the struggle.[3]

During these years, the church tried but failed to influence the debate through supporting individual candidates and establishing a pro-church party. In attempting to do so, however, it succeeded in antagonizing many. The decision of Monseigneur Bernard (the last European bishop of Brazzaville) that prohibited priests from participating in the political process and discouraged teachers and monitors from standing for political office brought a particularly hostile reaction since Abbé Fulbert Youlou was a leading political figure with avid supporters in Bacongo and the Kongo regions neighboring Brazzaville. In fact, the church's action strengthened Youlou's hand, for it separated him from association with the white church hierarchy. Declaring he would not step down from political engagement, he was removed from the priesthood by the church authorities and went on to be elected mayor of Brazzaville and the first president of the new republic.[4]

In the course of these contestations, missionary priests in Bacongo were attacked and wounded by angry crowds when Youlou and his Union Démocratique pour la Défense des Intérêts Africains lost an election in 1956.[5] Women and their families were caught in the violence and harassment at different points in time. In 1959, over a hundred people died and many were wounded as the capital was embroiled in an ethnicization of politics that brought about a divide between "northerners" (mainly Mbochi from the Alima region) and "southerners" (mainly Lari from the Pool region).[6] The Sisters of Saint Joseph of Cluny wrote of "caravans of women and children" trying to make their way across the town from Poto-Poto (largely the domain of northerners) to Bacongo and vice versa, while the Franciscan sisters reported 250 women and children seeking shelter from the "mothers" at their Poto-Poto convent over six days. Sisters and lay women prepared hundreds of meals for prisoners and refugees from both sides at gathering points throughout the city.[7] The sisters were also touched by the violence. When a young Congolese sister was stopped by party militants near her Bacongo community, a European sister negotiated her safe passage, but the superior thought the situation sufficiently grave to order a temporary withdrawal to the safer location of the community in the central city. At Linzolo, in the early heartland of mission Catholicism, the sisters were in the territory of Youlou supporters. French parachutists were sent in to guard the buildings and the sisters recalled to Brazzaville by their provincial superior.[8] As young women activists carried the struggle into the Brazzaville general hospital, the European nursing sisters were targets of verbal abuse as foreigners drawing wages from taxes collected from the people. They also came under attack as vehicles of imperialism from members of the important church-connected trade union, Confédération Africaine des Travailleurs Croyants (African Federation of Believing Workers, CATC), which included monitors and teachers from the Catholic schools.[9] Four years later, at the time of the *Trois Glorieuses,* the Sisters of the Divine Providence in Ouenze reported hand-to-hand combat going on around them and their convent being searched by young men who thought that Youlou might be hiding there.[10] Yet, the sisters reassured their superiors in Europe that overall they were treated with respect by party militants as they carried out their traditional roles of *bonnes soeurs.*

After the overthrow of Youlou and in the early years of the socialist revolution, women gathered in prayer meetings as popular African clergy were imprisoned and tortured.[11] Among them was Abbé Louis Badila, the editor of the Catholic weekly, *La semaine africaine,* who had published articles questioning the directions of the socialist government; another was Emile Biayenda, the future cardinal, who was later murdered.[12] Relations between church and state improved or at least reached something of a modus vivendi by the mid-1970s under President Marien Ngouabi, who integrated the practice of religion with his conceptualization of Congolese socialism. In an interview with the magazine *Jeune afrique,* he replied to a question on the special character of the Congo revolution:

> For us, we think that when one talks of Marxist-Leninism and of scientific so-
> cialism in Africa, or at least in Congo, one cannot make denial of God a start-
> ing point. In Congo, the people believe in God, in the cult of the ancestors. . . .
> There is no question of restricting them in their practice or in their faith; they
> are Congolese whatever their religion, their tribe. Congo belongs to them and
> they to Congo. The people have understood that the socialist revolution is not
> in opposition to their faith in any way but only against neo-colonialism, trib-
> alism, and imperialism.[13]

Yet the tensions remained. Many in the church hierarchy interpreted events as the advance of communism, and party members and civil servants trained in religious schools cut their links with the church and lived in a "deChristianized milieu." Non-attendance at church and non-participation in church activities were prerequisites for party membership, and civil servants could lose their jobs for attending Mass.[14] Their wives, many of whom had been educated in the sisters' schools, were not usually party members and continued to attend Mass and participate in church activities. Some members of the women's wing of the party, the Union Révolutionnaire des Femmes du Congo (URFC), who had attended the sisters' schools also continued their church attachment and were members of the fraternity movement. This was in itself a comment on the political sphere as a largely male affair, whereas religious practice remained a legitimate domain for women as it had always been.[15] Still, on a broader front, the line between the domain of religious action and what constituted a political act was often tested. Lay leaders and clergy had to be cautious when party militants thought their authority and the validity of the state were being contested, and when political tensions were high party militants launched attacks on activist Christians.[16] It was only after the mid-1970s that a rapprochement was reached under President Ngouabi and his successors.

Power struggles in the political arena occurred throughout the country but were intensely experienced in the towns. In the last half of the twentieth century, Congo became one of the most highly urbanized countries in Africa. The flood of migrants from the rural areas started after the Second World War when the colonial power funded large construction projects that drew in labor from long-exploited and poor rural areas. At the time of political independence, Moyen-Congo had a larger proportion of its population in cities than any other country in tropical Africa, with most of the people in the capital and southern towns, and the vast majority having arrived in the previous twenty

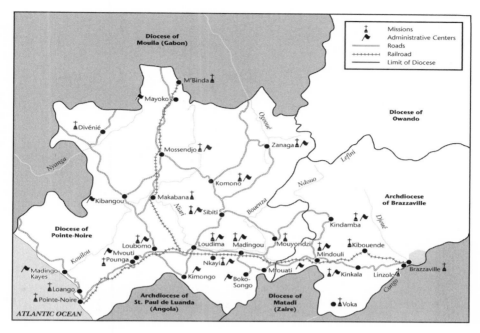

Map 3. Diocese of Pointe-Noire, 1970s.

years. The population of Brazzaville rose from around 40,000 in 1940 to 125,000 twenty years later.[17] Young women as well as men poured into the towns, so that by 1960 the numbers of women and men in Brazzaville had almost achieved parity. Whereas a majority of men surveyed said they had come to find work, women said they had arrived in the town to join their husbands or marry young men who had preceded them. A study of women in the Brazzaville economy in 1979–80 found that 82 percent of those surveyed said family reasons had been most important in bringing them to town either as children or as young women.[18]

As migrants poured into the cities, the Catholic church became predominantly an urban church, targeted by missionaries who saw better results for their proselytization there than in the thinly populated rural areas.[19] In the twenty years before nationalization, the missionary church was the recipient of large subsidies from the colonial government for schools that drew in children who became baptized church members. According to official church statistics, the Catholic population doubled between 1950 and 1969, when a third of Congo's official population was Catholic, the great majority in Brazzaville and the towns of the lower Congo.[20] Unlike earlier in the century, when mission stations were largely male spaces, the urban church of the later twentieth century became mainly a church of women, who actively recruited other women in their neighborhoods. It was women who supported the priests, maintained the buildings, did social work, and turned out for parish activities. At a popular level, women were active in furthering the transition from a missionary church to an African church and used their religious affiliation to channel their own search for community and spiritual empowerment. This chapter discusses further the conditions that helped bring women into the church, and the following chapter considers more specifically the emergence and popularity of the fraternity movement.

A Church of the People

Two developments in the 1960s created large openings for lay participation. One was the nationalization of schools and the termination of church youth movements by the state in favor of a single-party youth movement. As one informant put it, "the Party did the church a favor," for it encouraged clergy and laity to seek alternative avenues of involvement instead of those imported from Europe.[21] The pronouncements of the Second Vatican Council (1962–65) were also a profound source of change, for they defined the church as the whole "People of God," encouraged liturgical reform including the use of local languages and elements of indigenous culture, and portrayed the church as a pastoral body open to the needs and aspiration of all.[22] For women, it became a more welcoming place.

Voices demanding change had been heard for at least two decades before the dramatic events of the 1960s. In some respects, the groundwork for phasing out the missionary church had already been laid. The struggle that most claimed attention developed in private schools, where missionaries were never able to pay teachers and monitors on the same level as the state and suffered retention problems.[23] The sisters wrote home about the discontent of their staff, some of whom were leaving for better-paying jobs. The classes in Bacongo were short-staffed, and some had been cancelled, so that the more advanced students had to walk to the sisters' school in central Brazzaville to finish their course work. Furthermore, the provincial superior blamed the Congolese staff for radicalizing students; she wrote, "The monitors have become the masters of many young consciences."[24] Students were becoming more assertive and creating discipline problems, especially in the dormitories, where they complained about the food and ganged up against young, inexperienced teachers who did not know the language well.[25] Student action in Catholic and Protestant schools was mutually reinforcing. In a strike that lasted eight days at a Protestant mission school over food, quality of teachers, and scholarships, students refused to get out of bed or go to services.[26]

Independently and through their trade union, teachers and monitors were leaders in demands for equal pay. The more radical elements were already advocating nationalization of schools before independence. In 1958, the CATC organized a strike by teachers in private schools and a march through the streets of the capital. According to Jean-Claude Ganga, one of the organizers, the demonstrators received encouragement from the parents' association.[27] Ganga himself had attended the mission primary school in Bacongo and went on to the prestigious Collège Chaminade, where he graduated as a school teacher. His autobiographical account is instructive, for it is a story of his own radicalization and his relations with his devout Catholic parents. He tells of his posting to Nganga-Lingolo, fifteen kilometers from Linzolo, where he bicycled on Sundays to attend Mass. Just as his father had taken his "fiancée" to Mère Marie in Brazzaville to prepare for baptism and marriage in the 1920s, so Ganga took his future wife, Albertine Bazebissa, to the sisters at Linzolo. Becoming interested in radical ideas, he started meeting with other activists and was eventually elected president of the Christian trade union for the Pool, Djoué, and Niari-Bouenza region. He received additional training in labor law and writing by taking correspondence courses through the French branch of his union. According to his account, his activism brought the ire of his missionary employers, and an article in *La semaine africaine* (still under European direction at the time) accused him of wanting to tear down religious symbols in the schools and nationalize education. He maintained that this was a smear campaign and his only goal was equal pay. An audience with Monseigneur Bernard brought no meeting of the minds, and he left his teaching position to become a leader of the local CATC, which united workers across denominational lines.[28]

Ganga's account of his relations with his mother and father are illustrative of the tensions within many families and the kind of situations that brought women to gather in devotional meetings for mutual support. A generation of young people raised in devout Catholic homes and church schools joined the new political movements, some becoming leaders in the socialist government and others joining the militant party youth wing, the Jeunesse du Mouvement National de la Révolution (JMNR).[29] Ganga tells of being called home to account for his actions by his parents, who were both members of the confraternity of the Sacred Heart. According to his account, it was a painful experience on all sides. They had given their four children a "Christian education with a rigorous moral training," and the family attended Mass together on Sundays. His father had sought to give his household "a modern image." He had emphasized "good manners" and "he dressed us correctly." Ganga's mother, Catherine Soueneta, "was part of a generation of women who only seemed to have two goals in her life: to be a mother and to devote her life to her household, especially her children." She was an "indefatigable worker" who went on foot to her manioc farm some fifteen kilometers from the town, taking her children to work with her during their school vacations.[30] The appearance of the article, his defiance of the bishop, and his decision to leave the church thus caused his parents a great deal of pain, for they could not understand his position. He received an "indignant" and "angry" letter from them summoning him back to Brazzaville to answer the accusations that he and his comrades were bent on chasing the missionaries from Congo and destroying holy objects. For his parents it was an act of treachery that had brought shame on the family. They asked him to end his union activities and his association with undesirable influences. Again, Ganga protested that he and the other teachers had been misrepresented and that their only goal was equal pay with the teachers in government schools. At the same time, he wrote of his new conviction that he had been too long duped by the heroic images of missionaries, whom he now saw as an arm of colonialism.[31] While at times the account of his family may be over-romanticized and reads like the vindication of a party activist, it is instructive as a reminiscence of a "good" Catholic family and the divisions that political change might bring about.

The 1965 Education Act was thus, in part, the culmination of an anti-missionary movement, a strand in the decolonization process. In the legislation, schooling became a universal right, compulsory for all children between six and sixteen years of age. Education was put under state control and schools had to respect all beliefs and accept students from all backgrounds. Private teaching establishments such as seminaries and novitiates were allowed, but they were not to receive state support.[32] It was further mandated that church youth groups such as Scouts and Guides were banned in favor of the single-party youth organization; religious teaching such as catechism classes had to be conducted outside school hours; and all school-related property was confiscated without compensation.

Following a meeting between the superiors of various missionary congregations and the archbishop of Brazzaville, Monseigneur Mbemba, almost all the European congregations decided to remain in Congo, maintain a united front, and refuse to accommodate any requests to teach in schools under pro-Marxist secular authorities.[33] Some teaching sisters were called back to Europe, and some were reassigned to other African missions. The bishop advised that when government representatives arrived, the keys to the schools should be handed over quietly. At Bacongo, the separation of church and state was graphically marked by barbed wire strung out between the sisters' community and the primary school.[34] The schools reopened on time but without adequate books, with a lack of teachers, and in some confusion. The Congolese teachers largely welcomed nationalization as a necessary part of the nationalist and socialist agendas. The government received technical assistance, including teachers from the Soviet Union, Cuba, and China.

Although women and girls continued to interact with the sisters, both European and increasingly African, the relationship was not as close as it had been for earlier generations who had attended the church schools, especially the boarding schools. Even without the coming to power of a Marxist-Leninist government, changes in the religious geography of the country were underway with the rapid growth of urban parishes and the organization of congregations around parish churches with African clergy. The action of the state and the directions advocated by the Second Vatican Council further promoted alternative sources of energy and activism in rural villages and urban neighborhoods. Overall, the practice of Catholicism became more popular. The church historian Sylvain Makosso-Makosso, who lived through these times, wrote of the changes wrought by nationalization:

> There only remained in the dioceses the Legion of Mary, some groups meeting in Christian homes, and some *scholas populaires*. The Church did not welcome these measures with enthusiasm, that goes without saying! Out of concern for a neutral education, the catechism was forbidden in the schools; the children gathered together in the evening in the neighborhoods, under the trees, around volunteer catechists. The missionaries found themselves in a state of "apostolic unemployment." But in the towns and larger villages, missionaries, African priests and Christians were well heard and together they tried to proclaim and practice their message.[35]

The recommendations of the Second Vatican Council made communication and participation in this "church of the people" easier for women who were unable to read or follow the liturgy in Latin or French. The use of vernacular languages was introduced, and indigenous arrangements of church music, new songs, and elements of traditional ritual were integrated into religious observances. A sister describing Good Friday celebrations at Kindamba noted the popularity of liturgical adaptations. The harmonium had been replaced by the *ngongi* that provided the rhythm for Kilari songs composed by priests and laity, and customary funerary practices had been integrated with Catholic forms.

This year Good Friday saw the staging of elaborate ceremonies. In the morning along the Way of the Cross, groups of the faithful carried a large cross of five meters which was planted in the ground at the fourteenth station at the entrance to the mission; and, in the evening, there was the *ndizi* ceremony, the traditional funeral wake in Congolese families. At the end of the religious service, the faithful, more numerous than ever, gathered at the foot of the large cross. . . . One of the Christians, according to custom, eulogized the deceased; readings from the Gospel were interspersed with prayers and chants taken up by the crowd to the rhythm of the *ngongi,* drums, and hand-clapping.

The celebration lasted twenty-three hours.[36]

Openings for women to participate more fully and take leadership roles in church activities were increased through the establishing of local groups of Catholics called *mabundu* (Kilari/Kikongo, sing. *dibundu*), variously translated as "community," "family," or "family meeting" but used in a religious context to convey the spiritual bonds that joined members together. According to Père Guy Pannier, parish priest and then vicar general of the Pointe-Noire diocese for many years, groups of Christians had started to meet together "somewhat spontaneously" with the encouragement of priests, who emphasized that the laity must provide leadership in village communities and urban parishes. By the late 1960s, the *mabundu* were organized and had become a cornerstone of the "domestic church."[37] Various factors contributed to their rapid growth: the enthusiasm and participation of ordinary church members, the growing numbers of baptized Catholics, the aging and dwindling number of European missionaries, the small number of African clergy, the advocacy of inculturation by the Second Vatican Council, the indigenization of beliefs and practices by Congolese Christians themselves, and the monopoly of schools and youth movements by the state. The *mabundu* were alternative spaces in the dynamic practice of religious community that dovetailed with local understandings.

Not all *mabundu* functioned in the same way, but they all gave women the chance to actively participate and organize. Made up of individuals who knew each other on a daily basis, each *dibundu* accepted responsibility for the spiritual and material well-being of its members. Meetings always included prayers that spoke to the links between belief, practice, and daily life issues. Leaning on local meanings of family life, this was, according to the account of some Congolese sisters, the "Christian family of the village" enlarging solidarity beyond the kin group and engaging in "collective godparenting."[38] In regions where populations were thinly scattered and visits by priests sporadic, they became critical in the everyday operation of the church. In the mid-1970s, for example, the old Kindamba mission was located in the midst of a region larger than a French *dé-*

Figure 5.1. Three young women catechists in a Pointe-Noire neighborhood, c. 1970.
Reproduced from Pannier, *L'église de Pointe-Noire.*

partment, with a population estimated at eighteen thousand, of whom some four
to five thousand were baptized church members in some nine hundred villages.
In 1978, there were forty-five functioning *mabundu* charged with practicing the
faith, transmitting it to others, caring for the material needs of members, and
contributing to the life of the wider village community. They gave catechism instruction and decided when an individual was ready to be presented for baptism
and admission to the sacraments. Well-functioning *mabundu* held regular meetings, usually in the comfortable environment of someone's home, with prayers,
hymn-singing, and discussions on the meaning of talks given by catechists or
visiting priests. Other functions included visitation of widows and the sick and
help with essential family expenses. The oversight and "christianization" of
burials and mourning was another responsibility, with the *mabundu* sometimes
inviting another popular church organization, the *scholas populaires,* to participate. Started by Abbé Barthélemy Batantu in 1957, these were part choirs and
part advocacy groups that attended funerals and "animated" them with singing,
readings from the Bible, and prayers on certain conditions: no "evil talk of the
dead," no palm wine or other drinks, and no accusations of sorcery.[39] *Mabundu*
also carried out similar functions on their own.

In the Kindamba region, village *mabundu* had communal workdays on Wednesday, based on the Kongo practice of not going to the fields every fourth day, when the ancestors would be cultivating their land and not brook interference. Instead, members would get together on common work projects such as repairing the chapel or the itinerant priest's house or helping the community with work on houses, bridges, and roads. Land claims, clan disputes, and marriage might also be brought for arbitration before the most respected members, who served on an elected council and represented the *dibundu* when matters had to be taken before local chiefs. Satisfactory resolution of disputes ended in the traditional Kongo manner with the washing of hands and throwing away the water, symbolic for setting aside the problems that had divided the adversaries.

In all these activities, women participated fully, for the hierarchies associated with the old catechist posts and European authority were no longer as evident. Those who were experienced and respected could be elected to the *dibundu* council and attend the annual synod, which met at the parish center. Girls and young women who had been to school, especially in villages where they were the first generation educated, might act as the group secretary. The advance in girls' education after the Second World War also meant that young women were now serving as catechists, but more in towns than in the countryside. Women also worked in teams as they did in the normal practice of agriculture, clearing the ground and helping each other with planting and harvesting. At Kingoyi, they worked in the fields of those outside their community and earned money to buy new hymn books and a drum, to mend the roof of the church, and to provide food for the visiting priest. Thus, through such groups based on a Christian democracy, women were increasingly drawn into religious communities, and the popularization of the church continued under a radical socialist regime, although with caution when under the scrutiny of party militants.

The Relevance of School

The storm of the 1965 Education Act brought to an end two decades of remarkable expansion in education in which the church played a leading role, especially in girls' schooling. In their formative years, many of the girls who attended the sisters' schools forged lifelong bonds with each other and went on to marry influential men and enter the wage-labor market. Significantly for the future directions of the church, many of the generation that attended the sisters' schools in the postwar years not only were professional women and well-positioned in Congolese society in later years, but they continued their religious affiliation.

By the late 1950s, school attendance and literacy rates in Congo were among the highest in Africa. After decades of neglect, large-scale investment in social programs by the colonial state grew out of the "native policy" of Governor-General Eboué, the recommendations of the 1944 Brazzaville conference, and the new *outre-mer* orientation of France.[40] At the same time, the new generation of townspeople were demanding better education for their children. As part of the development program, the "flagrant imbalance" of boys' and girls' education was to end. "Girls must not be left out" but be given a "serious education," "parallel" to that of boys.[41] On the eve of nationalization, Congo had the highest rate of attendance among school-age children in francophone Africa, with 80 percent of those of school age in school: 27 percent of these were girls, the greatest proportion in francophone Africa.[42] The partnership between church and state in the postwar years meant that the state underwrote half the cost of school building projects, allowing the missions to open primary schools in new locations. On the eve of nationalization, about 42 percent of children were in state schools and 58 percent in church schools, with the great majority of girls attending schools run by the Catholic sisters.[43] In 1963, 13 percent of those entering secondary education were girls.[44]

The knowledge that girls might acquire in school and the consequences of school attendance were now more relevant for families than previously, especially for those who were flooding into the towns. In the countryside, it was a different story: enrolments were sluggish and attendance irregular, especially when girls lived at a distance from the schoolhouse or their labor was needed in peak farming seasons. Girls might show up for their first class when they were quite old and leave soon thereafter to be married. The kind of knowledge needed by wives and mothers was still more pertinent when it was transmitted through mothers and lineage structures rather than in the classroom. In 1942, the Sisters of Saint Joseph of Cluny finally established a community at Linzolo where, over six decades, the work with girls had remained in the hands of priests and lay Catholic "mothers." The sisters opened a school, but the results were disappointing, with only sixty girls enrolled in school ten years later. "In the bush, the parents don't understand the importance of education for girls," wrote one mother-superior.[45] At Kindamba, the enthusiasm that greeted the sisters when they arrived to establish a community in the 1920s had waned, with only 72 girls in school in 1952, compared to 730 boys in the priests' school. According to the sisters' report, the girls were mostly interested in farming and sewing. Reading and writing were less relevant, and even sewing was seen as impractical in the long term, given lack of materials when they returned to the village. "The girls are still promised in marriage at an early age," wrote the sister.[46]

In the towns, however, the sisters could hardly keep up with the demand by mothers, uncles, and fathers to enroll their daughters, since a classroom education was now thought significant for "getting on" as a wife, mother, and working women. The goals for a young woman had little changed, but a growing number of authority figures now thought that the knowledge necessary for adult life could no longer be provided by mothers alone. The relevance and appropriateness of education was the issue as it had always been. Jeanne-Françoise Vincent in her study of women in the Bacongo and Makélékélé districts of Brazzaville (1962–63) and Emilienne Raoul-Matingou in her study of women in Brazzaville (1979–80) found that informants considered the education girls received from their mother very important and believed that the mother-daughter bond could not be replaced. Those who lived in Bacongo, whatever their background and religion, emphasized the moral education received at home, especially virtues of respect and honesty. Yet, Vincent concluded from her interviews with some five hundred women that mothers and daughters were less close when girls were at school all day and had different preoccupations in urban daily life. The old Kongo adage "like mother, like daughter" was less true than before. Some mothers were ambivalent about their daughters going to school because they feared "bad boys" in the streets, but this was not sufficient reason for them to try to prevent girls from attending school if their daughters and their uncles or fathers wanted it, even if the mothers had never been to school themselves and did not really understand what went on.[47] Vincent concluded: "It seems that today, parents, especially the father, give to school teachers not only the task of instructing but training children. But classes are so big that children are less prepared than before for adult life."[48]

Many who attended the sisters' schools dropped out or were removed by their parents when they reached marriageable age, while those who stayed wanted wage-earning jobs and improved marriage prospects. Scholastique Dianzinga, who first attended Sainte-Agnès school in Bacongo before transferring to Collège Javouhey for secondary studies, commented: "Families who hid their girls in the 1930s wanted them to go to school after the Second World War. Before they only wanted boys to go to school to get jobs. But after there were jobs in offices for women. There was amazing development in a few years."[49] Vincent found that women who were wage earners had great prestige with their neighbors and there was little disapproval of those who were gone all day. Educated children were useful, for they were often the first generation literate and could help their elders who could not read and write. Mothers wanted a daughter to be able to support her children if the husband's income was erratic or the marriage failed.[50] On the eve of nationalization, the sisters were already phasing out some of their classes in response to criticism from parents. "Domestic science is no longer popular, neither the parents nor girls want it. All want classes that will allow them to work in an office. We have put together some secretarial classes with more success," wrote one.[51]

Education as a means to a good marriage continued to be a prime goal, and in the towns demands for a wife educated at the sisters' schools paralleled the transition of the male elite to an African middle class after the Second World War.[52] Bernard Mambeke-Boucher, one of the first students at Ecole Rénard, who became a teacher and civil servant before serving in the Opangault government, noted of his generation:

> There was a current of people moving about, a transformation in the ways of life. In the towns, there was the influence of foreigners and other cultures. Some of us traveled to other countries such as Togo, Libreville, Bangui, for example. We saw other cultures and started to introduce them.... The means were different and some of us had more money.... There was a bit of snobbishness that you could see at burials, for example.... Now families have to put on a good show.[53]

Marie-Thérèse Metereau, who attended Collège Javouhey, said:

> By that time there were men in politics, black deputies. If they wanted to advance, both men from this side and those from the Belgian Congo, they were looking for girls from the *Collège.* They wanted a girl who knew French, who could express herself. They could receive westerners in their home, so they wanted wives who had the necessary education to be at ease.[54]

Marriage of a daughter to such a man was considered a "social promotion" for a family.[55] Materially, it involved a large degree of social ostentation, especially in upper-class neighborhoods such as "Quartier Chic" in Bacongo, where wives might flaunt their domestic possessions and structure their days according to their children's and husbands' schedules.[56] Yet very few girls could expect to become *bamama ya midi* (Lingala, "mothers of noon") as those who shopped at supermarkets in the middle of the day later in the century were jokingly called.[57] While the education of girls had improved, labor policies practiced by European officials and employers were designed in masculine terms, and men were slotted into better wage-paying jobs to the disadvantage of women.[58]

Debate on the substance of an "equal" or "parallel" education for girls continued in the late colonial and early postcolonial times with a heavy cultural and gendered component. Vincent found in her Bacongo survey that an "ideal" woman should have "some education," meaning that she should be able to read and write and be "cultured" but that "too much education" led to "excessive independence." Josephine Ambiera Oboa carried out an inquiry about marital relations in Brazzaville households in her capacity as assistant secretary of the Action catholique des familles. She found that many men mistrusted educated young women, especially monitors and teachers, when it came to choosing a spouse since they were thought too independent and "demanding."[59] Practices surrounding marriage and family were debated by young men who in the 1950s published articles in the magazine *Liaison* with titles such as "The Evolution of the African Woman"; "What I Think of Present-Day Marriages"; and, "No Confidence in Women!"[60] Writers claimed that continuing ties of women to their matrilineal kin were barriers to a modern marriage. In the context of "Marriage and Divorce," one contributor claimed: "She does what the family tells her so it is the notion of what constitutes a family that needs to be changed. It is the continuation of the old system that creates unstable households." Another writer blamed women's prolonged visits to their home village as a cause of family instability in an article entitled "When the Married Woman 'Leaves for a Vacation.'"[61] In one of the few contributions by a woman, written as a letter to the editor, Madeleine M'Bombo took the magazine and the male writers to task for the repetitive themes that blamed women for marriage and family problems:

> Since no. 7 of *Liaison*, you and your contributors have been totally preoccupied with questions of bridewealth, the African woman, and marriage. . . . But what are you really doing, each in his private life? How many of you are taking the trouble to educate your wives? You heap blame on her relations. . . . But once again, what action are you taking? . . . On the occasion of the birth and baptism of our first child, my husband and I gave a reception and all the male guests arrived by themselves having left their wives and children behind at home. Some were even accompanied by their female "friends" although the reception was held by a serious household expecting to be honored by legitimate couples surrounded by their dear children.[62]

Some mothers and grandmothers continued to mistrust the education their daughters received in school, not only because of the loss of labor but because they lost control over the daughters' preparation for marriage and motherhood. This is documented in attempts to retain elements of *kumbi* in a modified form in the face of resistance from schoolgirls. One writer in *Liaison* described the custom as "greatly detested by marriageable young girls." His school friend, Joséphine Lembe, had been invited by her maternal relatives to visit a village near Pointe-Noire. "On returning, some distance from the village, two women ambushed her and took her by force to the *tchicoumbi* house. Joséphine cried out but could do nothing. This was on Saturday. On Sunday she was bathed in warm water, washed with a red color and shut in the house." The author does not detail how long the girl missed classes but said that his friend "greatly regretted her studies being interrupted."[63]

Testimonies collected from three women in the 1970s in Pointe-Noire indicate modifications in the practice to meet the demands of schoolgirls while satisfying older women that the essentials of *kumbi* were preserved. According to the three women, their seclusion had lasted from one to five weeks and had taken place at their mother's or aunt's home. The layering of *tukula* paste on the body remained an essential part of the ritual; the *tchikumbi* was dressed in a special costume with a raffia skirt, bracelets, and rings on the legs; and oversight was in the hands of an aunt or a woman chosen by the women of the family. Yvette, who was secluded for several weeks, said that the honor of the family demanded she go through the ritual. The customs were a link to the spirits of the ancestors, who would bless her with fertility, help her pregnancy, and guard her children from death. She played card games with the younger girls who were her companions, and her neighborhood friends signed their names on the planks of the house where she was secluded. That the event was in women's domain and an expression of their joint responsibility was also preserved. Even if girls returned to school and did not marry immediately, older female relations insisted that the ritual must still be practiced in some form. In the case of Yvette, her father wanted her to return to school. It was her grandmother who was afraid that she might become pregnant before going through the *tchikumbi* process, given the freedom of young people in the towns. Of the three young women who recorded their *tchikumbi* experiences, two returned to school. A third said that her uncle had arranged her marriage and insisted that she leave school.[64]

Anxieties over control of girls' sexuality continued as old forms of initiation practices died out. While the mission churches railed against the practice as they had done over decades, *Nzambi-Bougie,* the church of the prophet Zéphérin Simon Lassy with many adherents in the Loango and Mayombe regions, integrated key aspects of *kumbi* into its rituals.[65] It prohibited the seclusion of marriageable young women in a "house of paint" and substituted the seclusion of a girl at home, where she wore a white cloth (church members were distinguished by their white robes with insignia such as a cross and a star), drenched her body with perfumes, and bathed several times a day. This "modernizing" of the institution brought control of girls at puberty within the purview of the church and made membership more acceptable to older women.[66] In 2000, some women still remembered *kumbi*-related events, but they said that one would have to travel to a "remote area" to find it still practiced. One woman said that with the prevailing conditions in towns, modern culture, and the splintering of some families, many young people did what they wanted. The missionary sisters' denial of a girl's sexuality was at the heart of Andrée Blouin's scathing account of the convent boarding school.[67] Others said that their education as Christian "mothers of families" had been restricted to the practical details of running the household and child-rearing.

Religious Sisters and Mothers Challenged

The demand for girls' education was fortuitously paralleled by an increase in the number of young women entering religious orders in France after the Second World War, and the missionary congregations responded to requests for reinforcements from the bishops of the Brazzaville and Pointe-Noire dioceses with many well-qualified sisters, not only those belonging to congregations already in Congo, such as the Sisters of Saint Joseph of Cluny, the Franciscan Missionaries of Mary, and the Spiritan sisters, but congregations such as the Sisters of the Divine Providence of Ribeauvillé, an Alsatian teaching order whose mistress of novices was the sister of Monseigneur Biéchy, bishop of Brazzaville at the time.[68] Reinforcements also came from a new generation of well-educated African sisters, who took up positions as teachers and nurses and provided leadership as European sisters aged and retired.

At the time of nationalization in Brazzaville, 2,830 girls were enrolled at Ecole Javouhey and in Bacongo. The level of achievement was still modest, however, since only sixty girls passed the primary school certificate between 1960 and 1965.[69] The long experience of the Cluny sisters in schooling African girls not only in Congo but in other French colonies such as Senegal and Madagascar caused the colonial government to select them to open the Collège Javouhey (that gave the equivalent of a middle school education). In 1965, the school had 334 students taking basic academic subjects and receiving religious education. Some of the best students also took courses at the Collège Chaminade, the prestigious boys' secondary school. In 1965, the first student who had been trained by the Cluny sisters passed the *baccalauréat* (the secondary school graduation certificate on the French model).[70] At their schools in Ouenze, Voka, and Mouléké, the Ribeauvillé sisters had about 2,500 girls enrolled when they handed their schools over to the state. They wrote of trying to hold down enrollments, but it was difficult to turn away girls when their parents insisted. Very few children came from Catholic homes, but this was not a barrier; older folk said they were too old for the new religion, but they did not oppose their children attending catechism classes and being baptized.[71]

Figure 5.2. Schoolgirls waiting outside their classrooms, Brazzaville, c. 1960. Archives, Sisters of the Divine Providence of Ribeauvillé.

The Franciscan sisters, who for many years had been working in upper Congo, were also called to the capital to service the growing demand for girls' education. Whereas the Sisters of Saint Joseph of Cluny had some skills in Kikongo and Kilari, the Franciscans' knowledge of Lingala was essential in Poto-Poto and Moungali, where 2,307 were enrolled by 1964.[72] The six-year curriculum had classes on the catechism, home hygiene, sewing, math, science, history, and geography. While Collège Javouhey was developing a secondary school academic stream, the Franciscans with their practical, technical orientation moved "household management" onto a more professional level.[73] In 1958, they opened a post-primary technical school, Ecole Professionelle, partially funded by a government subsidy. Students followed a three-year course of study: the first in general academic subjects, after which students were streamed to give them qualifications for jobs as social workers, domestic science teachers, childcare specialists, nurses, and commercial and secretarial workers.[74]

Finally, girls' schooling was also transformed in the diocese of Pointe-Noire that included much of the lower Congo (see map 3).[75] In 1953, an official Spiritan visitor toured the thirteen mission stations of the lower Congo and found that only one, Pointe-Noire, had a community of sisters. He concluded: "Because of this lack of Sisters, all the missions seem to be inhabited by men only. There is no work with girls except at Pointe-Noire. *It is a Christianity of boys!*"[76] In the Pointe-Noire region, the Spiritan sisters, like other congregations, financed the expansion of their work through their own income as teachers and nurses and government subsidies for half the costs of new buildings. In Pointe-Noire, they supervised three schools, including one with secondary classes. Six European sisters also worked at the general hospital training nurses and medical technicians. At the time of nationalization in the Pointe-Noire diocese, there were 7,761 girls in church primary schools, 150 in secondary schools, and 242 in household management courses.[77]

The break that came with nationalization was a huge blow to the sisters and to many of their students. One sister wrote home that handing over the keys to the schools was "like handing over the souls of our children."[78] Another wrote of the sadness at Ouenze when the older girls carried the religious objects and symbols from the school buildings to the sisters' community.[79] At the girls' boarding house at the Javouhey convent in central Brazzaville, a large statue of Notre Dame de Lourdes was carried in procession to a new location in the convent garden.[80] At Bacongo in the early months of nationalization, the sisters reported that after school the girls had begun to find their way to the community around the "iron curtain" (the barbed wire) between Sainte-Agnès primary school and the convent building. Women had also arrived to discuss how their study groups and sewing and knitting classes could be reorganized in the changed circumstances.[81] Some women trained in the sisters' schools recalled with nostalgia their relations with their religious mothers, especially those with whom they were particularly close, such as those after whom they were named or who were their godmothers.

The experience of Marie-Antoinette Mouanga is illustrative of the bonds that could be forged in formative years. Born into a "very religious family"— her uncle was Cardinal Emile Biayenda and her aunt, a sister of Saint Joseph of Cluny—she attended the sisters' primary school in Baratier (Kibouende) as a boarder and then transferred to the Collège Javouhey in 1964. About nationalization a year later, she recalled:

> But I stayed in touch with the Sisters for it was a sudden break like that. We missed the Sisters. We were more or less like orphans because there was no one, we were cut off. At first, it was necessary that we not go to catechism classes and not have contact with the nuns. They had installed what they called in the countries of the east the Pioneers, all of that. Since I came from a religious family, we did not go to these lay movements. Never. So, the Sisters were forbidden to continue movements such as the Brownies, the Scouts, Guides and so on. Little by little, since we did not want to be cut off from the Sisters, we went to see them in the afternoon. It began with small sewing classes, cooking classes, singing lessons, so like that our contacts with the Sisters grew.

She went on to say that when she was about fourteen or fifteen years old, she became a catechist in the Parish of Saint-Pierre in Bacongo. She also elaborated further on how the church organized:

> They authorized the *Rassemblement des cathéchistes* to gather the catechists in different parishes together to strengthen the group. . . . During the holidays we went on a mission to the bush. We stayed at the mission that received us and we gathered the catechumens from several villages. Together with the children who taught the catechism there, we gathered at a grand meeting to take communion, a great retreat.

In later years, she maintained her friendships with other former students of the sisters' schools through her membership in the *Amicale Javouhey* and a newsletter the sisters mailed out.[82]

For the sisters, the major challenge of the post-1965 years was to reconfigure their work, keep up their recruitment of Congolese sisters, and retool. Overall, the flow of energy was away from convent schools to work in neighborhoods alongside the laity. While they earned necessary income through wage-earning jobs at the hospital, polio treatment centers, and social centers, they also organized catechism classes, trained volunteer teachers, taught sewing, visited the sick and widows, helped with child care, talked to prisoners, gave advice on minor ailments, and worked with young people. Such activities channeled some into the church.[83] Reflecting on the work, the provincial-superior of the Sisters of Saint Joseph of Cluny reported in 1973: "The face of the Congolese church is changing. At all levels, leaders are able to read the 'signs of the times' and after the tempest that claimed so many victims and made necessary complete readjustments, the church has taken on a new lease of life . . . we are fully integrated with these 'people of God.'"[84] Soeur Johanna Ammeux, who worked as a teacher in Pointe-Noire and was called home at the time of nationalization to be superior-general of the Spiritan sisters, concluded "nationalization was good for the church," for it forced missionary congregations to adjust, to work more closely with the people, and to increase efforts to train African sisters and lay women in leadership roles.[85]

Recruiting more African women into the female congregations was a pressing concern, but recruitment by foreign congregations was now jeopardized by the priorities and nationalist orientation of what was now an African church. Following a meeting of the Congolese bishops, the superiors of the female missionary orders received a letter announcing the creation of an inter-diocesan congregation of Congolese nuns, the Soeurs de Notre Dame du Rosaire. Archbishop Théophile Mbemba wrote that "the time has come to take a new step and to prepare for a future in keeping with new African aspirations." To give the new congregation of Congolese nuns the chance to succeed, he wrote, "I am asking the European missionary congregations to stop their recruitment and to direct their female religious vocations to the Congregation of Congolese Religious."[86] Thanking the European congregations for their work in training some seventy Congolese nuns over the years, he quoted from the findings of the Second Vatican Council on the need "in the new Christianity to develop forms of religious life in keeping with the character and local customs of people and their conditions of life."[87] An association of Oblates du Rosaire for older women who had received their calling to a religious commitment later in life—for example, widows and those who had been divorced and had grown children—was also established.[88] Following these strictures on local recruitment, the European missionary congregations struggled to maintain their work through some bleak years that were also a time (c. 1969–75) when persecutions of church workers by party militants was at a high. In 1973, Mère Marie Budinger wrote home that "from year to year our novitiate is emptied."[89] Recovery only came slowly after Cardinal Biayenda lifted the ban on recruitment in 1975.

At the heart of these institutional struggles lived and worked African religious women. The path to profession might start through their contacts with sisters or through parish priests and devotional communities. Some were from devout religious families. In the case of the first two Congolese Sisters of Notre Dame of Ribeauvillé, who took their vows in 1962, the father of Soeur Marie-Thérèse Nkouka was a catechist and the father of Soeur Jeanne-Françoise Oumba, a primary school teacher.[90] Yet even in devout families there could be sustained opposition to daughters' choosing a religious vocation. In a society where motherhood was the mark of a successful and adult woman, even a freely chosen childlessness was a source of sadness and suffering. A Congolese sister in Pointe-Noire wrote of her experience:

> While I was in primary school at Notre-Dame, I knew a nun called Soeur Martha who was principal of the school at the time. Her presence affected me greatly. I started catechism at Notre-Dame during the first year. At that time, we also learnt it in school at the end of classes. And I used to go to mass at Saint Christophe every Sunday with my parents. There I met the Sisters who came to pray. In 1968, I took my first communion. From then, I felt a strong call deep within me, a call from God that I knew at once. After my confirmation, I knew some Sisters who were friends of my mother but I didn't dare say anything about my vocation for lack of courage, and also in case they spoke to my parents. I knew from the bottom of my heart that I wanted to be like them.
>
> One day I had the courage to speak to the priest in my parish of Saint Christophe. That was Abbé Mwati, today the Bishop of Pointe-Noire. Before

me, others had also thought of the religious life. Without waiting, the priest asked the Soeurs de la Visitation to help us explore our vocation in order to respond to God's calling. I went with the others without knowing there were different congregations. Thus, it was at the Visitation that I started to see the importance of prayer in a religious life.

She then decided to return to school, and the testimony goes on to relate how the influence of her secular, academic milieu, her neighborhood friends, and thoughts of marriage diverted her from the religious life. Then:

> At a given moment, I felt my calling for the religious life again, my way started to open but I was incapable of getting out of the deep waters immediately. To arrive where I am today was difficult. . . . My parents were always aware of my desire to be a nun but when I decided to leave them, there was opposition. At present, a young girl who goes to the convent is very strange, she will not marry, she will not have children, and my parents will never cradle my small child. That is very hard for certain parents to accept. I was sure of my choice. I decided to stick with my decision in spite of opposition from my family. I ignored everything people would say: "your parents are against it, they will put a curse on you." After I left home, my parents accepted my decision as good Christians, although it did not lessen their sacrifice.[91]

Whether or not a girl was from a Catholic background, she could encounter mockery from her peers as a barren woman, harassment from boys and young men in her family, and fierce opposition from elders.[92] Furthermore, there was the added problem of criticism within the church community itself. In the nationalist period and in the early days of the Marxist state, the affiliation of Congolese sisters to foreign congregations made them vulnerable to criticism from young priests who saw the formation of a Congolese congregation as part of the development of the national church. The publication in *La semaine africaine* of the archbishop's pastoral letter concerning the new inter-diocesan congregation and the reluctance of European congregations to give up their own novitiates was especially disconcerting for Congolese sisters, who thought it painted then as "counter-revolutionaries" and "slaves of the Europeans," whereas, they argued, their congregations were not against the new order but only the archbishop's position that it should have a monopoly on recruitment. Each order needed to maintain it own novitiate, they said, so that novices could "learn the way of the congregation." Those who had already taken permanent vows to a foreign congregation were in a difficult situation, and some of them, now mothers-superior, went to argue their case with the archbishop.[93]

Yet it was family opposition that was most difficult for girls and young women to bear. According to the Ribeauvillé sisters, consent from the uncle could facilitate the handing over of a daughter, although the church, given its model of a Christian family, would include the parents in any negotiations.[94] At Kibouende, the European novice mistress of the Sisters of Saint Joseph of Cluny wrote that the ongoing attachment of the postulants and novices to their families "is a source of great concern. As long as the family is not in agreement with them, they are tormented. If there is a difficulty in their family, they ask for permission to go and help mediate the palavers. Certainly, it is not France."[95] The superior of the Vice-Province of Congo (SSJC) also reported: "The closeness of the families of Congolese Sisters creates serious problems through too frequent contacts, the influence certain parents wield over their children, and the bad advice given."[96]

Such "problems" caused the congregations to revise their policies and refuse to take on a girl if the family opposed it. One retired sister remembered: "It was not worth it. If the family did not agree, we did not take her."[97] At the same time, the openings encouraged by the Second Vatican Council and the subsequent revision of the constitutions of missionary congregations allowed far-reaching changes to be introduced, the most visible of which was the modification or giving up of religious habits, a more humane novitiate experience (previously dominated by notions of "sacrifice and "discipline"), an end to distinctions between different ranks of sisters, and a more liberal approach to their daily lives.[98]

Joan Burke's research on changes within her own congregation, the Sisters of Notre Dame de Namur in the Lower Congo (DRC), has shown how rites of incorporation into a religious order were Africanized and expressed in local categories, thus making them more meaningful for religious women and their families. She cites practices that could be understood in the context of the seclusion and intense education that young Kongo women underwent at puberty, namely the seclusion of postulants and novices for a period of time under the supervision of a "designated professional" who passed on the "ancestral knowledge" needed to serve the "clan." Thus, the whole process of a young woman leaving her mother's household and entering a community of women religious could be understood as the passage from one life stage to another and from one family to another.[99]

In a document entitled "Asking for the Consent of the Parents," the Sisters of Saint Joseph of Cluny described how a young woman's kin were incorporated into the process of entering the religious life through the metaphor of a marriage agreement between families. "Customary marriage rituals" were used to "remove the fear of our young Sisters that they do not have their family's blessing." The "marriage" negotiations that took place once the novice had completed her time in the novitiate were illustrated through a particular case:

We were about ten Sisters accompanying the novice, armed with the traditional wine, that was: a demijohn of 10 liters of palm wine, 2 bottles of red wine, some bottles of beer and lemonade. At the agreed time, we went to the family compound where the paternal and maternal families of the young woman were already awaiting us.

Soeur Solange, knowing the language of these families perfectly, took the lead in explaining the purpose of our visit. She started by introducing us all and the families in their turn introduced themselves. She then continued: so, your daughter has been with us for three years. We know that you are in agreement but before she enters our religious family completely, we want to make clear to you these new obligations. As in marriage, she is going to belong to another family. We, members of the new family, have come to make an alliance with you. From now on, we are all your daughters and we think of you like our parents.

She continued:

Your daughter is going to enter an international religious family, implying that she may be sent to another country in Africa, Europe or America. For now, she will stay in Congo The congregation will look after her completely. She has thus nothing to ask of you. Anything you want to give her will belong to all the Sisters. In a family, one gives what is needed, so don't be surprised or sad if you see something you have given to your daughter being used by another Sister, for is she not also your daughter? We live in true communism.

The spokesperson went on to assure the family that their daughter was not abandoning them, that she would visit them from time to time and that they could visit her, although she should not be "distracted by small matters" from her responsibilities to her religious family. The congregation would do what it could to help families in need, but if the daughter earned a wage it belonged to the community, not her family. There was then an explanation of how the ritual of profession would be conducted. Finally:

Then, the novice with a glass of palm wine in one hand and a bottle of wine in the other approached her father, knelt before him, put down the bottle, and with glass in hand, her voice choking with emotion, asked for the consent of her father. An impressive silence fell on those gathered. The father poured a little wine on the ground for the ancestors, swallowed a mouthful, passed the glass to his daughter who did the same, retook the glass and drank. The novice then did the same in front of the head of the maternal family.

The whole occasion ended with a celebration.[100]

The ritual of profession also incorporates the novice's family, for the young woman walks down the aisle escorted by her mother and father. When the novice mistress calls her name the novice advances to the altar with her father and mother, who then give her to the mother-superior of the congregation. The church rituals associated with taking vows then proceed.[101] Such ceremonies were a spectacle, with massed clergy in their most elaborate vestments and the full ritual of the church. In 1989, the rite of profession for five African sisters was conducted at the cathedral by the archbishop of Brazzaville, the bishop of Nkayi, and the apostolic administrator of Owando, with ten priests, sisters from different congregations, and over two thousand others in attendance. Later in the year, a similar ceremony for five sisters of the congregation of Notre Dame du Rosaire at the parish church in Makélékélé was presided over by the archbishop of Brazzaville, the bishop of Pointe-Noire, many clergy and sisters, and a crowd numbered in the thousands.[102]

By the end of the century, it was much more acceptable for a family to give up one of its daughters to a religious congregation, although there were always some who were opposed to the loss of a woman and the children she might bear. While the sense of vocation is not in question, there were clearly many practical advantages to be had: security, education, a career, access to networks within the church, and opportunities for families. In 1986, Soeur Marie-Michelle drove her jeep all over the lower Congo on both sides of the river visiting families whose daughter had been recommended as a potential postulant by a local priest. Along the way, she would be asked by women with many children and little support to take a girl to the novitiate. Although from the region herself, she talked of the problem of discerning "vocations" and the difficulty of returning girls to their families if they proved unsuitable for the religious life.[103] The sisters are now much more concerned about levels of education and the potential of novices for professional careers, not least because of the rise in education standards in the general population and the need for respect. Sisters from different orders have attained higher degrees in medicine, social work, nursing, education, theology, linguistics, and economics at Université Marien Ngouabi in Brazzaville and overseas. They are also sent to Europe for courses in spiritual formation. In 1994 of the 130 Congolese sisters, 21 were overseas for education or on mission-related business.[104] Some voice concern at their vows of poverty and their relative affluence in the midst of so much poverty.

Joan Burke's study *We Sisters Are All Mamas!* expands on her basic thesis that the metaphor of maternity has allowed sisters' families to come to terms with the loss of their daughters and their vow of celibacy. She writes:

> These young adults often explain their motive for becoming members of
> the religious congregation in terms of maternity of a kind that makes them

"mothers of all the people." Their choice of this alternative way of living is presented as more of an affirmation than a denial of the matrifocal Kongo valuation of women in terms of motherhood.[105]

She also points out:

> It is a quite common practice in the lower Zaire for Catholic Sisters—whether they are local or expatriate women—to be addressed as *"Mama."* . . . The application to the celibate Sisters of the title *"Mama,"* the usual form of address to a Kongo woman who has borne her people children, presumes a different perception of Sisters from that held by Westerners. The fact that most of the Sisters are teachers of children, or work in the dispensary caring for the sick, strongly reinforces this perception.[106]

From their arrival in Loango, when the first missionary sisters remarked on the children who shouted *"zi mèle!"* to more recent times, when the newly arrived sisters from Ribeauvillé wrote home of those along the route from the airport calling out *"mamas,"* European sisters, especially young women, were struck by the terminology of local people. *Mama* was, of course, also a title of respect for women of an older generation as well as biological or social mothers. While the in-depth and "insider" research that led Joan Burke to her conclusions has not been carried out on the Brazzaville side of the river, the common matrifocal groundings of Kongo society and the integration of local practices in rites of religious profession lend some credence to the conclusion that a situation similar to that of the sisters of Namur may pertain north of the river.

Conclusion

In the second half of the twentieth century, the Catholic church in Congo changed from being missionary-dominated to being a "church of the people." The popularization of Catholicism began almost as soon as Christianity arrived in Congo, but it now was given impetus through political transformations, the rapid growth of urban parishes, and the recommendations of the Second Vatican Council on inculturation. The practice of the faith flowed not only from directives of the clergy but from local initiatives as people created and appropriated openings and filled them with expressions of their own needs and understandings. In the "church of the people," members of *mabundu* took responsibility for their local meetings, young women taught catechism classes under the trees, and members of *scholas populaires* helped "christianize" rituals surrounding death. Women's participation grew and their numbers increased with a new generation of Catholics who attended the sisters' schools in the postwar years and brought their children to be baptized. In 1964, church women established their own associations, described by a bishop twenty years later as "a great reality in the life of the Congolese church." Through the fraternities the church further evolved so that it became primarily a church of women.[107]

6. Women Together

In a special edition marking the centenary of the Congolese church in 1983, *La semaine africaine* highlighted historical landmarks and key features of the contemporary church. Among the photographs is one of women in cloths and head-scarves signifying membership of different church groups, with a caption referring to the "vast movement of the women's fraternities" and "a social phenomenon whose spiritual and pastoral aspects have still not been sufficiently analyzed."[1] Six years later, the Mass for the fraternities' twenty-fifth anniversary was attended by delegations of women from Senegal, Côte d'Ivoire, Guinée (Conakry), Cameroon, Central African Republic, and Zaire as well as bishops, clergy, sisters, and lay representatives. Reviewing the history of women in the Congolese church, the bishop of Ouesso noted how they had remained in the background for decades, but went on to say: "Through the women's fraternities created in the 1960s, we have at last found the place of women in the Congolese church. But the road has not been easy." He noted that at the outset fraternity activities had been confined to prayer meetings, novenas, recitation of the rosary, and anniversary celebrations. The women had then added mutual aid functions similar to those in secular society. Concerning the "difficult road," he noted that there had been too much public display, competition between groups, and tensions between leaders who were educated and wealthy and other members who were poor. Yet, he concluded, in spite of these problems, the women's work had collectively grown so that fraternity members now provided essential services in the church and community. Overall, they merited praise:

The development of the fraternities, it must be recognized has sometimes been out of step with the rhythms of Congolese church life, and they have not always fulfilled the hopes raised among the clergy. The result has been a great deal of criticism and times of discouragement.... But, thanks be to God, a great deal has been accomplished.... The Congolese ecclesiastical hierarchy is proud and sincerely thanks Mme. Malékat, National President of all the Fraternities and, with her, all the members for the existence of these precious movements, instruments for the evangelization of our laity.... For 25 years, they have ensured catechism teaching; the proclamation of the Gospel and liturgical services; the distribution of communion to the sick; assistance to communities of priests, gatherings for communion, and institutes for religious training; advice for members of households; support for widows and for those divorced, etc.... But there are many difficulties that remain to be overcome, as is the case with other apostolic movements throughout the church.[2]

The bishop's words summed up the contradictions that the fraternities presented for the clergy as the women's organizations grew in popularity and became the dynamic core at the heart of the church. As the women developed their own priorities, they were at times out of step with other church organizations and drew criticism from those in the secular world, but they also had avid supporters. "Committed" and "disciplined" were adjectives I heard to describe fraternity women even as they were the object of negative comment. The parish priests intervened little, for they recognized that fraternity power contributed to the spiritual and social well-being of Catholic urban communities: women clean the church, cook for the priests, attend Mass, visit the sick, help widows, and give substantial monetary support. Furthermore, throughout the Marxist period and after they evidenced the continued spiritual vitality of the church. Several of the African clergy I talked with admired women's religious fervor and contribution to the everyday life of the parishes.[3]

The fraternities were by no means the first organized women's group associated with the church, but they were different, for they were created and developed by church women out of their own circumstances and religiosity.[4] As has been shown in studies elsewhere in Africa, it was common for missionaries, especially missionary wives, to start up groups modeled after those in the European church. In Congo, the earliest—not surprisingly given the missionary preoccupation with women as "mothers of families"—was an Association des Mères Chrétiennes (Association of Christian Mothers) started by the sisters in Bacongo at the behest of the male missionaries and based on similar associations in French parishes. An account of the 1912 Corpus Christi celebrations described the various groups that participated in the procession around the cathedral: "the *Schola* in the robes of the choir," "the youth club with its banners flying in the wind," and "in the middle of the procession the Christian mothers and their offspring under the banner of Saint Anne."[5] In 1918, about one hundred women attended meetings of the association, which seem to have continued, probably with reinforcements from the women who had passed through the sisters' "fiancées" classes. In 1930, two hundred women attended a meeting where they heard a priest talk on the moral responsibility of motherhood, recited the Rosary, and received communion.[6] Otherwise, there is not much information on the content of programs, and the association does not seem to have drawn much enthusiasm, perhaps because meetings were high on moral advice and low on the kind of practical information that interested most women.

Another group of Catholic women, although not a church organization, was the Amicale des Anciennes Elèves (Former Students' Association) started by the sisters with former students from their Brazzaville school. Soeur Clothilde, who arrived in Brazzaville in 1923, recalled the meetings. Photographs taken at annual meetings in 1937 and 1942 show young women wearing the European-style dresses and stockings that were trendy with the elite at that time. As already noted, such contacts between former "Javouhey" students have continued up till the present with branches in France.[7] Women also participated in church organizations such as the Legion of Mary or mixed choirs, but it was the fraternities that allowed them to create an organization that most met their spiritual and material needs.

Aimée Gnali, in an article decrying the scarcity of women in leadership positions in Congolese public life, blamed low levels of education and poor access to economic opportunity, but she also noted that women were generally less vocal in public arenas when men were present, and their independence and leadership roles more likely to be constricted.[8] Two priests in a Pointe-Noire parish agreed that women were less assertive in church groups if men were present even when women were in the majority.[9] Léontine Bissangou, president of the Pointe-Noire fraternities, also remarked that although women were in the great majority in the parishes, men "often lay down the law."[10] Through the fraternities, women found their voice.

From Javouhey to Poto-Poto, Bacongo, and Beyond

Fraternity women date the origins of their movement to a specific moment in time. The first to be founded, the *Fraternité Saint-Joseph,* traces its origins to 1964 and the days that followed the overthrow of the Youlou government by young revolutionaries. For mothers, the 1950s and 1960s were traumatic years as family members took to the streets. According to one account, those whom leaders mobilized to attack opponents in pro-Youlou demonstrations in 1956 included boys of twelve to fifteen years old.[11] The crowds of the *Trois Glorieuses* uprisings included many young people, and after 1965, it was militants in the party youth wing who were virulent in their attacks on "counter-revolutionaries."[12] The difficult meeting of Jean-Claude Ganga with his devout Catholic parents when he cut his ties with the church and joined the socialist party was likely repeated in other families with young people who became radicalized. It was in these troubled times, with husbands and sons and brothers fighting in the streets, family members leaving the church, church sympathizers losing their jobs, lay leaders harassed, and priests imprisoned and tortured, that the fraternities were born. According to the founders, they were a spontaneous response by Catholic women to personal suffering and social upheaval.

Some of this was conveyed to me by Firmine Malékat, a founding member of the first fraternity and president of the Brazzaville fraternities when I met her in 1986. She explained:

> Mère Marie used to hold annual reunions for former students of the Ecole Ja-
> vouhey in Brazzaville. Europeans, *métisses* from the orphanage, and Africans,
> we all would come. On 21 November 1964 (the Feast of the Presentation of the
> Virgin Mary), Mère Hortense invited all the former students from Bacongo
> and Poto-Poto to come together for a reunion, as usual just a social gather-
> ing with drinks, cookies, exchanging news of professional accomplishments,
> families, and so on. Then, we had the idea of going to the Grotto of Lourdes to
> pray together, two by two, as we had done during our schooldays. We did this
> and Mère Marie called on me to lead the group in prayers given the troubled
> conditions in the town. There were about 50 or 60 of us of all ages from twenty
> to seventy at this first gathering. We decided to ask Abbé Badila to organize
> a mass for us. He agreed but just at that point he was arrested. Political prob-
> lems had arisen. A few days later another mass was arranged at Saint Anne's
> and we women met from 2 PM to 9 PM to pray for his release. Then we heard
> that Abbé Badila had been freed. 21 November 1964 is taken as the beginning
> of the fraternities with *Fraternité Saint-Joseph* as the oldest. On the release of
> Abbé Badila there was a day of retreat at the cathedral beginning with a mass
> led by him and then the women walked through the streets in procession to
> Javouhey. In December 1964, we organized another retreat and mass for our
> group. At Javouhey, we followed the Stations of the Cross.[13]

This narrative that locates fraternity beginnings in a group of women going to pray to Our Lady of Lourdes at the convent Grotto is now commonly told and is included in the official fraternity history that is the preamble to the statutes.

The story symbolically confirms what women maintain, that they are drawn together through the practice of their faith and the spiritual empowerment they receive. From this, all other activities such as mutual aid and social action flow. For the original members the bonds created in their school days also helped to strengthen their new communities.[14]

Firmine Malékat went on to relate how following these events about thirty women began to meet at her home in Poto-Poto to talk about their individual and social problems, hold prayer meetings, and discuss how they might contact other former students of the Catholic schools. Then: "The next year was very heated. They nationalized education and the youth movements in the church. Priests were arrested. It was very difficult to meet on a regular basis but the group continued to attract members and eventually we had to move our meetings to Saint Anne's."[15] By 1968, members decided to establish an executive committee, and other fraternities that had come into existence did likewise. Following the example of the Javouhey graduates, those who had attended other Catholic schools started associations named after the saints that they knew well from their student days. Thus, the Fraternité Saint-Joseph was followed by the Fraternité Sainte-Thérèse after the Franciscan school in Poto-Poto, the Fraternité Sainte-Agnès after the primary school in Bacongo, and the Fraternité de l'Immaculée Conception after the school of the Ribeauvillé sisters in Ouenze. The idea of such women's groups then spread to women in the parishes, some of whom had a formal education and others who had never attended school. With each infusion of new members, the fraternities became more popular.

From these beginnings membership increased, and the leaders decided that structures were necessary to integrate what was becoming a broad movement of church women. In particular, the two "camps" of fraternities, those started by the graduates of the sisters' schools and those originating in the parishes, needed to be unified in a single organization. Thus, in 1972, with seven groups in existence in Brazzaville, the leaders approached Monseigneur Biayenda, who gave them official recognition. The women appointed a president and vice-president to assume direction of all the fraternities, established a central office and parish offices, and requested the bishop to appoint chaplains and sister-counselors. Each group was to develop its own statutes with guidelines for admission, the timing of meetings, and members' dues. New members were to receive a small manual with the rules of the fraternity, and the overall goals were summed up in the motto: "Prayer, conversion and penitence, mutual aid, and evangelism."[16]

The sociologist Michèle O'Deyé, in a study (1985) comparing urban associations in Dakar and Brazzaville, found that over 70 percent of those who lived in the Congo capital were members of an association but concluded that with church associations "their religious aspects do not seem to be significant."[17] While this may be true of some groups, members of the Catholic fraternities insist they exist primarily as devotional groups, and outsiders who observe the long hours women spend in prayer meetings, retreats, and vigils agree. In 1986, a social worker compared the fraternities with the URFC:

> The fraternities are more popular with women than the revolution. Women like to pray. It is a religious motivation that causes fraternity women to turn out to clean the hospital; it is their idea of charity that causes them to help those who have suffered. . . . The URFC tries to organize women traders and farmers, for example around Brazzaville, to help themselves and women in general but it doesn't deal with women on a personal level and their problems with husbands and families as the fraternities do.

She added that lack of adequate schooling meant that the great majority of women did not understand what Marxism and the revolution were about: "Prayers are more important than the revolution."[18] As women came to the town from rural areas, they gravitated to religious groups, in part because they evoked recognition from previous experience. In rural areas, fertility cults continued to be central in the lives of many women. Marie-Claude Dupré's research in the 1960s and 1970s, for example, concerned a women's fertility and therapeutic cult based on a water spirit that had spread from the Kongo region to Teke-Tsaayi, probably in the nineteenth century, and persisted at the time of her research. Spirit possession could rid a woman of misfortunes such as sickness, infertility, and fear of robbery, and it could fight witchcraft. New relationships and networks of women formed and continued after possession and its treatment were finished. The spirit was seen as dangerous by men, who sought to neutralize it since a possessed woman had rights that could invert men's position in a society where they dominated women.[19] With religious practice so much recognized as a women's domain through customary practices and in the mission church, it seems likely that those who arrived in the towns, where the tools of political, economic, and coercive power were largely in male hands, looked for alternative sources of spiritual and social empowerment and that some found them with other women within the "modern" institution of the Catholic church. Together with their fraternity sisters they found a degree of protection not only from social and economic threats but from the threats of *ndoki,* which remained a powerful explanatory force of misfortune and uncertainties.

In fraternities, women also found an inclusive group that welcomed them regardless of their status or stage in life: those married with children, those without children, divorced and single women, and widows. They were all Catholic women, *mamas,* as the priests addressed their gatherings. Furthermore, and importantly, fraternities gave recognition to those within the church who could not be full members because of their marital status, such as those who could not receive communion because they had customary marriages, had children by more than one father, or were divorced. Fraternities differed from religious groups that missionaries had introduced from Europe such as the Legion of Mary, for those were rigid where fraternities were more flexible. According to one retired missionary who spent some forty years in Congo, "The Legion of Mary is too strict, very strict. You have to have a Christian marriage to be a member and many do not have that for many reasons. So, the fraternities provide the means of coming together and that creates strong bonds."[20] Church women felt it keenly when they could not take the sacrament, but the fraternities at least gave them recognition and a place to participate along with others in religious observances that spoke to them.[21]

Fraternities also evolved into mutual aid organizations to help members with heavy costs relating to sickness, death, wakes, burials, mourning, and *matanga.*[22] For those that lacked support from kin and even for those who did, these expenses could be crushing. Death in the city is expensive, with mortuary fees and transportation to the cemetery several miles away and families obliged to put their resources into the finest *matanga* they can afford or lose social status.[23] Michèle O'Deyé found that "marriage payments are difficult but there are more possibilities of getting around them in Brazzaville. But all the ceremonies surrounding death are indispensable."[24] Beyond expense, just as burdensome for women are the obligatory rituals in which they must participate. The whole process of mourning, so linked to respect for the ancestors, fear of retaliation from spirits or society, and upholding of family honor that bore so heavily on village women, continued in different forms in the towns. Joseph Tonda has written that "the time and space of mourning is female." It is a highly gendered enactment, part of the larger working out of the social relations of men and women, as he sees it.[25] Describing what happens in urban circumstances, he writes:

> In Brazzaville it is the women who, massively, carry out and bring an end to mourning. In the vigils for the dead, the taking of the corpse to the morgue, in funeral processions, at burials, women are distinguished probably less by their numbers than by the huge amount of physical and emotional energy they expend and by a more or less marked transformation of their appearance. It is they who weep ("a man does not cry" prescribes a traditional education). Today, in Brazzaville, it is the women more than men who sleep on mats or cloths at the place of the vigil. They cut their hair, braid it or cover it with a black or white head scarf. More than men, they follow the hearse in

measured steps and close order to the church or the home of the dead person, barefooted or in sandals. It is always they more than men who animate the vigils with their singing. Easily falling into a trance, some of them roll on the ground and make witchcraft accusations.[26]

Women's mourning may continue for months, even years, until they decide the time to end it has arrived and start organizing the *matanga*. Catholic families might call on the *scholas populaires* to attend the vigil to sing Christian hymns, lead the prayers, and comfort the bereaved, but increasingly where women were fraternity members they turned to their sisters for personal, practical, and ritual support. Indeed, fraternity women are obliged in their statutes to help "christianize" burial and mourning rituals. They must discourage what the church calls "disrespect" for the deceased, comfort bereaved sisters who might neglect their hair and wear old, dirty clothes, and counsel each other not to take their mourning to extremes. Members should spend the night at the vigil for a deceased member or her parents, and they should hold Masses for the deceased and attend in their uniforms.[27] Firmine Malékat said that when her father and mother died and she was distraught, it was her fraternity sisters who gave her the support she needed: "Congolese women like to throw themselves around when they are in mourning, wailing, and tearing their clothes. A fraternity member can visit them and tell them that it is not getting them anywhere."[28] Léontine Bissangou explained a major reason for the popularity of fraternities: "In case of sickness, the sisters can do something. When you have no parents and family around you, you have a family in the fraternity. One is surrounded by all the sisters. A fraternity sister need not suffer, even without family a sister need not suffer. When she is in the hospital, the sisters in the fraternity go there to visit. In the case of death and misfortune, the sisters help."[29]

Dues to fraternities are primarily structured around sickness and death and the size of an individual fraternity. In 1986, Yvonne Miayedimina of the Fraternité Bienheureuse Anne-Marie Javouhey told me that the annual dues in her fraternity were ten thousand francs. Money would then build up in the common fund and be paid out depending on the exigency: five thousand francs when a member died, one thousand francs when a family member of a fraternity woman died, and five hundred francs when a member was celebrating a special event such as a birth, baptism, confirmation, marriage, or *matanga*. "Assistance is automatic; it is written in the statutes."[30] The statutes also laid down that the fraternity will cover the costs where the member has no family. A common commitment to attend to their obligations is part of fraternity culture. "They pay a monthly fee at a fixed rate, and the fraternity will pay the expenses when there is a death in the family. The fraternities are more regular in their payments than a *kitemo*," said one Congolese sister.[31] "They help to keep each other honest," said one woman. "Their moral sense of being a religious community helps them negotiate money problems. As with other mutual aid associations there are always problems over money. To be charitable is difficult when one calls on the others for several gifts in the same year. The fraternities provide a safer environment than some other associations." Discussing the anger of some men when their womenfolk are gone long hours from home attending to fraternity responsibilities, she added, "Men often admire the fraternities, even if reluctantly. For example, the women keep records very carefully and they are financially more honest than some other groups."[32]

Through their ability to meet women's spiritual and social needs, fraternities grew rapidly. In 1989, twenty-five years after their founding, there were forty-three in Brazzaville, ten in Pointe-Noire, and three in the smaller towns of Nkayi and Kinkala in the lower Congo. There were also three in Owando and one in Ouesso, regional centers in upper Congo.[33] By 2000, there were over fifty in the Congolese capital, with several fraternities in some parishes; the smallest had one hundred to two hundred members and the largest approaching a thousand. In Pointe-Noire, there were fifteen fraternities, the largest with about two hundred members and the smallest one with fifty to eighty. Others continued to be established in small towns and regional centers, especially in lower Congo.[34] Fraternities have remained an urban phenomenon. In rural areas, the *mabundu* remain at the center of grass-roots Catholic activity and the major source of evangelization.

Saints and Celebrations

In a collection of essays entitled *Christianity and the African Imagination*, David Maxwell describes Christianity as a "fluid medium," "sensitive to the varied and varying needs of youth, women, old men and labour migrants, urban and rural dwellers."[35] He also concludes that "African popular Christianity was by no means purely instrumental. African Christians were motivated by a genuine pious urge, a sincere desire to act decisively on their beliefs."[36] Fraternity women practiced their piety within the dictates of the church but especially embraced and elaborated the "feminine" side of Catholicism first introduced by Spiritan priests and brothers and missionary sisters. For the women, Mary the Mother of God remained central in their devotions. Historically a multivalent figure, she is described in one account that follows her through the centuries as "A Woman for All Seasons—and for All Reasons."[37] Fraternity women found in her a protector, intercessor, simple believer, and suffering mother. In an interview in 1992,

Firmine Malékat was asked about the place of Mary in members' spirituality. She answered: "But she is the Patron of all the Fraternities! The Mother! Our Lady of Seven Sorrows." When asked why this particular attribute of their patron was chosen, the fraternity president, herself the mother of thirteen children, answered:

> You see a woman is always struggling. . . . I have just lost my son. I am unhappy. This morning I was sobbing. Fortunately, a fraternity sister came to visit me. She soothed me. She gave me some good advice. . . . I always see Mary with her divine son. Each fraternity has the name of a patron saint but Mary is the Queen of all the Saints and Angels. Why? Because she accepted the death of her Son. That kind of sorrow, no one can accept it naturally. It is too hard. It is a dagger, truly.[38]

Yet, although all the Brazzaville fraternities come together annually on the feast day of Our Lady of Seven Sorrows, it is their "invention" of a cult of saints that has been most striking in giving them a distinct identity within the church.[39] As ancestors could mediate relations with the divine, so saints were supernatural beings with specialized powers who through prayers might be convinced to intercede in a wished-for way. They come in "all shapes and sizes" and historically have been "more or less constructed" subject to the context of the times.[40] They are like global ancestors within the modern, universal, Catholic church. Saints do not detract from the veneration of Jesus and Mary, fraternity members said; rather they are an additional means of approaching these two figures who are closest to God.

Women choose their fraternity for a variety of reasons, some more mundane than others. They do not necessarily join one in the parish where they live, but may travel across town to find the one where they feel "at ease."[41] In principal, membership of each fraternity is mixed in terms of age, class, and ethnicity, and this generally pertains. In some parishes, one ethnicity will predominate and will thus constitute a majority of fraternity members, but it is not by design. In the case of the Fraternité Sainte-Monique, one of the early groups, started in 1969 by women who had attended the "Javouhey" school between 1930 and 1944, members were older women.[42] Some of the newer fraternities have more youthful membership that makes them attractive to other young women. In the case of the Fraternité Bienheureuse Anne-Marie Javouhey, established by women who had attended Collège Javouhey before nationalization, class is something of a distinguishing factor. Members include professional women, high civil servants, and the wives of powerful and wealthy men. In some cases where members may want to keep their fraternity limited in number, admission is restricted, but anyone can apply since the constitution of all the fraternities states that membership should be open. Mothers may ask that junior family members be admitted, perhaps to take the place of a deceased member. Admission is not granted at once; rather anyone interested must attend fraternity meetings for at least six months and pay dues before admission.

Of all the reasons women gave for choosing a particular fraternity, "I liked the saint" was most common. It is the patron saint that gives a fraternity its identity, guides its spiritual life, and unites members as a cohesive force for common action. Women liked the stories of saints' lives, their struggles and their triumphs over human predicaments. Their telling and the repetition of devotional prayers, some written by the women themselves, helped draw fraternity members together, create a common identity, and propel them into action. Suzanne Tchitembo, a devout Catholic but not a fraternity member herself, explained the success of fraternities: "Saints are models and around this ideal, they organize. They live this ideal in a community, in a fraternity: solidarity, assistance, a true mobilization. It can be a hundred women who live like that. Within the fraternity there is such good organization that it can function well."[43]

While the first fraternities chose patrons like Saint Joseph whose life they had celebrated as schoolgirls, the first fraternities in parishes might adopt the patron saint of their local church. Elisabeth Koutana said that she and her husband were active members of the parish council of Saint Bernadette in Pointe-Noire. She told of helping establish the first fraternity in her parish:

> The fraternities started in Pointe-Noire in 1974, first Saint Catherine and then Saint Rita. It was a difficult time when the Party opposed activities in the church. In fact, organizations lost members but they returned gradually. In 1978, the president of the parish council asked me and some other women to create a fraternity since there were none in the parish of Saint Bernadette. We decided to call it Saint Bernadette since there were no others with that name. We researched her prayers and wrote our own and presented the organization to the parish. We designed a cloth with her image. We followed the statutes of the fraternities. When a woman wants to join, she copies the prayers of Saint Bernadette into her notebook. She receives a bible and a cloth. Now there are many young women in the fraternity. Some of them are not married.[44]

Léontine Bissangou told of helping to establish a fraternity in another Pointe-Noire parish where a group of women were especially worried about the morality of young women and the number of unmarried mothers.[45] They chose as their patron a young African sister who had held fast to her vows and died a martyr. They were also attracted by an African woman who although she had not yet been canonized had been officially acknowledged as "Blessed," a stepping-stone to sainthood.

I helped start the *Fraternité Bienheureuse Anuarite*. There were fraternities in other parishes and we needed one. When we started, we were a small group of women. Then, we met over three days and discussed our beliefs and what was important to us and we made our choice. We chose *Bienheureuse Anuarite*, an African, because of her witness. She died in 1964 at the time of the war in Congo-Zaire. At that time, the rebels arrived in the region and did shocking things. There were the convents and the priests, too. They entered the convent and threatened the nuns with death. You know that in a group there was always a chief. This one, he was interested in Soeur Anuarite. He said to his soldiers, "I must have her for myself. She must belong to me." She refused all his advances and he became enraged and said "I will kill you." Fortunately, that chief could not get her and he moved away. But later others came and abused her and killed her. She was, in any case, a good example, especially for young girls. She stood by her vows to God even when she was close to death. She said "no, I have consecrated myself to God." We ordered books from Zaire to learn more about her, then we wrote our prayers and songs and stories. When a woman wants to be a member, she comes and asks for the prayers and we give her a copy.[46]

A single saint can be made meaningful through different attributes, depending on the petitioner, as shown by the number of causes for which saints have been designated patrons. In choosing their saints, women were often drawn to those who, like many of them, had suffered physical pain and emotional anguish, those who would understand their anxieties.[47] Several fraternities took Saint Rita, a fifteenth-century nun, as their patron saint. She had been a wife, mother, and widow; her husband of eighteen years had been cruel and bad-tempered. When he was murdered, she entered an Augustinian convent, where she was reported to have conducted many miracles, leading to her later canonization. She became the patron saint of seemingly impossible causes, victims of abuse, those who suffered from infertility, and widows. A fraternity member said: "Some women had heard of Saint Rita and they researched her life and her prayers. She was married and had children and she became a nun after the death of her husband. She had experienced great suffering and lived through many problems like we do. Her intervention in our lives can help us."[48]

Saint Catherine Labouré, a nineteenth-century French nun, was another favorite of church women, who said that she had struggled in life as they did. As a young novice, she had a vision of the Virgin Mary, who instructed her to strike a medal with a special design. Her confessor told the bishop, who authorized thousands of medals, but Catherine herself lived a humble and obedient life in obscurity, working for forty years in terrible conditions in a hospice for old men. A member of the fraternity who had visited the shrine of Saint Catherine at the mother house of the Daughters of Charity in Paris told the story. She had brought back images and pamphlets with information about the saint's life, and the fraternity had subscribed to a magazine until it had to stop due to lack of funds.[49] Other fraternities chose Saint Anne, the patron saint of pregnant women and women in labor.[50] Sainte-Monique was another favorite. She had a bad-tempered, adulterous husband and a son who led a wild life, but through her constant prayers both had converted. She was the patron saint of difficult marriages, alcoholics, disappointing children, and victims of unfaithfulness.

Thus, fraternity women who were experiencing daily life adversity in towns and cities where conditions were deteriorating, political violence was never far away, and old social networks were fragmenting appropriated the saints as models of faith and fortitude, for they, too, had also experienced illness, bad marriages, "wild" sons, daughters pregnant before marriage, and abusive spouses. They had suffered from childlessness, an almost intolerable problem for some of those who sought community in fraternity. In her sociological inquiry (1979–80), Raoul-Matingou found that 8.5 percent of the women she interviewed in Brazzaville were without children; 37.5 percent had one to three children, but that was "not enough" since infant mortality was 60.4 percent and children were considered the best insurance in old age, the best means of cementing a union with a man, and necessary to fulfill social roles.[51] Jeanne-Françoise Vincent in her study of women in Bacongo and Makélékélé found that those who had not been to school wanted as "many children as possible." Even if they had few resources, women with some schooling wanted five or six children. Not to have children was a great sorrow and generally led to divorce.[52]

The fraternities also embraced the festive and communal side of popular Catholicism that resonated with both the exuberance of village celebrations and the processions and festivities of the feast days in the Catholic calendar. While individual groups met regularly, the anniversary celebrations of a fraternity were a highlight of the year, to which representatives of the other fraternities were invited. At these Sunday events, there was an extended Mass with the parish congregation, visitors, representatives from other fraternities, and curious onlookers in attendance. They integrated traditions of the universal Catholic church with fraternity innovations. One such occasion conveyed a sense of vitality, organization, and community.

The tenth-anniversary celebrations of the Fraternité Sainte-Cathérine Labouré were held at the parish church of Saint Charles Lwanga in Makélékélé, a suburb of Brazzaville, in November 1986. Some two thousand were crammed on the benches inside the church, and hundreds more watched through the windows and stood around in the church yard. The women's preparations had

Figure 6.1. "Postulants," Fraternité Sainte-Cathérine Labouré, Brazzaville, 1986.
Photograph by Phyllis M. Martin.

started well in advance. For days, they had been discussing arrangements, practicing songs, and holding prayer meetings. They had commissioned new cloths
from a well-known local cloth-maker, decorated the church, engaged a band,
printed programs for visitors, gathered food to be distributed to the needy, and
prepared food for the guests. Before the start of the Mass, representatives from
each of the visiting fraternities gathered in the yard, including a group from
the sister Fraternité Sainte-Cathérine Labouré of Pointe-Noire, who had made
the overnight train journey to the capital. As explained by some of the women,
their brightly colored uniforms with the image of a saint and the name of the
fraternity spoke to their faith and their solidarity with their sisters. Some wore
cloths commissioned for the pope's visit to Brazzaville in 1980; that of the Fraternité Anne-Marie Javouhey had been designed and produced for the centenary
of the Sisters of Saint Joseph of Cluny's Congo mission earlier in the year (see
figure 4.1). They were a blend of the deeply rooted Congolese appreciation of the
symbolism of bodily adornment, the donning of special garments by religious
practitioners, and the women's experience of uniforms in the Catholic schools
and youth movements. Congolese women are well-versed in "reading" cloth and
clothing, and as one writer has put it, "uniforms ask to be taken seriously."[53]

Figure 6.2. Members waiting to enter the church. Fraternité Sainte-Cathérine Labouré, Brazzaville, 1986. Photograph by Phyllis M. Martin.

As the other attenders moved into the church, the members of the host fraternity, some three hundred women, lined up outside. They wore blue and white batik cloths and head-scarves carrying the image of Saint Catherine, the medal for which she was famous, and the words "Fraternité Sainte-Cathérine Labouré" inscribed along the border. They also wore white T-shirts with their fraternity name and the saint's image printed in blue on the front and the words "10th Anniversary" printed on the back. Standing to the side were two groups. One with young men in matching red shirts was a youth fraternity mentored by their fraternity "mothers," who encouraged them to lead good, moral lives. Standing separately were the "postulants," those who had completed their training and were to make their "Promise" and be admitted into the organization. They wore the same white T-shirts and cloth but no head-scarf since the donning of the head-gear was a sign of full membership in the organization. The practice of the European religious orders was reproduced from the naming of the saint to the postulants and to the president of all the fraternities being called the "mother-general." It was one of several signals that the fraternities had placed themselves squarely within the church even as they adapted their practice and organization to suit their own needs and sensibilities.

Inside the church a live band of three electric guitars, drums, a tambourine, double-gong, and rattles played popular religious music, and eventually the procession of the host fraternity members entered, moving in a swaying motion down the central aisle and carrying aloft two portraits of Saint Catherine dressed in the blue dress and high, white, starched cornette of the Daughters of Charity. One the Makélékélé fraternity had owned previously; the other had just been received as an anniversary present from the sister fraternity from Pointe-Noire. As they moved to their seats the fraternity members sang of their patron saint, asking for her intercession with Jesus and Mary:[54]

Refrain:

Sainte-Cathérine Labouré,	Saint Cathérine Labouré,
Ecoute-nous, toi notre patronne	Listen to us, you our Patron,
Prie pour nous sans cesse	Pray for us without ceasing
auprès de Jésus	at the side of Jesus.
O Cathérine.	Oh Catherine.
A plusieurs reprises elle a rencontré Marie	Several times she met Mary
qui l'a tenue en promesse	who had her promise
au service du Seigneur et celui des pauvres	to serve the Lord and the poor.
O Cathérine	Oh Catherine.
Quelle joie ce dut être pour elle	What joy must it have been for her
quand elle reçut cet habit	when she received that habit

ce fût le rêve de ses douze ans	this was the dream of her twelve years
qui s'est réalisé	that was realized.
O Cathérine	Oh Catherine.
Messagère de Marie immaculée	Messenger of Mary Immaculate
aide-nous à vivre de la simplicité	help us to live in simplicity,
la pureté et la charité	purity and charity
comme tu l'as su vivre	as you knew to live.
O Cathérine	Oh Catherine.
O Sainte Cathérine que le salut	Oh Saint Catherine may the salvation
de Jésus	of Jesus
brille dans toute notre vie	shine in all our life
pour que le monde d'aujourd'hui	so that the world today
découvre ton espérance	discovers your hope.
O Cathérine	Oh Catherine.

The paintings were placed in front of the congregation below the altar, where the three presiding clergy also took their place. The Mass then proceeded through its usual segments, interspersing songs, prayers, and responses in French, Kilari, and Lingala. Before the liturgy of the Eucharist, two parts of the service showed the integration of church priorities and women's innovations: the rituals for the admission of new members and the offering.

The sixteen postulants lined up below the altar in front of the congregation to be presented by their fraternity president. The ceremony followed a format laid out in a document authorized by the diocesan chaplain, "The Ceremony of Admission of New Members" and interspersed questions from the chaplain and the responses of the aspirants.[55] For example, "Dear sisters what do you want?" and the answer, "I want to renew the commitment of my Baptism in the midst of our sisters of the Fraternité Sainte-Cathérine Labouré. . . . I also want to learn to pray, to practice mutual aid and to spread the word of God in words and actions." The chaplain then addressed the president: "Mother-President, have you followed these sisters . . . ?" and she answered, "Yes, Father Chaplain these sisters and I, we have followed them and we think they can live out their commitment to their fraternity." The postulants then turned to face the audience and the chaplain asked, "Dear sisters of all the women's Christian fraternities who are here present, can you accept these sisters to be members of the Fraternité Sainte-Cathérine Labouré?" and the response, "Yes, father. We can and we accept them." Another question to the prospective members: "Have you the agreement of your family and your husband?" to which the reply was "yes"; each then gave the mother-president a note giving permission. There then followed the Litany of the Fraternities read by the mother-general—the names of each of the thirty-one Brazzaville fraternities, and after each the response, "Pray for Us." Finally, there was the "Renunciation of Satan" directed at those who still turned to traditional diviners, healers, and anti-witchcraft specialists to ward off evil, and those who might deviate from the moral teachings of the church. "You have renounced Satan but do you know what that means? You have thus renounced all practices of magic, all fetishes and all sects such as the *Rose-Croix,* the *Mahikari,* the *Feu,* the *Dambage,* etc., that lead people astray by marketing their success and goodwill," and the response, "I renounce them." Then, "Do you renounce the practice of prostitution, adultery, and abortion?" and the response, "I renounce them." Finally, there was the Profession of the Faith, the Fraternity Promise, and the donning of head-scarves that were first blessed by the priest. The new members received bibles, rosaries, and candles, and, once again, there was a prayer for all the fraternities of the town, each one named in turn followed by the response, "Pray for Us."

Another high point of the celebrations that generated considerable excitement was the offering, the *makabu* (Kikongo/Kilari) modeled after the bringing of gifts in kind by guests at village celebrations such as the out-dooring of babies, marriages, and the end-of-mourning festivities. Accompanied by band music, jubilant singing, and hand-clapping, a procession made its way down the central aisle. Leading the way were several girls, barefooted and carrying candles, which they handed to the priests, who then used them to light other candles around the altar. Following them came a line of women carrying the offering on their heads: basins with smoked fish, manioc bread, flagons of wine, boxes of sugar, bags of rice, and chickens; a live goat was also carried in by two women. Baskets were passed around for those who wanted to deposit cash in the usual manner.

The whole Mass finished with the liturgy of the Eucharist, thanks from the mother-president of the Fraternité Sainte-Cathérine Labouré, and short speeches from the mother-general of the Brazzaville fraternities, the fraternity chaplain, the president of the parish council, and the parish priest. Outside the church some four hours after their arrival, people milled about and moved into the large yard, where tables had been set up. As they gathered, the sound of hand-clapping and singing started up and into the midst of the crowd came the members of the Fraternité Sainte-Cathérine Labouré, dancing, and carrying aloft the two pictures of Saint Catherine. After the jubilation, the hosts appeared to serve baguettes, *kwanga,* and fish and chicken soup to the guests.

These occasions are repeated on many Sundays across the capital and other towns as different fraternities mark their anniversaries and celebrate their saints. They follow the same pattern; only the level of elaboration varies with the weight

Figure 6.3. Celebrating with Sainte-Cathérine Labouré after Mass, Brazzaville, 1986. Photograph by Phyllis M. Martin.

of the occasion.[56] The lavishness of the display is among the aspects of fraternity life most criticized by the clergy and other church members, but for the women these are essential affirmations of their belief in the power of the saints, the bonds of sisterhood, and pride in their organization. The activities go beyond celebration, for they are performing their convictions and making tangible the abstract.[57] Unlike in cults of saints in other parts of the world, Congolese Catholics lack relics to venerate or saintly sites to visit.[58] Yet fraternity women have created other means of affirming their devotion and community: notebooks of prayers members have written and others have copied; cloths they have inscribed with their saint's image; portraits that focus their devotions; music, songs, and prayers they have composed; and anniversary occasions that reinvigorate identity and sisterhood.

Fraternities and Their Critics

The Bishop of Ouesso's references to the fraternities as "out of step with the rhythms of Congolese church life," to the clergy experiencing "times of discouragement," and to the "many difficulties that remain to be overcome" all point to the tensions that the women's movement created in the postcolonial church, even as it helped increase church membership and maintain church vitality under the authoritarian state. A state of ambivalence existed, an admiration for fraternity achievements on the one hand and women "out of control" on the other. According to one parish leader, "The fraternities started right but they have gone off the rails."[59] A graduate of the Catholic schools said, "The clergy need to bring the fraternities into line," but thus far the church hierarchy has been unable or unwilling to reverse problematic elements in fraternity practice.[60] For centuries, the tendency of fraternities to independence and innovation made them unpopular with European clergy and inspired various effort to "clean them up."[61] Indeed, the confraternities of the Sacred Heart and the Legion of Mary had originated in attempts by the European church to replace popular groups with clerically controlled organizations. Like their European counterparts, the church authorities in Congo also tried to address the main "problems" posed by the fraternities through drawing up constitutions to which they were expected to conform.

The 1984 statutes of the Brazzaville fraternities, revised and incorporated in the national fraternity constitutions of 1987, are very detailed and cover a wide range of topics, from the fraternities' responsibilities (spiritual, pastoral, and material) to conditions for admission, dues, relations to parishes and dioceses, and specifics on mutual aid. Attached recommendations to chaplains and a later diocesan report give indications of areas where the church authorities saw the fraternities in need of reform.[62] Four examples and some criticisms are given here as further indication of how fraternity women selectively developed their own popular practice.

The style and substance of devotional life was a cause for concern. The obligations of the women were many: attendance at the weekly fraternity Mass and Sunday Mass; individual Bible reading and daily meditation; novenas in preparation for anniversary celebrations, Christmas, Easter, and the day of Our Lady of Seven Sorrows; Friday meditations on the Way of the Cross; vigils and support at a sister's death; and Masses to be said in her memory. Women's zeal was not at issue; the practice of their devotions was. Study of the Gospels was being neglected, although all members received a bible when they were admitted to the organization. Silent meditation was not sufficiently observed, and singing was taking precedence over prayer. "Is this a choir?" asked the diocesan report on the conduct of weekly meetings. A further problem was inattentiveness to the Virgin Mary and the prominence of patron saints. Such a situation was contrary to the teachings of the church; indeed, the 1987 constitution emphasized the centrality of Marian devotions. Article 60 read:

Among the models to follow, the church gives first place to Mary, the first human and the first Christian; Mary has a place of choice in the church and she
is Our Mother who is close to her son Jesus. Each member of the fraternity
should have a special devotion for Mary the Mother of God and recite a rosary
every day.

As a means of countering the predilection for saints, more time should be given
to reciting the Rosary at fraternity meetings:

> The diocesan chaplain's team having noted the lesser place given to Mary pro-
> poses that instead of a decade of the rosary, the whole rosary or three decades
> be recited at the start of the meeting and two other decades before the end.
> After these two last decades, there will be a recitation of the Magnificat fol-
> lowed by the prayer of the Patron Saint.[63]

In general, the problem could be solved by greater attention to the process of
admission, which was flawed. The chaplains were reminded that they had the
responsibility to meet with the "postulants" on a regular basis so that new members could be "rigorously" tested in elements of their Catholic faith. Priests also
needed to meet frequently with the fraternities in their parish, but such oversight
was difficult for already overburdened clergy. The diocesan team in Pointe-Noire
concluded that priests were bowing to pressures from some fraternity women
to admit new members before they were ready, and, as a result, some members
lacked a solid understanding of the faith. Clearly the membership was much less
uniform than it had been in the early days, when the founders of the movement
had all received a rigorous religious training in Catholic schools.

Questions of money and mutual aid also claimed the attention of the church
authorities. Here, there was some ambivalence, for fraternities gave good financial and material support to the church, yet their financial obligations were
heavy. Apart from dues for assistance to fellow members, women had to make
a fixed annual contribution to support the central office of the fraternities, contribute to the work of the bishop, and contribute to the funeral costs of a bishop,
priest, deacon, or sister.[64] Support to the parishes was also critical. While the
comments of the diocesan clergy recognized the contributions of fraternities
and the many assiduous women who found a means of paying their dues even
when resources were tight, some areas needed improvement. Negotiations on
money matters occupied too much time at fraternity meetings, and more time
should be devoted to prayer: "The sisters are all reminded that prayer alone is the
source of charity. A person who does not pray cannot practice charity."[65] Also,
whereas the early leadership was in the hands of educated women with some
understanding of financial records, some positions had been filled by women

with little formal schooling. The church authorities suggested that the chaplains should have more oversight and that the president of a fraternity should be "someone who can take notes and knows how to oversee the Treasurer's notebook." Some "mothers" were not doing their job well and ought to be dismissed, and terms of office should be limited.[66] The fraternity leadership was asked to consider exemptions for women of little means, and by 2000 the Pointe-Noire diocesan team reported that the whole question of payments needed to be reconsidered, for they were "taxing the household budget" and even draining precious resources from children.[67]

The practice of offering *makabu* in kind at the annual celebrations was also in need of reform, for it undercut the cash income on which the clergy depended. The recommendation read:

> During the celebration of the saint, the team of Chaplains and Diocesan Counselors has been shocked at the exorbitant nature of the offerings (*makabu*). It is not a question of forbidding the practice of making some *makabu* but the manner of doing so needs to be reconsidered. The following questions are posed for consideration by all the fraternities: why are you making these *makabu*? where do your *makabu* come from? and who are they for?
>
> To avoid causing a real sensation and even a certain amount of waste, the team wishes that another way of making the *makabu* should now be put in place. That, at a celebration, a fraternity make an offering of some "symbolic" items, and that it should then provide an envelope for the Poor of the parish, an envelope for the training colleges that can be sent to the Seminary Savings Fund, an offering for the team of diocesan chaplains to cover expenses of transportation and office work (paper, ink for copier), and, lastly, an offering for the parish.[68]

Women were not about to give up performing the *makabu*, however, for it had become a central part of their annual celebrations and had grown out of familiar ways of gift-giving in the past. The 2000 Pointe-Noire diocesan report not only called for a review of the practice, calling it "wasteful," but referred to "abuse of funds for the celebrations, uniforms, invitations, for glory and personal pride." All this needed to be "reconsidered."

A third source of criticism was a tendency by the fraternities to independent action that had a potentially unsettling impact for the church. The fraternities needed to maintain their roots in the parishes under the oversight of the priests and parish council. There should be no question of their developing alternative lines of authority; indeed, the very definition of a fraternity in the constitution was a "group of women living in the same parish."[69] The predilections of some women to join fraternities where they might feel more at ease or liked the patron saint could not be permitted. Nor could they drop their membership in one group and join one in another parish, unless in special circumstances. If a member dropped her membership, she was not allowed to join another fraternity. In the structures of the church, such a state of affairs was considered unmanageable since it could lead to tensions and competition between fraternities for members, and create difficulties for the clergy, who needed to keep track of the women in their parish where their services were needed.[70] The attempt to retain women in a parish also seems to have remained a dead letter, for oral sources all maintained that women could choose which fraternity to join and that a preference for a saint, good management of mutual aid, and the draw of friends most guided them in their choice.

Other developments relating to fraternity initiatives were also questioned by the diocesan inquiry in 2000. Several fraternities had independently started youth fraternities in their parish (such as the one in attendance at the celebrations for Saint Catherine Labouré). These were questioned and the policy reiterated: "The basic foundation must be the parish structure. The youth groups mentored by the fraternities must instead be part of the church youth organization." By century's end, the centralization of fraternity activities in Brazzaville was also called in question, as the need for fraternities to take joint action not only in the church but in a larger arena had resulted in the growth of organization outside the parish structure. For the church, this caused some anxiety in its potential to undermine traditional lines of authority: "The national administration is too demanding and does not respect the liberty of parish."[71]

The main complaint by critics, however, concerned the amount of time that women devoted to prayer meetings, parish work, and mutual aid. For working women with families, critics maintained their families suffered. Article 12 in the constitution read: "The fraternity must not serve as a pretext for the neglect of civic, family and professional obligations."[72] Likewise, the recommendation to chaplains and counselors in 1984 included: "Some fraternities being almost all week at the parish, we ask them to reduce their days of activities for the parish so that the sisters may be true wives and true mothers of families, staying at home with their children."[73]

Members and observers agreed that the commitment to fraternity activities and to each other could have a negative impact on women's ability to take care of their family responsibilities. For some, being "mothers of the parish" had affected their mothering of families. Suzanne Tchitembo, not a fraternity member but sympathetic to the women, stated the problem:

> The fraternities are strong but they are perhaps hindered by an excess of zeal. Women are so loyal to the fraternity that at times they sacrifice the needs of

their children for the fraternity. They are not present enough for them because if a fraternity has 100 members, in a society like ours that means 100 families and that means there will be 10 members who have problems with mourning and you must assist. Everyone must go to assist and pay the amount due. Then, they spend the night at the house for you know with us there is the wake for the dead. . . . There were so many complaints from husbands that they had to abolish the wakes during the night and women must assist their sister during the day.[74]

Two professional women, who had attended Catholic schools but were not fraternity members, were more harsh:

They leave their children. They have nothing to eat. They say "*mama* has gone to pray." Some women have these priorities. Our mothers went to pray in the afternoon but they returned in the evening. Now there are many separations because of these fraternities. The mother is at church all day.[75]

Another commented:

The fraternity women are away from home too much but the priests need the income from women as well as their resources. They cook their food, they clean the church, they visit the sick, so they let them go their own way.[76]

Several women said that they had left the fraternities because of the burden of responsibility. One put the problem simply: "I used to be a member but the demand on my time and money was too great."[77] The potential problem was also expressed by Yvonne Miayedimina of the Fraternité Bienheureuse Anne-Marie Javouhey:

Sometimes commitments can cause problems, for example preparation for the annual celebrations involves nine days of prayers and practicing songs. Husbands complain of absences from the house, so do the children. Working women usually plan food for the week on Sundays and this doesn't get done. . . . Some men have gone to the bishop and complained. Now a woman must have her husband's consent before she can join. But husbands can feel threatened, too. For example, if there is trouble in a marriage several fraternity women may come to counsel him and his wife. Women discuss their personal problems not with the larger group but with friends in a smaller group. Or they may discuss personal problems with the President.[78]

Such tensions between fraternity women and their husbands or other men in their families were reminiscent of the confrontations of the 1930s, when men in Bacongo had tried to bar the path of women making their way to the church for days of prayer, but they had been exacerbated through the social conditions of the later century.[79] The fraternities' constitution does indeed include a clause that to become a member the postulant must "have the agreement of the husband, guardian, or one in a similar position."[80] This had been written into the regulations when men complained to the clergy about the absence of women from home, explained more than one informant. It was not that men necessarily wanted to go out with women they were close to, for men and women often spent leisure time separately.[81] Rather men expected their wives and the mothers of their children to be at home taking care of the family and household tasks, and they could feel threatened when women disappeared for long hours on fraternity business. On the other hand, informants said men seldom exercised the authority to stop women joining a fraternity, for that would be socially unacceptable and could cause a man embarrassment, for religious groups and mutual aid associations were entirely legitimate spheres for women's involvement. Addressing some of the charges leveled at fraternity members, Firmine Malékat said:

> At first men liked fraternities since they helped women through times of bereavement and expense. But then there were problems as fraternities grew and more time was spent away from home, and Brazzaville grew and it took more and more time to cross the city to events. Now only representatives from fraternities are invited to major events. . . . All organizations have good and bad members and so do fraternities. There are those who tell their husbands they are going off to a meeting and instead are visiting friends.

She and other leaders talked of their ongoing responsibility for the "education" of members and the need to revise the fraternity constitution.[82]

If the fraternities have elicited negative criticisms, they have also drawn admiration. Their contribution to the church is widely recognized by priests and sisters. For example, Soeur Lydia Portella commented: "The women are so involved in the church. If you want something done, they will do it. The church does not want to be responsible for problems in home life." She especially pointed to the pastoral care given by fraternity women in the parishes and noted the networks across the city that can take action: "Fraternity women work with other women in daily life, where women meet in the markets, at work, in the streets, where they exchange news. . . . When something needs to be done they can spread the word."[83] Fraternities are also admired, albeit sometimes grudgingly, in the wider society for their organization and their ability to mobilize members. During the Marxist period, they collaborated with the URFC and other women in public service, for example, cleaning up the road to the airport when a visiting dignitary was expected. Some militant URFC members saw the fraternities as counter-revolutionary, but others were members of both organizations and saw no contradiction since both were advocates of women's power. Among those who were high up in the party and government were those who had attended Catholic schools with women now fraternity leaders, and all might be practicing Catholics.[84] Marie-Thérèse Avemeka, once a URFC member, who was appointed after democratization as minister for women's integration in development in the Pascal Lissouba government, was enthusiastic about the fraternity movement and its potential in advancing women's issues nationwide. She said:

> Personally, I have always supported the Catholic fraternities, also the fraternities of other religions. The Catholics have the largest and the most organized women's associations in Congo. Through their fraternities, women organize their activities: prayer, social action in the hospitals, visiting the sick and old people, giving service to the church, and helping women with their basic survival. That is to say, one can use their meetings and their members to touch a maximum number of women in all the activities one wants to promote. Thus, when I was minister we worked with the fraternity women in food production and nutrition, for example. We had a meeting at Saint Anne's. They are very important for family life. . . . The fraternities are important as women's organizations for they give a means of talking about their problems. . . . It is a base for an important work and we can also help them in their lives. They are women and citizens whom we can direct to projects. When women are organized like that, they are much easier to work with than other women.

She added that her office had worked with other women's associations such as *tontines* and market women, but the Catholic fraternities had the advantage of cutting across social, economic, and regional interests, and their membership was larger than other groups. On questions of mutual aid, she said:

> The fraternities have a solidarity and they help women with little means. In part, they exist to deal with poverty. So when they are together they can give 5 francs, and then 5 francs more to help someone or someone who is sick. So, women come because they can find assistance. They bring nothing. There is no social security, there is no assistance but the fraternities are there to help.[85]

Whereas the fraternity members would doubtless agree with the minister, they would likely want to add that it was their spiritual life that provided the basis for their social action and commitment to each other.

Conclusion

As Robert Orsi found in his study of Italian immigrant women's devotion to the Madonna in New York, local circumstances, ordinary lives, and personal and corporate assessment of "what matters" create the dynamic elements in popular religion.[86] Congolese women, like their American counterparts, want a meaningful religion that relates to their problems: family, home life, social relations, immiseration, childbirth, sickness, and ensuring a decent death. Elizabeth Isichei talks of a religiosity that comes from "the realm of experience, of the heart," something that is part of the church but different from official structures and priorities.[87] Devotion to saints, those who had struggled in their earthly lives and gone on to an afterlife to which petitioners aspired, sprang from their humanity as well as their mediation in the world of the spirits.

In fraternities, members have devised an organization that is flexible, innovative, and appealing to women who come from different backgrounds. They can be intimate yet mobilize large numbers for common priorities. Fraternities cannot be simply categorized as mutual aid societies, although they have characteristics in common with other associations dealing with death, burial, and mourning. They are deeply rooted in religious belief like the cults of healing common in the history of the region. Like therapeutic cults and prophetic churches they are part of an ongoing search "to ameliorate and stabilize daily life" by religious means, and this process goes on as much within the "mainstream" churches as in the prophet churches that have claimed so much attention in the lower Congo.[88] Originating in the political violence of the postcolonial state, the fraternities evolved to address personal struggles in urban society. They also developed a modern organizational base that allows women to act on issues beyond their parochial concerns. In the 1990s, with the country experiencing dramatic political change and horrendous civil wars, the fraternities were pulled onto a national stage.

Epilogue: Mothers and Sisters in War and Peace

It is now time to return to the 1998 peace conference convened by the Mamans Chrétiennes Catholique de l'Afrique Centrale that was the starting point of this book. The letter of invitation from the conference president, Joséphine Songuemas-Mampoumba of Brazzaville, and the vice president, Cécile Mboyo Ekota-Nsombe of Kinshasa, had set out the purpose of the conference. In part, it read:

> Confronted by problems of all kinds, drowning in the plague of politics, sti-
> fled by socio-economic burdens, suffocating in ethno-tribal quarrels and wars
> between brothers, and having submitted for years to the sad events that have
> ravaged Africa, we, Christian mothers of the Catholic women's fraternities
> of Congo-Brazzaville and the movement of Catholic Mothers in the Demo-
> cratic Republic of Congo-Kinshasa indicate through this letter, our wish to
> come together in a conference to reflect and meditate on the deep causes of
> the conflicts and moral problems that lead to war, the systematic destruction
> of our continent, and the elimination of our youth, in particular. Yesterday,
> it was war in Rwanda, in Burundi, in Congo-Kinshasa; today it is war in
> Congo-Brazzaville; and tomorrow whose turn will it be? . . . In this confer-
> ence, we want to join together with our sisters in similar Catholic associations
> in dioceses throughout Central Africa, so that through the power of the Holy
> Spirit, we will share and meditate on the present conditions in our country,
> the common road we need to take, and the most effective means to eliminate
> obstacles to spiritual, moral, and material development. Together, we want to

reflect on our responsibility, the reasons for our apathy, and our culpability in our silence. All have and still are contributing to the situation.[1]

The conference opened with a Mass at the National Assembly building, where all the plenary sessions were also held, an indication of the fraternities' standing as a national women's organization. Over an eight-day period, the main proceedings included prayers and Masses; speeches by prominent church women, both laity and sisters; and debates and workshops on the causes of conflict, the role of youth, the impact on children, and the actions that must be taken to advance reconciliation and social reconstruction. Social gatherings gave opportunities for informal contacts and networking. Women's responsibilities as mothers was a pervasive theme in the devotional aspects of the proceedings and in the practical issues addressed. Indeed, they reinforced each other.[2]

In Congo-Brazzaville, the conference convened at the end of ten years of economic collapse, profound social disruption, unstable governments, and widespread violence. In 1989, the government of the one-party state cracked and caved in under external and internal pressures, forcing President Sassou-Nguesso, a military officer who had assumed power ten years earlier, to agree to a democratization conference on a model similar to that in other francophone countries such as Benin. The National Conference held from February to June 1991 drafted a new constitution and created a Higher Council of the Republic to lead the country to a referendum on the constitution and elections for the National Assembly. Women were very poorly represented at the conference, with only 62 among 1,202 delegates, and in the elections that followed.[3] In the elections of 1993 there were 24 women among 774 candidates, a situation that Aimée Gnali, president of the Mouvement des femmes engagées du Congo (Movement of Women Activists in Congo) attributed to politics being costly, most of the money for electoral campaigns finding its way into male hands, and women's lack of access to remunerative sectors of the economy.[4] At the time, women constituted 60 percent of the workforce but earned 10 percent of the monetary income of the country.[5]

In August 1992, presidential elections had brought to power Pascal Lissouba, a former prime minister imprisoned and exiled during the Marxist period, but his government was unable to stabilize the political situation or develop the conditions necessary for reconciliation. On the contrary, underlying tensions between political leaders with their local and foreign support—including funding from major oil companies and soldiers from neighboring states—led the capital to explode in civil wars that continued sporadically between May 1993 and January 1994. The violence and destruction far surpassed that of the 1950s but was mainly waged by the same "big men" who had dominated Congo politics since independence, supported by army units and private militias.[6] Thousands of armed, disaffected, and unemployed youth, often under the influence of drugs and alcohol, raised barricades to seal off their territories and engage in unpredictable violence. Personalized cults and magical practices ritualized the identities of politicians-turned-warlords and energized their supporters. One analysis has suggested that the link established since the 1960s between religion and politics has not been emphasized enough and that "the two domains can be so closely mixed that one can speak today of an 'absorption' of the political field by the religious, at least that tendency."[7] Militias engaged in ethnic killings, looted and destroyed property, and terrorized women and girls. In 1993, the conflict was mainly in Brazzaville: over two thousand died, thirteen thousand houses were destroyed, and over one hundred thousand were forced to flee as refugees. During the wars of the 1990s, an estimated sixty thousand women were raped, a quarter of them between twelve and fifteen years old.[8] In June 1997, the fragile peace was again broken on a much larger scale, spilling over into the Pool region with some fighting in the north of the country as well. Over ten thousand died, and half a million fled the capital. The former president, Denis Sassou-Nguesso, with decisive help from Angolan forces emerged victorious in October 1997, appointed himself as president, and promised elections in 2000. It was not the end of violence, however, for a third war broke out in the Pool region, resulting in tens of thousands again fleeing as refugees and continued economic disruption accentuated by guerilla attacks on the CFCO line. Only in 2000 and 2002 were treaties signed and a semblance of peace restored to an exhausted country.[9]

Individual Christians fought on all sides, but the Catholic church, like other churches, was an instigator of peace initiatives. At the time of the National Conference, people looked to it as an institution that had outlasted state persecution and survived the murder of its cardinal. As one of the few legitimate long-standing national institutions, it might be instrumental in returning morality to political life. On a practical level, it was one of the few institutions in civil society with the contacts and resources to provide assistance in the void of the failed state. The standing of the church was shown in the appointment of Monseigneur Ernest Kombo, the bishop of Owando, as president of the democratization conference and the Higher Council of the Republic. A special Mass in the National Assembly building also confirmed the place of the church at a turning point in Congolese history. At the National Conference, representatives of the large churches—including Catholics, Protestants, the Salvation Army, and Kimbanguists—acted as interrogators of those who had wielded political power. Throughout the 1990s, the episcopal conference continued to issue pastoral letters calling for national unity, non-violence and "a peaceful evolution of our institutions towards democracy." Working with representatives from other churches, Catholic leaders were active in an ecumenical council that assessed the situation and met with political leaders to urge the disbanding of militias, the lowering of roadblocks, and an end to the fighting.[10] The civil wars showed the limitations of the church's influence in the face of political, economic, and social disintegration, but religious communities did succeed in receiving and distributing international aid, gathering people together for mutual support, and invoking the spiritual power that could engage that of the politicians in a "war of religion."

Not only did the fraternities gain from being part of a mainstream institution that somehow functioned in the midst of widespread insecurity, their continued popularity among women from diverse backgrounds was part of a generalized effervescence of religion in the 1990s, when armed struggle, far from holding back religious practice, encouraged it in all its dimensions. According to Elisabeth Dorier-Apprill and Abel Kouvouama, who have researched this topic in some depth, the proclamation of religious freedom by the National Conference gave impetus to a growth in mainline churches and to a host of independent, pentecostalist, and charismatic churches and cults. Many also functioned as mutual aid associations.[11] They write: "Religion appeared as the only recourse in the face of the growing difficulties of daily life linked to economic crisis, political fragmentation, the crisis of families, and the unemployment of young people."[12]

Heavily engaged in peace work, sheltering refugees, and helping the wounded were the Catholic sisters, now in the large majority Congolese women. They joined with fraternity and other church women in prayer meetings, vigils, peace marches, and appeals over the radio. In 1992, with the coming to power of the new Lissouba government, fraternity leaders and some sisters organized the first of several demonstrations. Soeur Fabienne remembered: "We marched carrying placard and banners: 'Peace, Peace, Peace!' Many, many women. It was truly a march of women in silence and praying, We marched all through the town to the office of the President and were welcomed. Another time we marched to the Palais de Congrès and then we had a Day for Youth at St. Anne's."[13]

In 1997, sisters in Brazzaville and the lower Congo had to flee the violence like much of the rest of the population. Some convents and hospitals were looted and destroyed. At Linzolo, militias arrived with their wounded and enlisted the help of three sisters in the dispensary. When supplies ran out and they were threatened with violence, the sisters fled into the forest, where they were sheltered by villagers for several months before finding their way across the frontier to the Democratic Republic of Congo. In June 1997, the convent of the Sisters of Saint Joseph of Cluny in central Brazzaville was caught in the crossfire between the forces of Sassou-Nguesso and Lissouba; some European sisters were evacuated by French paratroopers, while others found shelter locally or went north to Ouesso, from where they traveled to a community of their sisters in southern Cameroon. The Franciscans at Poto-Poto were also in the center of heavy fighting. They escaped to Ouenze, a part of the city less touched by the fighting, where they were taken in by the Ribeauvillé sisters. From there, they crossed the river to the Kinshasa side. The community of Spiritan sisters in Pointe-Noire remained outside the war zone and received sisters from missions in the lower Congo.

Many of the sisters, like the rest of the population, returned to rebuild their work in 1998. Some opened new projects in Pointe-Noire, a city flooded with refugees from the interior. With the fall of the Marxist regime, the Ministry of Education sought to return some schools to the church authorities. In Brazzaville, the sisters decided to work from the bottom up, starting with nursery children and kindergartens. The Ecole Anne-Marie Javouhey was reopened by the Sisters of Saint Joseph of Cluny in 1995, closed during the 1997 war, and then again reopened. In 2000, there were four classes with about four hundred girls. The Ribeauvillé sisters at Ouenze also restarted their nursery and primary school, with a sister coordinating the work with lay teachers. In Poto-Poto, the Saint Jean Bosco technical school was returned to the Franciscans by the state in 1995. The Union of Mother-Superiors agreed to run it as a joint project directed by six sisters from different congregations, two priests, and twenty-five state teachers.[14] Individual sisters turned their administrative skills and overseas contacts to establishing foundations and work with NGOs for the benefit of war victims. Soeur Brigitte Yengo of the Soeurs Congolaises du Rosaire was appointed treasurer of the National Conference in 1991 and a member of the executive committee of the High Council of the Republic. Trained as a chiropractor in Chicago, she became the director of the Fondation Cardinal Emile Biayenda, which promotes peace work and social reconstruction, and also set up an NGO to work with disabled people, street children, and orphaned children. Soeur Marie-Thérèse Nkouka of the Soeurs de la Divine Providence de Ribeauvillé, a linguist and faculty member of the Université Marien Ngouabi, is also prominent among Congolese sisters. She coordinates a project of lay workers and Caritas-Congo to establish rehabilitation centers for children and young people traumatized by war and promote a "culture of peace." She and the provincial superior of the Sisters of Saint Joseph of Cluny are working to rebuild the hospital at Linzolo and to start up the polio center again.

Catholic women have mobilized to distribute aid and work on the more difficult task of reconciliation. Pointe-Noire became a major receiving point for refugees. According to the president of the fraternities, "We welcomed everyone and organized help in different parishes. Caritas was there. They sent drugs and food, a little rice. We helped give this out and collected some clothes. In hospitals and prisons, we tried to help. We are involved with necessities to the level of the means we have."[15] During the wars, some fraternity women were inevitably on opposite sides and caught up in supporting family and ethnic loyalties, but the historical origins of the associations between fraternity women and their basic ideology seems to have helped mediate tensions. Marie-Thérèse Avemeka referred to the background of the fraternity founders in the sisters' schools, where there was ethnic mixing, and to the persecutions under the Marxist state that drew them together for common action in the first place. She explained: "In principal, these associations allow for mixing." She also thought that being members of a national organization helped mitigate divisions, although these did surface at times.[16] Two Franciscan sisters also related that during the war the fraternity women of Bacongo and Makélékélé prayed for those involved in Poto-Poto and Moungali, where opposing forces fought each other. They agreed that "there were some bad and weak women," but "in general, the faith is what is most important."[17] Léontine Bissangou of the Pointe-Noire fraternities also said of tensions: "We did not feel it so in the fraternities. As mothers, we tried to stay together. This kind of division does not do any good. We tried to remain united. Where there were problems in some parishes, we talked about them and we prayed for the problems of war. On the contrary, we welcomed those coming to Pointe-Noire from all the different regions."[18] Of the fraternity women, Soeur Lydia Portella also said of the women in Pointe-Noire: "As people reacted to rumors coming from Brazzaville, some fraternity women tried to help women sort through what was happening. There was more of conflict in some neighborhoods than others since some are mixed and others are more associated with a single ethnicity. . . . The bishop called on the fraternities to help create peace in the parishes and pray for peace in the diocese."[19]

Turning back to the fraternity conference, it can also be placed in the context of a national women's peace movement that embraced a new activism. During the 1993 war, some women had established a National Committee of Women for Peace (Comité National des Femmes pour la Paix) to initiate contacts between protagonists, gather information, issue public statements, and stage peace demonstrations. According to the claims of the vice president, "this contributed greatly to ending the hostilities and establishing peace," but in 1997 efforts to stop "the infernal machine, to bring men to reason, and to calm hearts and spirits" were in vain. In December, the organization brought together women from the northern and southern districts of Brazzaville, where the opposing forces were located, to gather information on what had happened and to start a process of reconciliation. On a larger front, the committee proposed the organization of victims and offenders, the working out of reparations, and the appointment of a Committee for Pardon and Reconciliation.[20]

The International Women's Day for Peace celebrated around the world each year on 8 March was particularly meaningful in 1998 as Congolese women addressed postwar recovery. In the capital and other towns, numerous events were planned under the auspices of the Minister of Family and Integration of Women in Development with the theme "Peace: an analysis of the situation in Congo." According to a newspaper report, activities were spread over five days and included a service of repentance at the National Assembly building, work by commissions, exhibitions, and the giving of gifts to widows and orphans of the war dead. Speeches by prominent women leaders addressed the low numbers of women in political office and women's economic vulnerability with the majority in agriculture, "one of the least remunerative of activities."[21] To symbolize peace, a flame was lit and the torches carried by the women to different Brazzaville neighborhoods, where candles were lit.[22]

Following the celebrations that marked International Women's Day for Peace in the capital, women in Pointe-Noire also found their voice and staged a peace demonstration. According to one participant:

> Even if dispersed in the community, women are a true force. With all that the country experienced during the last few years, it was necessary for women to rise up and say "enough, enough." The women even became heads of families, so many were killed. They supported their families, they buried their families, so that today in spite of some bad women, Congolese women are in the midst of positioning themselves. . . . Here, we have an NGO, called the Kouilou Regional Coordination. All the women's associations are members. So, the executive committee visited all the associations to say that our voice must be unanimous. It is the voice of peace for no one here wants war. Why do we not have the courage to go to men in politics and say, stop this fighting?

She then recalled:

> And so, we too, like the sisters in the fraternities undertook a march. . . . It was after the celebrations of 8 March. We had meetings and drew up a document and marched to the offices of the regional administration. We said, "we cannot take this any longer. We are tired. We brought you into the world. We are your mothers, your sisters, why do you continue to kill us? We are all from the same country." The women made their voice heard. Certainly, it is difficult to

say that this led to an end in the fighting but I believe it did show there was a segment of society opposed to all the destruction that was now rising up to say, "enough is enough."[23]

The fraternity peace conference can thus be located in the renewed vitality of popular religious movements and women's initiatives for peace and reconstruction that reached across national divides. Action grew out of moral outrage, terrible suffering, and an overwhelming desire to find solutions. In the final resolutions and recommendations of the conference, the fraternity women expressed their demands in both social and religious terms, but also demonstrated that for them mothers' rights were women's rights and human rights. Firstly, they addressed church women, who must "live the Gospel and translate it in action," "respect the law," "access information," "spread around themselves a culture of peace," "leave lethargy behind and take an active role in the church and civil society," "be vigilant in the choice of political leaders," "create regional centers to monitor and mediate socio-political tensions," "validate themselves through meeting with men to discuss the issues," and "end hostility to other women for we have a common cause."

Secondly, addressing the church, the women said it must "support the *mamans* in their efforts," "have the courage to denounce the evils that consume our societies," "create parish movements to be responsible for girl-mothers and street children," and "preach Peace everywhere and in all circumstances." Thirdly, the women made demands of the state. It must "show respect for life and the dignity of death," "respect the Charter of Human Rights that it signed," "reduce the arms budget and direct the funds to the creation and promotion of Cooperatives for Youth to fight against unemployment and laziness," "combat poverty and ensure an equitable distribution of the wealth of the country," "ensure the education and health of the people by restructuring the two systems presently in a state of asphyxiation," "encourage women to engage in political life," "authorize Family Allowances sufficient for all mothers—Heads of Families, wage-earners or not"; "take responsibility for street children by creating centers for rehabilitation and providing space for competent NGOs," and "ensure social support for children abused by their families." The document ended with several resolutions including the establishment of the peace organization Mouvement pour la Paix des Mamans Chrétiennes Catholiques de l'Afrique Centrale (MOPAX).[24]

The conference closed with a pontifical Mass with several bishops, priests from Central African countries, sisters, and dignitaries, including two cabinet ministers and several high-ranking officials, in attendance. The previous day, the conference delegates had again marched in the streets of the capital from the basilica of Saint Anne in Poto-Poto to the residence of the president in Mpila.

There, they were met by President Denis Sassou-Nguesso, a public recognition of the emergence of fraternities as a national women's movement with international dimensions. According to critics, it was also likely a public relations move influenced by Marie-Antoinette Sassou-Nguesso, well-known for her Catholic background and her charity work. The president of the Congolese fraternities and of the conference, Joséphine Songuemas-Mampoumba, addressed the president on behalf of the women, reviewing the circumstances that had led to the meetings: "*mamans* traumatized by conflicts and fratricidal war," "tortured and tormented by fear," "the systematic destruction of our country," and "the elimination of our young people, the principal victims in these dramas." "Great evils need great remedies," she told him. Thanking the president for granting permission for the conference to meet and acknowledging a new openness to peace, she asked him to convey the results of the conference to other Central African heads of state. She then called on the secretary-general of the conference, Véronique Kokolo Kitsisi of the Democratic Republic of Congo, to read aloud the recommendations and resolutions.[25]

The response of the president demonstrated the vulnerability of women with limited political and economic power and the ways in which the discourse on motherhood could be inverted. In his speech, he projected himself as a man of peace and pointed to the culpability of Christians themselves in the Central African wars, not only in the two Congos but in Rwanda, "a deeply Christian nation." Christians were among the worst perpetrators of ethnically inspired violence, he charged. He further blamed Christians in Congo-Brazzaville for creating instability during the democratization process through mounting "wildcat strikes," "dragging the chief through the mud before us all" (a reference to attacks on the credibility of Monseigneur Kombo), and abusing the democratic process by creating "more than a hundred political parties based on ethnicity." He, on the other hand, had launched the democratization movement "with many sacrifices," signed the documents, and ceded power peacefully in elections.

The president then took up his vision of maternal responsibility, ignoring the resolutions of the conference but rather using them to counter women's aspirations for a broader role in national decision making. Given the occasion, he may also have been framing his response with the teachings of the church, as he interpreted them. Maternal responsibilities, he said, involved prayer, children, and pride in households and neighborhoods. He was especially scathing about educated women who overreached in public life to the neglect of their "true" responsibilities as mothers:

> Christian women and women of the city, that is to say those who are truly participating in national reconstruction and development projects—I am

not thinking in this case of Catholics who live in the city and are members of numerous associations and NGOs but who cannot organize women in the neighborhood, so that each woman cuts the grass, picks up the rubbish, and sweeps in front of her house.

I also go around the city. As recently as last Saturday, I toured Brazzaville in an ordinary car. You did not see me but I saw you. I was at the Cataracts near the Djoué river, a beautiful tourist spot where we all used to go at the weekends. Now it is abandoned to forest. . . . I toured Brazzaville, I always leave from here, the Avenue de France, the Avenue de la Paix, as far as the Palais du Parlement. The whole way, in front of the houses of the *mamans,* there was rubbish, grass. The Christian, Catholic *mamans* sell food amidst the grass and rubbish.

Thus, the beautiful resolutions from your conference make the Christian, Catholic *mamans* responsible for this situation. In the course of some of my interviews with the religious authorities, they said that the Christian Catholic *mamans* in the fraternities are the best organized. How is it, then, that the Basilica Saint Anne, even if bombed lies abandoned like that in the grass? Where are the Christian, Catholic *mamans*? Why are they not organizing themselves at least to clean up around the ruin? We will, of course, take responsibility for restoring the cathedral. But the surrounding area should be kept clean.

He then addressed women with greater pretensions:

So, I think that Christian, Catholic *mamans* can play their role in prayer and in the care of the city and children. Women in the world are more numerous than men. I acknowledge that they are engaged in production more actively than men, especially in the countryside. In these conditions, I understand their right to claim their just place in decision-making circles. I think you have the right to pose the problem in these terms. But all this is a struggle. Don't think the men will give you that without a fight on your part, and this fight is not only by the Christian *mamans* of Central Africa. It is worldwide. The women have returned from the congress in Peking. You have met women from other continents, the problem exists for them in the same way. In an old civilization like France, women only received the right to vote after the Second World War. When a woman is admitted to the *Académie Français,* that is treated as an event. Thus, it is a long struggle. You must engage in it fully.

Ignoring his contribution to the violence and destruction of the time, the president then reminded his audience of his accomplishment in turning the country over to democracy in 1991. After five years of misrule and violence, however, he must now clamp down on dissidents who might again set alight the flames of violence. He was not the one who had started the violence of June 1997, he claimed; rather he had gone to war in self-defense, and now his government's actions were directed to peace and national reconciliation. He finished by saying he would show the resolutions to the other Central African heads of state and present them at the forthcoming Organization of African Unity summit in Ouagadougou.[26] A delegate from Pointe-Noire summed up the meeting with the president with the understatement, "He was unreceptive."[27]

The whole episode of the conference and the subsequent meeting with the president revealed a growing activism among Catholic women in the face of political chaos and destruction. It also demonstrated how motherhood remained subject to a range of definitions, with the women using it as a platform for action on a broad front and the president using it to bolster his discourse on domesticity. The conversation was not academic, for it came from very real situations. It did, however, mirror the scholarly debate that continues between those who see motherhood as a restricted category, a "collusion of patriarchy," and part of a discourse to restrict women's rights, and others who see it as a means of mobilizing African women more effectively than around issues of gender, given that identity as mothers is so rooted in women's historical experience.[28] Like the Argentinean mothers who gathered in the Plaza de Mayo in Buenos Aires to express their anger and suffering at the "disappearance" of their children who had been kidnapped and killed by the military junta, Congolese women were expressing their sorrow and moral outrage at the civil wars that had inflicted so much suffering on children and society. Beyond that they were setting out an agenda for political, economic, and social action. One Argentinean woman who knew her son had been killed and would not return was reported to have said she was demonstrating for others, for "I have socialized my maternity."[29] On this front, Congolese women can claim long experience of social motherhood, for maternity was never restricted to biological children but extended to lineage, clan, and community.

The story that has been told here is only in part about mothers for, as was made clear in the introduction, that is a strand in a broader history about Catholic women who have lived in a region characterized by violence and neglect for much of the colonial period and subject to social and political upheavals in postcolonial times. While a church wedding and a marriage to an elite (generally church-educated) man allowed some Catholic women and their daughters to gain increased social status, only after the Second World War, with the rapid expansion of girls' education, did the church give some women the means to improve also their political and economic status, which had long been undermined through developments in the nineteenth and earlier twentieth centuries. Perhaps most positively, women within Catholic communities did find a measure of security and room to negotiate their position as "mothers of families," a domain as important to the missionaries as it was to them. Drawing on social capital of acting together in work, healing, family life, and mutua women helped create new communities that were not only a basis for social tion but expressions of a spirituality in which they selectively incorporated el ments of Catholicism. They met together in devotional groups, prayer meetings, and retreats, and in the later twentieth century entered fully into the life of the *mabundu*. In the practice of their religion, women also drew on the teachings of religious sisters and the early generations of Catholic women who were their mentors and mothers. It was within the fraternities in the later twentieth century that urban women were particularly inventive in opening up avenues for mutual aid and expressions of Catholicism meaningful to them.

Notes

Introduction

1. *Colloque des Mamans Chrétiennes Catholiques de l'Afrique Centrale, Rapport final des Travaux* (Brazzaville: MOPAX, 1998, unpublished); "Colloque des mamans chrétiennes catholiques de l'Afrique Centrale: Un enfant est né: son nom est: Mo.Pax," *La semaine africaine* 2162 (4 June 1998). Invitations were also sent to Catholic organizations in Angola, Burundi, Central African Republic (CAR), Gabon, Chad, and Rwanda, but the women could not attend. Two representatives from Benin were present as observers.

2. "Adresse du Président Denis Sassou-Nguesso," *Rapport final;* "Vous êtes le socle de la société!" *La semaine africaine* 2162 (4 June 1998). The events of the conference, the context, and the president's speech are dealt with more fully in the epilogue.

3. "Fraternités féminines chrétiennes catholiques du Congo: 25 ans déjà," *La semaine africaine* 1815 (Oct. 1989).

4. Patrice Yengo, "Un recours endémique à la violence," *Afrique contemporaine* 186 (April–June 1998): 33–45; also, Théophile Obenga, *L'histoire sanglante du Congo-Brazzaville (1959–1997)* (Paris: Présence Africaine, 1998).

5. Jan Vansina, *Paths in the Rainforest: Toward a History of Political Tradition in Equatorial Africa* (Madison: University of Wisconsin Press, 1990), 251; also, 60, 143–46.

6. Jane Guyer, "Wealth in People, Wealth in Things: Introduction," *JAH* 36, no. 1 (1995): 86.

7. On the Central African slave trade, see Joseph C. Miller, *The Way of Death: Merchant Capitalism and the Angolan Slave Trade, 1730–1830* (Madison: University of Wisconsin Press, 1988), 130 and passim, and "Central Africa during the Era of the Slave Trade, c. 1690s–1850s," in *Central Africa and Cultural Transformations in the American Diaspora*, ed. Linda Heywood (Cambridge: Cambridge University Press, 2002), 21–69; and Claire C. Robertson and Martin A. Klein, eds., *Women and Slavery in Africa* (Madison: University of Wisconsin Press, 1983).

8. Jane I. Guyer and S. M. Elo Belinga, "Wealth in People as Wealth in Knowledge: Accumulation and Composition in Equatorial Africa," *JAH* 36, no. 1 (1995): 120, and *passim*.

9. Vansina, *Paths in the Rainforest,* 255–57.

10. Guyer and Belinga, "Wealth in People as Wealth in Knowledge," 115–16.

11. Wendy James, "Matrifocus on African Women," in Shirley Ardener, ed., *Defining Females: The Nature of Women in Society* (Oxford: Berg, 1993), 132, 139.

12. Ibid., 132.

13. For example, the classic work of J. Van Wing, *Etudes Bakongo: sociologie-religion et magie*, 2nd ed. (Brussels: Desclée de Brouwer, 1959), 83–8; Georges Balandier, *The Sociology of Black Africa* (London: Deutsch, 1970), 303; and Jeanne-Françoise Vincent in her study of those living in the Bacongo neighborhoods of Brazzaville, *Femmes africaines en milieu urbain* (Paris: ORSTOM, 1966), 33–37, 59.

14. Simon Bockie, *Death and the Invisible Powers: The World of Kongo Belief* (Bloomington: Indiana University Press, 1993), 19–20; Balandier, *Sociology of Black Africa*, 303–304. Also, for a more extensive discussion of kinship terminology, see Wyatt MacGaffey, *Custom and Government in the Lower Congo* (Berkeley and Los Angeles: University of California Press, 1970), 84–100; and "Lineage Structure, Marriage and the Family amongst the Central Bantu," *JAH*, 24, no. 2 (1983): 173–87.

15. Vansina, *Paths in the Rainforest*, 152–55. *Nkàzi* is also used for someone respected in a position of authority.

16. For a classic account of kinship by a social anthropologist of the older generation, see Audrey Richards, "Some Types of Family Structures amongst the Central Bantu," in *African Systems of Kinship and Marriage*, ed. A. R. Radcliffe-Brown and D. Forde (London: Oxford University Press, 1950), 297–351, who chose the Mayombe variant to illustrate a type of matriliny.

17. Pauline E. Peters, "Introduction," *Critique of Anthropology* 17, no. 2, special issue on "Revisiting the Puzzle of Matriliny in South-Central Africa" (1997): 125–46.

18. MacGaffey, "Lineage Structure"; Anne Hilton, "Family and Kinship among the Kongo South of the Zaire River from the Sixteenth to the Nineteenth Centuries," *JAH* 24, no. 2 (1983): 189–206; John K. Thornton, "The Origins and Early History of the Kingdom of Kongo, c. 1350–1550," *IJAHS* 34, no. 1 (2001): 89–120; Phyllis M. Martin, "Family Strategies in Nineteenth Century Cabinda," *JAH* 28, no. 1 (1987): 70–1. Also, for the Bobangi peoples north of the Pool region, see Robert W. Harms, *River of Wealth, River of Sorrow: The Central Zaire Basin in the Era of the Slave and Ivory Trade, 1500–1891* (New Haven, Conn.: Yale University Press, 1981), 168.

19. Cherryl Walker, "Conceptualising Motherhood in Twentieth Century South Africa," *JSAS* 21, no. 3 (Sept. 1995): 417–37.

20. See chapter 3; also, in general, Julia Clancy-Smith and Frances Gouda, eds., *Domesticating the Empire: Race, Gender, and Family Life in French and Dutch Colonialism* (Charlottesville: University Press of Virginia, 1998): see especially "Introduction" by the editors, 1–20, and Alice L. Conklin, "Redefining 'Frenchness': Citizenship, Race, Regeneration, and Imperial Motherhood in France and West Africa, 1914–1940," 65–83; and Elinor A. Accampo, Rachel G. Fuchs, and Mary Lynn Stewart, eds., *Gender and the Politics of Social Reform in France, 1870–1914* (Baltimore, Md.: Johns Hopkins University Press, 1995). Also, Anna Davin, "Imperialism and Motherhood," *History Workshop* 5 (1978): 9–65; Carol Summers, "Intimate Colonialism: The Imperial Production of Reproduction in Uganda, 1907–25," *Signs* 16 (1991): 787–807.

21. See the influential study of missionary-Tswana interactions interpreted as a "long conversation": John Comaroff and Jean Comaroff, *Of Revelation and Revolution*, 2 vols. (Chicago: University of Chicago Press, 1991); and, more generally, Dagmar Engels and Shula Marks, eds., *Contesting Colonial Hegemony: State and Society in Africa and India* (London: British Academic Press, 1994).

22. See the landmark collection of essays edited by Karen Tranberg Hansen, *African Encounters with Domesticity* (New Brunswick, N.J.: Rutgers University Press, 1992), that deals with struggles over the contents and meanings of domesticity and the personal troubles and public issues they provoked; Jean Allman, "Making Mothers: Missionaries, Medical Officers and Women's Work in Colonial Asante, 1924–1945," *History Workshop Journal* 38 (Autumn 1994): 23–47; Nancy Rose Hunt, "Domesticity and Colonialism in Belgian Africa: Usumbura's Foyer Social, 1946–1960," *Signs* 15, no. 1 (1990): 447–74; LaRay Denzer, "Domestic Science Training in Colonial Yorubaland, Nigeria," in *African Encounters with Domesticity*, ed. Hansen, 116–42; and Estelle Pagnon, "'Une oeuvre utile?' La scolarisation des filles par les missionnaires catholiques dans le sud-est du Nigéria (1883–1930)," *Clio* 6 (1997): 35–59.

23. I visited fully enrolled sewing classes and talked with some of the women in Pointe-Noire in 2000.

24. Nancy Rose Hunt, "Placing African Women's History and Locating Gender," *Social History* 14, no. 3 (1989): 361, and passim. Also, Nancy Rose Hunt, Tessie P. Liu, and Jean Quartaert, eds., *Gendered Colonialisms in African History* (Oxford: Blackwell, 1997), previously published as a collection of essays in *Gender and History* (1995). For surveys of the historiography of African women at various points in time, see Margaret Strobel, "African Women: A Review," *Signs* 8, no. 1 (1982): 109–31; Margaret Jean Hay, *Queens, Prostitutes and Peasants: Historical Perspectives on African Women, 1971–1986* (Boston: African Studies Center, Boston University, 1988); and Iris Berger, "African women's history: themes and perspectives," *Journal of Colonialism and Colonial History* 4, no. 1 (2003), http://muse.jhu.edu/journals/journal_of_colonialism_and_colonial_history.

25. Walker, "Conceptualising Motherhood," 423. Apart from South Africa, there is a growing literature on certain aspects of motherhood such as the management, medicalization, and politicization of pregnancies and child care. See, for example, Nancy Rose Hunt, *A Colonial Lexicon of Birth Ritual, Medicalization, and Mobility in the Congo* (Durham, N.C.: Duke University Press, 1999); and Lynn M. Thomas, *Politics of the Womb: Women, Reproduction, and the State in Kenya* (Berkeley and Los Angeles: University of California Press, 2003). The social role of mothers, however, is often subsumed under other categories such as marriage, family, and occupations, and can bear bringing out of the shadows. Neither "mother" or "motherhood" appear in the index of two recent important collections of essays: Dorothy L. Hodgson and Sheryl A. McCurdy, eds., *"Wicked" Women and the Reconfiguration of Gender in Africa* (Portsmouth, N.H.: Heinemann, 2001); and Jean Allman, Susan Geiger and Nakanyike Musisi, eds., *Women in African Colonial Histories* (Bloomington: Indiana University Press, 2002). For a historiographical review of some of the literature, see Anne Hugon, "L'historiographie de la maternité en Afrique subsaharienne," *Clio* 21 (2005): 212–29, special issue on motherhood.

26. AbdouMaliq Simone, *For the City Yet to Come: Changing Life in Four African Cities* (Durham, N.C.: Duke University Press, 2004), 225, 224–43. In the large literature on urban associations by scholars from various disciplines, see for its representative essays, Arne Tostensen, Inge Tvedten, and Mariken Vaa, eds., *Associational Life in African Cities: Popular Responses to the Urban Crisis* (Uppsala, Sweden: Nordiska Afrikainstitutet, 2001), and, for a comparison of Brazzaville and Dakar associations, Michèle O'Deyé, *Les associations en villes africaines: Dakar-Brazzaville* (Paris: L'Harmattan, 1985).

27. Interview with Suzanne Tchitembo, Pointe-Noire, 1 July 2000.

28. See chapter 6 and epilogue. On the *manyanos*, Deborah Gaitskell, "Devout Domesticity? A Century of African Women's Christianity in South Africa," in *Women and Gender*

in Southern Africa to 1945, ed. Cherryl Walker (London: James Currey, 1990), 251–52; and "'Wailing for Purity': Prayer Unions, African Mothers and Adolescent Daughters, 1912–1940," in Shula Marks and Richard Rathbone, eds., *Industrialisation and Social Change in South Africa* (Harlow, UK: Longman, 1982), 338–57. Church women's prayer unions, *ruwadzanos,* mobilized around motherhood were also dynamic aspects of the missionary church in colonial Zimbabwe: see Barbara A. Moss, "'And the Bones Come Together': Women's Religious Expectations in Southern Africa, c. 1900–1945," *Journal of Religious History* 23, no. 1 (Feb. 1999): 108–27, and "Mai Chaza and the Politics of Motherhood in Colonial Zimbabwe," in *Stepping Forward: Black Women in Africa and the Americas,* ed. Catherine Higgs, Barbara A. Moss, and Earline Rae Ferguson (Athens: Ohio University Press, 2002), 143–57; also, Marja Hinfelaar, *Respectable and Responsible Women: Methodist and Roman Catholic Women's Organizations in Harare, Zimbabwe (1919–1985)* (Zoetermeer, Neth.: Boeckencentrum, 2001).

29. Recently, the name of the congregation has been translated in English as Fathers of the Holy Spirit but the older name, Holy Ghost Fathers (or the commonly used Spiritans), will be retained here, given the historical nature of this study. The fullest treatment of the early history of the region is Phyllis M. Martin, *The External Trade of the Loango Coast, 1576–1870: The Effects of Changing Commercial Relations on the Vili Kingdom of Loango* (Oxford: Clarendon Press, 1972).

30. The name of the French colony that was ruled from Libreville in modern Gabon until the capital was moved to Brazzaville (1904) and the name changed to French Equatorial Africa (AEF) five years later. The literature on Christianity in the Kongo kingdom is large. The main starting point in English is the work of John Thornton and Richard Gray. See, for example, John K. Thornton, *The Kingdom of Kongo: Civil War and Transition, 1641–1718* (Madison: University of Wisconsin Press, 1983); "The Development of an African Catholic Church in the Kingdom of Kongo, 1491–1750," *JAH* 25, no. 2 (1984): 147–67; and *The Kongolese Saint Anthony: Dona Beatriz Kimpa Vita and the Antonian Movement, 1684–1706* (Cambridge: Cambridge University Press, 1998). Also, Richard Gray, *Black Christians and White Missionaries* (New Haven, Conn.: Yale University Press, 1990).

31. P. Jerôme Merolla da Sorrento, "A Voyage to Congo and Several Other Countries in Southern Africa (1682)," in *A Collection of Voyages and Travels,* compiled by Awnsham and John Churchill (London: J. Walthoe, 1732), 1:651–52; Louis Jadin, "Essai d'évangélisation du Loango et du Kakongo, 1766–1775," *Zaire* 7 (1953): 1053–65.

32. Abbé Proyart, *Histoire de Loango, Kakongo, et autres royaumes d'Afrique* (Paris: C. P. Berton, 1776), 203–382; Jean Cuvelier, *Documents sur une mission française au Kakongo, 1766–1776* (Brussels: IRCB, 1953).

33. Jean Ernoult, *Les spiritains au Congo de 1865 à nos jours* (Paris: Congrégation du Saint-Esprit, 1995), 27.

34. See, for example, Dennis Pelletier, *Les catholiques en France depuis 1815* (Paris: La Découverte, 1997), 26–43; and J. P. Daughton, *An Empire Divided: Religion, Republicanism, and the Making of French Colonialism, 1880–1914* (Oxford: Oxford University Press, 2006), 34–41, 267.

35. The names of the vicariates changed over time as did their boundaries. Where this is significant, it is mentioned in the text.

36. Frederick Cooper and Ann Laura Stoler, eds., *Tensions of Empire: Colonial Culture in a Bourgeois World* (Berkeley and Los Angeles: University of California Press, 1997); also Georges Balandier, "La situation colonial: approche théoretique," *Cahiers internationaux de sociologie* 11 (1951): 44–79.

37. On Libermann, his beliefs and priorities, see the collection of essays in Paul Coulon and Paule Brasseur, eds., *Libermann, 1802–1852: une pensée et une mystique missionniaires* (Paris: Cerf, 1988). The most accessible source on the Spiritans in English is Henry J. Koren, *To the Ends of the Earth: A General History of the Congregation of the Holy Ghost* (Pittsburgh: Duquesne University Press, 1983); see 200–22, 247–62 on Libermann, his life, doctrine, and achievements. For Spiritan ideology and practice in Eastern Africa, see Paul V. Kollman, *The Evangelization of Slaves and Catholic Origins in Eastern Africa* (Maryknoll, N.Y.: Orbis Books, 2005).

38. Useful studies by Spiritan scholars are by Ernoult, *Les spiritains au Congo;* and Guy Pannier, *L'église de Pointe-Noire (Congo-Brazzaville): évolution des communautés chrétiennes de 1947 à 1975* (Paris: Editions Karthala, 1999). Also of interest since it gives insights from the perspectives of African priests who passed through the Spiritan seminary is the work by Côme Kinata, *La formation du clergé indigène au Congo Français, 1875–1960* (Paris: L'Harmattan, 2004).

39. Protestant missionaries from the *Svenska Missionsförbundet* (Swedish Evangelical Church) crossed the border from Belgian Congo into the French colony in 1910. Their presence was much smaller than that of Catholics, but important nevertheless, for their schools and training of an educated elite and for periodic "revivals" that drew in converts. Spiritan reports complained of the great resources of the Swedish missionaries, who constituted severe competition for them; at times this was likely the case but it was also good strategy in appeals for increased financial support. The literature on the Protestant missions is mainly in Swedish, but see the insights offered by Ephraim Andersson, himself a missionary in Congo for twenty years, *Churches at the Grass-Roots: A Study of Congo-Brazzaville* (London: Lutterworth Press, 1968).

40. Adrian Hastings's comment that "the Christian advance was a black advance or it was nothing": Hastings, *The Church in Africa, 1450–1950* (Oxford: Clarendon Press, 1994), 437–38.

41. Ruth Slade, *English-Speaking Missions in the Congo Independent State, 1878–1908* (Brussels: Académie Royale des Sciences Coloniales, 1959), 20, and Jadin, "Essai d'évangelisation du Loango et du Kakongo," 1061–62; both are quoted in Joan F. Burke, *These Catholic Women are all Mamas: Towards the Enculturation of the Sisterhood in Africa, an Ethnographic Study* (Leiden, Neth.: Brill, 2001), 13. John Thornton has shown, although in different circumstances, the powerful appeal of a female religious leader: see Thornton, *The Kongolese Saint Anthony.* According to Louis Jadin, plans to establish a convent at Mbanza Kongo, came to nothing in 1612 and 1626: see Jadin, "Essai d'évangélisation du Loango et du Kakongo," 1062.

42. Ralph Gibson, *A Social History of French Catholicism, 1789–1914* (New York: Routledge, 1989), 105–107, 117–20, and "Female Religious Orders in Nineteenth Century France," in *Catholicism in Britain and France since 1789,* ed. Frank Tallett and Nicholas Atkin (London: Hambledon Press, 1996), 105–15. See Gibson's discussion of conditions in nineteenth-century France that gave impetus to this movement. Also, Pelletier, *Les catholiques en France,* 28–32; Claude Langlois, *Le catholicisme au féminin: les congrégations françaises à supérieure générale au XIXe siècle,* 4 vols. (Paris: Cerf, 1984); and Elisabeth Dufourcq, *Les congrégations religieuses féminines hors d'Europe de Richelieu à nos jours,* 4 vols. (Paris: Librairie de l'Inde, 1903). While the word "nuns" will sometimes be used here interchangeably with "sisters," it tends to be more used for women who belong to contemplative orders.

43. Judith Stone, "Anticlericals and *Bonnes Soeurs:* The Rhetoric of the 1901 Law of Associations," *French Historical Studies* 23 (2000): 103–28; Pelletier, *Les catholiques en France,* 30.

44. The *Soeurs Missionnaires du Saint-Esprit* (Spiritan sisters), the *Franciscaines Missionnaires de Marie* (Franciscan Missionaries of Mary), and the *Soeurs de la Divine Providence de Ribeauvillé* (Sisters of the Divine Providence of Ribeauvillé) become important in my account after c. 1940 and will be dealt with in more detail in chapter 5.

45. Paule Brasseur, "Anne-Marie Javouhey (1779–1851)," in Coulon and Brasseur, *Libermann*, 647.

46. There are several biographies of Anne-Marie Javouhey, the most recent by Geneviève Lecuir-Nemo, *Anne-Marie Javouhey: fondatrice de la congrégation des Soeurs de Saint-Joseph de Cluny (1779–1851)* (Paris: Karthala, 2001); also, *La tradition vivante: appelées pour la mission: les Soeurs de Saint Joseph de Cluny* (Paris: Editions CIF, 1985), 11, 30; and *Les Soeurs de Saint-Joseph de Cluny en Afrique Centrale, 1886–1986* (Kinshasa: Imprimerie Saint Paul, 1986). Well over a thousand of her letters are extant. See Jean Herbert and Marie-Cécile de Segonzac, eds., *Anne-Marie Javouhey: Correspondance.* 4 vols. (Paris: Cerf, 1994).

47. Elizabeth A. Isichei, *A History of Christianity in Africa from Antiquity to the Present* (Grand Rapids, Mich.: Eerdmans, 1995), 87. Edited collections of essays on missions in Africa show few chapters on Catholic sisters compared to Protestant missionary women. See, however: Sister Mary Aquina Weinrich, "An Aspect of the Development of the Religious Life in Rhodesia," in T. O. Ranger and John Weller, eds., *Themes in the Christian History of Centra Africa* (Berkeley and Los Angeles: University of California Press, 1975), 218–37; and Joan F. Burke, "These Catholic Sisters Are All Mamas! Celibacy and the Metaphor of Maternity," in Fiona Bowie, Deborah Kirkwood, and Shirley Ardener, eds., *Women and Missions: Past and Present: Anthropological and Historical perspectives* (New York: Oxford University Press, 1993), 251–66. Among works on Catholic missions where sisters are prominent, see Hugo F. Hinfelaar, *Bemba-Speaking women of Zambia in a Century of Religious Change (1892–1992)* Leiden, Neth.: Brill, 1994); Brigitta Larsson, *Conversion to Greater Freedom? Women, Church, and Social Change in North-Western Tanzania under Colonial Rule* (Stockholm: Almquist and Wiksell, 1991); and Kathleen R. Smythe, *Fipa Families: Reproduction and Catholic Evangelization in Nkansi, Ufipa, 1880–1960* (Portsmouth, N.H.: Heinemann, 2006), and, "African Women and White Sisters at the Karema Mission Station, 1894–1920," *Journal of Women's History* 19, no. 2 (2007): 59–84; Anene Ejikene, "Mission and Motherhood: Towards a History of Catholic Women and Education in Onitsha, Nigeria, 1885–1964," Ph.D. thesis, Columbia University, 2003; also, Nicholas Creary, "Jesuit Missionary Perspectives on the Formation of African Clergy and Religious Institutes in Zimbabwe, c. 1922–1959," *Le fait missionnaire* 14 (July 2004), 117–45. See also Burke, *These Catholic Women Are All Mamas,* based on her anthropological research in a community of her own congregation, the Sisters of Notre Dame of Namur in the Lower Congo (Zaire). The literature in French on missionaries in Africa in general and nuns in particular is slight, but, see for example, Yvonne Knibiehler and Régine Goutalier, *La femme au temps des colonies* (Paris: Stock, 1985), chapter 5; and Pagnon, "Une oeuvre inutile?" Also, for the role of the White Sisters in the health service in colonial Rwanda, Anne Cornet, "Action sanitaire et contrôle social au Ruanda (1920–1940): femmes, missions et politiques de santé," Ph.D. thesis, Université Catholique de Louvain, 2005. For upper Congo and Brazzaville, there is the unpublished account by a Franciscan missionary, Odile de Langavant, "Les Franciscaines Missionnaires de Marie au Congo," c. 1996; Phyllis M. Martin, "Celebrating the Ordinary: Church, Empire and Gender in the Life of Mère Marie-Michelle Dédié (Senegal, Congo, 1882–1931)," *Gender and History* 16, no. 2 (2004): 289–317; and, Ghislain de Banville, *Kalouka et Zoungoula: les deux premières religieuses de Brazzaville, au Congo 1892–1909* (Paris: Karthala, 2000).

48. Helen Rose Ebaugh, "Patriarchal Bargains and Latent Avenues of Social Mobility: Nuns in the Roman Catholic Church," *Gender and Society* 7, no. 3 (1993): 400–14; Mary Taylor Huber and Nancy C. Lutkehaus, eds., *Gendered Missions: Women and Men in Missionary Discourse and Practice* (Ann Arbor: University of Michigan Press, 1999), especially the introduction by the editors and the chapters by Huber and by Lutkehaus on Catholic missionaries in New Guinea. The essays on Africa concern Protestant missions. Also, for Catholic missionary relations in Papua, see the very readable Diane Langmore, *Missionary Lives: Papua, 1874–1914* (Honolulu: University of Hawaii, 1989); and for the centuries-long struggles of lay and religious women to assert their place within the church, both Catholic and Protestant, see Mary T. Malone, *Women and Christianity*, 3 vols. (New York: Orbis Books, 2003), especially vol. 3, *From the Reformation to the 21st Century*.

49. There is a large literature on the subject: for example, Thomas A. Kselman, *Miracles and Prophecies: Popular Religion and the Church in Nineteenth Century France* (New Brunswick, N.J.: Rutgers University Press, 1983), 89–112; Gibson, *A Social History of French Catholicism*, 131, 135–55; Pelletier, *Les catholiques en france*, 22–27; Caroline Ford, "Female martyrdom and the politics of sainthood in nineteenth century France: the cult of Sainte-Philomène," in Tallett and Atkin, 115–34.

50. Dorothy Hodgson, *The Church of Women: Gendered Encounters between Maasai and Missionaries* (Bloomington: Indiana University Press, 2005). Others who have considered women's devotional life within the church are Kathleen Smythe, "The creation of a Catholic Fipa society: conversion in Nkansi District, Ufipa," in *East African Expressions of Christianity*, ed. Thomas Spear and Isaac N. Kimambo (Athens: Ohio University Press, 1999), 129–49; Deborah Gaitskell, "'Prayer and Preaching': The Distinctive Spirituality of African Women's Church Organizations," in *Missions and Christianity in South African History*, ed. Henry Bredekamp and Robert Ross (Johannesburg: Witwatersrand University Press, 1995), 211–32; Hugo F. Hinfelaar, *Bemba-Speaking women of Zambia*; Larsson, *Conversion to Greater Freedom?*

51. Brian Stanley, ed., *Missions, Nationalism, and the End of Empire* (Grand Rapids, Mich.: Eerdmans, 2003), 2.

52. Hodgson, *The Church of Women*.

53. Wendy James and Douglas H. Johnson, "Introduction," in *Vernacular Christianity: Essays in the Social Anthropology of Religion presented to Godfrey Lienhardt*, ed. James and Johnson (New York: Lillian Barber Press, 1988), 10. Also, Terence Ranger, "New Approaches to the History of Mission Christianity," in Toyin Falola, ed., *African Historiography: Essays in Honour of Jacob Ade Ajayi* (Harlow, UK: Longman, 1993), 180–94.

54. Pierre Vennetier, ed., *Atlas de la République Populaire du Congo* (Paris: Jeune Afrique, 1977), 22–29, and passim. I am using the term "Kongo-related peoples" to refer to those whose homeland is the region of lower Congo between Brazzaville and the Atlantic Ocean. Occasionally, I will refer to a sub-group (Vili, Nsundi, Beembe, Lari, etc.) to delineate the reference more precisely, while noting that although some of these groups were identified thus at the time, others received their specific present-day meaning as ethnicity became politicized in the twentieth century. Scholars have written of the history of some of these groups and their appellation but have also remarked on the close linguistic and cultural affinity of the Kongo-related peoples who live north of the Congo river (present-day Republic of Congo, Cabinda, and Democratic Republic of Congo): see, for example: Bernard Pinçon and Dominique Ngoïe-Ngala, "L'unité culturelle kongo à la fin du XIXe siècle. L'apport des études céramologiques," *CEA* 30, no. 2 (1990): 157–78; K. E. Laman, *The Kongo*, 4 vols. (Uppsala, Sweden: Studia Ethnographica Upsaliensia, 1953–68); Balandier, *Sociology of Black*

Africa, 292–97; Marcel Soret, *Les Kongo Nord-Occidentaux* (Paris: Presses Universitaires de France, 1959), 1–6; René Mavoungou Pambou, *Proverbes et dictons du Loango en Afrique centrale* (Jouy-le-Moutier, France: Bajag-Meri, 1997), 12; Wyatt MacGaffey, *Kongo Political Culture: The Conceptual Challenge of the Particular* (Bloomington: Indiana University Press, 2000), 70–71; Phyllis M. Martin, *Leisure and Society in Colonial Brazzaville* (Cambridge: Cambridge University Press, 1995), 40–41, 66–70, 199–200. Dunja Hersak has warned of the dangers of overstating a single Kongo universe, however, and urged attention be given to the "particularities within Kongo tradition." See Dunja Hersak, "There Are Many Kongo Worlds: Particularities of Magico-Religious Beliefs among the Vili and Yombe of Congo-Brazzaville," *Africa* 71, no. 4 (2001): 614–40.

55. My original intention was to cover the whole country, but I reluctantly abandoned that plan for several reasons: the scope was too large and the people too diverse; the region of upper Congo has received much less scholarly attention than the south, and thus the background on which to base this work was still lacking; and political insecurities in the north and difficulties of communication made the original plan too difficult to manage.

56. During the period of the Marxist-Leninist regime (1969–90), the country was known officially as the People's Republic of Congo. The country is called Congo-Brazzaville to distinguish it from the better known and much larger Democratic Republic of Congo (DRC), with its capital at Kinshasa on the opposite side of Malebo Pool, a body of water several miles wide formed by the Congo River before it hurtles downstream through the region of the cataracts.

57. Special issue of *Politique africaine* 31 (Oct. 1988) on Congo, see, Bahjat Achikbache and Francis Anglade, "Les villes prises d'assaut: les migrations internes," 7–14. The four largest towns, Brazzaville, Pointe-Noire, Loubomo (formerly Dolisie), and Nkayi (formerly Jacob), are in lower Congo.

58. Vansina, *Paths in the Rainforest;* Gilles Sautter, *De l'Atlantique au fleuve Congo: une géographie du sous-peuplement,* 2 vols. (Paris: Mouton, 1966); Rita Headrick, "The Impact of Colonialism on Health in French Equatorial Africa," Ph.D. thesis, University of Chicago, 1987, and *Colonialism, Health, and Illness in French Equatorial Africa, 1885–1935,* ed. Daniel R. Headrick (Atlanta: African Studies Association, 1994).

59. Frederick Cooper, *Africa since 1940: The Past of the Present* (Cambridge: Cambridge University Press, 2002), 48.

60. Catherine Coquery-Vidrovitch, "Investissements privés, investissements publiques en AEF, 1900–1940," *African Economic History* 12 (1983): 13–16; and, *Le Congo au temps des grandes compagnies concessionnaires, 1898–1930* (Paris: Mouton, 1972).

61. The study of town life has largely been carried out by anthropologists, sociologists, urban geographers, and development specialists. The seminal work of Georges Balandier and other scholars from ORSTOM (Paris) during the last decade or so of colonial rule laid the groundwork for other studies after independence; see, for example, Georges Balandier, *Sociologie des Brazzavilles noires,* 2nd ed. (Paris: Presses de la Fondation Nationale des Sciences Politiques, 1985); and Pierre Vennetier, *Pointe-Noire et la façade maritime du Congo-Brazzaville* (Paris: ORSTOM, 1968). For more recent social histories, see Martin, *Leisure and Society in Colonial Brazzaville,* and Ch. Didier Gondola, *Villes miroirs: migrations et identités urbaines à Kinshasa et Brazzaville, 1930–1970* (Paris: L'Harmattan, 1997).

62. Catherine Coquery-Vidrovitch, "Histoire des femmes d'Afrique," *Clio* 6 (1997): 7; also, see the comprehensive discussion on African women and the practice of history in France by Odile Goerg, "Femmes africaines et pratique historique en France," *Politique africaine* 72 (1998): 130–44; and for a consideration of the lack of interest in research on colonial

and African women in francophone as opposed to anglophone scholarship and a review of the literature in French, see Sophie Dulucq and Odile Goerg, "Le fait colonial au miroir des colonisées. Femmes, genre et colonisation: un bilan des recherches francophones en histoire de l'Afrique subsaharienne (1950–2003)," in Anne Hugon, ed., *Histoire des femmes en situation coloniale: Afrique et Asie, XXe siècle* (Paris: Karthala, 2004), 43–70.

63. Hugon, ed., "Introduction," in *Histoire des femmes en situation coloniale*, 5; and Odile Goerg, ed., *Perspectives historiques sur le genre en Afrique* (Paris: L'Harmattan, 2007).

64. Scholastique Dianzinga, "Les femmes congolaises du début de la colonisation à 1960," Ph.D. thesis, Université de Pau, 1998.

65. For example, Martial Sinda, *Le messianisme congolais et ses incidences politiques* (Paris: Payot, 1972); and, among the Swedish publications in English, Andersson, *Churches at the Grass-Roots*.

66. These publications are fully referenced in the notes for the epilogue.

1. Mothers at Risk

1. The phrase is borrowed from the history of early Christianity in northern Namibia by Meredith McKittrick, *To Dwell Secure: Generation, Christianity, and Colonialism in Ovamboland* (Portsmouth, N.H.: Heinemann, 2002). See also MacGaffey, *Kongo Political Culture*, 24, but his reference to those who sought protection at the Swedish Protestant mission stations does not distinguish between men and women.

2. P. Carrie, *Coutumier de l'oeuvre des enfants dans le vicariat apostolique du Congo Français* (Loango: Imprimerie de la Mission, 1890); "Communauté de Marie-Immaculée à Loango" (hereafter Loango), *Bulletin de la Congrégation des Soeurs de Saint-Joseph de Cluny (BCSSJC)* 17 (March 1890), 589; "Communauté du Sacre-Coeur de Loango" (hereafter Loango), *Bulletin de la Congrégation des Pères du Saint-Esprit (BCPSE)* 20 (1899–1900), 404. Also, for a similar policy by the vicar apostolic of upper Congo, Mgr. Augouard, see Archives, Oeuvres Pontificales Missionnaires, Lyons (AOPM), G35, Mgr. Augouard to Propagation de la Foi (PF), 31 Dec. 1907.

3. Adrian Hastings, "Were Women a Special Case?" in *Women and Missions*, ed. Bowie, Kirkwood, and Ardener, 111, 112; also, Dorothy L. Hodgson, "Engendered Encounters: Men of the Church and the 'Church of Women' in Maasailand, Tanzania, 1950–1993," *Comparative Studies in Society and History* 41, no. 4 (1999): 758, 758n3.

4. See Sautter, *De l'Atlantique au fleuve Congo*, 1:19–207, 331–582.

5. Vansina, *Paths in the Rainforest*, 239, 369n1; see also, Côme Kinata, *Les ethnochefferies dans le Bas-Congo français: collaboration et résistance, 1896–1960* (Paris: L'Harmattan, 2001); Coquery-Vidrovitch, *Le Congo au temps des grandes compagnies concessionaires;* Headrick, *Colonialism, Health, and Illness in French Equatorial Africa.*

6. Based on accounts by those who traveled along the Loango-Brazzaville route between 1883 and 1898. See, for example, Elisabeth Rabut, *Brazza Commissaire Général: le Congo Français, 1886–1897* (Paris: Editions de l'EHESS, 1989), 98, 105, 301, 311–12, 381; Marc Michel, *La mission Marchand, 1895–1899* (Paris: Mouton, 1972), passim; Marcel Guillemot, *Notice sur le Congo Français* (Paris: J. André, 1901), 89–90; L. Girard, "Brazzaville," *BCAF* (March 1916): 31; Archives Générales de la Congrégation des Pères du Saint-Esprit, Chevilly (AGCPSE), 510/B/VI, Report of Mgr. Augouard to Sainte-Enfance, 2 Sept. and 18 Oct. 1897; Elie Gandziami, "De Loango à Tandala par la piste de caravanes," *Liaison* 49–50 (1955), 26–30; Vennetier, *Pointe-Noire et la façade maritime*, 94–96.

7. Colonel Baratier, *Au Congo: souvenirs de la Mission Marchand* (Paris: Arthème Fayard, 1914), 62.

8. Rabut, *Brazza Commissaire Général*, 89, 157, 159, 301; P. Christophe Marichelle, *Tablettes d'un congolais: Sainte-Marie de Kouilou* (unpublished, 1909), 16; Vennetier, *Pointe-Noire et la façade maritime*, 104; Sautter, *De l'Atlantique au fleuve Congo*, 1:621, 624–25. The major work is by Headrick, "The Impact of Colonialism on Health in French Equatorial Africa," and *Colonialism, Health and Illness in French Equatorial Africa*.

9. AGCPSE, 176/B/VIII, Mgr. Derouet, "Mission de Congo Français, 1903–1904"; 177/A/IV, P. Koffel to Mgr. Derouet, Bouanza, 30 Sept. 1905; P. Zimmerman to Mgr. Derouet, Bouanza, 2 Feb. 1908; Mayeul de Dreuille, *La Bouenza, 1892–1992: les sources de l'église au Congo* (Paris: Beauchesne, 1994), 22–135.

10. *BCPSE* 21 (1900–1902), Report from Lucula, 717–18; and 23 (1902–1905), 196, 198. This mission was in the Cabinda region of the southern Mayombe.

11. Headrick, *Colonialism, Health and Illness in French Equatorial Africa*, 29–43, 93, 311–83, 400–19; Sautter, *De l'Atlantique au fleuve Congo*, 1:621, 624–25; Vennetier, *Pointe-Noire et la façade maritime*, 104–105.

12. Authors who have worked on Kongo-related groups have emphasized the association of power, wealth, and trade: see, for example, Martin, *The External Trade of the Loango Coast*, passim, especially 158–74; Norm Schrag, "Boma and the Lower Zaire: a Socio-Economic Study of a Kongo Trading Community, 1785–1885," Ph.D. thesis, Indiana University, 1985, passim, especially 231–63; MacGaffey, *Kongo Political Culture*, 72, and *Art and Healing of the Bakongo: Commented by Themselves* (Stockholm: Folkens Museum-Etnografiska, 1991), 98; John Janzen, *Lemba, 1650–1930: A Drum of Affliction in Africa and the New World* (New York: Garland, 1982), passim, especially 1–79. As will become evident in later chapters, the social and economic transformations introduced by Christian missionaries contributed to these "uncertainties."

13. Martin, *The External Trade of the Loango Coast*, 153–57, 156n3; Jean-Luc Vellut, "L'économie internationale des côtes de Guinée Inférieure au XIXe siècle," in *Reunião internacional de história de Africa: Relação Europa-Africa no 3.o quartel do Séc. XIX* (Lisbon: Instituto de Investigaçao Científica e Tropical, 1989), 135–49; Mgr. Carrie, "Congo Français," *Les Missions Catholiques* (*MC*) 1402 (April 1896): 182; AGCPSE, 177/A/III, P. Mintier to Henri, Loango, 14 Dec. 1908; Vennetier, *Pointe-Noire et la façade maritime*, 81–7; Pierre-Philippe Rey, *Colonialisme, néo-colonialisme et transition au capitalisme: exemple de la "Comilogue" au Congo-Brazzaville* (Paris: Maspero, 1971), 288–91.

14. Jean Dybowski, *La route du Tchad: du Loango au Chari* (Paris: Librairie de Firmin-Dido, 1893), 15.

15. Vennetier, *Pointe-Noire et la façade maritime*, 95.

16. Beatrix Heintz, "Colonial ambitions as blind passengers: the case of German explorers in West-Central Africa (1873–86)," in *A Africa e a instalação do sistem colonial, (1885–1930)* (Lisbon: Centro de Estudos de História e Cartografia Antigao, 2000), 20–26.

17. Eduard Pechuël-Loesche, *Volkskunde von Loango* (Stuttgart: Verlag von Strecker und Schröder, 1907), 100.

18. For example, S. P. H. Naber, ed., *Samuel Brun's Schiffarten (1624)* (The Hague: M. Nijhoff, 1913), 9–11; Olfert Dapper, *Naukeurige Beschrijvinge der Afrikaensche Gewesten*, 2nd ed. (Amsterdam: J. van Meurs, 1676), 151; Proyart, *Histoire de Loango*, 14–57, 65–66; Pechuël-Loesche, *Volkskunde*, 213–14; D. José Franque, *Nós, os Cabindas: história, leis, usos e costumes dos povos de N'goio* (Lisbon: Editora Lisboa, 1940), 123–27, 167–71. For a detailed account of women's economic activities, see Dianzinga, "Les femmes congolaises," 39–77.

19. Dianzinga, "Les femmes congolaises," 41, 58.

20. Cuvelier, *Documents sur une mission française au Kakongo*, 51.

21. Pechuël-Loesche, *Volkskunde*, 214.

22. Deleval, "Les tribus Kavati du Mayombe," *Revue Congolaise* 3 (1913): 180; also, Albert Doutreloux, *L'ombre des fétiches: société et culture yombe* (Louvain: Editions Nauwelaerts, 1967), 62. For similar practices in other Kongo-related groups, see Laman, *The Kongo*, 1:48, 115–21 (Nsundi); and Sautter, *De l'Atlantique au fleuve Congo*, 1:485–515, 605–18.

23. Sautter, *De l'Atlantique au fleuve Congo*, 1:502–503; Dianzinga, "Les femmes congolaises," 47–49; Georges Dupré, *Les naissances d'une société: espace et historicité chez les Beembé de Congo* (Paris: ORSTOM), 307–308; interview with Veronique Mbemba, Brazzaville, 17 June 1989.

24. Pechuël-Loesche, *Volkskunde*, 100.

25. Ibid., 100, 104; Mavoungou Pambou, *Proverbes et dictons du Loango*, 98, 111.

26. This composite picture is based on European observations in the late nineteenth and early twentieth centuries. Laman, *The Kongo*, contains accounts based on information collected by his male informants around the first decade of the twentieth century, see 2:1–22. Théophile Obenga's article, "Naissance et puberté en pays Kongo au XVIIe siècle," *CCAH* 9 (1984): 19–30, draws heavily on the accounts in Dapper and Proyart and also deals with what he terms the Kongo "cultural zone," including the region of the old Kongo kingdom south of the Congo river.

27. MacGaffey, *Art and the Healing of the Bakongo*, 4–6, 9, and *Kongo Political Culture*, 12, 80; Laman, *The Kongo*, 2:59 and 3:67–75, 173–80; Doutreloux, *L'ombre des fétiches*, 238–48; Frank Hagenbucher-Sacripanti, *Les fondements spirituels du pouvoir au royaume de Loango* (Paris: ORSTOM, 1973) 29–34, 104–109; Mavoungou Pambou, *Proverbes et dictons*, 63–76; John M. Jansen, "Ideologies and Institutions in the Pre-colonial History of Equatorial African Therapeutic Systems," *Social Science and Medicine* 13B, 4 (1979), 317–20. Particularly fascinating is the work of Janzen and MacGaffey in translating from the Kikongo and commenting on many of the original notebooks containing the testimonies collected by Kongo male teachers and catechists using questionnaires distributed by the Swedish missionary Karl Laman between about 1912 and 1919. These have been the basis for much of their work. See, for example, Janzen, *Lemba*; MacGaffey, *Art and Healing of the Bakongo*, and *Kongo Political Culture*.

28. MacGaffey, *Art and Healing of the Bakongo*, 4.

29. R. E. Dennett, *Seven Years among the Fjort* (London: Sampson Low, Marston, Searly and Rivington, 1887), 62, 67–68, 67n12. Dennett was an employee of the Hatton and Cookson company. He worked at factories along the northern Angolan and Loango coast from 1879 to 1902 and recorded his observations in three books. MacGaffey, *Art and Healing of the Bakongo*, 11–13, gives information on a variant of the Mabyala *nkisi* drawn from the notebooks of Laman's informants. Photos of various Mabyala *nkisi*, as well as his wife holding a child, and paraphernalia associated with the cult that exist in Western museums are included and discussed in the exhibition catalogue by Wyatt MacGaffey and Michael D. Harris, *Astonishment and Power* (Washington, D.C.: Smithsonian Institution Press, 1993), 34–39. See also on *nkondi*, MacGaffey, *Art and Healing of the Bakongo*, 121, 141, and *Kongo Political Culture*, 98–99, 101, 108. Such nail figures are featured prominently in many museum catalogues since they are among the Kongo sculptures best-known in the West.

30. Janzen, *Lemba*, 55–57. Janzen's work has remained the definitive analysis of this important association. The historical sources include: Dapper, *Naukeurige Beschrijvinge*, 179; Adolf Bastian, *Die Deutsche Expedition an der Loango-Küste* (Jena, Germany: Hermann Costenoble, 1874), 1:170–73; Paul Güssfeldt, Julius Falkenstein, and Eduard Pechuël-Loesche, *Die Loango-Expedition ausgesandt von der Deutschen Gesellschaft zur Erforschung Aequatorial-Africas, 1873–1876* (Leipzig: P. Frohberg, 1879–1907), 1:71, 106.

31. Pechuël-Loesche, *Volkskunde*, 463; for late-nineteenth- and early-twentieth-century accounts of raising children and consultations with *nganga*, see, Bastian, *Die Deutsche Expedition an der Loango-Küste*, 1:168–69, 173–75, 183–84; Pechuël-Loesche, *Volkskunde*, 361, 370, 461–63; Laman, *The Kongo*, 3:133–34, 157–58; MacGaffey, *Art and Healing of the Bakongo*, 11–12, 39, 47, 51–2.

32. Laman, *The Kongo*, 1:1.

33. Hagenbucher-Sacripanti, *Les fondements spirituels*, 31–34.

34. Georges Dupré, *Les naissances d'une société*, 304.

35. Vincent, *Femmes africaines en milieu urbain*, 37.

36. Herbert Pepper collected songs, dance music, and music for orchestras and single instruments in Congo and Gabon while working for ORSTOM. This lullaby is from a published collection (disks and text): *Anthologie de la vie africaine (Moyen-Congo et Gabon)* (Paris: Ducretet-Thomson, 1958). The lullaby is on disc 1, side 1, number 1, and the text is published on page 13.

37. For examples of maternity sculptures for different Kongo-related peoples, see Raoul Lehuard, *Art Bakongo: les centres de style* (Arnouville, France: Arts d'Afrique Noire, 1993), vols. 1 and 2, passim, and *Les Phemba du Mayombe* (Arnouville, France: Arts d'Afrique Noire, 1977), 89–103.

38. Lehuard, *Les Phemba du Mayombe*, 8, 104. See, also, the review of this book by John M. Janzen in *African Arts* 11 (1978), 88–9.

39. Mary Nooter Roberts, "Imagining Women in African Art: Selected Sculptures from Los Angeles Collections," in Mary Nooter Roberts and Alison Saar, *Body Politics: the Female Image in Luba Art and the Sculpture of Alison Saar* (Los Angeles: UCLA Fowler Museum, 2000), 62, 74. For an overview of maternity figures from various African regions and a discussion of individual pieces, see the text and photographs in Roy Sieber and Roslyn Adele Walker, *African Art in the Cycle of Life* (Washington, D.C.: Smithsonian Institution Press, 1987), 28–44.

40. Nooter Roberts, "Imagining Women in African Art," 62.

41. Sylvia Williams in comparing several *pfemba* figures has suggested that they may have been made by different carvers from the same "school": see "A Yombe Maternity: A Case Study," lecture delivered to the Ethnic Arts Council, Los Angeles, Jan. 1984, in *Speeches Given by Sylvia H. Williams, 1935–1996* (Washington, D.C.: Smithsonian Institution, 1996).

42. The ones I have seen in catalogues and in the sizable collection at the Musée Royal de l'Afrique Centrale at Tervuren are about twelve inches tall or smaller.

43. Lehuard, *Les Phemba*, 46–67. Most catalogues on Kongo art include at least one example of a *pfemba* figure with a commentary. See, for example, Kate Ezra and Hans-Joachim Koloss, comment on "Kneeling Women and Child" in *Art of Central Africa: Masterpieces from the Berlin Museum für Völkerkunde*, ed. Koloss (New York: Metropolitan Museum of Art, 1990), 34; Lehuard, *Art Bakongo*, 2:452–597; G. Verswijver et al., eds., *Treasures from the Africa-Museum* (Tervuren, Belgium: Royal Museum for Central Africa, 1995), 59, 289, 290; G. Verwijver et al., eds., *Masterpieces from Central Africa* (Munich: Prestel, 1996), plate 15, and 146–47. A fully gendered analysis of the pieces has not been carried out. For a model of how this might be attempted see Mary Nooter (Roberts), "Luba Arts and Polity: Creating Power in a Central African Kingdom," Ph.D. thesis, Columbia University, 1991, especially 236–81.

44. MacGaffey, *Kongo Political Culture*, 27, 85.

45. Ibid., 207.

46. Janzen's work, *Lemba*, 54–57, has been particularly important in contextualizing historically the fertility cults, using the German sources.

47. Pechuël-Loesche, *Volkskunde,* 385–87; for new and competing *nkisi* dealing with fertility and reproductive problems in women and men, see also Bastian, *Die Deutsche Expedition,* 2:163–64.

48. Marie-Claude Dupré, "Les femmes mukisi des Téké Tsaayi rituel de possession et culte anti-sorcier (République Populaire du Congo)," *Journal de la société des africanistes* 44, no. 1 (1974): 53–69. Wyatt MacGaffey, commenting on a *pfemba* figure, in Verswijver et al., eds., *Masterpieces,* 146, notes that "the more we look into these figures, the more puzzling they turn out to be." Part of the mystery concerns the figure of the child, who at times appears to be lifeless and at other times is nursing. See also, Lehuard, *Les Phemba,* 62–64; Janzen review of *Les Phemba,* 88; Williams, "Speech Given at Edinburgh Festival, August 10, 1984" and "A Yombe Maternity."

49. Lehuard, *Les Phemba,* 45.

50. Ibid., 64–73, 106, 108; Williams, "A Yombe Maternity."

51. Doutreloux, *L'ombre des fétiches,* 63–64.

52. Lehuard,104–108; Janzen, review of *Les Phemba,* 88; Williams, "A Yombe maternity"; Koloss and Ezra, *Art of Central Africa,* 34.

53. Martin, *The External Trade of the Loango Coast,* 24–25; Pechuël-Loesche, *Volkskunde,* 163. For the Kongo kingdom south of the river, see John K. Thornton, "Elite Women in the Kingdom of Kongo: Historical Perspectives on Women's Political Power," *JAH* 47, no. 3 (2006): 437–460.

54. As summed up by Pechuël-Loesche based on seventeenth century sources: *Volkskunde,* 163.

55. Ibid., 163–64.

56. In a manner similar to that discussed by Iris Berger, "Fertility as Power: Spirit Mediums, Priestesses, and the Precolonial State in Interlacustrine East Africa," in *Revealing Prophets: Prophecy in East African History,* ed. David M. Anderson and Douglas H. Johnson (London: James Currey, 1995), 65–82; and, "'Beasts of Burden' Revisited: Interpretations of Women and Gender in Southern African Societies," in Robert W. Harms et al., eds., *Paths towards the Past: African Historical Essays in Honor of Jan Vansina* (Atlanta: African Studies Association Press, 1994), 123–41. In the household economy, see Dorothy L. Hodgson, "Pastoralism, Patriarchy, and History: Changing Gender Relations among Maasai in Tanganyika, 1890–1940," *JAH* 40, no. 1 (1999): 41–65.

57. Vansina, *Paths in the Rainforests,* 59–61, 80, 143–51, 159.

58. MacGaffey, *Kongo Political Culture,* 47, 72.

59. MacGaffey, *Art and Healing of the Bakongo,* 98; interview with Veronique Mbemba, Brazzaville, 17 June 1989.

60. Doutreloux, *L'ombre des fétiches,* 42.

61. Vansina, *Paths in the Rainforest,* 152–53; Balandier, *Sociology of Black Africa,* 332–34.

62. Archives de la Congrégation des Soeurs de Saint-Joseph de Cluny, Paris (ACSSJC), 2A/u.1.6, M. St. Charles to Mère-Générale (MG), Loango, 6 Aug. and 6 Dec. 1888.

63. "Chronique," 3 April 1909, *Le mémorial du Vicariat du Loango* (Loango: Imprimerie de la Mission), vol. 3 (1907–09), 156.

64. Soeur Jerôme, letter from Loango, published in *MC* 46 (1914).

65. Archives Nationales, Centre des Archives d'Outre-Mer, Aix-en-Provence (AOM), AP 668, Père Scao to Minister of Colonies, Paris, 28 Nov. 1916.

66. Dapper, *Naukeurige Beschrijvinge,* 152, 200.

67. Proyart, *Histoire de Loango,* 86–7.

68. Dapper, *Naukeurige Beschrijvinge,* 152.

69. Auguste-Réné Gambou, "Le mariage en Afrique centrale précoloniale: le problème de la nubilité féminine," *CCAH* 7 (1982): 34; Hagenbucher-Sacripanti, *Les fondements spirituels,* 47–8.

70. The main contemporary sources are Bastian, *Die Deutsche Expedition,* 1:151–52, 175–77; Pechuël-Loesche, *Volkskunde,* 113, 159; R. E. Dennett, *Notes on the Folklore of the Fjort (French Congo)* (London: Folk-Lore Society, 1898), 20; *At the Back of the Black Man's Mind* (London: Macmillan, 1906), 38; *Seven Years among the Fjort,* 160, 160n3; Cyrille van Overbergh, *Les Mayombe* (Brussels: A. De Wit, 1907), 237–38; Deleval, "Les tribus Kavati," 109, 172–73; Laman, *The Kongo,* 1:22, 2:27–28; Marichelle, *Tablettes,* 23; Jean-Marc Bel, *Rapport sur une mission au Congo Français, 1906–1907* (Paris: Imprimerie Nationale, 1908), 148–49; See also comments by Dybowski, Voulgré, and Castellani cited in notes 90, 91, and 92 in this chapter.

71. René Dembi, "'Tchicoumbi' ou réclusion des filles nubiles chez le Mayombe," *Liaison* 32 (Feb. 1953), 29–31; J. Pouabou, "Le peuple Vili ou Loango," *Liaison* 58 (July–Aug. 1957), 50–53; A. Poaty, "Rite traditionnel du Tchicoumbi dans la région du Kouilou," 23 Aug. 1984, unpublished, and oral testimonies in "Documents, Soeur Lydia, 1976," in Courtois papers, Pointe-Noire. See Robert Courtois, "Devenir des rites d'initiation de puberté dit *tchikoumbi* face à modernité (ethnies Ki-Vili, Sud-Congo)," M.A. thesis, Université François Rabelais de Tours, 1995; unfortunately, I have not been able to access a copy of this work. See also, Ndjimbe-Tshiende, "'L'initiation 'kumbi' chez les Woyo du Zaire: ébauche d'interprétation philosophique," *Zaire-Afrique* 18e année, 128 (Oct. 1978), 473–84; Coppée-Samuel Bicouncou, "La Tchikoumbi ou Bikoumbi," unpublished, 1954—based on interviews he conducted with informants while acting as a research assistant for Herbert Pepper (in IRD, Pepper Papers); Franque, *Nós, os Cabindas,* 110–14; Obenga, "Naissance et puberté," 19–30. Also, see Doutreloux, *L'ombre des fétiches,* 72–73; Hagenbucher-Sacripanti, *Les fondements spirituels,* 33–46; José Martins Vaz, *No mundo dos Cabindas: estudo etnográfico* (Lisbon: Editorial L.I.A.M., 1970), 210–17.

72. "Le rite de Tschikumbi," Musée Regional 'Ma Loango,' n.d. The pamphlet also uses extracts from the work of Hagenbucher-Sacripanti. Interview with the museum curator, Joseph Kimfoko Madoungou, Diosso and Pointe Noire, 14 and 16 June 2000; and with Frank Hagenbucher-Sacripanti, Paris, 13 April 2005.

73. The circumcision of boys and the initiation rituals are not discussed here. The boys were younger than the *tchikumbi* when they went through initiation rites.

74. The word *tukula* is from the Portuguese and reflects the long presence of the Portuguese and the trade they conducted along the coast from the fifteenth century. The Kikongo word is *kisesi.* For its early history in trade, see Martin, *The External Trade of the Loango Coast,* 35, 39–40, 47, 57.

75. By the mid-twentieth century, the leg rings were no longer worn. There is some confusion about when and for how long the initiate wore them earlier in the century. Marichelle, the missionary, treats the heavy leg rings as part of the "oppression" he observed, and says that she wore them "for several months." Photographs from the period show *tchikumbi* girls wearing the bracelets and rings around their legs, but they do not tell us much since we do not know the context in which the photographs were taken (see, for example, Lehuard, *Art Kongo,* 2:71).

76. Joseph Voulgré, *Le Congo Français: Le Loango et la vallée du Kouilou* (Paris: Librairie Africaine et Coloniale, 1897), 164.

77. Dybowski, *La route du Tchad,* 22–23.

78. Charles Castellani, *Les femmes au Congo* (Paris: Ernest Flammarion, 1898), 67.

79. For examples of songs, see Pepper, *Anthologie*, disc 1, side 1, numbers 18–20, with the text on pages 19–20. Also, Hagenbucher-Sacripanti, *Les fondements spirituels*, 35–46.

80. Gambou, "Le mariage en Afrique centrale précoloniale," 33; Scholastique Dianzinga, "Le décret du 15 juin 1939 et la condition des femmes en Afrique Equatoriale Française," *CCAH* 13 (1993): 57.

81. Ndjimbe-Tshiende, "L'initiation 'kumbi,'" particularly emphasizes the community-building aspects of these events.

82. Marichelle, *Tablettes*, 23.

83. The idiom in Kikongo for death through witchcraft. There is not space here to deal in any detail with the large topic of Kongo cosmology except insofar as to provide a basis for understanding some of the early responses to missionaries. Kongo religious beliefs and practices as well as their interpretations of the whites who arrived on their shores from the fifteenth century have been widely detailed and interpreted in, for example: Richard Gray, *Black Christians and White Missionaries*; Wyatt MacGaffey, *Religion and Society in Central Africa: The Bakongo of Lower Zaire* (Chicago: Chicago University Press, 1986), *Kongo Political Culture*, 27–31, and "The West in Congolese Experience," in *Africa and the West: Intellectual Responses to European Culture*, ed. Philip D. Curtin (Madison: University of Wisconsin Press, 1972), 49–74. Also, Thornton, "The Development of an African Catholic Church," 147–67, and "Religious and ceremonial life in the Kongo and Mbundu areas, 1500–1700," in *Central African and Cultural Transformations in the American Diaspora*, ed. Heywood, 71–90; Doutreloux, *L'ombre des fétiches*, 246–47, 260–62; Kinata, *La formation du clergé indigène*, 18–68; Sigbert Axelson, *Culture Confrontation in the Lower Congo* (Falköping, Sweden: Gummersons, 1970), 289–92; Efraim Andersson, *Churches at the Grass-Roots*, 44–53; and Florence Bernault, "Body, Power, and Sacrifice in Equatorial Africa," *JAH* 47, no. 2 (2006): 207–39.

84. ACSSJC, 2A/u.1.6, M. St. Charles to MG, Loango 9 Aug. 1887.

85. ACSSJC, 2A/u.1.6, M.. St. Charles to MG, Loango 9 Jan. 1888.

86. J. Delcourt, *Au Congo Français, Mgr. Carrie, 1842–1904* (Brazzaville: Maison Libermann, n.d.), 70–1; and BCPSE 15 (1889–91), 551–52: "Communauté du Sacre-Coeur à Loango" (hereafter Loango). For the celebrated regional spirit, Bunzi, see Doutreloux, *L'ombre des fétiches*, 212–19.

87. Richard Gray, *Black Christians and White Missionaries*, 5–6.

88. ACSSJC, 2A/u.1.6, M. St. Charles to MG, Loango, 7 July 1887.

89. *BCSSJC* 156 (March 1925), report from Loango.

90. Proyart, *Histoire de Loango*, 328–51.

91. Andersson, *Churches at the Grass-Roots*, 47. He is writing of his work and study among the Dondo, a Kongo-related subgroup.

92. Based on the monthly letters of the mothers-superior to the mother house in Paris between 1886 and 1900, at which point the Loango mission was closed due to the deaths of the sisters and children, leaving only two sisters and six girls to be transferred up the coast to Mayumba in Gabon. For more details, see, Phyllis M. Martin, "Life and Death, Power and Vulnerability: Everyday Contradictions at the Loango Mission, 1883–1904," *Journal of African Cultural Studies* 1, no. 15 (2002): 61–78.

93. As heard by the writer of the letter. This was the local word for "the" and the local pronunciation of the French word *mères*.

94. ACSSJC, 2A/u.1.6, M. St. Charles to MG, 8 Jan. 1888, 4 Jan. 1889, 26 Jan. and 26 June 1897; 2A/u.1.7, and M. St. Prix to MG, 22 Dec. 1898, 18 June 1899, 7 Feb. and 21 April 1900 (all, Loango); Robert Witwicki, *Marie et l'évangélisation du Congo* (Brazzaville: Centre Chaminade, 1995), 1:328–38.

95. Dennett, *Seven Years among the Fjort*, 44; Witwicki, *Marie et l'évangélisation du Congo*, 1:121.

96. *BCPSE* 17 (1893–96), Loango, 484.

97. Ibid., 591.

98. AGCPSE, 189/B/II, Mgr. Carrie to Mgr. Le Roy, Loango, 25 Jan. 1899; 178/A/IV, Mgr. Carrie to P. Mintier, Loango, May 1898 and Jan. 1899.

99. ACSSJC, 2A/u.1.6, M. St. Charles to MG, Loango, 9 July 1889; 2A u.1.7, M. St. Prix to MG, Loango, 22 Feb. and 17 July 1899, and 7 Feb. 1900.

100. "L'oeuvre des jeunes filles du Loango," *AA* 25 (June 1909): 164.

101. François Gaulme, *Le pays de Cama: un ancien état côtier du Gabon et ses origines* (Paris: Karthala, 1981), 332–33.

102. André Raponda-Walker and Roger Sillans, *Rites et croyances des peuples du Gabon* (Paris: Présence Africaine, 1962), 243–46.

103. Paul B. du Chaillu, *Voyages et aventures dans l'Afrique équatoriale* (Paris: M. Lévy, 1863), 332–34.

2. The First Generation

1. J. Derouet, "Les lunettes de Mère Agnès," *AA* 26 (1910): 278–82.

2. AGCPSE, 177/A/XIII, "Comptes de Saint-Joseph en Linzolo avec l'oeuvre des rachats, 1899–1929." The cost is registered in francs, although the actual transaction was likely in goods.

3. Interview with P. Gaston Schaub, Brazzaville, 15 Oct. 1986; interview with Paul Bouanga, Pointe-Noire, 29 June 2000; Balandier, *Sociology of Black Africa*, 307–13; P. Bonnefond and Jean Lombard, "Notes sur les coutumes Lari," *BIEC* 2, no. 2 (1946), 141–76; Dianzinga, "Les femmes congolaises," 79–83.

4. "Communauté de Saint-Joseph de Linzolo" (hereafter Linzolo), *BCPSE* 15 (1888–91), 587.

5. "Communauté de Saint-Louis de l'Oubangui," *BCPSE* 18 (1896–97), 609.

6. Duchesse d'Uzès, *Le voyage de mon fils au Congo* (Paris: Librairie Plon, 1894), 60.

7. AGCPSE, 177/B/I, Père Kraft to Mgr. Carrie, Linzolo, 2 June 1884, 1 Oct. 1884, 29 Aug. 1885.

8. A theme that appears in various secondary works but that is covered for West-Central Africa in Vellut, "L'économie internationale," 136. Also, Rey, *Colonialisme, néo-colonialisme*.

9. The literature on Kongo slavery is large and can be followed in sources such as: Thornton, *The Kingdom of Kongo*; Susan H. Broadhead, "Slave Wives, Free Sisters: Bakongo Women and Slavery, c. 1700–1850," in *Women and Slavery in Africa*, ed. Robertson and Klein, 160–81; Miller, *Way of Death*, especially, 3–140; and Martin, *The External Trade of the Loango Coast*. Also, slavery is discussed in anthropological accounts with a historical dimension: for example, MacGaffey, *Custom and Government in the Lower Congo*; Georges Dupré, *Les naissances d'une société*, 110–16, 211–14; Balandier, *Sociology of Black Africa*, 337–39; and Sautter, *De l'Atlantique au fleuve Congo*, 1:622–23. Jan Vansina in his study of the Tio kingdom that dominated the plateau regions north of the Pool distinguishes five categories of slavery; see *The Tio Kingdom of the Middle Kongo, 1880–1892* (London: Oxford University Press, 1973), 365–71.

10. Martin, "Celebrating the Ordinary," 298–99; AGCPSE, 177/B/1, P. Sand to Mgr. Carrie, Linzolo, 1 July 1890, 10 Feb. 1891, 20 May 1891.

11. AGCPSE, 177/B/II, P. Bouleuc to Mgr. Carrie, 8 Jan. 1900, Linzolo.

12. Dominique Ngoïe Ngalla, *Les Kongo de la vallée du Niari: origines et migrations XIII–XIXe siécles* (Brazzaville: Les Editions CELMAA, 1982); Balandier, *Sociology of Black Africa*, 331–2; Sautter, *De l'Atlantique au fleuve Congo*, 1, 475–7; Andersson, *Churches at the Grass-Roots*, 15.

13. Georges Dupré, *Les naissances d'une société*, 6, 25–27, 45–47, 96, 101–16, 211–14.

14. Baratier, *Au Congo*, 60–69; Chavannes to De Brazza, Brazzaville, 11 Jan. 1888, in Rabut, *Brazza Commissaire Général*, 311–12; Sautter quoting a 1909 administrative report, *De l'Atlantique au fleuve Congo*, 1:622–23; Vansina, *The Tio Kingdom*, 256–57, 274–77, 365–71, 450–51; Harms, *River of Wealth, River of Sorrow*, 183–84.

15. ACSSJC, 2A/u.1.6, M. St. Charles to MG, Loango, 9 Oct. 1888; *BCPSE* 16 (1891–93), Linzolo, 504.

16. Mgr. Augouard report to Propaganda Fide, Brazzaville, Dec. 1899, published in *BCPSE* 20 (1899–1900), 470–75; François Bontinck, "Le rachat d'enfants esclaves dans les rivières équatoriales (1889–1897)," *Revue africaine de théologie* 11, no. 19 (1987), 51–64; William J. Samarin, *The Black Man's Burden: African Colonial Labor on the Congo and Ubangi Rivers* (Boulder, Colo.: Westview Press, 1989), 88–113, 204–10.

17. R. P. Allaire, *Le R. P. Allaire: missionnaire au Congo d'après ses écrits et sa correspondance* (Paris: Librairie Religieuse H. Oudin, n.d.).

18. Mgr. Carrie to Société Antiesclavagiste, 28 March 1896, quoted in Denise Bouche, *Les villages de liberté en Afrique Noire Française, 1887–1910* (Paris: Mouton, 1968), 190; AOPM, Fond Augouard II/3, Mgr. Augouard to P. Ebenrecht, 10 Oct. 1899.

19. AGCPSE, B708/I, Journal of Père Zimmerman, 57, 58

20. Ibid., 53, 62, 66.

21. Ibid., 58.

22. Castellani, *Les femmes au Congo*, 275. Emphasis in the original.

23. "Communauté du Sacre-Coeur à Brazzaville" (Brazzaville), *BCSSJC* 43 (Sept. 1896), 658, 659.

24. "Orphanage" was an imprecise term used by the missionaries. The children were not necessarily without living parents. It is used here as it was used in the contemporary documents, however.

25. ACSSJC, 2A/u.1.6, M. Saint-Charles to MG, Loango, 10 Dec. 1892, 26 Dec. 1984; AGCPSE, 177/B/II, P. Luec to Mgr. Carrie, Linzolo, 1 Feb. 1898; Prosper P. Augouard, *28 années au Congo* (Poitiers, France: Société française d'Imprimerie et de Librairie, 1905), 422, 449; and *36 années au Congo* (Poitiers, France: Société française d'Imprimerie et de Librairie, 1914), 380.

26. Letter of P. Rémy, *MC* 25 (Sept. 1893): 427.

27. Augouard, *28 années*, 448–49.

28. AGCPSE, 177/B/II, P. Luec to Mgr. Carrie, Linzolo, 17 Jan. 1897.

29. AGCPSE. 177/A/XIII, "Comptes de Saint-Joseph en Linzolo;" also, Olivier Ouassongo, "Les aspects financiers du Vicariat de l'Oubangui," *Mémoire spiritaine* 14 (2001): 113–27.

30. Troy Feay, "Mission to Moralize: Slaves, Africans, and Missionaries in the French Colonies, 1815–1852," Ph.D. thesis, University of Notre Dame, 2003, for example, 4–12, 217–90, 301–303; Alice L. Conklin, *A Mission to Civilize: The Republican Idea of Empire in France and West Africa, 1895–1930* (Stanford, Calif.: Stanford University Press, 1997), especially introduction, and chapters 3 and 4.

31. De Brazza to Minister of Colonies, Libreville, 19 Jan. 1895, in Rabut, *Brazza Commissaire Général*, 153.

32. AGCPSE, 510/B/VI, "Oeuvres de la Sainte-Enfance," Brazzaville, 14 Oct. 1903; 177/B/III, P. Doppler, Linzolo, 12 March 1905; 177/B/VIII, P. Derouet, "Oeuvres de la Sainte-Enfance," Dec. 1906, Dec. 1908; Bouche, *Les villages de liberté en Afrique Noire Française*, 238.

33. Quoted in Jean Ernoult, "L'abbé Charles Maondé (+/-1865–1907): premier prêtre du vicariat apostolique de Loango," *Mémoire spiritaine* 14 (2001), 55. See also, Delcourt, *Au Congo*, 323. Initial church support for the policy stemmed from the 1888 encyclical *In Plurimis* of Pope Leo XIII that was greatly promoted in Europe and Africa by Cardinal Lavigerie, the archbishop of Algiers. For the wider background, see Bouche, *Les villages de liberté*, 177–200.

34. AGCPSE, 177/B/II, P. Bouleuc to P. Schmitt, Linzolo, 8 April 1898

35. AGCPSE, 177/B/II, P. Bouleuc to Mgr. Carrie, Linzolo, 15 April 1898.

36. AGCPSE, 177/B/II, P. Bouleuc to Mgr. Carrie, Linzolo, 31 Aug. 1898; 178/A/IV, Mgr. Carrie to P. Gerrer, Loango, 1 Sept. 1898.

37. AGCPSE, 176/B/IV, "Oeuvres de la Sainte-Enfance," Mgr. Carrie, Loango, 30 June 1904; 177/B/I, P. Huet to Mgr. Carrie, 21 Jan. 1893; 510/B/VI, Mgr. Augouard, "Oeuvres de la Sainte-Enfance," Brazzaville, 14 Oct. 1903 and 15 Oct. 1905; *BCSSJC* 43 (Sept. 1896), Brazzaville, 658. See also chapter 3.

38. AGCPSE, 708/I, Journal of P. Zimmerman, Linzolo, 1904, 57; 510/B/VI, "Oeuvres de la Sainte-Enfance," Mgr. Augouard, Brazzaville, 20 Jan. 1909; *BCPSE* 23 (1905–1906), Bouanza, 122.

39. AGCPSE, 510/B/VI, "Oeuvres de la Sainte-Enfance," Mgr. Augouard, Brazzaville, 31 Dec. 1909; Mgr. Augouard to Propagation de la Foi, Brazzaville, 1 Dec. 1915, 1 Dec. 1916, 1 Nov. 1917.

40. Martin, "Life and Death, Power and Vulnerability," 67–68.

41. See Ernault, *Les spiritains au Congo*, 47–217.

42. AGCPSE, 176/B/IV, "Oeuvres de la Sainte-Enfance," Mgr. Carrie, Loango, 28 Dec. 1900.

43. AGCPSE, 176/B/IV, "Oeuvres de la Sainte-Enfance," Mgr. Carrie, Loango, 1 Nov. 1889.

44. AGCPSE, 176/B/IV, "Oeuvres de la Sainte-Enfance," Mgr. Carrie, Loango, 26 Oct. 1890.

45. Père Gaston Schaub worked at the Linzolo mission from 1925 to 1945. I had two interviews with him, 14 and 15 Oct. 1986. His interview with the Catholic newspaper *La semaine africaine* was featured in a special edition for the centennial celebration of the church in Congo in 1983. See "Les origines de l'église du Congo racontées à l'occasion du centenaire de l'évangelisation du Congo à Linzolo," *La semaine africaine* 1543–45 (Aug. 1983). See also Kinata, *La formation du clergé indigène*, 33n2.

46. AGCPSE, 177/B/I, P. Sand to Mgr. Carrie, Linzolo, 7 Aug. and 30 Sept. 1889; *BCPSE*, 15 (1889–91), Linzolo, 583, and 16 (1889–93), Loango, 495; Delcourt, *Au Congo*, 354.

47. AGCPSE, 177/B/I, P. Sand to Mgr. Carrie, Linzolo, 9 March 1890.

48. AGCPSE, 177/B/I, P. Sand to Mgr. Carrie, Linzolo, 11 May and 11 June 1890.

49. Malone, *Women and Christianity*, 3:197.

50. Deleval, "Les tribus Kavati du Mayombe," 109.

51. *BCPSE* 21 (1901–1902), "Mission de Congo Français: Aperçu Générale," 619.

52. AGCPSE, 177/B/III, P. Doppler to Mgr. Derouet, Linzolo, 14 April 1910.

53. AGCPSE, 513/A/VI/ P. Jaffré to Mgr. Friteau, Linzolo, 30 June 1922.

54. De Dreuille, *La Bouenza*, 55; de Banville, *Kalouka et Zoungoula*, 49–51; P. Carrie, *Coutumier de l'oeuvre des enfants*).

55. *Le mémorial du Congo Français* 1 (Nov. 1891): 382–33; AGCPSE, 177/B/II, P. Luec to Mgr. Carrie, Linzolo 4 Dec. 1891; *BCPSE* 16 (1891–93), Linzolo, 295; de Banville, *Kalouka et Zoungoula*, 51.

56. Based on letters from the sisters to the mother-general in Paris, especially those of the two superiors of the Loango convent, Mère Saint-Charles, 1886–98, and Mère Saint-Prix, 1898–1900: see ACSSJC, 2A/ u.1.6 and 2A/u.1.7.

57. AGCPSE, 177/A/ XIII; see, de Banville, *Kalouka et Zoungoula*, 51, for a copy of the document.

58. AGCPSE, 177/B/II, P. Luec to Mgr. Carrie, Linzolo, 17 Jan. 1897. Jeanne Mpolo was listed as a postulant in 1894. She was probably the girl listed in the mission account book as "Mpollo, jeune fille" in 1891. Since Mpolo was quite a common name she was not necessarily related to Agnès.

59. I first heard of these women when I visited Linzolo in October 1986 and had their importance confirmed by those from the region and by former missionaries: interviews and conversations with Marie-Thérèse Oumba, Bloomington, 15 Aug. 1993; Marie-Antoinette Mouanga, Paris, 11 Nov. 1998; Père Paul Coulon, Chevilly, 20 Sept. 1998; and Père Robert Gévaudan, Pointe-Noire, June 2000.

60. AGCPSE, 177/B/III, P. Doppler to Mgr. Carrie, Linzolo, 7 Nov. 1903 and 20 Jan. 1904.

61. A. Fraisse, "Une viste à Linzolo," *AA* 27 (April 1911): 110; AGCPSE, 512A/I, P. le Gallois to Mgr. Derouet, Linzolo, 13 Aug. 1913; *BCPSE* 27 (1910–13), Linzolo, 66–67, and 28 (1914–18), Linzolo, 165.

62. Derouet, "Les lunettes de Mère Agnès," 278–79.

63. Ibid., 280–81.

64. Ibid., 281.

65. For the Loango mission, Martin, "Life and Death, Power and Vulnerability," 61–65; and for the Zimbabwe experience, Terence Ranger, "Taking Hold of the Land: Holy Places and Pilgrimages in Twentieth Century Zimbabwe," *Past and Present* 117 (1987): 158–94. In general, Ute Luig and Achim von Oppen, eds., "The Making of African Landscapes," in a special issue of *Paideuma* 43 (1997); see especially the introductory essay. Also, Christopher Gray, *Colonial Rule and Crisis in Equatorial Africa: Southern Gabon, 1850–1940* (Rochester, N.Y.: University of Rochester Press, 2002), 136–41; Tamara Giles-Vernick, *Cutting the Vines of the Past: Environmental Histories of the Central African Rain Forest* (Charlottesville: University of Virginia Press, 2002, 97–115, 139–40, 176–79; Vansina, *Paths in the Rainforest*; and Florence Bernault, "The politics of enclosure in colonial and post-colonial Africa," in *A History of Prison and Confinement in Africa*, ed. Bernault (Portsmouth, N.H.: Heinemann, 2003), 5–7, 41n15, 16.

66. Martin, *Leisure and Society in Colonial Brazzaville*, 72–83.

67. *BCPSE* 24 (1906–1908), "Mission du Loango: Aperçu Générale, (1905–07)," Loango, 259; R. P. Alphonse Fraisse, "Informations diverses: Oubanghi," *MC* 42 (1910): 498.

68. P. Grillot, "Dans le Haut-Congo Français," *MC* 46 (1914): 140–41.

69. AGCPSE, B706, *Brazzaville Mission Journal*, 29 May 1908; L. Girard, "Brazzaville," *Bulletin de la Comité de l'Afrique Française: Renseignements Coloniaux (BCAF)* (March 1916), 38–9; Grillot, "Dans le Haut-Congo Français," 140–41.

70. Interview with Bernard Mambeke-Boucher, Brazzaville, 1 Dec. 1986.

71. Quoted in Shula Marks and Richard Rathbone, "The History of the Family in Africa: Introduction," *JAH* 24, no. 2 (1983): 156.

72. Delcourt, *Au Congo Français*, quoted in Witwicki, *Marie et l'évangélisation du Congo*, 1:103–104.

73. I visited this exhibition in June 2000.

74. Testimony of Anne-Marie Kambissi, Loango, 15 Nov. 2000. I am grateful to Père Pierre Wauters for making the text of this interview available to me and for the several conversations we have had in which he shared his fifty years' experience in the Loango region. See also Emile Zimmerman, *Mémoire d'un Congolais, 1896–1941* (Madingou: Imprimerie de la Mission, 1941), 19, 22; and *Le Mémorial de Loango* (1911), 4:303.

75. Kinata, *La formation du clergé indigène*, 24.

76. *BCPSE* 20 (1899–1900), "Mission du Congo Français (1899–1900): Aperçu Générale," 402.

77. Mgr. Carrie, "A ses missionnaires sur l'installation et la direction des catéchistes dans le Vicariat," *Le mémorial du Congo Français* 2 (Dec. 1898): 162–72.

78. *APF,* Congo Français Inférieur, New Series, vol. 97, Five-year report of Mgr. Carrie, Rome, 9 April 1896.

79. I have not been able to ascertain her last name.

80. P. Marichelle, "Une école rurale," *MC* 30 (1898): 584, 607; AGCPSE, 177/A/III, P. Christophe Marichelle, "Sainte-Marie du Kouilou," 25 July 1913; *BCPSE* 18 (1896–97), Loango, 543, and 23 (1905–1906), Loango, 413. Communication from P. Pierre Wauters, 18 Nov. 2000.

81. AGCPSE, 177/A/III P. Marichelle, "Sainte-Marie du Kouilou," 25 July 1913; *BCPSE* 28 (1914–18), Loango, 264.

82. Interview with Veronique Mbemba, Brazzaville, 17 June 1989.

83. AGCPSE, 177/B/VIII, Reports of Père Doppler, Linzolo, 10 March 1903, 7 March 1904, 10 March 1905.

84. Mgr. Carrie, "A ses missionnaires sur l'installation et la direction des catéchistes dans le vicariat," *Le mémorial du Congo Français* 2 (Dec. 1898): 161–72; C. Berthet, "L'oeuvre des catéchistes à Linzolo," *AA* 24 (1908): 203–208, 224–30, 250–54; Sylvain Makosso-Makosso, "Le catéchiste africain aux XIXème et XXème siècles," *CCAH* 12 (1991): 83–86; Kinata, *La formation du clergé indigène*, 184–88.

85. Letter of Père Houchet, Kindamba, in *APSE* (Oct. 1933), 241.

86. "Rapport annuel du Lieutenant-Governeur du Moyen-Congo," 1932, quoted in Kinata, *La formation du clergé indigène*, 216.

87. See Phyllis M. Martin, "Contesting Clothes in Colonial Brazzaville," *JAH* 35, no. 3 (1994): 401–405.

88. Père Doppler, "Un auxiliaire des missionnaires," *AA* 23 (June 1907): 129. This composite picture of the catechist and his wife and their responsibilities is based on missionary accounts, old photographs, and conversations with informants.

89. For example, AGCPSE, 513/A/III, Mgr. Guichard to Governor-General, Brazzaville, 16 Oct. 1926, and Administrator of Moyen-Congo to Mgr. Guichard, Brazzaville, 26 Oct. 1926; AOM, 5D 128, Mgr. Guichard to Lieutenant-Governor, Moyen-Congo, 9 Aug. 1933; 5D 139, Governor-General to the Chief Administrator of Moyen-Congo, 28 April and 4 Nov. 1934; Mgr. Guichard to Governor-General, 1 May 1934.

90. Ranger, "Taking Hold of the Land."

91. Père Doppler, *BCPSE* 23 (1905–1906), Linzolo, 124.

92. Ibid., 124–25.

93. Derouet, "Les lunettes de Mère Agnès," 278, 282.

94. AGCPSE, 276/A/V, Annual reports of the Vicariat Apostolique de Loango, 1919–48, and Mgr. Friteau to Propaganda Fide, Loango, 1 Nov. 1927.

95. AGCPSE, 513/B/VII, Annual Reports, Vicariat Apostolique de Brazzaville, 1924–36.

3. Means of Transition

1. ACSSJC, 2B/ u.2.1, M. Jerôme to MG, Loango, 19 Oct. 1914, and 4 May 1915.

2. P. Fraisse, "Une visite à Linzolo," *AA* 27 (May 1911): 138.

3. AGCPSE, 512/A/I, Report of P. Rémy, Brazzaville, 20 April 1920.

4. AGCPSE, 177/A/XIII, "Comptes de S. Joseph en Linzolo."

5. Quoted in Ernoult, *Les spiritains au Congo*, 227.

6. *BCPSE* 30 (1921–22), 821; P. Bonnefont, "La formation de la famille chrétienne en pays Bacongo," *AA* 40 (July–Aug. 1924): 111; *ASSJC* 22 (1929), Brazzaville, 27; *BCSSJC* 187 (Nov. 1928–Aug. 1933), Brazzaville, 538.

7. The phrase is taken from the title of the book by Kristin Mann on marriage in Lagos, although the circumstances were quite different: see *Marrying Well: Marriage, Status and Social Change among Educated Elite in Colonial Lagos* (Cambridge: Cambridge University Press, 1985).

8. Ranger, "New Approaches to the History of Mission Christianity," 187.

9. Richard Roberts, "Representation, Structure, and Agency: Divorce in the French Soudan during the Early Twentieth Century," *JAH* 40, no. 3 (1999): 390–93.

10. Kinata, *Les ethnochefferies dans le Bas-Congo français*; Florence Bernault, *Démocraties ambiguës en Afrique Centrale: Congo-Brazzaville, Gabon: 1940–1965* (Paris: Karthala, 1996).

11. Gilles Sautter, "Notes sur la construction du chemin de fer Congo-Océan (1921–1934)," *CEA* 7 (1967): 259–56; report from the mission station at Nséssé, 1926, quoted in Ernoult, *Les spiritains au Congo*, 203; Svenska Missionsförbundet, Riksarchivet (Stockholm), F.1., Dagbök, Brazzaville, 21 Jan. 1917; Martin, *Leisure and Society in Colonial Brazzaville*, 37–39;

12. Raymond Bafouetela, "Le travail sous la période coloniale au Congo (1897–1945)," *CCAH* 6 (1981): 85, 91; Rey, *Colonialisme, neo-colonialisme*, 373; Marcel Homet, *Congo: terre de souffrances* (Paris: Editions Montaigne, 1934), 59–70, 95–101.

13. AGCPSE, 513/A/IV, Administrator Marchand to Mgr. Guichard, Brazzaville, 9 Jan. 1924.

14. ACSSJC, 2B/u.2.1, M. Jerôme to MG, Loango, 8 Sept. and 10 Nov. 1923; Ernoult, *Les spiritains au Congo*, 203, 241–42, 266, 271, 282–7, 332–4; Vennetier, *Pointe-Noire et la façade maritime*, 132–57, 261–78.

15. Martin, *Leisure and Society in Colonial Brazzaville*, 28–30, 45–46; Vennetier, *Pointe-Noire et la façade maritime*, 146; S. Christiane Masseguin, "Pointe-Noire," *Pentecôte* 9 (May–June, 1939), 10.

16. AGCPSE, 177/B/I, P. Huet to Mgr. Carrie, Linzolo, 12 April 1893.

17. AGCPSE, 513/A/V, "Dispenses matrimoniales: station de Linzolo, 1918–1936."

18. For some discussion of relationships, permissible marriage patterns, and the difficulty of sorting them out, see, for example, MacGaffey, *Custom and Government*, 144–47; Janzen, *Lemba*, 40–42; Balandier, *Sociology of Black Africa*, 302–13, 367; Georges Dupré, *Les naissances d'une société*, 204–13, 218–24. For canon law on age and consanguinity in the 1918 Marriage Code, see Joseph M. O'Hara, *The Laws of Marriage Simply Explained according to the New Code* (Philadelphia: Peter Reilly, 1918), 54–59.

19. AGCPSE, 513/A/V, dispensation request from Jean Baptiste Nkondia and Rosalie Ndembo to P. Rémy, Brazzaville, May 1917.

20. AGCPSE, 513/A/V, dispensation request from Silvestre Nkodi and Françoise Nzombe granted by P. le Duc, Brazzaville, 6 Jan. 1937.

21. AGCPSE, 513/A/V, dispensation request from Prosper Mounkala and Martine Thérèse Oumba adjudicated by Mgr. Guichard, Brazzaville, 30 Sept. 1926.

22. O'Hara, *The Laws of Marriage,* 48.

23. AGCPSE, 177/B/II, P. Luec to Mgr. Carrie, Linzolo, 15 March 1897.

24. AGCPSE, 512/A/III, correspondence relating to the case, 1–9 June 1915.

25. AGCPSE, 512/A/III, P. Kranitz to Mgr. Guichard, Linzolo, 1 June 1927.

26. AGCPSE, 513/A/V, dispensation request from Jean Souamounou and Thérèse Matala to P. Rémy , Brazzaville, 18 Aug. 1918.

27. AGCPSE, 513/A/V, dispensation request from P. Jaffré on behalf of Marguerite Nkassa granted by Mgr. Augouard, Brazzaville, 11 Oct. 1918.

28. AGCPSE, 513/A/V, dispensation request from P. Jaffré on behalf of Henriette Nlolo granted by P. Rémy, Brazzaville, 17 Sept. 1920.

29. AGCPSE, 513/A/V, dispensation request from P. Kranitz on behalf of Catherine granted by Mgr. Guichard, Brazzaville, 21 Jan. 1925.

30. AGCPSE, 513/A/V, dispensation request from P. Kranitz on behalf of Martha Louvoudou, Linzolo, 30 Dec. 1930.

31. Conversations with retired missionaries at Chevilly, June 2003.

32. AGCPSE, 513/A/I, "Causes Matrimoniales: Dispenses." The date of the document is not given, but it is signed by Monseigneur Guichard and seems to come from the early part of his tenure as vicar apostolic in Brazzaville (1922–36).

33. Over different issues but also relating to control of women, see, Nancy Rose Hunt, "Noise over Camouflaged Polygamy, Colonial Morality Taxation, and a Woman-Naming Crisis in Belgian Africa," *JAH* 32, no. 3 (1991): 471–94.

34. *JOAEF,* 15 Oct. 1910, 528.

35. Conklin, *A Mission to Civilize,* 87–88, 280n40, 281n43.

36. Georges Bruel, *La France Equatoriale Africaine* (Paris: Larose, 1935), 444.

37. AGCPSE, 276/A/VIII, Report of Mgr. Friteau, "Le mariage et la famille," Loango, Nov. 1937; Mgr. Guichard, "Oeuvres de la Sainte-Enfance," 25 Sept. 1933.

38. Antoine-Marie Aïssi, "Le système juridictionnel au service de l'ordre colonial: essence de la *justice indigène, CCAH* 2 (1978): 29–38; André Even, "Quelques coutumes des tribus badondos et bassoundis," *BSRC* 13 (1931): 18–19; Catherine Coquery-Vidrovitch, *African Women: A Modern History* (Boulder, Colo.: Westview Press, 1997), 64–5. Basic research on women's legal position as it was implemented in the gendered world of colonial legal enforcement has not been carried out for colonial Congo, however.

39. AOM, 5D 302, in particular contains an exchange of letters between the church and state authorities in the 1920s. Correspondence also exists in the Spiritan archives, for example: AGCPSE, 513/A/III, Mgr. Guichard to Gov.-Gen., Brazzaville, 16 Oct. 1926; 513/A/IV, correspondence between the administrator of Boko subdivision and the director of the mission at Linzolo, Sept. 1923; Marchand to Mgr. Guichard, Brazzaville, 9 Jan. 1924; Chief administrator of the Circumscription of Bas-Congo to the Lieut.-Gov. of Moyen Congo, Kinkala, 6 Jan. 1932.

40. AOM, 4(2) D53, Annual report of the Lieut.-Gov. of Moyen-Congo, 1932. See Kinata, *La formation du clergé indigène,* 211–17. Alice Conklin has drawn attention to the inequalities experienced by French women at home and the colonial impact: "French refusal to intervene in civil customs affecting women generally seems to have persisted throughout the colonial period. It is presumably linked to a similar refusal in the metropole to grant women the same rights as men under the Third Republic" (Conklin, *A Mission to Civilize,* 281n43). See also, Dianzinga, "Le décret du 15 juin 1939," 55–69.

41. Dianzinga, "Le décret du 15 juin 1939," 56–57, 60.

42. Feay, "Mission to Moralize," 4–12, 217–90, 301–303.

43. AGCPSE, 177/A/III, P. Marichelle, "Sainte-Marie du Kouilou," 25 July 1913.

44. Barbara Cooper, *Marriage in Maradi: Gender and Culture in a Hausa Society in Niger, 1900–1989* (Portsmouth, N.H.: Heinemann, 1997), 21, 34–35; also, Henrietta L. Moore and Megan Vaughan, *Cutting Down Trees: Gender, Nutrition, and Agricultural Change in the Northern Province of Zambia, 1890–1990* (Portsmouth, N.H.: Heinemann, 1994), 140–77, and Rachel Jean-Baptiste, "Une ville libre? Marriage, Divorce, and Sexuality in Colonial Libreville, Gabon, 1849–1960," Ph.D. thesis, Stanford University 2005.

45. For example, AOM, AP 2286, "Rapport politique et social, AEF, 1939–46," Directeur des Affaires Politique; 5D 36, M. Bayardelle, Directeur des Affaires Politiques, circular memo. to administrators in Moyen-Congo, 5 Feb. 1946.

46. See Introduction.

47. AGCPSE, 278/A/III, Report of P. Jaffré, Brazzaville, 1926–31.

48. AGCPSE, 513/A/VI, P. Kranitz, annual reports, Linzolo, 1 July 1926, 1 July 1927; and 512/A/VI, 19 July 1928.

49. Interview with Anne Ngondjo, Brazzaville, 15 June 1989. Mfoa was the name of the trading village and market at the Pool where the French established the administrative post that became Brazzaville. The town was still referred to in this way by those who lived in the Pool region during the colonial period. See Martin, *Leisure and Society in Colonial Brazzaville,* 16–18, 21.

50. Interview with Antoine Boudzoumou, Brazzaville, 16 Nov. 1986. A similar comment was made in a conversation with Maya Alden, a Swedish missionary of the Evangelical Church who arrived in Brazzaville with her husband in 1937 (10 Dec. 1986).

51. Martin, *Leisure and Society in Colonial Brazzaville,* 58–60; Jean-Claude Ganga, *Combats pour un sport africain* (Paris: L'Harmattan, 1979), 51.

52. The record on health was somewhat better. Influenced by the need for labor and a wide tax base and alarm at high mortality rates and low fertility, the colonial government allocated more funds to counter the sleeping sickness epidemic, for example. See Ralph A. Austen and Rita Headrick, "Equatorial Africa under Colonial Rule," in *History of Central Africa,* ed. David Birmingham and Phyllis M. Martin (Harlow, UK: Longman, 1983), 2:63.

53. Ibid., 70.

54. Girard, "Brazzaville," 34, 40; David E. Gardinier, "Schooling in the States of Equatorial Africa," *CJAS* 5, no. 3 (1974), 519; and "Education in French Equatorial Africa, 1842–1945," in *Proceedings of the Third Annual Meeting of the French Colonial Historical Society* (Lanham, Md.: University Press of America), 121–37.

55. Georges Hardy, "L'enseignement aux indigènes dans les possessions françaises d'Afrique," in *L'enseignement aux indigènes* (Brussels: Institut Colonial International, 1931), 390.

56. AOM, 5D27, "AEF: Gouvernement Général: Inspection de l'Enseignement, 1928–29."

57. AOM, 63/B41, Fond Guernot, Report of Governor-General Reste, Brazzaville, 12 July 1936.

58. Elikia M'Bokolo, "Forces sociales et idéologies dans la décolonisation de l'AEF," *JAH* 22, no. 3 (1981): 398.

59. Rabut, *Brazza Commissaire Général,* 83, 138, 148–50, 153; AOM, AP667(2), report from Mgr. Augouard to Minister of Colonies, Paris, 16 Sept. 1919; Ouassongo, "Les aspects financiers du Vicariat de l'Oubangui," 224. The 1905 anti-clerical laws that prohibited religious congregations from teaching in French schools were not applied to equatorial Africa.

60. AOM, AP 667(2), Report of Mgr. Augouard to Minister of Colonies, Paris, 16 Sept. 1919.

61. AOM, 5D27, Annual report on schools in Moyen-Congo, 3 July 1934.

62. Joseph-François Reste, *Action politique, économique et sociale en Afrique Equatoriale Française* (Brazzaville: Imprimerie Officielle, 1938), 171.

63. Mann, *Marrying Well*, 78. The beginning of a small African professional class in AEF was signaled by the first medical students, who began their courses in 1937, but these men did not receive the same training or privilege as Europeans according to the testimony of the first AEF physician. See Austen and Headrick, "Equatorial Africa under Colonial Rule," 75–76, 78.

64. See Martin, *Leisure and Society in Colonial Brazzaville*.

65. Interview with Paul Bouanga, Pointe-Noire, 29 June 2000, and Augustine Bouanga, Pointe-Noire, 15 June 2000.

66. See, for example, the sociological study of Marcel Soret, *Démographie et problèmes urbains en AEF: Poto-Poto-Bacongo-Dolisie* (Montpellier: Imprimerie Chanté, 1954), 26.

67. Ganga, *Combats pour un sport africain*, 46–47.

68. Ibid., 50–51.

69. For tensions between the sisters and the priests on various topics including education, see chapter 4.

70. For a comparable situation, see Deborah Gaitskell, "At home with hegemony? Coercion and consent in the education of African girls for domesticity in South Africa before 1910," in *Contesting Colonial Hegemony*, ed. Engels and Marks, 113.

71. Christiane Masseguin, *A l'ombre des palmes: l'oeuvre familiale et missionnaire des Soeurs de Saint-Esprit* (Paris: Editions Spes, 1942), 58.

72. Ibid., 59.

73. Interview with Joséphine Peka, and Anne Ngondjo, Brazzaville, 15 June 1989.

74. Interview with Martin Balossa, Brazzaville, 17 June 1989; interview with Joséphine Peka, Brazzaville, 15 June 1989; ACSSJC, Congo E, Lettres, M. Alphonse to MG, Brazzaville, 5 Sept. 1938.

75. S. Maria Viers, "Au travail," *Pentecôte* 4 (March–April 1935): 8, and "Loango-Mayumba: la moisson blanchit," *Pentecôte* 5 (March–April 1936): 11.

76. ACSSJC, 2B/u.7.2, "Compte rendu de la visite de règle par S. Anne du Précieux Sang, Communauté du Sacre-Coeur à Brazzaville," c. 1937.

77. See also chapter 5.

78. Allman, "Making Mothers," 23–47; and, Anne Hugon, "La redéfinition de la maternité en Gold Coast des années 1920 aux années 1950: projet colonial et réalités locales," *Histoire des femmes en situation coloniale*, ed. Hugon, 145–71, and "L'historiographie de la maternité," 212–29.

79. Teresa A. Barnes, *"We Women Worked So Hard": Gender, Urbanization and Social Reproduction in Colonial Harare, Zimbabwe, 1930–1956* (Portsmouth, N.H.: Heinemann, 1999), 101. Also, the essays in Hansen, ed., *African Encounters with Domesticity*; for sewing, Kathleen Sheldon, "'I Studied with the Nuns, Learning To Make Blouses: Gender Ideology and Colonial Education in Mozambique," *IJAHS* 31, no. 3 (1998): 595–625; Samuel S. Thomas, "Transforming the Gospel of Domesticity: Luhya girls and the Friends Africa Mission, 1917–1926," *African Studies Review* 43, no. 2 (2000): 1–27; and Hunt, *A Colonial Lexicon of Birth Ritual, Medicalization, and Mobility in the Congo*.

80. See Phyllis M. Martin, "Power, Cloth, and Currency on the Loango Coast," *African Economic History* 15 (1986), 1–12; and "Contesting Clothes in Colonial Brazzaville."

81. AFMM, Rapports annuels de Belgique et de Congo, 12e série, Lékéti, 1921–40, and AGCPSE 512/B/VI, Letters from M. Marie Baudoin to Mgr. Guichard, Lékéti, 1926–35.

82. For this aspect of women's work, see the rich ethnographic data in Dianzinga, "Les femmes congolaises," 61–70.

83. Carrie, *Coutumier de l'oeuvre des enfants,* 43–44.

84. Based on reports by the Sisters of Saint Joseph of Cluny on their schools in Brazzaville, Loango, and Kindamba, c. 1900–1930; also, Augouard, *36 années,* 281–82.

85. Interview with Martin Balossa, Brazzaville, 17 June 1989.

86. ACSSJC, Congo E, Lettres, M. Alphonse to MG, Brazzaville, 4 July 1932.

87. Andrée Blouin, *My Country, Africa: Autobiography of the Black Pasionaria* (New York: Praeger, 1983), 34.

88. Ibid., 67, 84, 119, 123, 127.

89. AGCPSE, 513/B/V, P. Le Duc to PF, Annual Report, Brazzaville, 28 Aug. 1935; 7/A/VII, Report of Mgr. Biéchy, Brazzaville, 3 Sept. 1937; BCSSJC 202 (Dec. 1938), Brazzaville, 581–82.

90. Blouin, *My Country, Africa,* 115.

91. See Bockie, *Death and the Invisible World,* 23–31.

92. Martin, "Celebrating the Ordinary," 291–93, 305–307.

93. R. P. Jaffré, "De Plougastel au Congo," *ASSJC* 23 (1930): 1–3.

94. Martin, "Contesting Clothes in Colonial Brazzaville"; Jean Allman, ed., *Fashioning Africa: Power and the Politics of Dress* (Bloomington: Indiana University Press, 2004).

95. Interviews conducted in Brazzaville in 1989.

96. ACSSJC, Congo D, Lettres, M. Marie to MG, Brazzaville, 24 May 1921.

97. Interview with Veronique Mbemba, Brazzaville, 15 Dec. 1986.

98. Interview with Adèle Nsongolo, Brazzaville, 16 June 1989.

99. Interview with Adèle Koudayou, Brazzaville, 14 June 1989.

100. Interview with S. Clothilde, Brazzaville, 10 Nov. 1986. The documentation on this point is especially good for the Urban School in Brazzaville: ANB, GG479(1), Attendance lists, 1913; Principal's report, 31 March 1914; and, GG481, Principal of the Urban School to Lieutenant-Governor of Moyen-Congo, 31 Dec. 1913, and Report of the Urban School, 1917.

101. ACSSJC, 2B/u.2.1, S. Joseph to MG, Loango, 7 Jan. and 12 Sept. 1935.

102. See chapter 1 above: also, Marie-Claude Dupré, "Les femmes mukisi des Tèkè Tsayi rituel de possession et culte anti-sorcier"; Laman, *The Kongo,* 2:85–100; Ragnar Widman, *The Niombo Cult among the Babwende* (Stockholm: Etnografiska Museet, 1967), 19–20.

103. Homet, *Congo,* 189; Sinda, *Le messianisme congolais et ses incidences politiques*; Kinata, *La formation du clergé indigène,* 217–19; Martin, *Leisure and Society,* 59–60, 68–69; interview with S. Clothilde, 10 Nov. 1986; ACSSJC, Congo E, Lettres, M. Alphonse to MG, Brazzaville, 29 May 1934.

104. The documents concerning the mayor's inquiry and the official report are in AOM, 5D/118, Report of the Mayor of Brazzaville to Administrator, Moyen-Congo, Brazzaville, 14 May 1934.

105. See chapter 6; also, David Blackbourn, "The Catholic Church in Europe since the French Revolution. A Review Article," *Comparative Studies in Society and History* 33, no. 4 (1991): 785.

106. Martin, *Leisure and Society in Colonial Brazzaville,* 128–30, 140–41.

107. Bastille Day in France.

108. Based on interviews conducted in Brazzaville in 1986 and 1989 while researching *Leisure and Society in Colonial Brazzaville.* See in that book 24, 34–35, 129.

109. Interview with Adèle Nsongolo, Brazzaville, 16 June 1989.

110. On Protestant missionary views on dancing, see Andersson, *Churches at the Grass-Roots* 177–78. For Catholic views, see J. Van Wing, "Les danses Bakongo," *Congo: Revue générale de la Colonie Belge* 2, no. 2 (July 1937): 121–28; and Jean Cuvelier, "Les missions catholiques en face des danses des Bakongo," *Africanae fraternae ephemerides romanae* (1939): 143–76.

111. AOM, 4(2)D65, "Compte rendu de M. Brouillet, Adjoint Principal des Services Civiles à Monsieur l'Administrateur Maire au sujet des dépositions contre M. Le Reverend Père Moyssan à l'occasion des fêtes du 14 juillet," 28 July 1934. Deposition of Augustine Mbonga.

112. AOM, 4(2)D65, Deposition of Emilie. Also, depositions of Albertine, and Hélène Koye, 28 July 1934.

113. AOM, 4(2)D65, Depositions of Augustine Mbonga and Antoinette Akolombi, 28 July 1934.

114. AOM, 4(2)D65, Mayor of Brazzaville to Administrator in Chief, Moyen-Congo, 3 Aug. 1934.

115. AOM, 4(2)D65, Administrator of Civil Affairs, Moyen-Congo, to the Director of Political Affairs, Governor-General's Office, 8 Aug. 1934.

116. Linda L. Clark, "The Primary Education of French Girls: Pedagogical Prescriptions and Social Realities, 1880–1940," *History of Education Quarterly* 21, no. 3 (1981): 411–28.

117. Archives, Musée Royale d'Afrique Centrale, Ethnographic Division, Administrative Reports, E. Chapeaux, "Dossier District Bas-Congo: étude des coutumes indigènes du groupement de Vili," c. 1933; also, Deleval, "Les tribus Kavati du Mayombe," 255, 256.

118. Interview with Augustine Bouanga, Pointe-Noire, 15 June 2000

119. Interview with Paul Bouanga, Pointe-Noire, 29 June 2000.

120. ACSSJC, 2B/u.2.1, S. Joseph to MG, Loango, 20 Oct. 1935; also, the testimony of four Vili women given confidentially and collected in 1976. See chapter 5.

121. Ephraim Andersson, *Messianic Popular Movements in the Lower Congo* (Uppsala, Sweden: Almquist and Wiksells Boktryekeri AB, 1958), 11.

4. Religious Sisters and Mothers

1. See map 2.

2. Burke, *These Catholic Sisters Are All Mamas!* 23–25.

3. The comment of Marie-Thérèse Avemeka, interviewed in Paris, 24 Nov. 1998.

4. Reintegration with family and society was an important consideration for those who left religious orders. See, for example, Monica Baldwin, *I Leapt over the Wall: Contrast and Impressions after Twenty-Eight Years in a Convent* (New York: Rinehart, 1950); Deborah Larsen, *The Tulip and the Pope* (New York: Alfred A. Knopf, 2005); and the fictional account of a sister-nurse in Belgian Congo by Kathryn Hulme, *The Nun's Story* (New York: Little, Bown, 1956), made famous in film.

5. I have written more about these letters and the personal ones Mère Marie's family generously allowed me to consult in Martin, "Celebrating the Ordinary."

6. The monthly reports from the mothers-superior of other communities in the lower Congo to Paris are also reasonably complete.

7. The sources for her life are in the notes to the introduction.

8. At the Brazzaville community, there were two mothers-superior who were in the position for long periods of time: Mère Marie Dédie (1892–1931) and Mère Marie Budinger (1945–74).

9. ACSSJC, 2A/u.1.3, "Croquis de la Maison à Loango montrant le Règlement de la Communauté," n.d., c. 1892; 2A/u.1.6, M. St Charles to MG, Loango, 2 Feb. 1887, 8 May 1889; 2B/u.2.4, M. Marie to MG, Brazzaville, 8 June 1896. The Saint Joseph sisters were primarily a teaching order and sent qualified nurses to Congo only in the 1930s. Their "dispensaries" treated minor ailments and proved to be a means of attracting candidates for baptism.

10. See also Colleen McDannell, *Material Christianity: Religion and Popular Culture in America* (New Haven, Conn.: Yale University Press, 1995); also, Cynthia Radding, *Wandering Peoples: Colonialism, Ethnic Spaces, and Ecological Frontiers in Northwestern Mexico, 1700–1850* (Durham, N.C.: Duke University Press, 1997).

11. Martin, "Celebrating the Ordinary," 291–93.

12. Blackbourn, "The Catholic Church in Europe since the French Revolution," 783; Gibson, *Social History of French Catholicism*, 251–53.

13. Witwicki, *Marie et l'évangélisation du Congo*, 1:88.

14. MacGaffey, *Religion and Society in Central Africa*, 198–200.

15. Richard Gray, *Black Missionaries and White Christians*, 102–104; Doutreloux, *L'ombre des fétiches*, 261.

16. Monseigneur Carrie admonished those in his vicariate "to put themselves energetically to language learning" and thus avoid being "useless missionaries." Quoted in Ernoult, *Les spiritains au Congo*, 425; for language manuals and religious texts translated into various Congolese languages by priests, 426–47. For girls' education in French parochial schools, see, Curtis, *Educating the Faithful*, 141, and passim. Other information gleaned through conversations with the Cluny sisters and Spiritan fathers.

17. ACSSJC, Congo B, Lettres, S. Xavier to MG, Brazzaville, 16 Oct. 1892.

18. Witwicki, *Marie et l'évangélisation du Congo*, 1:421.

19. ACSSJC, 2A/u.1.6, M. St Charles to MG, Loango, 10 Oct. 1887, 9 Oct. 1888, 28 Jan. 1891; 2A/u.2.4, M. Marie to MG, Brazzaville, 15 Jan. 1894, 8 June 1896, 1 Aug. 1896; BCSSJC 114 (June 1914), Loango, 441.

20. *APF*, Congo Français Inférieur, New Series, 238, *Catéchisme de la doctrine chrétienne á l'usage du vicariat du Congo Français*, Loango, 1894.

21. ACSSJC, 2A/u.1.6, M. St. Charles to MG, Loango, 8 April 1889. "Fiotes" was a word commonly used by Europeans to describe the inhabitants of the coastal regions.

22. ACSSJC, 2A/u,1,6, M. St. Charles to MG, Loango, 8 May 1889.

23. *BCSSJC* 57 (March, 1900), Brazzaville, 752.

24. Interview with Père Gaston Schaub, who worked at Linzolo, 1925–45, Brazzaville, 14 and 15 Oct. 1986.

25. Visit of author to Linzolo, Oct. 1986.

26. See Martin, *Leisure and Society in Colonial Brazzaville*, especially chapter 3.

27. ACSSJC, 2A/u.2.4, M. Marie to MG, Brazzaville, 5 Nov. 1892.

28. ACSSJC, 2A/u.1.2, "Règlement," Loango, 2 Feb. 1892.

29. *BCSSJC* 84 (Dec. 1906), Brazzaville, 481–82.

30. Interview with Mère Emilie, Moungali, 13 June 1989. She was not a sister; this was the name by which she asked to be identified.

31. Conversations with former students of the sisters' schools, Brazzaville, 1986 and 1989.

32. I did not, however, meet anyone with such negative experiences as those recorded by Andrée Blouin, who in her autobiography, entitled a chapter on her days in the sisters' boarding school for *métisses* girls, "Years of Misery, A Week of Happiness" (when her mother visited

her). One informant who had attended the boarding school at the same time suggested that Blouin, who went on to be a fervent African nationalist, a feminist, and chief of protocol in the government of Patrice Lumumba, had her own radical agenda and that her book was as much an attack on the Catholic church as it was on the sisters. See Blouin, *My Country Africa,* 226–75; also, Allison Drew, "Andrée Blouin and Pan-African Nationalism in Guinea and the Congo," in *Pan-African Biography,* ed. Robert A. Hill (Los Angeles: UCLA African Studies Center and Crossroads Press, 1987), 209–17.

33. ACSSJC, 2A/u.2.4, M. Marie to MG, Brazzaville, 5 Oct. 1892.

34. Colonel Moll, *Une âme de colonial: lettres du Lieutenant-Colonel Moll* (Paris: Emile-Paul, 1912), 14.

35. ACSSJC, 2A/u.1.4, Mgr. Carrie to MG, Loango, 13 Nov. 1898; also, J. Marthey, "L'oeuvre missionnaire pour la population féminine au Congo," *Revue française d'histoire d'outre-mer* 75 (July 1988): 80, and note 1.

36. AOPM, G85, Mgr. Girod, "Etat statistique de la mission à Loango," 19 Nov. 1918.

37. *BCSSJC* 43 (Sept. 1896), Brazzaville, 653.

38. It is not entirely clear why sisters were in short supply. It may be that in an expanding missionary congregation choices had to be made as to where sisters should be sent worldwide and that Congo was not a top priority. Certainly, Loango was so costly in terms of life and the priests so damning in their assessment of the quality of the sisters and their work that it may have dissuaded the mother-general from sending further reinforcements. The French anti-clerical laws and the prevailing climate also took their toll on the number of recruits for the congregation. In answer to a request from the Holy Ghost Fathers for sisters to open a new mission in upper Congo, the Cluny sisters declined, the superior-general writing: "We have lost a great number and young ones for some time. Our contingent of novices is weak. The women graduating are hardly enough to fill the places at existing missions."(AGCPSE, 510/A/III, S. Marie Sainte-Lutgarde to M. l'Abbé, Paris 1 March 1909; Augouard, *36 années,* 228). The fathers then turned to the Franciscan Missionaries of Mary, who sent the necessary sisters. (See map 2.) At Brazzaville, as demands by elites for convent-trained wives increased more sisters were sent in the 1920s and after.

39. ACSSJC, 2A/u.1.6, M. St Charles, to MG, Loango, 19 March 1892, and 13 July 1898; 2A/ u.1.4, P. Derouet to MG, Loango, 24 Aug. 1898.

40. ACSSJC, 2B/u.2.4, M. Marie to MG, 13 July 1898, and 25 Oct. 1901.

41. ACSSJC, 2A/u.1.6, M. St Charles to MG, 27 Dec. 1890; 2A/u.1.7, M. St Prix, to MG, 4 Dec. 1898.

42. Monseigneur Carrie, *Oeuvre des Soeurs de Saint-Joseph de Cluny dans la Mission du Congo Français* (Loango: Imprimerie de la Mission, 1897).

43. Based on statistics given in ACSSJC, "Etat de Personnel, Congo Français."

44. ACSSJC, 2A/u.2.4, M. Marie to MG, 14 April 1893 and 31 March 1895; S. Stanislas de Christ to M. Marie, Brazzaville, 11 Sept. 1899.

45. ACSSJC, 2A/u.1.6, M. St. Charles to MG, Loango, 8 May and 15 Nov 1889.

46. ACSSJC, Congo C, Lettres, M. Marie to MG, Brazzaville, 25 June 1902; Congo D, Lettres, M. Marie to MG, Brazzaville, 16 Jan. 1909 and S. Claire to MG, 25 June 1909; Chanoine Augouard, *La vie inconnue de Monseigneur Augouard* (Evreux: M. Poussin, 1934), 177, 341.

47. ACSSJC, Congo C, Lettres, M. Marie to MG, 14 March 1904. The emphasis and exclamation mark are in the original. "Cathedral" is the word given for the mission church in the French.

48. Stone, "Anticlericals and *Bonnes Soeurs*," 103–28.

49. ACSSJC, 2A/u.2.4, M. Marie to MG, Brazzaville, 28 Nov. 1893, 14 March 1904.

50. ACSSJC, 2A/u.2.4, M. Marie to MG, Brazzaville, 14 July 1893, 8 Oct. 1902, 14 Jan 1903.

51. ACSSJC, 2A/u.2.4, M. Marie to MG, Brazzaville, 28 Feb. 1900.

52. Julia Clancy-Smith and Frances Gouda, "Introduction," in *Domesticating the Empire,* ed. Clancy-Smith and Gouda, 8, 9–11; Martin, "Celebrating the Ordinary," 290, 299–304.

53. Baratier, *Au Congo,* 120.

54. ACSSJC, 2A/u.2.4, M. Marie to MG, Brazzaville,14 March 1893, 14 July 1893, 18 Jan. 1899, 14 March 1900, 10 Sept. 1900, 25 Oct. 1901; Coquery-Vidrovitch, *Le Congo,* 60.

55. BCSSJC, 114 (1914), Brazzaville, 437; Gabrielle M. Vassal, *Life in French Congo* (London: T. Fisher Unwin, 1925), 93–94.

56. ACSSJC, 2A/u.2.4, M. Marie to MG, Brazzaville, 28 Feb. 1900.

57. Administrator De Bonchamps to Commissioner-General of French Congo, "Rapport sur la Région de Brazzaville," Libreville, 1 May 1900, unpublished document. Many of these confrontations were over subsidies for the mission schools, which the colonial administration had agreed to in lieu of offering education itself but which were reduced or stopped altogether when anti-clericals came to power.

58. ACSSJC, 2A/u.2.4, M. Marie to MG, Brazzaville, 24 Oct. 1898; Congo C, Lettres, M. Marie to MG, Brazzaville, 28 Feb. 1900.

59. For missions, see the presentation by P. Pierre Charles given at the influential annual seminar at the University of Louvain, "Missiologie antiféministe," in *Le rôle de la femme dans les missions: rapport et compte rendu de la XXe Semaine de Missiologie de Louvain* (Brussels: L'Edition Universelle, 1950), 20–35; and, in general, Malone, *Women and Christianity,* 3 vols.

60. Vassal, *Life in French Congo,* 86.

61. ACSSJC, 2B/u.7.2, "Compte-Rendu de la visite de règle faite par le Révérende Mère Rose de St Jean-Baptiste, Communauté de Marie-Immmaculée à Loango," 3 April 1927.

62. ACSSJC, 2B/u.2, M. Alphonse to MG, Loango, 24 April 1927.

63. ACSSJC, 2B/u.2, M. Alphonse to MG, Loango, 12 Aug. 1927.

64. The distinctions between the sisters was laid out in the constitution of the Sisters of Saint Joseph of Cluny. See, for example, the landmark *Règle de la Congrègation des Soeurs de Saint Joseph de Cluny* (Rome: Imprimerie de Bernardo Morini, 1853). This constitution, promulgated on the death of Anne-Marie Javouhey, received the definitive approval of Rome in 1899. There was a revision in 1924, but it was only after the Second Vatican Council that the constitution and the lives of the sisters underwent dramatic change.

65. Mgr. Carrie, *Oeuvre des Soeurs de Saint Joseph de Cluny;* AGCPSE, 276/B/I, P. Rémy, "Règle provisoire du Tiers-ordre des Soeurs indigènes affiliées à la Congrégation des Soeurs de St Joseph de Cluny," Brazzaville, 1 Nov. 1900. Both documents are published in de Banville, *Kalouka et Zoungoula,* 185–210.

66. "Rapport Quinquennial," 1886–91, published in *Le mémorial du Congo Français,* 1:8.

67. Kinata, *Le clergé indigène du Congo Français,* 91–98.

68. Mgr. Carrie, *L'oeuvre des Soeurs de Saint-Joseph de Cluny;* AGCPSE, 276/B/I, P. Rémy, "Règle Provisoire du Tiers-Ordres des Soeurs indigènes."

69. See chapter 1.

70. ACSSJC, D3/2.b, M. Alphonse to MG, Loango, 1 Feb. 1929. A photograph of the first three novices and two postulants taken by P. Marichelle and in the possession of the woman interviewed—who may have been Suzanne Tchibassa—was given to the sisters at this point. It is published in de Banville, *Kalouka et Zoungoula,* 180.

71. ACSSJC, 2A/u.1.6, M. St Charles to MG, Loango, 13 Aug. 1895, 31 Dec. 1897; 2A/u.1.4, P. Derouet to MG, Loango, 24 Aug. 1898.

72. ACSSJC, D3/2.b, Former postulant's testimony to Mother-Superior Alphonse, Loango, 1 Feb. 1929.

73. ACSSJC, 2B/u.2.1, Mère Jerôme to MG, Loango, 26 July 1923.

74. Castellani, *Femmes au Congo*, 41, the caption wrongly identifies the place as Libreville; ACSSJC, 2B/u.2.4, M. Marie to MG, Brazzaville, 5 Nov. 1892, 13 May 1893, 2 June 1897, 17 Dec. 1897. Also, de Banville, *Kalouka et Zoungoula*, 43–51, 80–92.

75. ACSSJC, Congo C, Lettres, M. Marie to MG, Brazzaville, 10 Dec. 1902, 21 Dec. 1902, 11 Feb. 1903; S. Marie Stanislas to MG, Brazzaville, 11 Sept. 1899; de Banville, *Kalouka et Zoungoula*, 53–55.

76. ACSSJC, Congo B, Lettres, S. Alexandre to MG, Brazzaville, 30 May 1899; Congo C, Lettres, M. Marie to MG, Brazzaville, 23 Jan., 24 June, 16 Sept. 1901 and 8 Oct. 1902; also, 28 Dec. 1905 and 3 Dec. 1909. Kalouka and Zoungoula are buried in the churchyard by the Brazzaville cathedral. A single stone marks their graves and those of early European sisters. I have generally followed the dates in the contemporary reports of the Brazzaville sisters, which are occasionally at variance with those given by de Banville. His book is mainly a collection of documents that chart the two African sisters' lives and indicates the wider context. His work was published posthumously by fellow Spiritans.

77. Cooper and Stoler, *Tensions of Empire*, 3.

78. P. Rémy, "Une fleur noire," *La semaine religieuse de Poitiers* 14 (8 April 1906): 302–304; P. Rémy, "Une fleur congolaise," *AA* 22 (July 1906): 152–55; Mgr. Augouard, "Une fleur noire," *MC* (May–June 1906): 224–27; Augouard, *36 Années au Congo*, 424–36; Chanoine Louis Augouard, *Anecdotes congolaises* (Poitiers, France: Poussin, 1934), 170–79; also, *BC-SSJC* 84 (Dec. 1906), Brazzaville, 478. De Banville offers a critique of the various versions of the sisters' lives in *Kalouka et Zoungoula*, 162–75.

79. Ouassongo, "Les aspects financiers du Vicariat de l'Oubangui," 116–18.

80. Malone, *Women and Christianity*, 3:221; Robert Ellsberg, *All Saints* (New York: Crossroad Publishing, 1997), 427–29.

81. Jehan de Witte, *Un explorateur et un apôtre du Congo-Français: Monseigneur Augouard* (Paris: Emile-Paul Frères, 1924), 60, 61–6.

82. "Orphanage" continued to be used by the missionaries even when the children had living parents.

83. Anne L. Stoler, "Making Empire Respectable: The Politics of Race and Sexual Morality in Twentieth-Century Colonial Cultures," in *Situated Lives: Gender and Culture in Everyday Life*, ed. Louise Lamphere, Helene Ragoné, and Patricia Zavella (New York: Routledge, 1997), 374. (This chapter is a reprint of an article that appeared in *American Ethnologist* [1989]).

84. Jean-Loup Amselle, *Mestizo Logics: Anthropology of Identity in Africa and Elsewhere* (Stanford, Calif.: Stanford University Press, 1998), 32.

85. Mgr. Carrie, *Coutumier de l'oeuvre des enfants*.

86. Mgr. Carrie, *L'oeuvre des Soeurs de Saint-Joseph de Cluny*.

87. Martin, *Leisure and Society in Colonial Brazzaville*, 24–25, 36, 192–93. For French West Africa, which was often the model for Equatorial Africa, see Owen White, *Children of the French Empire: Miscegenation and Colonial Society in French West Africa, 1895–1960* (Oxford: Clarendon Press, 1999), and Alice K. Conklin, "Redefining 'Frenchness'," 65–83.

88. Owen White, *Children of the French Empire*: Conklin, "Redefining 'Frenchness'," 68, 71, 77; Accampo, Fuchs, and Stewart, *Gender and the Politics of Social Reform in France*;

Anne L. Stoler, "Sexual Affronts and Racial Frontiers: European Identities and the Cultural Politics of Exclusion in Colonial Southeast Asia," *Comparative Studies in Society and History* 34, no. 3 (1992), 514–51.

89. Martin, *Leisure and Society in Colonial Brazzaville,* 182–94.

90. Blouin, *My Country, Africa,* 58.

91. AOM, AP667 (2), Mgr. Augouard to Minister of Colonies, Poitiers, 16 Sept. 1919; Stoler, "Sexual Affronts and Racial Frontiers," 524–25.

92. AOM, AP 667 (2), Mgr. Augouard to Minister of Colonies, Paris, 5 Nov. 1919.

93. *BCSSJC,* 157 (1925), Brazzaville, 466–67, and 187 (1933), 539–40; ACSSJC, Congo D, Lettres, M. Marie to MG, Brazzaville, 10 Feb. 1923, and 10 May 1924.

94. ACSSJC, "Etat du personnel," 1931–60, "Orphelinat Augouard."

95. AGCPSE, 520/B/V, "Elèves métisses de l'Orphelinat Augouard."

96. AGCPSE, 520/B/VIII, P. de Louvre to Father-Superior, Kilomines (Ituri), 11 May 1936; G. Kesters to Father-Superior, Kinshasa, 11 Sept. 1937; Albert Mbuy to Mother-Superior, Léopoldville, 15 Dec. 1937.

97. Blouin, *My Country, Africa,* 58–60.

98. In 1916, Mgr. Augouard sent four girls from the Alima region to be postulants in Brazzaville, but "they could not adapt" and were sent back to their home region (*BCSSJC* 128 [Dec. 1917], 481; *Les Soeurs de Saint Joseph de Cluny,* 51).

99. ACSSJC, Brazzaville E, Lettres, M. Alphonse to MG, Brazzaville, 13 Nov. 1933, 21 Oct. 1935; 12 Sept. 1936; BSSJC 202 (Dec. 1938), Brazzaville, 583; AGCPSE, Mgr. Bièchy to Gov.-Gen., 14 May 1938.

100. When I first met the sisters in Brazzaville in 1986, the mother-superior of the convent and the superior for the Vice-Province of Central Africa were both graduates of the *métisses* program.

101. ACSSJC, D3/2.b, "Congo Français: Soeurs Affiliées."

102. Interview, Paris, 30 June 1997.

5. Toward a Church of Women

1. The "Trois Glorieuses" (the "Three Glories") are celebrated as a national holiday on 13, 14, 15 August each year. August 15 was also the anniversary of Congo's political independence. The origins of the term "Trois Glorieuses" date back to 1830, the deposition of the authoritarian Charles X, and the installation of a constitutional monarchy.

2. *Brazzaville janvier–février 1944: aux sources de la décolonisation* (Paris: Plon, 1988); Cooper, *Africa since 1940,* 40–49; Austin and Headrick, "Equatorial Africa under Colonial Rule," 82–86.

3. Bernault, *Démocraties ambiguës.* Gender is hardly mentioned in existing studies of the nationalist struggle in Congo. There is no in-depth work that deals with the participation of women comparable to that of Susan Geiger for Tanganyika or Elizabeth Schmidt for Guinea: see, *TANU Women: Gender and Culture in the Making of Tanganyikan Nationalism, 1955–1965* (Portsmouth, N.H.: Heinemann, 1997), and, *Mobilizing the Masses: Gender, Ethnicity, and Class in the Nationalist Movement in Guinea, 1939–1958* (Portsmouth, N.H.: Heinemann, 2005). Scholastique Dianzinga has a section on decolonization politics in her broad study of Congolese women. She did not find much evidence for women's participation at a popular level, but the subject warrants fuller treatment.

4. Youlou not only was a politician but was perceived as a powerful *nganga* among the Lari Matswaistes, who admired him not only for his superior education but for the possibility

that he could deliver them from misfortune and find André Matswa, whom many believed had not died in a colonial prison. See Sinda, *Le messianisme congolais*, 260–84; Kinata, *La formation du clergé indigène*, 243–45.

5. Various accounts of the period are in Jean-Michel Wagret, *Histoire et sociologie politiques de la République du Congo (Brazzaville)* (Paris: Librairie Générale de Droit de Jurisprudence, 1963); Réné Gauze, *The Politics of Congo-Brazzaville* (Stanford, Calif.: Hoover Institute Press, 1973); Ernoult, *Les spiritains au Congo*, 112; Kinata, *La formation du clergé indigène*, 211–48; Pannier, *L'église de Pointe-Noire*, 102–103; Elisabeth Dorier-Apprill and Abel Kouvouama, "Pluralisme religieux et société urbaine à Brazzaville," *Afrique contemporaine* 186 (1998): 58–76; Florence Bernault, *Démocraties ambiguës*, and "The political shaping of sacred locality in Brazzaville, 1959–1997," in *Africa's Urban Past*, ed. David M. Anderson and Richard Rathbone (Oxford: James Curry, 2000), 283–302; and Rémy Bazenguissa-Ganga, *Les voies du politique au Congo: essai de sociologie historique* (Paris: Karthala, 1997).

6. Bernault, "The Political Shaping of Sacred Locality," 283–7.

7. ACSSJC, Congo 2, Lettres G, M. Marie Budinger to MG, Brazzaville, 4 and 24 Feb., 21 June 1959; AFMM, Province de Marie-Mediatrice, Léopoldville (PMM), Rapport annuel, série 12, no. 17/60, M. M. Xavier Remy, Brazzaville, Aug. 1960; *BCSSJC* 267 (Dec. 1965), Brazzaville, 721.

8. ACSSJC, Congo F, Lettres, M. Marie Budinger to MG, Brazzaville, 4 Jan. 1955, and Congo 2, Lettres G, 7 and 8 Jan. 1956.

9. ACSSJC, Congo 2, Lettres G, M. Marie Budinger to MG, Brazzaville, 7 Feb. 1956, 27 Oct. 1957, 3 April 1961.

10. Archives des Soeurs de la Divine Providence de Ribeauvillé (ASDPR), Chronique Ouenze II, "Les trois glorieuses, journées de la révolution."

11. Interview with Firmine Malékat, Brazzaville, 17 Dec. 1986. See chapter 6.

12. *La semaine africaine*, 6 Aug. and 20 Oct. 1964. Cardinal Biayenda was murdered in 1977 shortly after the assassination of Marien Ngouabi, president of the People's Republic of Congo, 1969–77. The Military Committee of the Party blamed members of Ngouabi's family for the cardinal's death as an act of revenge since Biayenda was the last to have an audience with the president before his assassination. Rumor attributed the death of the president to a struggle of spiritual forces in which Biayenda's power weakened that of the president, making him vulnerable to attack. The Military Commission of the Party found the former president, Massemba-Débat, guilty of plotting Ngouabi's murder and had him executed. See the official account in *Etumba*, 9 April 1977, and the account of the cardinal's death in *La semaine africaine*, 27 March 1977. Also, Appolonaire Ngolongolo, *L'assassinat de Marien Ngouabi ou l'histoire d'un pays ensanglanté* (Vincennes: AutoEdition, 1988).

13. Jean-Pierre N'Diaye, "Prudence dans la révolution: une interview du président Marien N'Gouabi recueillie à Brazzaville" *Jeune afrique*, 710–11 (Aug. 1974): 34. Also, Marien Ngouabi, *Vers la construction d'une société socialiste en Afrique* (Paris: Présence Africaine, 1975), 29–59.

14. Sylvain M. Makosso, "L'église catholique et l'état au Congo de 1960 à nos jours," *Afrique contemporaine* 88 (Nov.–Dec. 1976), 11; Abraham Okoko-Esseau, "The Christian Churches and Democratisation in the Congo," in *The Christian Churches and the Democratisation of Africa*, ed. Paul Gifford (Leiden, Neth.: Brill, 1995), 149–51.

15. A law was passed in 1963 giving official recognition to seven churches, including the Catholic church. See Dorier-Apprill and Kouvouama, "Pluralisme religieux et société urbaine à Brazzaville," 58.

16. For example, Pannier, *L'église de Points-Noire,* 262–73; ACSSJC, Congo 2, Lettres M, M. Marie Budinger to MG, Brazzaville, 31 Jan. 1970, 26 Feb. 1972. Makosso, "L'église catholique," 6–11.

17. Wagret, *Histoire et sociologie politiques,* 121–23; Austen and Headrick, "Equatorial Africa under Colonial Rule," 89; Emilienne Raoul-Matingou, "Activités des femmes en milieu urbain: le cas de Brazzaville," Thèse de 3e cycle, Université des Sciences et Techniques de Lille, 1982, 5, 18, 27; Martin, *Leisure and Society in Colonial Brazzaville,* 28.

18. Raoul-Matingou, "Activités des femmes en milieu urbain," 18–30. The massive influx of migrants to the cities, their motives, economic fortunes, and daily lives were the subject of several studies by researchers from ORSTOM in the late 1940s and 1950s: for example, Balandier, *Sociologie des Brazzaville noires.* See also Martin, *Leisure and Society in Colonial Brazzaville,* 50–52.

19. Pannier, *L'église de Pointe-Noire,* 200–201.

20. The figures were based on the numbers baptized and official census figures. Since the latter could only be approximate, precise reckonings were hardly possible, but the figures can stand as broad estimates. See, Makosso, "L'église catholique," 6–7, where he quotes from the official *Annuaire statistique des missions catholiques,* 1970–71, 6–7; also, *Pentecôte sur le monde* 82 (1970): 11. Percentages for African Catholics in 1963 show a figure of 34% for the Republic of Congo; only Gabon and Réunion show more. See Marcel Merle, ed., *Les églises chrétiennes et la décolonisation* (Paris: Presses de la fondation nationale des sciences politiques, 1962), 98.

21. Interview with Marie-Paule Samba, Brazzaville, 13 Jan. 1987; also, interview with S. Marie, Pointe-Noire, 6 Jan 1987.

22. Especially the documents *Lumen Gentium, Sacrosanctum Concilium,* and *Gaudium et Spes.* See Walter M. Abbott, ed., *The Documents of Vatican II,* 2nd ed. (New York: Crossroad Publishing, 1989), 9–106, 133–316.

23. Those called monitors were usually teachers in primary schools. They were expected to have two or three years of education beyond primary school, but this was not always the case.

24. ACSSJC, Congo 2, Lettres G, M. Marie Budinger to MG, Brazzaville, 7 Feb. and 25 Aug. 1956.

25. ACSSJC, Congo, Lettres F, M. Marie Budinger to MG, Brazzaville, 16 Sept. 1947; Congo 2, Lettres G, M. Marie Budinger to MG, 11 Jan. 1961, and S. Marie Bernard to MG, Brazzaville, 3 April 1961.

26. ACSSJC, Congo 2, Lettres G, S. Marie Bernard to MG, Brazzaville, 3 April 1961.

27. Ganga, *Combats pour un sport africain,* 96–98. Also, Gérard Lucas, "Congo-Brazzaville," in *Church, State, and Education in Africa,* ed. David G. Scanlon (New York: Teachers College Press, 1966), 129.

28. Ganga, *Combats pour un sport africain,* 52–125.

29. Pierre Bonnafé, "Une classe d'âge politique: la JMNR de la République du Congo-Brazzaville," *CEA* 8, no. 31 (1968), 327–68. Ganga became director of the Office of Youth and Sports and eventually secretary-general of the Council for African Sports.

30. Ganga, *Combats pour un sport africain,* 51–52.

31. Ibid., 89–103. See, Pannier, *L'église de Pointe-Noire,* 106–107, 162–63 on the "climate of distrust" that existed between the teacher's union and missionary employers. The problems for some church families at the time were also conveyed to me by informants, for example, Firmine Malékat, 17 Dec. 1986, a leader of Catholic women's groups; and Veronique Mbemba, 15 Dec. 1986, a leader of women in the Evangelical Church.

32. ACSSJC, 2B/u.3.4. Education Act, 11 Aug. 1965. The act was to take effect for the new school year.

33. ACSSJC, 2B/ u.3.4. Minutes of a meeting of the superiors of religious congregations with Mgr. Mbemba, 16 Aug. 1965, Brazzaville. Mgr. Mbemba was the first Congolese archbishop.

34. ACSSJC, Congo 2, Lettres H2, S. Marie Guenaël to MG, Bacongo, 21 Sept. 1965.

35. Makosso, "L'église catholique," 11.

36. *BCSSJC* 267 (Dec. 1965), Kindamba, 737. The *ngongi* is a single, clapperless bell with a wooden handle that is struck with a piece of iron or wood.

37. Pannier, *L'église de Pointe-Noire,* 253–73.

38. This account of *mabundu* was written by Congolese sisters who worked in the Kindamba region: "Des communautés chrétiennes au Congo," *Cluny-Missions* 241 (May–June 1972): 44–47. Otherwise, this account of *mabundu* is based on conversations in 2000 with active church members in Pointe-Noire. Also, S. Solange Lozi, "Les communautés de base au Congo," *Annales de Notre-Dame du Sacré-Coeur* (Nov. 1978): 235–39; and accounts of various *mabundu* published in Witwicki, *Marie et l'évangélisation du Congo,* 1:499–502. Also, Elisabeth Dorier-Appril, Abel Kouvouama, and Christophe Appril, *Vivre à Brazzaville: modernité et crise au quotidien* (Paris: Karthala, 1998), 278–9.

39. On *scholas populaires,* see "Echos d'Afrique," *Ut sint unum* 52 (June 1966): 13–14; "Christianization," *Cluny-Mission* 219 (Sept.–Oct. 1968): 90; "Mbanza-Ndounga," in Witwicki, *Marie et l'évangélisation du Congo,* 1:500.

40. Félix Eboué, from the French West Indies, was the first black governor of a French African colony (Chad). He supported Free France and was appointed governor-general of AEF by Charles de Gaulle. His policies were laid out in *La nouvelle politique indigène* (Paris: Office Français d'Edition, 1941), but there is little reference to women.

41. ANB, GG 487, Report on Public Education, AEF, 1946; IGE 151, Report on Education, AEF, 1950; Jean-Rémy Ayouné, "La formation de la femme africaine en AEF," *Service de l'Information: Bulletin de Documentation, AEF* 158 (1952).

42. Wagret, *Histoire et sociologie politiques,* 147.

43. Vincent, *Femmes africaines en milieu urbain,* 62–68. Schools run by the Swedish Evangelical Mission and the Salvation Army are included in this figure, but the great majority of those who attended church schools attended Catholic schools, especially in regions where they were long established in Brazzaville and lower Congo. See also Gérard Lucas, "Congo-Brazzaville," 123–25, and Gardinier, "Schooling in the States of Equatorial Africa," 520–22.

44. Vincent, *Femmes africaines en milieu urbain,* 69.

45. BCCSJC 230 (Aug. 1953), Linzolo, 749.

46. BCCSJC 215 (Aug. 1948), Kindamba, 943; 230 (Aug. 1953), Kindamba, 751–52. Any assessment of low enrollments at Kindamba and Linzolo that were in the heart of Matswa country must also take into account a general turning away from the Catholic church at the time.

47. Vincent, *Femmes africaines en milieu urbain,* 2–3, 184–85. For a "generation gap" between young male party militants and their elders in the plateau region north of Brazzaville, see, Bonnafé, "Une classe d'âge politique," 334–45.

48. Vincent, *Femmes africaines en milieu urbain,* 185–86; Raoul-Matingou, *Activités des femmes en milieu urbain.*

49. Interview, Brazzaville, 17 Nov. 1986.

50. Vincent, *Femmes africaines en milieu urbain,* 111–12.

51. *BCSSJC* 267 (Dec. 1965), Bacongo, 724.

52. M'Bokolo, "Forces sociales et ideologies."

53. Interview with Bernard Mambeke-Boucher, Brazzaville, 17 Nov. 1986.

54. Interview with Marie-Thérèse Metereau, Paris, 30 June 1997.

55. The phrase is used in a report from S. Elise-Marie, who taught at the school of the Sisters of the Divine Providenc of Ribeauvillé in Ouenze: ASDPR, "Chroniques Ouenze," II, c. 1960.

56. See Dianzinga, "Les femmes congolaises," 330–32; Martin, *Leisure and Society in Colonial Brazzaville*, 64, 166–69. This small group of women also received tips from European women in the same manner as those in Usumbura written about in Nancy Hunt's article, "Domesticity and Colonialism in Belgian Africa."

57. I am grateful to Jean-Pierre Ngole, my Lingala teacher, for providing me with this phrase.

58. Similar situations were widespread in other parts of late colonial Africa. See Cooper, *Africa since 1940*, 32–33, 87, 124–27.

59. Josephine Ambiera Oboa, "Le rôle de l'épouse," in *Femmes africaines* (Paris: Les Editions du Centurion, 1959), 74–75.

60. Joseph Pouabou, "L'évolution de la femme Africaine," *Liaison* 15 (Sept. 1951): 14; Eugène Mikoto, "Ce que je pense de nos mariages actuels," *Liaison* 29–30 (Nov.–Dec. 1952): 13–14; Albert Locko, "L'enfant de base: l'enfant africain et les parents actuels," *Liaison* 31 (Jan. 1953); P. G. Tchipala, "Pas de confidence aux femmes!" *Liaison* 32 (Feb. 1953).

61. Victor Onanga and P. L. Tchibamba, "Mariage et divorce," *Liaison* 35 (May 1953): 16–17; Joseph Massengo, "Quand la femme mariée 'part en congé,'" *Liaison* 37 (July 1953): 15–16.

62. Madeleine M'Bombo, letter to the editor, *Liaison* 39 (Sept. 1953): 16–17.

63. Dembi, "'Tchicoumbi' ou réclusion des filles nubiles chez les Mayombe"; Pouabou, "Le peuple Vili ou Loango."

64. The testimonies are in the private papers of Gilbert Courtois. The informants asked that they remain anonymous.

65. The church was founded in 1953; its name can be translated literally as "God-Candles," for the extensive use of candles in ritual. The church spread from its original base in Pointe-Noire to Cabinda and surrounding regions. See Vaz, *No Mundo dos Cabindas,* 1:128–59, and Sinda, *Le messianisme congolais,* 340–47.

66. Vaz, *No mundo dos Cabindas,* 1:151.

67. Blouin, *My Country, Africa.*

68. The bishop of the Pointe-Noire diocese also called on the help of two small French congregations: the Soeurs de Saint-Charles de Lyon, who opened schools in lower Congo at Madingou and Mouyondzi, and the Soeurs de Saint-Méen, who established their missions at Zanaga, Sibiti, Komono, and Mossendjo. See Pannier, *L'église de Pointe-Noire,* 173.

69. *BCSSJC* 267 (Dec. 1965), Brazzaville, 720.

70. ACSSJC, Congo F, Lettres, M. Marie Budinger to MG, 5 Dec. 1959; *BCSSJC* 220 (Aug. 1953), Brazzaville, 741; 247 (April 1959), 810–12; 267 (Dec. 1965), 719–22. Communities of sisters also arrived at missions previously without sisters such as Linzolo, Kibouende, and Mindouli. See *Les Soeurs de Saint-Joseph de Cluny,* 68–82.

71. ASDPR, S. Elise-Marie, "Ouenze: Chronique"; S. Edouard-Joseph, "Ouenze, Sept. 1961," *Ut sint unum* 35 (Oct. 1961), 24, also, 20–21, S. Wendelina, Voka, Dec. 1961; and 57 (Oct. 1967): 14.

72. AFFM, PMM, 18/64, Rapport Annuel, Brazzaville, Aug. 1964. Also, 17/58, Brazzaville, Aug. 1958, and 17/59, Brazzaville, Aug. 1959.

73. *Bulletin d'information et de documentation*, Brazzaville, 66 (1950); ANB, IGE 151, Report on Education, 1950.

74. AFMM, PMM, 17/54, Rapport Annuel, Brazzaville, Aug. 1954; 17/60, Rapport Annuel, Brazzaville, Aug. 1960; and, 18/61, Rapport Annuel, Brazzaville, Aug. 1961.

75. See Pannier, *L'église de Pointe-Noire*, 100, for the reorganization of ecclesiastical boundaries in AEF in 1955.

76. Quoted in Pannier, *L'église de Pointe-Noire*, 90. The emphasis is in the original. The point is well made, but the inspector likely did not count the girls who were living with African women and receiving catechism training.

77. Ibid., 179. The Spiritan sisters also established schools in the towns of lower Congo such as Louboumou (Dolisie), Nkayi (Jacob), and Makabana.

78. ACSSJC, Congo 2, Lettres H2, S. Marie Guenaël to MG, Bacongo, 21 Sept. 1965.

79. ASDPR, Chronique Ouenze, c. 1965.

80. Interview with S. Marcel Meckler and S. Anna Perez-Cosio, 7 Jan. 1992, by P. Robert Witwicki: see Witwicki, *Marie et l'évangélisation du Congo*, 3:47.

81. ACSSJC, Congo2, Lettres H2, S. Marie Proxède de Jésus to MG, Bacongo, 28 Oct. 1965.

82. Interview with Marie-Antoinette Mouanga, Paris, 11 Nov. 1998.

83. ASDPR, "La nationalisation des écoles, October 1965"; interview with Firmine Malékat, 17 Dec. 1986. The summary of the nuns' activities is taken from letters and published reports and conversations with retired sisters in Europe.

84. *BCSSJC* 289 (Aug. 1973), 1102, "Vice-Province de l'Afrique Centrale, 1965–1973."

85. Interview with S. Johanna Ammeux, Paris, 18 Nov. 1998.

86. ACSSJC, 2B/u.2.3, Mgr. Théophile Mbemba to Mères-Supérieures Générales, Brazzaville, 8 Jan. 1968; AFMM, PMM, 35, "Procès verbale de la réunion des Supérieures chez Mgr. l'Archèveque," Brazzaville, 25 Jan. 1968; Superior-Générale des FMM to Mgr. Mbemba, Jan. 1968.

87. ACSSJC, 2B/u.2.3, Episcopal letter from Mgr. Théophile Mbemba, Brazzaville, Easter 1967.

88. ACSSJC, 2B/u.2.3, Mgr. Barthélemy Batantu, *Les Oblates du Rosaire: une nouvelle formule d'engagement des femmes à la vie consacrée*, Brazzaville, 2nd ed., 1985.

89. *BCSSJC* 290 (Aug. 1973), 1120, M. Marie Budinger, Baratier-Kibouende.

90. *Ut sint unum* 35 (Oct. 1961): 30, letter of S. Marie Xavier, 24 Sept. 1961; 105 (Jan. 1982): 19–20, "Nos soeurs de Congo et leurs familles."

91. ASMSE, Testimony of Anastasie Kembe Barros, c. 1978. The sister was 21 at the time she wrote down her testimony. The reference to the Soeurs de la Visitation is to a contemplative order of French nuns who established a convent on the site of the old Christian village of Saint Benoît at Loango in 1964.

92. This was still the experience of postulants whom I talked to in 2000, even if becoming a nun was more acceptable to society at large. See, also, Burke, *These Catholic Sisters Are All Mamas!* 81–82.

93. ACSSJC, Congo M, Lettres, S. Marie-Jésus de Béthanie to MG, Kibouende-Baratier, 5 March 1967; S. Françoise de Sainte-Marie to MG, Brazzaville, 9 March 1967; letter signed by twelve Congolese sisters to Mgr. Mbemba, Brazzaville, 17 April 1969.

94. Interview with S. Anne-Andrée, Ribeauvillé, 17 May 2001, and S. Marie-Rita, 15 May 2001.

95. ACSSJC, Congo 2, Lettres G, M. Marie Bernard to MG, Kibouende, 9 March 1962.

96. ACSSJC, 2B/u.7.2, Report of M. Marie Budinger, Brazzaville, 16 June 1969.

97. Interview with S. Marie-Rita, Ribeauvillé, 15 May 2001; and interview with S. Anne-Andrée, Ribeauvillé, 17 May 2001.

98. Words used in conversations with Congolese sisters who had passed through the novitiate in the 1950s and 1960s.

99. Burke, *These Catholic Sisters Are All Mamas!* 90–95, 104, 107–10, 127.

100. ACSSJC, Congo, 2B/u.7.1, "Demands de consentement des parents," c. 1981. Some congregations allowed a sister to give 50 percent of her income to her family. Since the congregations were self-supporting, they had to rethink their finances after the nationalization of schools and the loss of the teaching sisters' wages.

101. ACSSJC, Congo, 2B/u.7.1, "Cérémonie de profession religieuse," 20 Sept. 1981.

102. *La semaine africaine* 1801–02 (1989), and 1825 (1989).

103. Conversations with Soeur Marie-Michelle Biyela, Brazzaville, 25 Oct. 1986, and, Paris, 14 Nov. 1998.

104. "Religieux, religieuses, clergé diocésain au Congo, 1994," publication of the Conférence des Supérieur(e)s majeur(e)s du Congo.

105. Burke, *These Sisters Are All Mamas!* 83.

106. Ibid., 84.

107. "Centenaire de l'évangélisation du Congo," *La semaine africaine* 1542–45 (Aug. 1983).

6. Women Together

1. "Centenaire de l'évangélisation du Congo," *La semaine africaine* 1542–45 (Aug. 1983).

2. "Fraternités féminines chrétiennes catholiques du Congo: 25 ans déja," *La semaine africaine* 1815 (Oct. 1989).

3. Based on conversations with parish priests in Brazzaville, 1986, and Pointe-Noire, 2000.

4. An article in *La semaine de l'AEF* (4 Sept. 1952) announced that on the saint's day in 1952 a group of women from Dahomey-Togo had gathered at Saint Anne's cathedral for the first public event of their association. It had taken the form of a Mass followed by a social gathering at the home of the president of the Dahomean Association. The future plan was to open the women's association "to any Christian woman regardless of race." No details are given about who initiated the organization, and it sounds closer in its origins to the many ethnic associations in the town than to the later fraternity idea.

5. J. Rémy, "La Fête-Dieu à Brazzaville en 1912," in Augouard, *Anecdotes Congolaises,* 52.

6. *BCPSE* 28 (1914–18), Brazzaville, 158; AGCPSE, 513/B/VII, Report by Monseigneur Guichard, Brazzaville, 1925–30, and Report of Père Le Duc, Brazzaville, 28 Aug. 1935; interview with Soeur Clothilde, Brazzaville, 10 Nov. 1986.

7. Interview with Soeur Clothilde, 10 Nov. 1986. During a conversation with him, Brazzaville, 1 Dec. 1986, Bernard Mambeke-Boucher showed me photographs of his sister with her friends at meetings of the *Amicale* in the 1930s.

8. Aimée Gnali, "Des femmes engagées," *La semaine africaine* 168 (23 Sept. 1993). Aimée Gnali was a teacher and school inspector who then worked for UNESCO in Paris and Dakar. She first entered politics in 1963, when she was elected to the national assembly. In 2002, she was minister of culture, arts, and tourism.

9. Interview with Abbé Georges Loemba and Abbé Joachim Lelo, Pointe-Noire, 28 June 2000.

10. Interview with Léontine Bissangou, Pointe-Noire, 26 June 2000.

11. Wagret, *Histoire et sociologie politiques*, 65.

12. Bonnafé, "Une classe d'âge politique," passim.

13. Interview with Firmine Malékat, Brazzaville, 17 Dec. 1986.

14. A more elaborate version of the story of origins can also be found in Firmine Malékat's interview with Père Robert Witwicki in 1992. See Witwicki, *Marie et l'évangélisation du Congo*, 3:169–74; "La fraternité Saint-Joseph à 24 ans (paroisse Sainte-Anne)," *La semaine africaine* (May 1988); and "Statuts des fraternités chrétiennes catholiques, du Congo," 1987, iv–vii.

15. Interview with Firmine Malékat, Brazzaville, 17 Dec. 1986.

16. "Fraternités," *Cluny Mission* 252 (March–April 1974): 32–33; Firmine Malékat, interview with Witwicki in Witwicki, *Marie et l'évangélisation du Congo*, 3:173; "Statuts des fraternités," 1987.

17. O'Deyé, *Les associations en villes africaines*, 76, 82.

18. Interview with Marie-Paule Samba, Brazzaville, 13 Jan. 1987.

19. Marie-Claude Dupré, "Les femmes mukisi"; and "Comment être femme: un aspect du rituel Mukisi chez les Téké de la République Populaire du Congo," extrait des *Archives des Sciences Sociales des Religions*, 46, no. 1 (1978): 57–84.

20. Interview with Soeur Anne-Andrée, Ribeauvillé, 17 May 2001; also, Soeur Marie-Rita, Ribeauvillé, 15 May 2001. The Legion of Mary was an evangelical organization organized along military lines.

21. The problem of being barred from taking the sacrament was a point made by several fraternity members. Jeanne-Françoise Vincent carried out her research before fraternities existed, but when she asked women if they would like a church marriage, they said yes, "to be able to take the sacraments." See *Femmes africaines en milieu urbain*, 74.

22. For more on *tontines* (revolving savngs associations) and *musiki* (mutual aid associations), see Martin, *Leisure and Society in Colonial Brazzaville*, 140–42.

23. Interview with Bernard Mambeke-Boucher, Brazzaville, 17 Nov. 1986; interview with Marie-Paule Samba, Brazzaville, 13 Jan. 1987; also, see Martin, "Power, Cloth, and Currency," for funerals among the Kongo in precolonial times, and *Leisure and Society in Colonial Brazzaville*, for modifications in the city, especially the *matanga* celebrations, 138, 141–42, 144–48. Also, for a description of modern mourning and *matanga*, see Joseph Loukou, "Moeurs brazzavilloises," *Brazzaville: revue de l'action municipale* 9 (May–June, 1968), and for the costs of death (funeral parlors, burial at the municipal cemetery, etc.) see Ouabari, "La mort et les pompes funèbres municipales de Brazzaville," *Les Cahiers d'Outre-Mer* 44 (1991): 296–307.

24. O'Deyé, *Les associations en villes africaines*, 98.

25. Joseph Tonda, "Enjeux du deuil et négociation des rapports sociaux de sexe au Congo," *CEA* 157, no. 40 (2000): 7.

26. Ibid., 5. Also, see Florence Bernault, "Economie de la mort et reproduction sociale au Gabon," in *Mama Africa: hommage à Catherine Coquery-Vidrovitch*, ed. Odile Goerg and Issiaka Mande (Paris: L'Harmattan, 2005, 203–18.

27. "Fraternités," *Cluny Mission* 252 (March–April, 1974): 33; "Statuts," 1987, articles 63, 83–88.

28. Interview with Firmine Malékat, Brazzaville, 17 Dec. 1986.

29. Interview with Léontine Bissangou, Pointe-Noire, 26 June 2000.

30. Interview with Yvonne Miayedimina, Brazzaville, 25 Nov. 1986.

31. Interview with Soeur Gertrude Onghaïe, Brazzaville, 6 Nov. 1986. *Kitemo* is the Kilari word for a revolving credit association.

32. Interview with Yvonne Miayedimina, Brazzaville, 25 Nov. 1986.

33. "Les fraternités en RPC," *La semaine africaine* 1815 (Oct. 1989).

34. Figures provided by Léontine Bissangou, 26 June 2000; and, Abbé Louis Pambou, chaplain for the Pointe-Noire fraternities, Pointe-Noire, 20 June 2000.

35. David Maxwell with Ingrid Lawrie, *Christianity and the African Imagination: Essays in Honour of Adrian Hastings* (Leiden, Neth.: Brill, 2002), 4.

36. Ibid., 7.

37. Jaroslav Pelikan, *Mary through the Centuries: Her Place in the History of Culture* (New Haven, Conn.: Yale University Press, 1996), 215–23.

38. Witwicki, *Marie et l'évangélisation du Congo*, 3:172–73.

39. On the ability of popular religion to go beyond inculturation to invention, see Paul Rutayisire, "Popular Religiosity or the Failure of the Missionary Churches," *Pro Mundi Vita Studies* 6 (Nov. 1988): 37–38, quoted in Ranger, "New Approaches to the History of Mission Christianity," 181.

40. Philip Nord, "Catholic Culture in Interwar France," *French Politics, Culture, and Society* 21, no. 3 (2003): 6; Ford, "Female Martyrdom and the Politics of Sainthood in Nineteenth Century France," 24.

41. An expression used by Augustine Bouanga, Pointe-Noire, 15 June 2000; and Soeur Lydia Portella, Pointe-Noire, 19 June 2000.

42. Oral sources and BCSSJC 290 (Aug. 1973), Bacongo, 1114–15.

43. Interview with Suzanne Tchitembo, Pointe-Noire, 1 July 2000.

44. Interview with Elisabeth Koutana, Pointe-Noire, 22 June 2000.

45. Fears of the dangers of daughters loitering in the streets and falling under the influence of "bad boys" was a concern of mothers expressed to Vincent in her study of Bacongo women at an earlier period, also. See Vincent, *Femmes africaines en milieu urbain*, 184–85.

46. Interview with Léontine Bissangou, Pointe-Noire, 26 June 2000. Soeur Anuarite of the Soeurs de la Sainte Famille (Holy Family Sisters) was killed in eastern Zaire by guerillas in their uprising of 1964. She was beatified by Pope John Paul II in 1985.

47. Much of this information is drawn from informal conversations with fraternity members.

48. Interview with Anne-Marie Thérèse Pena, Pointe-Noire, 23 June 2000.

49. Ibid.

50. See chapter 2. The girls' dormitory at Linzolo was under her patronage.

51. Raoul-Matingou, *Activités des femmes en milieu urbain*, 52–57. Three centuries previously, sick and childless women were among the followers of Dona Beatriz Kimpa Vita, who claimed to be possessed by Saint Anthony: see Thornton, *The Kongolese Saint Anthony*, 131–33; and Richard Gray, *Black Christians and White Missionaries*, 52.

52. Vincent, *Femmes africaines en milieu urbain*, 182–83.

53. Paul Fussell, *Uniforms: Why We Are What We Wear* (New York: Houghton Mifflin, 2003), 3. Among many studies of the power of cloth and clothing in Africa, see for Congo, Martin, "Contesting Clothes in Colonial Brazzaville," and, for various African regions in the past and present, Allman, *Fashioning Africa*.

54. From the order of service: "10ème anniversaire de la fraternité 'Saint Cathérine Labouré,' le 23 novembre 1986, paroisse 'Saint Charles Lwanga,' Makélékélé."

55. "Aumonerie diocesaine des fraternités féminines chrétiennes," Brazzaville, n.d., c. 1983. What follows are extracts from the ceremony, not the whole.

56. The celebrations on this occasion followed much the same pattern, but more elaborate (for example, the celebrations and food after the Mass), as those for the fourteenth anniversary of the Fraternité Bienheureuse Anne-Marie Javouhey in October 1986.

57. In a manner similar to that of women who engaged in the African nationalist struggle: for example, Geiger, *TANU Women,* and Schmidt, *Mobilizing the Masses.*

58. Ford, "Female Martyrdom and the Politics of Sainthood in Nineteenth Century France," 123–24.

59. Interview, Pointe-Noire, 11 June 2000.

60. Interview, Pointe-Noire, 20 June 2000.

61. Blackbourn, "The Catholic Church in Europe since the French Revolution," 782–83; also, Gibson, *Social History of French Catholicism,* 57, 156.

62. "Statuts des fraternités paroissiales," Brazzaville, 1984, and an appendix with recommendations to chaplains and counselors; "Statuts des fraternités chrétiennes catholiques du Congo," 1987; and "Regard sur les fraternités," Diocèse de Pointe-Noire, c. 2000. Fraternity leaders also needed a frame of reference and were consulted by chaplains, but the ultimate sanctions came from the diocesan authorities. The 1987 fraternity constitution was still in operation when I visited Point-Noire in 2000, but the fraternity president said they needed a revised constitution since that of 1987 was out-of-date and did not reflect the realities of fraternity practice. Progress toward revisions had been delayed by the war in Brazzaville.

63. Appendix, "Statuts," 1984, 2.1.3.

64. Congo "Statuts," 1987, articles 33, 70, 71.

65. Appendix, "Statuts," 1984, 2.1.4.

66. Appendix, "Statuts," 1984, 2.4.1–2.4.3, and 3.1.1.

67. "Regard sur les fraternités."

68. Appendix, "Statuts," 1984, 2.3.1, 2.3.2.

69. Congo "Statuts," 1987, article 2.

70. Congo "Statuts," 1987, articles 58, 69, 92–4.

71. "Regard sur les fraternités."

72. Congo "Statuts," 1987.

73. Appendix, "Statuts," 1984, 2.2.4.

74. Interview with Suzanne Tchitembo, Pointe-Noire, 1 July 2000.

75. Interview, Brazzaville, 20 June 1989.

76. Interview, Pointe-Noire, 20 June 2000.

77. Interview, Pointe-Noire, 15 June 2000.

78. Interview with Yvonne Miayedimina, Brazzaville, 25 Nov. 1986.

79. See chapter 3.

80. Congo "Statuts," 1987, article 17.

81. Vincent, *Femmes africaines en milieu urbain,* 195–96; Josephine Ambiera Oboa, "Le rôle de l'épouse," in *Femmes africaines,* 74–75; Martin, *Leisure and Society,* 152–53.

82. Interview with Firmine Malékat, Brazzaville, 17 Dec. 1986. Also, Léontine Bissangou made similar points concerning the fraternities in Pointe-Noire, 26 June 2000.

83. Interview with Soeur Lydia Portella, Pointe-Noire, 29 June 2000; also, interview with Suzanne Tchitembo, Pointe-Noire, 1 July 2000.

84. Interview with Marie-Thérèse Avemeka, Paris, 24 Nov. 1998.

85. Ibid. Marie-Thérèse Avemeka was one of the most prominent Congolese women working on gender and women's issues. She has worked at UNESCO and led her country's delegation to the United Nations Commission on the Status of Women.

86. Robert Orsi, *The Madonna of 115th Street: Faith and Community in Italian Harlem, 1880–1950* (New Haven, Conn.: Yale University Press, 1985), xiii–xviii, and passim; and *Thank You, St. Jude: Women's Devotion to the Patron Saint of Hopeless Causes* (New Haven, Conn.: Yale University Press, 1996).

87. Elizabeth Isichei, ed., *Varieties of Christian Experience in Nigeria* (London: Macmillan Press, 1982), 1, 8.

88. Wyatt MacGaffey, *Modern Kongo Prophets: Religion in a Plural Society* (Bloomington: Indiana University Press, 1983), 147, and passim; Janzen, *The Quest for Therapy in Lower Zaire* (Berkeley and Los Angeles: University of California Press, 1978), 81–89, and passim; Sinda, *Le messianisme congolais.* Also, for contemporary cults of healing in the Pointe-Noire region, Frank Hagenbucher-Sacripanti, *Santé et rédemption par les génies au Congo* (Paris: Publisud, 1993), and *Le Prophète et le militant (Congo-Brazzaville)* (Paris: L'Harmattan, 2002).

Epilogue

1. *Colloque des Mamans Chrétiennes Catholiques de l'Afrique Centrale.* The letter of invitation was published before the conference in *La semaine africaine* 2157 (April 1998).

2. "Programme des travaux," *Rapport final des travaux,* 36–39; and "Interventions," 42–120.

3. Bazenguissa-Ganga, *Les voies du politique au Congo,* 375–76n55.

4. "Des femmes engagées," *La semaine africaine* 1968 (Sept. 1993). Aimée Gnali also blamed girls' education, as lagging behind that of boys. Lack of overall participation in politics did not mean that there were not a few highly influential women, however. In the Lissouba cabinet, for example, Claudine Munari was powerful as his chief of staff, while Albertine Lipou-Massala was minister of communications.

5. Joséphine Mazouka-Nsika, director of the Integration of Women in Development, "Déclaration de la femme à l'occasion de la journée internationale de la femme, le 8 mars 1993" (Brazzaville: Ministère du Plan, de l'Economie et de la Prospective, 1993).

6. See, for example, Obenga, *L'histoire sanglante du Congo-Brazzaville;* and Bazenguissa-Ganga, *Les voies du politique au Congo.*

7. Marc-Eric Gruénais, Florent Mouanda Mbambi, and Joseph Tonda, "Messies, fétiches et lutte de pouvoirs entre les 'grandes hommes' du Congo démocratique," *CEA* 35, no. 137 (1995), 163. Also, Jean-François Bayart, "Introduction," in *Religion et modernité politique en Afrique noire,* ed. Bayart (Paris: Karthala, 1993), 9–16; Bernault, "The Political Shaping of Sacred Locality in Brazzaville," and "Magie, sorcellerie et politique au Gabon et au Congo-Brazzaville," in *Démocratie et mutations culturelles en Afrique noire,* ed. Marc Mvé Bekale (Paris: L'Harmattan, 2005), 21–39.

8. Sidonie Matokot-Mianzenza, *Viol des femmes dans les conflits armés et thérapie familiales: cas de Congo-Brazzaville* (Paris: L'Harmattan, 2003), 23–27, and passim. The estimates are based on the writer's own research and data collected by Doctors Without Borders, the United Nations, Human Rights Watch, and the Congo branch of the International Federation of Human Rights. See, also, the results of an inquiry by Doctors Without Borders: Marc le Pape and Pierre Salignon, eds., *Une guerre contre les civils: réflexions sur les pratiques humanitaires au Congo-Brazzaville, 1998–2000* (Paris: Karthala, 2001).

9. The complexity of the events of the 1990s, analyses of the roots of violence, the shaping of new ethnicities, the rise of militias, and the ideologies that bolstered the power of individual men have been the subject of many studies. Only a few of the salient facts are given here as the context for Catholic women's struggle for survival and restoration of a semblance of normalcy. Among these studies are: Elisabeth Dorier-Apprill, "Jeunesse et ethnicités citadines à Brazzaville," *Politique africaine* 64 (Dec. 1996): 73–88; Bazenguissa-Ganga, *Les voies du politique au Congo,* and "The Spread of Political Violence in Congo-Brazzaville," *African Affairs* 98 (1999), 37–54; "Congo-Brazzaville: entre guerre et paix," *Afrique contemporaine* 186

(April–June 1998), special issue; Bernault, "The Political Shaping of Sacred Locality in Brazzaville, 1959–1997"; John Clark, "The Neo-colonial Context of the Democratic Experiment of Congo-Brazzaville," *African Affairs* 101 (2002): 171–92; and Patrice Yengo, *La guerre civile du Congo-Brazzaville, 1993–2002: "chacun aura sa part"* (Paris: Karthala, 2005).

10. Okoko-Esseau, "The Christian Churches and Democratization in the Congo," 148–67. See also, the chapters by Paul Gifford, Terence Ranger, and Adrian Hastings in the same volume; AOPM, *Documentation et informations africaines* (Kinshasa), "De notre envoyé spécial," Brazzaville, 15 April 1994; Dorier-Apprill and Kouvouama, "Pluralisme religieux," 66–67.

11. Elisabeth Dorier-Apprill, "Christianisme et thérapeutique à Brazzaville," *Politique africaine* 55 (Oct. 1994), 133–39; Elisabeth Dorier-Apprill, "Les enjeux sociopolitiques du foisonnement religieux à Brazzaville," *Politique africaine* 64 (Dec. 1996), 129–35; Dorier-Apprill and Kouvouama, "Pluralisme religieux," 58–76.

12. Dorier-Apprill and Kouvouama, "Pluralisme religieux," 59. Also, Dorier-Apprill, Kouvouama, and Apprill, *Vivre à Brazzaville.*

13. Interview with Soeur Fabienne, Strasbourg, 18 May 2001; interview with Elisabeth Koutana, Pointe-Noire, 22 June 2000.

14. Information concerning events of 1997–98 was mainly gathered from conversations with sisters (1998–2001) who returned to their mother-houses, in France and in Pointe-Noire, 2000; also from short reports in their newsletters; *BCSSJC* 359 (Dec. 2002), Vice-Province d'Afrique Centrale (1997–2002), 568–76; and Langavant, "Les Franciscaines Missionnaires de Marie au Congo-Brazzaville," 309–10.

15. Interview with Léontine Bissangou, Pointe-Noire, 26 June 2000.

16. Interview with Marie-Thérèse Avemeka, Paris, 24 Nov. 1998.

17. Interview with Soeur Nzenzili Mboma and Soeur Julienne Makosso, Rome, 19 Feb. 1999.

18. Interview with Léontine Bissangou, Pointe-Noire, 26 June 2000.

19. Interview with Soeur Lydia Portella, Pointe-Noire, 17 June 2000.

20. "Contribution du Comité National des Femmes pour la Paix au Forum National pour la Réconciliation, l'Unité, la Démocratie et la Reconstruction du Congo," Brazzaville, 5–11, Jan. 1998; Clémentine Portella, Vice-Président, "Message du Comité National des Femmes pour la Paix-CNFP (Congo Brazzaville)", in *Rapport final des travaux, Colloque des mamans chrétiennes catholiques,* 186–87.

21. Speech of Cécile Matingou, minister in the "Gouvernement d'Union Nationale et de Salut Public," as reported in "Les femmes congolaises s'engagent sur le chemin de la paix," *La semaine africaine* 2148 (March 1998).

22. "Les femmes congolaises s'engagent sur le chemin de la paix," *La semaine africaine* 2148 (March 1998).

23. Interview with Suzanne Tchitembo, Pointe-Noire, 1 July 2000.

24. *Communiqué Final: Résolutions et Recommandations, Colloque des Mamans Chrétiennes Catholiques.* Included here is a summary of major points, not a complete account of the whole document.

25. "Un enfant est né! Son nom est:Mo.Pax," *La semaine africaine* 2162 (4 June 1998).

26. "Adresse du Président Denis Sassou-Nguesso," *Communiqué Final: Colloque des Mamans Chrétiennes Catholiques;* "Vous êtes le socle de la société!" *La semaine africaine* 2162 (4 June 1998). The reference to Peking was to the Fourth World Conference on Women in Beijing.

27. Interview, Pointe-Noire, 25 June 2000.

28. This is a large literature: see, for example, some of the issues raised in Walker, "Conceptualising Motherhood"; and for a discussion generated, among others, by Nigerian scholars, see Ifi Amadiume, *Re-inventing Africa: Matriarchy, Religion, and Culture* (London: Zed Press, 1997); and Oyèrónké Oyewùmi, *The Invention of Women: Making African Sense of Western Gender Discourses* (Minneapolis: University of Minnesota Press, 1997), and "Abiaymo: Theorising African Motherhood," *Jenda: A Journal of Culture and African Women Studies* 4 (2003), http://www.jendajournal.com.

29. Marguerite Guzman Bouvard, *Revolutionizing Motherhood: the Mothers of the Plaza de Mayo* (Wilmington, Del.: Scholarly Resources, 1994), 177.

Bibliography

Interviews were carried out in Brazzaville and Pointe-Noire with some in Europe and a few in the United States. The informants represented a range of backgrounds, including those who had attended Catholic schools, missionaries, fraternity members, and those who had no church attachment. Congolese and European sisters from the four missionary congregations most active in the region and Spiritan fathers and Congolese priests were also interviewed. Conversations usually started with open-ended questions about the individual's life and their involvement, if any, with the Catholic church. More specific follow-up questions grew out of the replies and dealt with such topics as the education of girls, Congolese-missionary relations, church organizations, family life, and other issues according to individual experience and interests. The author conducted interviews in French, and research assistants carried out interviews in Kilari, Kikongo, and Lingala. I especially want to thank Léa Ngole and Honoré Ngonza for their work as research assistants and with translations. The names given are those by which informants identified themselves. Names of those who wanted to remain anonymous are not given.

Interviews

Alden, Maya. 7 November, 10 December 1986, Brazzaville.
Ammeux, Soeur Johanna. 18 November 1998, Paris.
Anne-Andrée, Soeur. 17 May 2001, Ribeauvillé.
Avemeka, Marie-Thérèse. 24 November 1998, Paris.
Badila, Abbé Louis. 8 December 1986, Brazzaville.
Ball, Soeur Bernadette. 25 June 2000, Pointe-Noire.
Balossa, Martin. 17 June 1989, Brazzaville.

Bihani, Augustine. 5 November 2004, Indianapolis.

Bissangou, Léontine. 26 June 2000, Pointe-Noire.

Biyela, Soeur Marie-Michelle. 25 October 1986, Brazzaville; 14 November 1998, Paris.

Blanchet, Soeur Madeleine. 24 June 2000, Pointe-Noire.

Bouanga, Augustine. 15 June 2000, Pointe-Noire.

Bouanga, Paul. 29 June 2000, Pointe-Noire.

Boudzoumou, Antoine. 16 November 1986, Brazzaville.

Clothilde, Soeur. 10 November 1986, Brazzaville.

Coulon, Père Paul. 13 June 1997, 20 September 1998, Chevilly.

Courtois, Gilbert. 15 June 2000, Pointe-Noire.

Dianzinga, Scholastique. 27 December 1986, Brazzaville; 8 June 1996, Pau.

Fabienne, Soeur. 18 May 2001, Strasbourg.

Fouemina, Jeanne. 21 June 2000, Pointe-Noire.

Gévaudan, Père Robert. June 2000, Pointe-Noire.

Hagenbucher-Sacripanti, Frank. 13 April 2005, Paris.

Henriot, Marcelle. 4 March 1999, Saint Raphael.

Koudayou, Adèle. 14 June 1989, Brazzaville.

Koutana, Elisabeth, 22 June 2000, Pointe-Noire.

Lannon-Unvoas, Maryanne. 26 November 1998, Brest.

Lelo, Abbé Joachim. 28 June 2000, Pointe-Noire.

Loemba, Abbé Georges. 28 June 2000, Pointe-Noire.

Madoungou, Joseph Kimfoko. 14 June 2000, Diosso; 16 June 2000, Pointe-Noire.

Makosso, Soeur Julienne. 19 February 1999, Rome; 2 July 2000, Pointe-Noire.

Malékat, Firmine. 17 December 1986, Brazzaville.

Mambeke-Boucher, Bernard. 17 November, 1 December 1986, Brazzaville.

Marie, Soeur. 6 January 1987, Pointe-Noire.

Marie-Louise, Soeur. 15 May 2001, Ribeauvillé.

Marie-Rita, Soeur. 15 May 2001, Ribeauvillé.

Marie-Thérèse, Soeur. 15 May 2001, Ribeauvillé.

Marie-Zita, Soeur. 17 May 2001, Strasbourg.

Mbemba, Veronique. 15 December 1986, 17 June 1989, Brazzaville.

Mboma, Soeur Nzenzili. 19 February, 16 March 1999, Rome.

Mère Emilie. 12, 13 June 1989, Brazzaville.

Metereau, Marie-Thérèse. 30 June 1997, Paris.

Miayedimina, Yvonne. 25 November 1986, Brazzaville.

Mouanga, Marie-Antoinette. 11 November 1998, Paris.

Ngole, Jean-Pierre. 13 October 1988, Bloomington.

Ngole, Sidone. 12 May 1988, Bloomington.

Ngondjo, Anne. 15 June 1989, Brazzaville.

Nsongolo, Adèle. 16 June 1989, Brazzaville.

Onghaïe, Soeur Gertrude. 6 November 1986, Brazzaville; 23 June 2000, Pointe-Noire.

Oumba, Marie-Thérèse. 15 August 1993, Bloomington.

Pambou, Abbé Louis. 20 June 2000, Pointe-Noire.

Pannier, Père Guy. 2 October 1998, Paris.

Peka, Stephanie Joséphine. 15 June 1989, Brazzaville.

Pena, Anne-Marie Thérèse. 23 June 2000, Pointe-Noire.

Portella, Soeur Lydia. 17, 29 June 2000, Pointe-Noire.

Samba, Marie-Paule. 13 January 1987, Brazzaville.

Schaub, Père Gaston. 14, 15 October 1986, Brazzaville.
Scholastique, Soeur. 3 November 1986, Brazzaville.
Sinant, Geneviève, 24 June 2000, Pointe-Noire.
Suzanne, Soeur. 15 May 2001, Ribeauvillé.
Tchitembo, Suzanne. 1 July 2000, Pointe-Noire.
Unvoas, Jeanette. 26, 27 November 1998, Brest.
Wauters, Père Pierre. 7 January 1987, Loango; 15 October 1998, Paris.

Archives

Archives de la Congrégation des Soeurs de Saint-Joseph de Cluny, Paris
Archives de la Musée Royale d'Afrique Centrale, Tervuren
Archives de l'Organization de la Recherche Scientifique et Technique Outre-Mer, Paris
Archives des Franciscaines Missionnaires de Marie, Rome
Archives des Oeuvres Pontificales Missionnaires, Lyons
Archives des Soeurs de la Divine Providence de Ribeauvillé, Ribeauvillé
Archives des Soeurs Missionnaires du Saint-Esprit, Paris
Archives Générales de la Congrégation des Pères du Saint-Esprit, Chevilly
Archives Nationales, Centre des Archives d'Outre-Mer, Aix-en-Provence
Archives Nationales du Congo, Brazzaville
Archivio de Propaganda Fide, Rome

Newspapers and Journals

The following are important primary sources. The dates given are the range of the articles
consulted. A few of the more important articles are listed in the bibliography. In all
cases, full references are given in the notes for the chapter where they are cited.
Annales apostoliques (*AA*), 1886–1926; became *Annales des Pères du Saint-Esprit,* 1927–39;
later, *Pentecôte sur le monde.*
Annales des Franciscaines Missionnaires de Marie, 1910–65; later, *Peuples du monde.*
Annales des Soeurs de Saint-Joseph de Cluny, (*ASSJC*) 1892–1960; later *Cluny-Mission.*
Bulletin de la Comité de l'Afrique Française (*BCAF*), 1893–1939.
Bulletin général de la Congrégation des Pères du Saint-Esprit (*BCPSE*), 1883–1960.
Bulletin de la Congrégation des Soeurs de Saint-Joseph de Cluny (*BCSSJC*), 1886–2000.
Bulletin de la Société des Recherches Congolaises (*BSRC*), 1922–39; later *Bulletin de l'Institut
d'Etudes Centrafricaines* (*BIEC*), 1945–60.
Etumba, Brazzaville, 1960s.
Journal Officiel du Congo-Français, 1904–10; became *Journal Officiel de l'Afrique Equatoriale
Française* (*JOAEF*), 1910–59.
La Semaine de l'AEF, 1952–60; became *La Semaine Africaine,* 1960–present.
Le bon message (*Bulletin mensuel de la Mission Catholique de Brazzaville*), 1933–38.
Le mémorial du Congo Français, 1888–1906; became *Le mémorial du Vicariat Apostolique du
Loango,* 1907–14.
Les missions catholiques (*MC*), 1881–1939.
Liaison, Brazzaville, 1950–59.
Pentecôte: Bulletin des Soeurs Missionnaires du Saint-Esprit, 1937–64; later integrated with
Pentecôte sur le monde.
Ut sint unum: Bulletin d'information et de liaison, Soeurs de la Divine Providence de Ribeauvillé,
1955–67.

Other Sources

Abbott, Walter M., ed. *The Documents of Vatican II*. 2nd ed. New York: Crossroad Publishing, 1989.

Accampo, Elinor A., Rachel G. Fuchs, and Mary Lynn Stewart, eds. *Gender and the Politics of Social Reform in France, 1870–1914*. Baltimore, Md.: Johns Hopkins University Press, 1995.

Achikbache, Bahjat, and Francis Anglade. "Les villes prises d'assaut: les migrations internes." *Politique africaine* 31 (1988): 7–14.

Aïssi, Antoine-Marie. "Le système juridictionnel au service de l'ordre colonial: essence de la justice indigène." *CCAH* 2 (1978): 27–53.

Allaire, R. P. *Le R. P. Allaire: missionnaire au Congo d'après ses écrits et sa correspondance*. Paris: Librairie Religieuse H. Oudin, n.d.

Allman, Jean. "Fathering, Mothering and Making Sense of *Ntamboa*: Reflections on the Economy of Child-Rearing in Colonial Asante." *Africa* 67, no. 2 (1987): 296–321.

———. "Making Mothers: Missionaries, Medical Officers and Women's Work in Colonial Asante, 1924–1945." *History Workshop Journal* 37 (Autumn 1994): 23–47.

———, ed. *Fashioning Africa: Power and the Politics of Dress*. Bloomington: Indiana University Press, 2004.

Allman, Jean, Susan Geiger, and Nakanyike Musisi, eds. *Women in African Colonial Histories*. Bloomington: Indiana University Press, 2002.

Amadiume, Ifi. *Re-inventing Africa: Matriarchy, Religion, and Culture*. London: Zed Press, 1997.

Amselle, Jean-Loup. *Mestizo Logics: Anthropology of Identity in Africa and Elsewhere*. Stanford, Calif.: Stanford University Press, 1998.

Andersson, Ephraim. *Churches at the Grass-Roots: A Study in Congo-Brazzaville*. London: Lutterworth Press, 1968.

———. *Messianic Popular Movements in the Lower Congo*. Uppsala: Almquist and Wiksells Boktryekeri AB, 1958.

Andrée, Marie S. *La femme noire en Afrique occidentale*. Paris: Payot, 1939.

Ardener, Shirley, ed. *Defining Females: The Nature of Women in Society*. Oxford: Berg, 1993.

Arnfred, Signe, ed. *Re-thinking Sexualities in Africa*. Uppsala: Nordiska Afrikainstitutet, 2005.

Augouard, Chanoine Louis. *Anecdotes congolaises*. Poitiers, France: M. Poussin, 1934.

———. *La vie inconnue de Monseigneur Augouard*. Evereux: M. Poussin, 1934.

Augouard, Prosper P. *28 années au Congo*. Poitiers, France: Société française d'Imprimerie et de Librairie, 1905.

———. *36 années au Congo*. Poitiers, France: Société française d'Imprimerie et de Librairie, 1914.

———. *44 années au Congo*. Evreux, France: Poussin, 1934.

Austen, Ralph A., and Rita Headrick. "Equatorial Africa under Colonial Rule." In *History of Central Africa*, ed. Birmingham and Martin, 2:27–94.

Axelson, Sigbert. *Culture Confrontation in the Lower Congo*. Falköping, Sweden: Gummersons, 1970.

Ayouné, Jean-Rémy. "La formation de la femme africaine en AEF." *Service de l'Information: Bulletin de Documentation, AEF* 158 (1952): 47.

Azevedo, Mario J. "Ethnicity and Democratization in Congo and Chad, 1945–1995." In *State Building and Democratization in Africa*, ed. Kidane Mengistead and Cyril Daddieh, 157–82. Westport: Praeger, 1999.

Bafouetela, Raymond. "Le travail sous la période coloniale au Congo (1897–1945)." *CCAH* 6 (1981): 77–94.

Balandier, Georges. "La situation coloniale: approche théorique." *Cahiers internationaux de sociologie* 11 (1951): 44–79.

———. *Sociologie des Brazzavilles noires.* 2nd ed. Paris: Presses de la Fondation Nationale des Sciences Politiques, 1985.

———. *The Sociology of Black Africa.* London: Deutsch, 1970.

Baldwin, Monica. *I Leapt over the Wall: Contrast and Impressions after Twenty-Eight Years in a Convent.* New York: Rinehart, 1950.

Banville, Ghislain de. *Kalouka et Zoungoula: les deux premières religieuses de Brazzaville, au Congo, 1892–1909.* Paris: Karthala, 2000.

Baratier, Colonel. *Au Congo: souvenirs de la Mission Marchand.* Paris: Arthème Fayard, 1914.

Barnes, Teresa A. *"We Women Worked So Hard": Gender, Urbanization and Social Reproduction in colonial Harare, Zimbabwe 1930–1956.* Portsmouth, N.H.: Heinemann, 1999.

Barthélémy, Pascale. "La professionnalisation des africaines en AOF (1920–1960)." *Vingtième siècle, revue d'histoire* 75 (juillet–sept. 2002): 35–46.

Bastian, Adolf. *Die Deutsche Expedition an der Loango-Küste.* 2 vols. Jena, Germany: Hermann Costenoble, 1874.

Bay, Edna, ed. *Women and Work in Africa.* Boulder, Colo.: Westview Press, 1982.

Bayart, Jean-François. *The State in Africa: The Politics of the Belly.* London: Longman, 1993.

———, ed. *Religion et modernité politique en Afrique noire: dieu pour tous et chacun pour soi.* Paris: Karthala, 1993.

Bazenguissa-Ganga, Rémy. *Les voies du politique au Congo: essai de sociologie historique.* Paris: Karthala, 1997.

———. "The Spread of Political Violence in Congo-Brazzaville." *African Affairs* 98 (1999): 37–54.

Beidelman, T. O. *Colonial Evangelism: A Socio-Historical Study of an East African Mission at the Grassroots.* Bloomington: Indiana University Press, 1982.

Bel, Jean-Marc. *Rapport sur une mission au Congo Français, 1906–1907.* Paris: Imprimerie Nationale, 1908.

Berger, Iris. "African Women's History: Themes and Perspectives." *Journal of Colonialism and Colonial History* 4, no. 1 (2003), http://muse.jhu.edu/journals/journal_of_ colonialism_and_colonial_history.

———. "'Beasts of Burden' Revisited: Interpretations of Women and Gender in Southern African Societies." In *Paths towards the Past: African Historical Essays in Honor of Jan Vansina,* ed. Robert Harms et al., 123–41. Atlanta: African Studies Association Press, 1994.

———. "Fertility as Power: Spirit Mediums, Priestesses, and the Precolonial State in Interlacustrine East Africa." In *Revealing Prophets: Prophecy in East African History,* ed. David M. Anderson and Douglas H. Johnson, 65–82. London: James Currey, 1995.

Berger, Iris, and E. Frances White. *Women in Sub-Saharan Africa: Restoring Women to History.* Bloomington: Indiana University Press, 1999.

Bernard, J. "La mutualité chez les Bacongo: le kitemo." *BSRC* 3 (1923): 9–14.

Bernault, Florence. "Body, Power and Sacrifice in Equatorial Africa." *JAH* 47, no. 2 (2006): 207–39.

———. *Démocraties ambiguës en Afrique Centrale: Congo-Brazzaville, Gabon: 1940–1965.* Paris: Karthala, 1996.

———. "Economie de la mort et reproduction sociale au Gabon." In *Mama Africa: hommage à Catherine Coquery-Vidrovitch*, ed. Odile Goerg and Issiaka Mande, 203–18. Paris: L'Harmattan, 2005.

———. "Magie, sorcellerie et politique au Gabon et au Congo-Brazzaville." In *Démocratie et mutations culturelles en Afrique noire*, ed. Marc Mvé Bekale, 21–39. Paris: L'Harmattan, 2005.

———. "The Political Shaping of Sacred Locality in Brazzaville, 1959–1997." In *Africa's Urban Past*, ed. David M. Anderson and Richard Rathbone, 283–302. Oxford: James Currey, 2000.

———. "The Politics of Enclosure in Colonial and Post-colonial Africa." In *A History of Prison and Confinement in Africa*, ed. Florence Bernault, 1–46. Portsmouth, N.H.: Heinemann, 2003.

Beti, Mongo. *The Poor Christ of Bomba*. London: Heinemann, 1971.

Birmingham, David, and Phyllis M. Martin, eds. *History of Central Africa*. 3 vols. Harlow: Longman, 1983, 1998.

Blackbourn, David. "The Catholic Church in Europe since the French Revolution. A Review Article." *Comparative Studies in Society and History* 33, no. 4 (1991): 778–90.

Blouin, Andrée. *My Country, Africa: Autobiography of the Black Pasionaria*. New York: Praeger, 1983.

Bockie, Simon. *Death and the Invisible World: The World of Kongo Belief*. Bloomington: Indiana University Press, 1993.

Bonnafé, Pierre. "Une classe d'âge politique: la JMNR de la République du Congo-Brazzaville." *CEA* 8, no. 31 (1968): 327–68.

Bonnefont, P. "La formation de la famille chrétienne en pays Bacongo." *AA* 40 (1924): 111.

Bonnefont, P., and Jean Lombard. "Notes sur les coutumes lari." *BIEC* 2, no. 2 (1946): 141–76.

Bontinck, François. "Le rachat d'enfants esclaves dans les rivières équatoriales (1889–1897)." *Revue africaine de théologie* 11, no. 19 (1987): 51–64.

Bouchaud, J. S. "Les missions catholiques." In *Afrique Equatoriale Française*, ed. Eugène Guernier, 579–87. Paris: Encyclopédie Coloniale et Maritime, 1950.

Bouche, Denise. *Les villages de liberté en Afrique Noire Française, 1887–1910*. Paris: Mouton, 1968.

Boucher, Mgr. A. *Au Congo Français: Les Missions Catholiques*. Paris: Librairie Pierre Téqui, 1928.

Bouvard, Margaret Guzman. *Revolutionizing Motherhood: The Mothers of the Plaza de Mayo*. Wilmington, Del.: Scholarly Resources, 1994.

Bowie, Fiona, Deborah Kirkwood, and Shirley Ardener, eds. *Women and Missions: Past and Present: Anthropological and Historical Perspectives*. New York: Oxford University Press, 1993.

Bozzoli, Belinda. *Women of Phokeng: Consciousness, Life Strategy, and Migrancy in South Africa, 1900–1983*. Portsmouth, N.H.: Heinemann, 1991.

Brasseur, Paule. "Anne-Marie Javouhey (1779–1851)." In *Libermann*, ed. Coulon and Brasseur, 643–48.

Brazzaville janvier–février 1944: aux sources de la decolonization. Paris: Plon, 1988.

Briault, Maurice. "Le cinquantenaire de la mission du Congo Français: Brazzaville, 1888–1938." *Revue d'histoire des missions* 15 (Dec. 1938): 504–22; 16 (Mar. 1939): 37–58.

Broadhead, Susan H. "Slave Wives, Free Sisters: Bakongo Women and Slavery, c. 1700–1850." In *Women and Slavery in Africa*, ed. Robertson and Klein, 160–81.

Brown, Peter. *The Cult of Saints: Its Rise and Function in Latin Christianity.* Chicago: University of Chicago Press, 1981.

Bruel, Georges. *La France Equatoriale Africaine.* Paris: Larose, 1935.

Burke, Joan F. "Research in a Post-missionary Situation: Among Zairian Sisters of Notre Dame de Namur." *Journal of the Anthropological Society of Oxford* 23, no. 2 (1992): 157–68.

———. "These Catholic Sisters Are All Mamas! Celibacy and the Metaphor of Maternity." In *Women and Missions,* ed. Bowie, Kirkwood, and Ardener, 251–66.

———. *These Catholic Sisters Are All Mamas! Towards the Inculturation of the Sisterhood in Africa, an Ethnographic Study.* Leiden, Neth.: Brill, 2001.

Cabanac, P. "Notes sur les tribus Ballalis et Bassoundis de la Subdivision de Manyanga (Moyen-Congo)." *BSRC* 7 (1925): 77–94.

Carozzi, Carlo, and Maurizio Trepolo. *Congo Brazzaville: Bibliographie Générale.* Turin: Edizione Libreria Cortina, 1991.

Carrie, P. *Coutumier de l'oeuvre des enfants dans le vicariat apostolique du Congo Français.* Loango: Imprimerie de la Mission, 1890.

———. *Oeuvre des Soeurs de Saint-Joseph de Cluny dans la Mission du Congo Français.* Loango: Imprimerie de la Mission, 1897.

———. *Règles des Frères de la Congrégation de Saint-Pierre Claver fondeé et approuvée par Mgr. Carrie.* Loango: Imprimerie de la Mission, 1891.

Castellani, Charles. *Les femmes au Congo.* Paris: Ernest Flammarion, 1898.

Catechism of the Catholic Church. English translation of the United States Catholic Conference. In Libreria Editrice Vaticana. New York: Doubleday, 1994.

"Catholicism in Southern Africa." Special issue of *Le fait missionnaire* 14 (July 2004).

Chaillu, Paul B. du. *Voyages et aventures dans l'Afrique équatoriale.* Paris: M. Lévy, 1863.

Charles, P. Pierre. "Missiologie antiféministe." In *Le rôle de la femme dans les missions: rapport et compte rendu de la XXe Semaine de Missiologie de Louvain.* Brussels: L'Edition Universelle, 1950.

Chrétien, Jean-Pierre, ed. *L'invention religieuse en Afrique: histoire et religion en Afrique noire.* Paris: Karthala, 1993.

Clancy-Smith, Julia, and Frances Gouda. "Introduction." In *Domesticating the Empire,* ed. Clancy-Smith and Gouda, 1–20.

———, eds. *Domesticating the Empire: Race, Gender and Family Life in French and Dutch Colonialism.* Charlottesville: University Press of Virginia, 1998.

Clark, Carolyn M. "Land and Food, Women and Power in Nineteenth Century Kikuyu." *Africa* 50, no. 4 (1980): 357–69.

Clark, Gracia. "Mothering, Work, and Gender in Urban Asante Ideology and Practice." *American Anthropologist* 101, no. 4 (1999): 717–29.

Clark, John. *The Failure of Democracy in the Republic of Congo.* Boulder, Colo.: Lynne Rienner, 2008.

———. "The Neo-colonial Context of the Democratic Experiment of Congo-Brazzaville." *African Affairs* 101 (2002):171–92.

Clark, John F., and David E. Gardinier, eds. *Political Reform in Francophone Africa.* Boulder, Colo.: Westview, 1997.

Clark, Linda L. "The Primary Education of French Girls: Pedagogical Prescriptions and Social Realities, 1880–1940." *History of Education Quarterly* 21, no. 3 (1981): 411–28.

Cohen, David William. "Doing Social History from Pim's Doorway." In *Reliving the Past: The World of Social History,* ed. Oliver Zunz, 191–235. Chapel Hill: University of North Carolina, 1985.

Cohen, William B. *The French Encounter with Africans*. Bloomington: Indiana University Press, 1990.

Colloque des Mamans Chrétiennes Catholiques de l'Afrique Centrale, Rapport final des Travaux. Brazzaville: MOPAX. Unpublished, 1998.

Comaroff, Jean. *Body of Power, Spirit of Resistance*. Chicago: University of Chicago Press, 1985.

Comaroff, John, and Jean Comaroff. *Of Revelation and Revolution*. 2 vols. Chicago: University of Chicago Press, 1991.

Comhaire-Sylvain, Suzanne. *Femmes de Kinshasa hier et aujourd'hui*. Paris: Mouton, 1968.

"Congo-Brazzaville: entre guerre et paix." Special issue, *Afrique contemporaine* 186 (April–June 1998).

Conklin, Alice L. *A Mission to Civilize: The Republican Idea of Empire in France and West Africa, 1895–1930*. Stanford, Calif.: Stanford University Press, 1997.

———. "Redefining 'Frenchness': Citizenship, Race, Regeneration, and Imperial Motherhood in France and West Africa, 1914–40." In *Domesticating the Empire*, ed. Clancy-Smith and Gouda, 65–83.

Cooper, Barbara. *Marriage in Maradi: Gender and Culture in a Hausa Society in Niger, 1900–1989*. Portsmouth, N.H.: Heinemann, 1997.

Cooper, Frederick. *Africa since 1940: The Past of the Present*. Cambridge: Cambridge University Press, 2002.

Cooper, Frederick, and Ann Laura Stoler, eds. *Tensions of Empire: Colonial Culture in a Bourgeois World*. Berkeley and Los Angeles: University of California Press, 1997.

Coquery-Vidrovitch, Catherine. *African Women: A Modern History*. Boulder, Colo.: Westview Press, 1997.

———. *Brazza et la prise de possession du Congo, 1883–1885*. Paris: Mouton, 1969.

———. "Histoire de femmes d'Afrique." *Clio, histoire, femmes et société* 6 (1997): 7–13.

———. "Investissements privés, investissements publiques en AEF, 1900–1940." *African Economic History* 12 (1983): 13–31.

———. *Le Congo au temps des grandes compagnies concessionnaires, 1898–1930*. Paris: Mouton, 1972.

Cornet, Anne. "Action sanitaire et contrôle social au Ruanda (1920–1940): femmes, missions et politiques de santé," Ph.D. thesis, Université Catholique de Louvain, 2005.

Coulon, Paul, ed. "La part des femmes dans la mission en Afrique, XIXe–XXe siècles." Special edition of *Mémoire spiritaine* 10 (1999).

Coulon, Paul, and Paule Brasseur, eds. *Libermann, 1802–1852: une pensée et une mystique missionnaires*. Paris: Cerf, 1988.

Creary, Nicholas. "African Inculturation of the Catholic Church in Zimbabwe, 1958–1977." *Historian* 61, no. 4 (Summer 1999): 765–81.

———. "Jesuit Missionary Perspectives on the Formation of African Clergy and Religious Institutes in Zimbabwe, c. 1922–1959." *Le fait missionnaire* 14 (July 2004): 117–45.

Curtis, Sarah A. *Educating the Faithful: Religion, Schooling and Society in Nineteenth Century France*. Dekalb: Northern Illinois University Press, 2000.

Cuvelier, Jean. *Documents sur une mission française au Kakongo, 1766–1776*. Brussels: IRCB, 1953.

———. "Les missions catholiques en face des danses des Bakongo." *Africanae fraternae ephemerides romanae* (1939): 143–76.

Dangarembga, Tsitsi. *Nervous Conditions*. Seattle, Wash.: Seal Press, 1998.

Dapper, Olfert. *Naukeurige Beschrijvinge der Afrikaensche Gewesten*. 2nd ed. Amsterdam: J. van Meurs, 1676.

Daughton, J. P. *An Empire Divided: Religion, Republicanism and the Making of French Colonialism, 1880–1914* (Oxford: Oxford University Press, 2006.

Davin, Anna. "Imperialism and Motherhood." *History Workshop* 5 (1978): 9–65.

Davison, Jean, with the Women of Matira. *Voices from Mutira: Lives of Rural Gikuyu Women*. Boulder, Colo.: Lynne Rienner, 1989.

Delcourt, J. *Au Congo Français, Mgr. Carrie, 1842–1904*. Brazzaville: Maison Libermann. n.d.

Deleval. "Les tribus Kavati du Mayombe." *Revue Congolaise* 3 (1913): 33–40, 103–15, 170–86, 253–64.

Dembi, René. "'Tchicoumbi' ou réclusion des filles nubiles chez les Mayombe." *Liaison* 32 (Feb. 1953): 29–31.

Dennett, R. E. *At the Back of the Black Man's Mind*. London: Macmillan, 1906.

———. *Notes on the Folklore of the Fjort (French Congo)*. London: Folk-Lore Society, 1898.

———. *Seven Years among the Fjort*. London: Sampson Low, Marston, Searly and Rivington, 1887.

Denzer, LaRay. "Domestic Science Training in Colonial Yorubaland, Nigera." In *African Encounters with Domesticity*, ed. Hansen, 116–40.

Derouet, J. "Les lunettes de Mère Agnès." *AA* 26 (1910): 278–82.

Dianzinga, Scholastique. "Le décret du 15 juin 1939 et la condition des femmes en Afrique Equatoriale Française." *CCAH* 13 (1993): 55–69.

———. "Les femmes congolaises du début de la colonisation à 1960." Ph.D. thesis, Université de Pau, 1998.

Dorier-Apprill, Elisabeth. "Christianisme et thérapeutique à Brazzaville." *Politique africaine* 55 (Oct. 1994): 133–39.

———. "Jeunesse et ethnicités citadines à Brazzaville." *Politique africaine* 64 (Dec. 1996): 73–88.

———. "Les enjeux sociopolitiques du foisonnement religieux à Brazzaville." *Politique africaine* 64 (Dec. 1996):129–35.

Dorier-Apprill, Elisabeth, and Abel Kouvouama. "Pluralisme religieux et société urbaine à Brazzaville." *Afrique contemporaine* 186 (1998): 58–76.

Dorier-Apprill, Elisabeth, Abel Kouvouama, and Christophe Apprill. *Vivre à Brazzaville: modernité et crise au quotidien*. Paris: Karthala, 1998.

Doutreloux, Albert. *L'ombre des fétiches: société et culture yombe*. Louvain: Editions Nauwelaerts, 1967.

Downey, Michael, ed. *The New Dictionary of Catholic Spirituality*. Collegeville, Minn.: Liturgical Press, 1993.

Dreuille, Mayeul de. *La Bouenza 1892–1992: les sources de l'église au Congo*. Paris: Beauchesne, 1994.

Drew, Allison. "Andrée Blouin and Pan-African Nationalism in Guinea and the Congo," In *Pan-African Biography*, ed. Robert A. Hill, 209–18. Los Angeles: UCLA African Studies Center and Crossroads Press, 1987.

Dubois, Collette. "Femmes d'Afrique centrale: une histoire sociale parcellaire et occultée." In *La recherche en histoire et l'enseignement de l'histoire en Afrique centrale francophone*. Aix-en-Provence: Publications de l'Université de Provence, 1997.

Dufourcq, Elisabeth. *Les congrégations religieuses féminines hors d'Europe de Richelieu à nos jours: histoire naturelle d'une diaspora*. 4 vols. Paris: Librairie de l'Inde, 1993.

Dulucq, Sophie, and Odile Goerg, "Le fait colonial au miroir des colonisées. Femmes, genre et colonisation: un bilan des recherches francophones en histoire de l'Afrique subsaharienne (1950–2003)." In *Histoire des femmes en situation coloniale,* ed. Hugon, 43–70.

Dupré, Georges. *Les naissances d'une société: espace et historicité chez les Beembé du Congo.* Paris: ORSTOM, 1985.

———. *Un ordre et sa destruction.* Paris: ORSTOM, 1982.

Dupré, Marie-Claude. "Comment être femme: un aspect du rituel Mukisi chez les Téké de la République Populaire du Congo." *Archives de Sciences Sociales des Religions* 46, no. 1 (1978): 57–84.

———. "Les femmes mukisi des Téké Tsaayi rituel de possession et culte anti-sorcier (République Populaire du Congo)." *Journal de la société des africanistes* 44, no. 1 (1974): 53–69.

Dybowski, Jean. *La route du Tchad: du Loango au Chari.* Paris: Librairie de Firmin-Didot, 1893.

Ebaugh, Helen Rose. "Patriarchal Bargains and Latent Avenues of Social Mobility: Nuns in the Roman Catholic Church." *Gender and Society* 7, no. 3 (1993): 400–14.

Eboué, Félix. *La nouvelle politique indigène en l'Afrique Equatoriale Française.* Brazzaville: Afrique Française Libre, 1941.

Einarsdottir, Jonina. *Tired of Weeping: Mother Love, Child Death and Poverty in Guinea-Bissau.* 2nd ed. Madison: University of Wisconsin Press, 2005.

Ejikene, Anene. "Mission and Motherhood: Towards a History of Catholic Women and Education in Onitsha, Nigeria, 1885–1964." Ph.D. thesis, Columbia University, 2003.

Ellsberg, Robert. *All Saints.* New York: Crossroad Publishing, 1997.

Emecheta, Buchi. *The Joys of Motherhood.* New York: Georges Braziller, 1979.

Engels, Dagmar, and Shula Marks, eds. *Contesting Colonial Hegemony: State and Society in Africa and India.* London: British Academic Press, 1994.

Ernoult, Jean. "L'abbé Charles Maondé (+/-1865–1907): premier prêtre du vicariat apostolique de Loango." *Mémoire spiritaine* 14 (2001): 45–57.

———. *Les spiritains au Congo de 1865 à nos jours.* Paris: Congrégation du Saint-Esprit, 1995.

Even, André. "Quelques coutumes des tribus badondos et bassoundis." *BSRC* 13 (1931): 18–19.

Ezra, Kate, and Hans-Joachim Koloss. "Kneeling Woman and Child." In *Art of Central Africa: Masterpieces from the Berlin Museum für Völkerkunde,* ed. Hans-Joachim Koloss. New York: Metropolitan Museum of Art, 1990.

Fabre, S. Marcienne. "Un centenaire au Congo, 1886–1986." Special issue, *Cluny-Mission* (Sept.–Oct. 1986): 88–92.

Fair, Laura. *Pastimes and Politics: Culture, Community, and Identity in Post-Abolition Urban Zanzibar, 1890–1945.* Athens: Ohio University Press, 2001.

Falola, Toyin, ed. *African Historiography: Essays in Honour of Jacob Ade Ajayi.* Harlow, UK: Longman, 1993.

Feay, Troy. "Mission to Moralize: Slaves, Africans, and Missionaries in the French Colonies, 1815–1852." Ph.D. thesis, University of Notre Dame, 2003.

Fields, Karen. *Revival and Rebellion in Colonial Central Africa.* Portsmouth, N.H.: Heinemann, 1997.

Flannery, Austin, ed. *Vatican Council II.* Northport, N.Y.: Costello Publishing, 1965.

Ford, Caroline. "Female Martyrdom and the Politics of Sainthood in Nineteenth Century France: The Cult of Saint Philomène." In *Catholicism in Britain and France since 1879,* ed. Frank Tallett and Nicholas Atkin, 115–34. London: Hambledon Press, 1996.

Franciscaines Missionnaires de Marie. *Notre Histoire.* 13 vols. Unpublished.

———. *Pour la Mission et ses risques, 1877–1984.* Grottaferrata, Italy: Imprimerie de FMM, 1985.

Franque, D. José. *Nós, os Cabindas: história, leis, usos e costumes dos povos de N'goio.* Lisbon: Editora Lisboa, 1940.

Fussell, Paul. *Uniforms: Why We Are What We Wear.* New York: Houghton Mifflin, 2003.

Gaitskell, Deborah. "At Home with Hegemony? Coercion and Consent in the Education of African Girls for Domesticity in South Africa before 1910." In *Contesting Colonial Hegemony,* ed. Engels and Marks, 110–30.

———. "Devout Domesticity? A Century of African Women's Christianity in South Africa." In *Women and Gender in Southern Africa to 1945,* ed. Cherryl Walker, 251–72. London: James Currey, 1990.

———. "Housewives, Maids or Mothers: Some Contradictions of Domesticity for Christian Women in Johannesburg, 1903–1939." *JAH* 24, no. 2 (1983): 241–56.

———. "'Prayer and Preaching': The Distinctive Spirituality of African Women's Church Organizations." In *Missions and Christianity in South African History,* ed. Henry Bredekamp and Robert Ross, 211–32. Johannesburg: Witwatersrand University Press, 1995.

———. "Wailing for Purity? Prayer Unions, African Mothers and Adolescent Daughters 1912–1940." In *Industrialisation and Social Change in South Africa,* ed. Shula Marks and Richard Rathbone, 338–57. Harlow, UK: Longman, 1982.

Gambou, Auguste-René. "Le mariage en Afrique centrale précoloniale: le problème de la nubilité féminine." *CCAH* 7 (1982): 33–38.

Gandziami, Elie. "De Loango à Tandala par la piste de carvanes." *Liaison* 49–50 (1955): 26–30.

Ganga, Jean-Claude. *Combats pour un sport africain.* Paris: L'Harmattan, 1979.

Gardinier, David E. "Education in French Equatorial Africa, 1842–1945." In *Proceedings of the Third Annual Meeting of the French Colonial Historical Society,* 121–37. Lanham, Md.: University Press of America, 1978.

———. "Schooling in the States of Equatorial Africa." *CJAS* 5, no. 3 (1974): 517–38.

Gaulme, François. *Le pays de Cama: un ancien état côtier du Gabon et ses origines.* Paris: Karthala, 1981.

Gauze, Réné. *The Politics of Congo-Brazzaville.* Stanford, Calif.: Hoover Institute Press, 1973.

Geertz, Clifford. *The Interpretation of Cultures.* New York: Basic Books, 1973.

Geiger, Susan. *TANU Women: Gender, and Culture in the Making of Tanganyikan Nationalism, 1955–1965.* Portsmouth, N.H.: Heinemann, 1997.

Geshiere, Peter. *The Modernity of Witchcraft: Politics and the Occult in Pre-colonial Africa.* Charlottesville: University Press of Virginia, 1997.

Gibson, Ralph. "Female Religious Orders in Nineteenth Century France." In *Catholicism in Britain and France since 1789,* ed. Frank Tallett and Nicholas Atkin, 104–15. London: Hambledon Press, 1996.

———. *A Social History of French Catholicism 1789–1914.* New York: Routledge, 1989.

Gifford, Paul, ed. *The Christian Church and the Democratization of Africa.* Leiden, Neth.: Brill, 1995.

Giles-Vernick, Tamara. *Cutting the Vines of the Past: Environmental Histories of the Central African Rain Forest.* Charlottesville: University Press of Virginia, 2002.

Girard, L. "Brazzaville." *BCAF*: Renseignements coloniaux (March 1916): 26–44.

Gnali, Mambou A. "La femme africaine, un cas: la Congolaise." *Présence africaine* 68 (1968): 17–31.

Goerg, Odile. "Femmes africaines et pratique historique en France." *Politique africaine* 72 (1998): 130–44.

———, ed. *Perspectives historiques sur le genre en Afrique.* Paris: L'Harmattan, 2007.

Gondola, Ch. Didier. *Villes miroirs: migrations et identités urbaines à Kinshasa et Brazzaville, 1930–1970.* Paris: L'Harmattan, 1997.

Gray, Christopher. *Colonial Rule and Crisis in Equatorial Africa: Southern Gabon, 1850–1940.* Rochester, N.Y.: University of Rochester Press, 2002.

Gray, Richard. *Black Christians and White Missionaries.* New Haven, Conn.: Yale University Press, 1990.

Grosz-Ngate, Maria, and Omari H. Kokole, eds. *Gendered Encounters: Challenging Cultural Boundaries and Social Hierarchies in Africa.* New York: Routledge, 1997.

Gruénais, Marc-Eric, Florent Mouanda Mbambi, and Joseph Tonda. "Messies, fétiches et lutte de pouvoirs entre les 'grandes hommes' du Congo démocratique." *CEA* 35, no. 137 (1995): 163–93.

Guernier, Eugène, ed. *Afrique Equatoriale Française.* Paris: Encyclopédie Coloniale et Maritime, 1950.

Guillemot, Marcel. *Notice sur le Congo Français.* Paris: J. André, 1901.

Güssfeldt, Paul, Julius Falkenstein, and Eduard Pechuël-Loesche. *Die Loango-Expedition ausgesandt von der Deutschen Gesellshaft zur Erforschung Aequatorial-Africas, 1873–1876.* 3 vols. Leipzig: P. Frohberg, 1879–1907.

Guyer, Jane I. "Wealth in People, Wealth in Things: Introduction." *JAH* 36, no. 1 (1995): 83–90.

Guyer, Jane I., and S. M. Elo Belinga. "Wealth in People as Wealth in Knowledge: Accumulation and Composition in Equatorial Africa." *JAH* 36, no. 1 (1995): 91–120.

Hafkin, Nancy J., and Edna G. Bay, eds. *Women in Africa: Studies in Social and Economic Change.* Stanford, Calif.: Stanford University Press, 1976.

Hagenbucher-Sacripanti, Frank. *Les fondements spirituels du pouvoir au royaume de Loango.* Paris: ORSTOM, 1973.

———. *Le prophète et le militant (Congo-Brazzaville).* Paris: L'Harmattan, 2002.

———. *Santé et rédemption par les génies au Congo.* Paris: Publisud, 1993.

Hansen, Holger Bernt, and Michael Twaddle, eds. *Christian Missionaries and the State in the Third World.* Athens: Ohio University Press, 2002.

Hansen, Karen Tranberg, ed. *African Encounters with Domesticity.* New Brunswick, N.J.: Rutgers University Press, 1992.

Hardy, Georges. "L'enseignement aux indigènes dans les possessions françaises d'Afrique." In *L'enseignement aux indigènes.* Brussels: Institut Colonial International, 1931.

Harms, Robert W. *River of Wealth, River of Sorrow: The Central Zaire Basin in the Era of the Slave and Ivory Trade, 1500–1891.* New Haven, Conn.: Yale University Press, 1981.

Hastings, Adrian. *African Catholicism.* London: SCM Press, 1989.

———. *The Church in Africa 1450–1950.* Oxford: Clarendon Press, 1994.

———. "Were Women a Special Case?" In *Women and Missions,* ed. Bowie et al., 109–25.

Hay, Margaret Jean. *Queens, Prostitutes and Peasants: Historical Perspectives on African Women 1971–1986.* Boston: African Studies Center, Boston University, 1988.

Hay, Margaret Jean, and Sharon Stichter, eds. *African Women South of the Sahara.* 2nd ed. Harlow, UK: Longman, 1995.

Headrick, Rita. *Colonialism, Health and Illness in French Equatorial Africa, 1885–1935.* Ed. Daniel R. Headrick. Atlanta: African Studies Association, 1994.

———. "The Impact of Colonialism on Health in French Equatorial Africa." Ph.D. thesis, University of Chicago, 1987.

Heintz, Beatrix. "Colonial Ambitions as Blind Passengers: The Case of German Explorers in West-Central Africa (1873–86)." In *A Africa e a instalação do sistem colonial (1885–1930)*. Lisbon: Centro de Estudos de História e Cartografia Antiga, 2000.

Herbert, Jean, and Marie-Cécile de Segonzac, eds. *Anne-Marie Javouhey: Correspondance*. 4 vols. Paris: Cerf, 1994.

Hersak, Dunja. "There Are Many Kongo Worlds: Particularities of Magico-Religious Beliefs among the Vili and Yombe of Congo-Brazzaville." *Africa* 71, no. 4 (2001): 614–40.

Heywood, Linda, ed. *Central Africa and Cultural Transformations in the American Diaspora*. Cambridge: Cambridge University Press, 2002.

Higgs, Catherine, Barbara A. Moss, and Earline Rae Ferguson, eds. *Stepping Forward: Black Women in Africa and the Americas*. Athens: Ohio University Press, 2002.

Hilton, Anne. "Family and Kinship among the Kongo South of the Zaire River from the Sixteenth to the Nineteenth Centuries." *JAH* 24, no. 2 (1983): 189–206.

———. *The Kingdom of Kongo*. Oxford: Clarendon Press, 1985.

Hinfelaar, Hugo F. *Bemba-Speaking Women of Zambia in a Century of Religious Change (1892–1992)*. Leiden, Neth.: Brill, 1994.

Hinfelaar, Marja. *Respectable and Responsible Women: Methodist and Roman Catholic Women's Organizations in Harare, Zimbabwe (1919–1985)*. Zoetermeer, Neth.: Boeckencentrum, 2001.

Hodgson, Dorothy L. *The Church of Women: Gendered Encounters between Maasai and Missionaries*. Bloomington: Indiana University Press, 2005.

———. "Engendered Encounters: Men of the Church and the 'Church of Women' in Maasailand, Tanzania, 1950–1993." *Comparative Studies in Society and History* 41, no. 4 (1999): 758–83.

———. "Pastoralism, Patriarchy, and History: Changing Gender Relations among Maasai in Tanganyika, 1890–1940." *JAH* 40, no. 1 (1999): 41–66.

Hodgson, Dorothy, and Sheryl A. McCurdy, eds. *"Wicked" Women and the Reconfiguration of Gender in Africa*. Portsmouth, N.H.: Heinemann, 2001

Homet, Marcel. *Congo: terre de souffrances*. Paris: Editions Montaigne, 1934.

Huber, Mary Taylor, and Nancy C. Lutkehaus, eds. *Gendered Missions: Women and Men in Missionary Discourse and Practice*. Ann Arbor: University of Michigan Press, 1999.

Hugon, Anne. Introduction to *Histoire des femmes en situation coloniale: Afrique et Asie, XXe siècle*, ed. Hugon, 5–14.

———. "La redéfinition de la maternité en Gold Coast des années 1920 aux années 1950: projet colonial et réalités locales." In *Histoire des femmes en situation coloniale: Afrique et Asie, XXe siècle*, ed. Hugon, 145–71.

———. "L'historiographie de la maternité en Afrique subsaharienne." *Clio* 21 (2005): 212–29.

———, ed. *Histoire des femmes en situation coloniale: Afrique et Asie, XXe siècle*. Paris: Karthala, 2004.

Hulme, Kathryn. *The Nun's Story*. New York: Little, Brown, 1956.

Hunt, Nancy Rose. *A Colonial Lexicon of Birth Ritual, Medicalization, and Mobility in the Congo*. Durham, N.C.: Duke University Press, 1999.

———. "Domesticity and Colonialism in Belgian Africa: Usumbura's Foyer Social, 1946–1960." *Signs* 15, no. 3 (1990): 447–74.

————. "Le bébé en brousse: European Women, African Birth Spacing and Colonial Intervention in Breast-Feeding in the Belgian Congo." *IJAHS* 21, no. 3 (1988): 401–32.

————. "Noise over Camouflaged Polygamy, Colonial Morality Taxation, and a Woman-Naming Crisis in Belgian Africa." *JAH* 32, no. 2 (1991): 471–94.

————. "Placing African Women's History and Locating Gender." *Social History* 14, no. 3 (1989): 359–79.

————. "'Single Ladies on the Congo': Protestant Missionary Tensions and Voices." *Women's Studies International Forum* 13, no. 4 (1990): 395–403.

Hunt, Nancy Rose, Tessie P. Liu, and Jean Quartaert, eds. *Gendered Colonialisms in African History.* Oxford: Blackwell, 1997.

Isichei, Elizabeth. *A History of Christianity in Africa from Antiquity to the Present.* Grand Rapids, Mich.: Eerdmans, 1995.

————, ed. *Varieties of Christian Experience in Nigeria.* London: Macmillan Press, 1982.

Jadin, Louis. "Essai d'évangélisation du Loango et du Kakongo, 1766–1775." *Zaire* 7 (1953): 1053–65.

Jaffré, R. P. "De Plougastel au Congo." *ASSJC* 23 (1930): 1–3.

James, Wendy. "Matrifocus on African Women." In *Defining Females*, ed. Ardener, 123–45.

James, Wendy, and Douglas Johnson, eds. *Vernacular Christianity: Essays in the Social Anthropology of Religion Presented to Godfrey Lienhardt.* New York: Lilian Barber Press, 1988.

Janzen, John, M. "Ideologies and Institutions in the Pre-colonial History of Equatorial African Therapeutic Systems." *Social Science and Medicines* 13B, no. 4 (1979): 317–26.

————. *Lemba, 1650–1930: A Drum of Affliction in Africa and the New World.* New York: Garland, 1982.

————. *The Quest for Therapy in Lower Zaire.* Berkeley and Los Angeles: University of California Press, 1978.

Janzen, John M., and Wyatt MacGaffey, eds. *An Anthology of Kongo Religion: Primary Texts from Lower Zaire.* Lawrence: University of Kansas, 1974.

Jean-Baptiste, Rachel. "Une ville libre? Marriage, Divorce, and Sexuality in Colonial Libreville, Gabon, 1849–1960." Ph.D. thesis, Stanford University, 2005.

Jeater, Diana. *Marriage, Perversion and Power.* New York: Oxford University Press, 1993.

Johnson-Hanks, Jennifer. *Uncertain Honor: Modern Motherhood in an African Crisis.* Chicago: University of Chicago Press, 2006.

Kanogo, Tabitha. *African Womanhood in colonial Kenya, 1900–1950.* Athens: Ohio University Press, 2005.

Kavuna, S. "Northern Kongo Ancestor Figures." *African Arts* 28, no. 2 (1995): 48–53.

Kinata, Côme. *La formation du clergé indigène au Congo Français, 1875–1960.* Paris: L'Harmattan, 2004.

————. *Les ethnochefferies dans le Bas-Congo français: collaboration et résistance, 1896–1960.* Paris: L'Harmattan, 2001.

Klieman, Kairn A. *"The Pygmies Were Our Compass": Bantu and Batwa in the History of West Central Africa, Early Times to c. 1900 C.E.* Portsmouth, N.H.: Heinemann, 2003.

Kniebiehler, Yvonne, and Régine Goutalier. *La femme au temps des colonies.* Paris: Stock, 1986.

Kollman, Paul V. *The Evangelization of Slaves and Catholic Origins in Eastern Africa.* Maryknoll, N.Y.: Orbis Books, 2005.

Koren, Henry J. *To the Ends of the Earth: A General History of the Congregation of the Holy Ghost.* Pittsburgh: Duquesne University Press, 1983.

Kouvouama, Abel. *La modernité en question.* Paris: Ed Paari, 2001.

Koven, Seth, and Sonya Michel. "Womanly Duties: Maternalist Politics and the Origins of the Welfare States in France, Germany, Great Britain, and the United States, 1880–1920." *American Historical Review* 95, no. 4 (Oct. 1990): 1076–1108.

Kselman, Thomas A. *Miracles and Prophecies: Popular Religion and the Church in Nineteenth Century France.* New Brunswick, N.J.: Rutgers University Press, 1983.

Kupalo, Ancilla. "African Sisters' Congregations: Realities of the Present." In *Christianity in Independent Africa,* ed. Edward Fasholé-Luko et al., 122–35. Bloomington: Indiana University Press, 1978.

Labou Tansi, Sony. *Les sept solitudes de Lorsa Lopez.* Paris: Seuil, 1992.

LaGamma, Alisa, ed. *Eternal Ancestors: The Art of the Central African Reliquary.* New York: Metropolitan Museum of Art, 2007.

Laman, K. E. *Dictionnaire Kikongo-Français.* Brussels: Librairie Falkfils, 1936.

———. *The Kongo.* 4 vols. Uppsala: Studia Ethnographica Upsaliensia, 1953–68.

Landau, Paul S. *The Realm of the Word.* Portsmouth, N.H.: Heinemann, 1995.

Langavant, Odile de. "Les Franciscaines Missionnaires de Marie au Congo." Unpublished, c. 1996.

———. "Les Franciscaines Missionnaires de Marie au Congo-Brazzaville: les débuts à Bondji, 1910–1937." *Mémoire spiritaine* 14 (2001): 128–50.

Langlois, Claude. *Le catholicisme au féminin: les congrégations françaises à supérieure générale au XIX siècle.* 4 vols. Paris: Cerf, 1984.

Langmore, Diane. *Missionary Lives: Papua, 1874–1914.* Honolulu: University of Hawaii, 1989.

Larsen, Deborah. *The Tulip and the Pope.* New York: Alfred A. Knopf, 2005.

Larson, Pier M. "Capacities and Modes of Thinking: Intellectual Engagements and Subaltern Hegemony in the Early History of Malagasy Christianity." *American Historical Review* 102 (1997): 969–1002.

Larsson, Birgitta. *Conversion to Greater Freedom? Women, Church and Social Change in North-Western Tanzania under Colonial Rule.* Stockholm: Almquist and Wiksell, 1991.

La tradition vivante, appelées pour la mission: les Soeurs de Saint-Joseph de Cluny. Paris: Editions CIF, 1985.

Lecuir-Nemo, Geneviève. *Anne-Marie Javouhey: fondatrice de la congregation des Soeurs de Saint-Joseph de Cluny (1779–1851).* Paris: Karthala, 2001.

Lehuard, Raoul. *Art Bakongo: les centres de style.* 2 vols. Arnouville, France: Arts d'Afrique Noire, 1993.

———. *Les Phemba du Mayombe.* Arnouville, France: Arts d'Afrique Noire, 1977.

Le Pape, Marc, and Pierre Salignon, eds. *Une guerre contre les civils: réflexions sur les pratiques humanitaires au Congo-Brazzaville (1998–2000).* Paris: Karthala, 2001.

Les Soeurs de Saint-Joseph de Cluny en Afrique Centrale, 1886–1896. Kinshasa: Imprimerie Saint Paul, 1986.

Lethur, R. *Etude sur le royaume de Loango et le peuple Vili.* Pointe-Noire, 1952. published as *Les Cahiers Ngonge* 2, 1960.

Lindsay, Lisa A., and Stephan F. Miescher, eds. *Men and Masculinities in Modern Africa.* Portsmouth, N.H.: Heinemann, 2003.

Lopes, Henri. *La nouvelle romance.* Yaoundé: Editions CLE, 1980.

———. *Sur l'autre rive.* Paris: Seuil, 1993.

Lorson, Pierre. *Les Soeurs de Ribeauvillé.* Paris: Editions Alsatia, 1946.

Lozi, S. Solange. "Les communautés de base au Congo." *Annales de Notre-Dame du Sacré-Coeur* (Nov. 1978): 235–39.

Lucas, Gérard. "Congo-Brazzaville." In *Church, State, and Education in Africa,* ed. David G. Scanlon, 109–34. New York: Teachers College Press, 1966.

Luig, Ute, and Achim von Oppen, eds. "The Making of African Landscapes." Special issue *Paideuma* 43 (1997): 5–252.

MacGaffey, Wyatt. *Art and Healing of the Bakongo: Commented by Themselves.* Stockholm: Folkens Museum-Etnografiska, 1991.

———. *Custom and Government in the Lower Congo.* Berkeley and Los Angeles: University of California Press, 1970.

———. *Kongo Political Culture: The Conceptual Challenge of the Particular.* Bloomington: Indiana University Press, 2000.

———. "Lineage Structure, Marriage and the Family amongst the Central Bantu." JAH 24, no. 2 (1983): 173–87.

———. *Modern Kongo Prophets: Religion in a Plural Society.* Bloomington: Indiana University Press, 1983.

———. *Religion and Society in Central Africa: The Bakongo of Lower Zaire.* Chicago: Chicago University Press, 1986.

———. "The Religious Commissions of the Bakongo." *Man,* new series 5, no. 1 (March 1970): 27–38.

———. "The West in Congolese Experience." In *Africa and the West: Intellectual Responses to European Culture,* ed. Philip D. Curtin, 49–74. Madison: University of Wisconsin Press, 1972.

MacGaffey, Wyatt, and Michael D. Harris. *Astonishment and Power.* Washington, D.C.: Smithsonian Institution Press, 1993.

Makosso, Sylvain. See under Makosso-Makosso, Sylvain.

Makosso-Makosso, Sylvain. "Le catéchiste africain au XIXème et XXème siécles." *CCAH* 12 (1991): 83–6.

———. "L'église catholique et l'état au Congo de 1960 à nos jours." *Afrique contemporaine* 88 (Nov.–Dec. 1976): 6–11.

———. "Les églises chrétiennes d'Afrique: Quel avenir?" *CCAH* 13 (1993): 71–82.

Maleissye, Marie-Thérèse de. "Femmes en mission: actes de la Xème session du CREDIC à Saint-Fleur." *Editions Lyonnaises d'Arte et d'Histoire* 9 (1991).

———. *Petite vie de Marie de la Passion.* Paris: Desclée de Brouwer, 1996.

Malone, Mary T. *Women and Christianity.* 3 vols. New York: Orbis Books, 2003.

Mann, Kristin. *Marrying Well: Marriage, Status and Social Change among Educated Elite in Colonial Lagos.* Cambridge: Cambridge University Press, 1985.

Manning, Patrick. *Francophone Sub-Saharan Africa, 1880–1985.* Cambridge: Cambridge University Press, 1988.

Marichelle, P. Christophe. *Dictionnaire Vili-français.* Loango: Imprimerie de la Mission, 1902.

———. *Tablettes d'un congolais: St. Marie du Kouilou.* Unpublished. 1909. Published in *Les Missions Catholiques* 42 (1910): 178–79, 190–91, 201–204, 213–15, 225–28.

Marks, Shula, ed. *Not Either an Experimental Doll: The Separate Worlds of Three South African Women.* Bloomington: Indiana University Press, 1987.

Marks, Shula, and Richard Rathbone. "The History of the Family in Africa: Introduction." JAH 24, no. 2 (1983): 145–61.

Marthey, J. "L'oeuvre missionnaire pour la population féminine au Congo." *Revue française d'histoire d'outre-mer* 75 (July 1988): 79–101.

Martin, Phyllis M. "Celebrating the Ordinary: Church, Empire and Gender in the Life of Mère Marie-Michelle Dédié (Senegal, Congo, 1882–1931)." *Gender and History* 16, no. 2 (2004): 289–317.

———. "Contesting Clothes in Colonial Brazzaville." *JAH* 35, no. 3 (1994): 401–26.

———. *The External Trade of the Loango Coast, 1576–1870: The Effects of Changing Commercial Relations on the Vili Kingdom of Loango.* Oxford: Clarendon Press, 1972.

———. "Family Strategies in Nineteenth Century Cabinda." *JAH* 28, no. 1 (1987): 65–86.

———. *Leisure and Society in Colonial Brazzaville.* Cambridge: Cambridge University Press, 1995.

———. "Life and Death, Power and Vulnerability: Everyday Contradictions at the Loango Mission, 1883–1904." *Journal of African Cultural Studies* 1, no. 15 (2002): 61–78.

———. "Power, Cloth, and Currency on the Loango Coast." *African Economic History* 15 (1986): 1–12.

———. "The Violence of Empire." In *History of Central Africa,* ed. Birmingham and Martin, 2:1–26.

Masseguin, Christiane. *L'ombre des palmes: l'oeuvre familiale et missionnaires des Soeurs de Saint-Esprit.* Paris: Editions Spes, 1942.

———. "Pointe-Noire." *Pentecôte* 9 (May–June 1939): 10.

Matokot-Mianzenza, Sidonie. *Viol des femmes dans les conflits armés et thérapie familiales: cas de Congo-Brazzaville.* Paris: L'Harmattan, 2003.

Mavoungou Pambou, René, *Proverbes et dictons du Loango en Afrique centrale: langue, culture et société.* Jouy-le-Moutier, France: Bajag-Meri, 1997.

Maxwell, David, with Ingrid Lawrie, eds. *Christianity and the African Imagination: Essays in Honour of Adrian Hastings.* Leiden, Neth.: Brill, 2002.

Mazouka-Nsika, Joséphine. "Déclaration de la femme à l'occasion de la journée internationale de la femme, le 8 mars 1993." Brazzaville: Ministère du Plan, de l'Economie et de la Prospective, 1993.

Mbembé, J-A. *Afriques indociles: christianisme, pouvoir et état en société postcolonial.* Paris: Karthala, 1988.

M'Bokolo, Elikia. "Comparisons and contrasts in equatorial Africa: Gabon, Congo and the Central African Republic." In *History of Central Africa,* ed. Birmingham and Martin, 3:67–96.

———. "Forces sociales et ideologies dans la décolonization de l'AEF." *JAH* 22, no. 3 (1981): 393–407.

McDannell, Colleen. *Material Christianity: Religion and Popular Culture in America.* New Haven, Conn.: Yale University Press, 1995.

McKittrick, Meredith. *To Dwell Secure: Generation, Christianity, and Colonialism in Ovamboland.* Portsmouth, N.H.: Heinemann, 2002.

Merle, Marcel, ed. *Les églises chrétiennes et la décolonisation.* Paris: Presses de la fondation nationale des sciences politiques, 1967.

Merolla da Sorrento, P. Jerôme. "A Voyage to Congo and Several Other Countries in Southern Africa (1682)." In *A Collection of Voyages and Travels,* compiled by Awnsham and John Churchill, 1:595–686. London: J. Walthoe, 1732.

Mianda, Gertrude. "Colonialism, Education, and Gender Relations in the Belgian Congo: The Évolué Case." In *Women in African Colonial Histories,* ed. Allman, Geiger, and Musisi, 144–63.

Michel, Marc. *La mission Marchand, 1895–1899.* Paris: Mouton, 1972.

Miller, Joseph C. "Central Africa during the Era of the Slave Trade, c. 1690s–1850s." In *Central Africa and Cultural Transformations in the American Diaspora,* ed. Heywood, 21–69.

———. *Way of Death: Merchant Capitalism and the Angolan Slave Trade, 1730–1830.* Madison: University of Wisconsin Press, 1988.

Moll, Colonel. *Une âme de colonial: lettres du Lieutenant-Colonel Moll*. Paris: Emile-Paul, 1912.

Moore, Henrietta L., and Megan Vaughan. *Cutting Down Trees: Gender, Nutrition, and Agricultural Change in the Northern Province of Zambia, 1890–1990*. Portsmouth, N.H.: Heinemann, 1994.

Moorman, Marissa. *Intonation: A Social History of Music and Nation, Luanda, Angola, 1945–Recent Days*. Athens: Ohio University Press, 2008.

Morier-Genoud, Eric, and Didier Péclard, eds. "Catholicism in Southern Africa." Special issue *Le fait missionaire* 14 (July 2004).

Moss, Barbara A. "'And the Bones Come Together': Women's Religious Expectations in Southern Africa, c. 1900–1945." *Journal of Religious History* 23, no. 1 (Feb. 1999): 108–27.

———. "Mai Chaza and the Politics of Motherhood in Colonial Zimbabwe." In *Stepping Forward*, ed. Higgs, Moss, and Ferguson, 143–57.

Mouyeke, Pierre. "L'oeuvre sociale des missionnaires catholiques dans la société Bakongo au Congo Français, 1880–1930." Mémoire, EHESS, Paris: 1976.

Mudimbe, V. Y. *The Invention of Africa: Gnosis, Philosophy, and the Order of Knowledge*. Bloomington: Indiana University Press, 1988.

Musisi, Nakanyike. "The Politics of Perception or Perception as Politics: Colonial and Missionary Representations of Baganda Women, 1900–1945." In *East African Expressions of Christianity*, ed. Spear and Kimambo, 95–115.

Naber, S. P. H., ed. *Samuel Brun's Schiffarten (1624)*. The Hague: M. Nijhoff, 1913.

N'Diaye, Jean-Pierre. "Prudence dans la révolution: une interview du président Marien N'Gouabi recueillie à Brazzaville." *Jeune afrique* 710–11 (Aug. 1974): 32–34.

Ndinga-Mbo, Abraham. *Pour une histoire du Congo-Brazzaville: méthodologie et réflexions*. Paris: L'Harmattan, 2004.

Ndjimbe-Tshiende. "L'initiation 'kumbi' chez les Woyo du Zaire: ébauche d'interprétation philosophique." *Zaire-Afrique* 18e année, 128 (Oct. 1978): 473–84.

Ngoïe Ngalla, Dominique. *Les Kongo de la vallée du Niari: origines et migrations XIII–XIXe siècles*. Brazzaville: Les Editions CELMAA, 1982.

Ngolongolo, Appolonaire. *L'assassinat de Marien Ngouabi ou l'histoire d'un pays ensanglanté*. Vincennes: AutoEdition, 1988.

Ngouabi, Marien. *Vers la construction d'une société socialiste en Afrique*. Paris: Présence Africaine, 1975.

Nooter Roberts, Mary. "Imagining Women in African Art: Selected Sculptures from Los Angeles Collections." In *Body Politics: The Female Image in Luba Art and the Sculpture of Alison Saar*, ed. Mary Nooter Roberts and Alison Saar, 62–77. Los Angeles: UCLA Fowler Museum, 2000.

———. "Luba Arts and Polity: Creating Power in a Central African Kingdom." Ph.D. thesis, Columbia University, 1991.

Nord, Philip. "Catholic Culture in Interwar France." *French Politics, Culture, and Society* 21, no. 3 (2003): 1–20.

O'Barr, Jean, Deborah Pope, and Mary Wyer, eds. *Ties That Bind: Essays on Mothering and Patriarchy*. Chicago: Chicago University Press, 1990.

Obenga, Théophile. *L'histoire sanglante de Congo-Brazzaville (1959–1997)*. Paris: Présence Africaine, 1999.

———. "Naissance et puberté en pays kongo au XVIIe siècle." *CCAH* 9 (1984): 19–30.

Oboa, Josephine Ambiera. "Le rôle de l'épouse." In *Femmes africaines*, 72–81. Paris: Les Editions du Centurion (1959).

O'Deyé, Michèle. *Les associations en villes africaines: Dakar-Brazzaville*. Paris: L'Harmattan, 1985.

O'Hara, Joseph M. *The Laws of Marriage Simply Explained according to the New Code*. Philadelphia: Peter Reilly, 1918.

Okoko-Esseau, Abraham. "The Christian Churches and Democratisation in the Congo." In *The Christian Churches and the Democratisation of Africa*, ed. Gifford, 148–67.

Orsi, Robert A. *The Madonna of 115th Street: Faith and Community in Italian Harlem 1880–1952*. New Haven, Conn.: Yale University Press, 1985.

———. *Thank You St. Jude: Women's Devotion to the Patron Saint of Hopeless Causes*. New Haven, Conn.: Yale University Press, 1996.

Ouabari. "La mort et les pompes funèbres municipales de Brazzaville." *Les Cahiers d'Outre-Mer* 44 (1991): 296–307.

Ouassongo, Olivier. "Les aspects financiers du Vicariat de l'Oubangui." *Mémoire spiritaine* 14 (2001): 113–27.

Oyewùmi, Oyèrónké. "Abiyamo: Theorising African Motherhood." *Jenda: a Journal of Culture and African Women Studies* 4 (2003), http://jendajournal.com.

———. *The Invention of Women: Making African Sense of Western Gender Discourses*. Minneapolis: University of Minnesota Press, 1997.

———, ed. *African Women and Feminism: Reflecting on the Politics of Sisterhood*. Trenton, N.J.: Africa World Press, 2003.

Pagnon, Estelle. "'Une oeuvre inutile?' La scolarisation des filles par les missionnaires catholiques dans le sud-est du Nigéria (1885–1930)." *Clio* 6 (1997): 35–59.

Pannier, Guy. *L'église de Pointe-Noire (Congo Brazzaville): évolution des communautés chrétiennes de 1947–1975*. Paris: Editions Karthala, 1999.

Parpart, Jane L. "'Where Is Your Mother?': Gender, Urban Marriage, and Colonial Discourse on the Zambian Copperbelt, 1924–1945." *IJAHS* 27, no. 2 (1994): 241–71.

Paulme, Denise, ed. *Femmes d'Afrique Noire*. Paris: Mouton, 1960.

Pechuël-Loesche, Eduard. *Volkskunde von Loango*. Stuttgart: Verlag von Strecker und Schröder, 1907.

Peel, J. D. Y. *Religious Encounter and the Making of the Yoruba*. Bloomington: Indiana University Press, 2000.

Pelikan, Jaroslav. *Mary through the Centuries: Her Place in the History of Culture*. New Haven, Conn.: Yale University Press, 1996.

Pelletier, Dennis. *Les catholiques en France depuis 1815*. Paris: La Découverte, 1997.

Pepper, Herbert. *Anthologie de la vie africaine (Moyen-Congo et Gabon)*. Paris: Ducretet-Thomson, 1958 (music collection).

Peters, Pauline E. "Introduction." *Critique of Anthropology* 17, no. 2, special issue on "Revisiting the Puzzle of Matriliny in South-Central Africa" (1997): 125–46.

Peterson, Derek, and Jean Allman. "Introduction: New Directions in the History of Missions in Africa." *Journal of Religious History* 23, no. 1 (1999): 1–7.

Pinçon, Bernard, and Dominique Ngoïe-Ngala. "L'unité culturelle kongo à la fin du XIXe siècle. L'apport des études céramologiques." *CEA* 30, no. 2 (1990): 157–78.

Pouabou, Joseph. "Le peuple Vili ou Loango." *Liaison* 58 (July–Aug. 1957): 50–53, 59–60.

Pourtier, Roland. "1997: les raisons d'une guerre 'incivile'." *Afrique contemporaine* 186 (April–June, 1998): 7–32.

Proyart, L. B. *Histoire de Loango, Kakongo et autres royaumes d'Afrique*. Paris: C. P. Berton, 1776.

Rabut, Elisabeth. *Brazza Commissaire Général: le Congo Français, 1886–1897.* Paris: Editions de l'EHESS, 1989.

Radding, Cynthia. *Wandering Peoples: Colonialism, Ethnic Spaces, and Ecological Frontiers in Northwestern Mexico, 1700–1850.* Durham, N.C.: Duke University Press, 1997.

Ranger, Terence. *Dance and Society in Eastern Africa, 1890–1970: The Beni Ngoma.* London: Heinemann, 1975.

———. "New Approaches to the History of Mission Christianity." In *African Historiography,* ed. Falola, 180–94.

———. "Religious Movements and Politics in Sub-Saharan Africa." *African Studies Review* 29 (1986): 1–69.

———. "Taking Hold of the Land: Holy Places and Pilgrimages in Twentieth Century Zimbabwe." *Past and Present* 117 (1987): 158–94.

Ranger, T. O., and John Waller, eds. *Themes in the Christian History of Central Africa.* Berkeley and Los Angeles: University of California Press, 1975.

Raoul-Matingou, Emilienne. "Activités des femmes en milieu urbain: le cas de Brazzaville." Thèse de 3e cycle, Université des Sciences et Techniques de Lille, 1982.

Raponda-Walker, André, and Roger Sillans. *Rites et croyances des peuples du Gabon: Essai sur les pratiques religieuses d'autrefois et d'aujourd'hui.* Paris: Présence Africaine, 1962.

Règle de la Congrégation des Soeurs de Saint-Joseph de Cluny. Rome: Imprimerie de Bernardo Morini, 1853.

Reste, Joseph-François. *Action politique, économique et sociale en Afrique Equatoriale Française, 1936–1938.* Brazzaville: Imprimerie Officielle, 1938.

Retel-Laurentin, Anne. *Infécondité en Afrique noire: maladies et conséquences sociales.* Paris: Masson, 1974.

Rey, Pierre-Philippe. *Colonialisme, néo-colonialisme, et transition au capitalisme: exemple de la "Comilogue" au Congo-Brazzaville.* Paris: Maspero, 1971.

Rich, Jeremy. "Maurice Briault, André Raponde Walker and the Value of Missionary Anthropology in Colonial Gabon." *Le fait missionnaire* 19 (Dec. 2006).

———. *A Workman Is Worthy of His Meat: Food and Colonialism in the Gabon Estuary.* Lincoln: University of Nebraska Press, 2007.

Richards, Audrey. "Some Types of Family Structures amongst the Central Bantu." In *African Systems of Kinship and Marriage,* ed. A. R. Radcliffe-Brown and D. Forde, 297–351. London: Oxford University Press, 1950.

Roberts, Richard. "Representation, Structure, and Agency: Divorce in the French Soudan during the Early Twentieth Century." *JAH* 40, no. 3 (1999): 389–410.

Robertson, Claire. "Women's Education and Class Formation in Africa, 1950–1980." In *Women and Class in Africa,* ed. Claire Robertson and Iris Berger, 92–113. New York: 1986.

Robertson, Claire C., and Martin A. Klein, eds. *Women and Slavery in Africa.* Madison: University of Wisconsin Press, 1983.

Sacre-Coeur, Soeur Marie-André du. *La femme noire en Afrique Occidentale.* Paris: Payot, 1939.

Samarin, William J. *The Black Man's Burden: African Colonial Labor on the Congo and Ubangi Rivers.* Boulder, Colo.: Westview Press, 1989.

Sanneh, Lamin O. *Translating the Message: The Missionary Impact on Culture.* Maryknoll, N.J.: Orbis, 1989.

Sautter, Gilles. *De l'Atlantique au fleuve Congo: une géographie du sous- peuplement.* 2 vols. Paris: Mouton, 1966.

———. "Notes sur la construction du chemin de fer Congo-Océan (1921–1934)." *CEA* 7 (1967): 219–300.

Schmidt, Elizabeth. *Mobilizing the Masses: Gender, Ethnicity, and Class in the Nationalist Movement in Guinea, 1939–1958*. Portsmouth, N.H.: Heinemann, 2005.

———. *Peasants, Traders, and Wives: Shona Women in the History of Zimbabwe, 1870–1939*. Portsmouth, N.H.: Heinemann, 1992.

Schrag, Norm. "Boma and the Lower Zaire: A Socio-Economic Study of a Kongo Trading Community, 1785–1885." Ph.D. thesis, Indiana University, 1985.

Schwartz, Stuart B., ed. *Implicit Understandings: Observing, Reporting, and Reflecting on the Encounters between Europeans and Other Peoples in the Early Modern Era*. Cambridge: Cambridge University Press, 1994.

Scott, James C. *Weapons of the Weak: Everyday Forms of Peasant Resistance*. New Haven, Conn.: Yale University Press, 1985.

Scully, Pamela. *Liberating the Family? Gender and British Slave Emancipation in the Rural Western Cape, South Africa, 1823–1853*. Portsmouth, N.H.: Heinemann, 1997.

Sheldon, Kathleen. "I Studied with the Nuns, Learning to Make Blouses: Gender Ideology and Colonial Education in Mozambique." *IJAHS* 31, no. 3 (1998): 595–625.

———. *Historical Dictionary of Women in Sub-Saharan Africa*. Lanham, Md.: Scarecrow Press, 2005.

Sieber, Roy, and Roslyn Adele Walker. *African Art in the Cycle of Life*. Washington, D.C.: Smithsonian Institution Press, 1987.

Simone, AbdouMaliq. *For the City Yet to Come: Changing African Life in Four Cities*. Durham, N.C.: Duke University Press, 2004

Sinda, Martial. *Le messianisme congolais et ses incidences politiques*. Paris: Payot, 1972.

Skard, Torild. *Continent of Mothers, Continent of Hope: Understanding and Promoting Development in Africa Today*. London: Zed Books, 2003.

Slade, Ruth. *English-Speaking Missions in the Congo Independent State, 1878–1908*. Brussels: Académie Royale des Sciences Coloniales, 1959.

Smythe, Kathleen R. "African Women and White Sisters at the Karema Mission Station, 1894–1920." *Journal of Women's History* 19, no. 2 (2007): 59–84.

———. "The Creation of a Catholic Fipa Society: Conversion in Nkansi District, Ufipa." In *East African Expressions of Christianity*, ed. Spears and Kimambo, 129–49.

———. *Fipa Families: Reproduction and Catholic Evangelization in Nkansi, Ufipa, 1880–1960*. Portsmouth, N.H.: Heinemann, 2006.

Soiri, Ini. *The Radical Motherhood: Namibian Women's Independence Struggle*. Uppsala: Nordiska Afrikainstitutet, 1996

Soret, Marcel. *Démographie et problèmes urbains en AEF: Poto-Poto-Bacongo-Dolisie*. Montpellier: Imprimerie Chanté, 1954.

———. *Les Kongo Nord-Occidentaux*. Paris: Presses Universitaires de France: 1959.

Spear, Thomas, and Isaac N. Kimambo, eds. *East African Expressions of Christianity*. Athens: Ohio University Press, 1999.

Stanley, Brian, ed. *Missions, Nationalism, and the End of Empire*. Grand Rapids, Mich.: Eerdmans, 2003.

Staunton, Irene, ed. *Mothers of the Revolution: The War Experience of Thirty Zimbabwean Women*. Bloomington: Indiana University Press, 1990.

Stoler, Ann L. "Rethinking Colonial Categories: European Communities and the Boundaries of Rule." *Comparative Studies in Society and History* 31, no. 1 (1989): 134–61.

———. "Sexual Affronts and Racial Frontiers: European Identities and the Cultural Politics of Exclusion in Colonial Southeast Asia." *Comparative Studies in Society and History* 34, no. 3 (1992): 514–51.

―――. "Making Empire Respectable: The Politics of Race and Sexual Morality in Twentieth-Century Colonial Cultures." In *Situated Lives: Gender and Culture in Everyday Life*, ed. Louise Lamphere, Helena Ragoné, and Patricia Zavella, 373–99. New York: Routledge, 1997. Reprint of an article published in *American Ethnologist* 16, no. 4, (Nov. 1989): 634–60.

Stone, Judith F. "Anticlericals and *Bonnes Soeurs:* The Rhetoric of the 1901 Law of Associations." *French Historical Studies* 23 (2000): 103–28.

Strobel, Margaret. "African Women: A Review." *Signs* 8, no. 1 (1982): 109–31.

―――. *Muslim Women in Mombasa, 1890–1975.* New Haven, Conn.: Yale University Press, 1979.

Summers, Carol. *Colonial Lessons: Africans' Education in Southern Rhodesia, 1918–1935.* Portsmouth, N.H.: Heinemann, 2002.

―――. "Intimate Colonialism: The Imperial Production of Reproduction in Uganda, 1907–25." *Signs* 16 (1991): 787–807.

Tenga, Nakazael, and Chris Maina Peter. "The Right to Organise as Mother of All Rights: The Experience of Women in Tanzania." *Journal of Modern African Studies* 341 (1996): 143–62.

Thomas, Lynn M. *Politics of the Womb: Women, Reproduction, and the State in Kenya.* Berkeley and Los Angeles: University of California Press, 2003.

Thomas, Samuel S. "Transforming the Gospel of Domesticity: Luhya Girls and the Friends Africa Mission, 1917–1926." *African Studies Review* 43, no. 2 (2000): 1–27.

Thompson, Robert F., and Joseph Cornet. *Four Moments of the Sun: Kongo Art in Two Worlds.* Washington, D.C.: National Gallery of Art, 1981.

Thornton, John K. "The Development of an African Catholic Church in the Kingdom of Kongo, 1491–1750." *JAH* 25, no. 2 (1984): 147–67.

―――. "Elite Women in the Kingdom of Kongo: Historical Perspectives on Women's Political Power." *JAH* 47, no. 3 (2006): 437–60.

―――. *The Kingdom of Kongo: Civil War and Transition, 1641–1718.* Madison: University of Wisconsin Press, 1983.

―――. *The Kongolese Saint Anthony: Dona Beatriz Kimpa Vita and the Antonian Movement, 1684–1706.* Cambridge: Cambridge University Press, 1998.

―――. "The Origins and Early History of the Kingdom of Kongo, c. 1350–1550." *IJAHS* 34, no. 1 (2001): 89–120.

―――. "Religious and Ceremonial Life in the Kongo and Mbundu Areas, 1500–1700." In *Central Africa and Cultural Transformations in the American Diaspora,* ed. Heywood, 71–90.

Tonda, Joseph. "Enjeux du deuil et négociation des rapports sociaux de sexe au Congo." *CEA* 157, no. 40 (2000): 5–24.

―――. *La guérison divine en African centrale (Congo, Gabon).* Paris: Karthala, 2002.

―――. *Le souverain moderne: le corps du pouvoir en Afrique Centrale (Congo, Gabon).* Paris: Karthala, 2005.

Tostensen, Arne, Inge Tvedten, and Mariken Vaa, eds. *Associational Life in African Cities: Popular Responses to the Urban Crises.* Uppsala: Nordiska Afrikainstitutet, 2001.

Troillot, Michel-Rolph. *Silencing the Past.* Boston: Beacon, 1995.

Turner, Victor. *The Drums of Affliction.* London: Oxford University Press, 1968.

Urban-Mead, Wendy. "'Girls of the Gate': Questions of Purity and Piety at Mtshabezi Girls' Primary Boarding School in Colonial Zimbabwe, 1908–1940." *Le fait missionnaire* 11 (Sept. 2001): 77–98.

Uzès, Duchesse d'. *Le voyage de mon fils au Congo*. Paris: Librairie Plon, 1894.

Van Overbergh, Cyrille. *Les Mayombe*. Brussels: A. De Wit, 1907.

Vansina, Jan. *Art History in Africa*. Harlow, UK: Longman, 1984.

———. *Paths in the Rainforest: Toward a History of Political Tradition in Equatorial Africa*. Madison: University of Wisconsin Press, 1990.

———. *The Tio Kingdom of the Middle Kongo, 1880–1892*. London: Oxford University Press, 1973.

Van Wing, J. *Etudes Bakongo: sociologie-religion et magie*. 2nd ed. Brussels: Desclée de Brouwer, 1959.

———. "Les danses Bakongo." *Congo: Revue générale de la Colonie Belge* 2, no. 2 (July 1937): 121–28.

Vassal, Gabrielle M. *Life in French Congo*. London: T. Fisher Unwin, 1925.

Vaughan, Megan. *Curing Their Ills: Colonial Power and African Illness*. Stanford, Calif.: Stanford University Press, 1991.

Vaz, José Martins. *No mundo dos Cabindas: estudo etnográfico*. Lisbon: Editorial L.I.A.M., 1970.

Veistroffer, Albert. *Vingt ans dans la brousse africaine: souvenirs d'un ancien membre de la Mission Savorgnan de Brazza dans l'Ouest africain, 1881–1903*. Lille, France: Mercure de Flandre, 1931.

Vellut, Jean-Luc. "Itinéraires croisées de la modernité Congo Belge, 1920–1950." *Cahiers Africains/Afrika Studies* 43/44 (2000): 7–13.

———. "L'économie internationale des côtes de Guinée Inférieure au XIXe siècle." In *Reunião internacional de história de Africa: Relação Europa-Africa no 3.o quartel do Séc. XIX*. Lisbon: Instituto de Investigaçao Cientifica e Tropical, 1989: 135–49.

———. "Préface: Itinéraires et vies des objets dans les rencontres Afrique-Europe." In *Makamba ya ndocki: l'art africain au travers des pratiques de sorciers et devins*. Namur, Belgium: Musée africain de Namur, 2001.

———. "Quelle profondeur historique pour l'image de la Vierge Marie au Congo?" *CJAS* 33, no. 2/3 (1999): 530–47.

Vennetier, Pierre. *Pointe-Noire et la façade maritime du Congo-Brazzaville*. Paris: ORSTOM, 1968.

———, ed. *Atlas de la République Populaire du Congo*. Paris: Editions Jeune Afrique, 1977.

Verswijver, G., et al., eds. *Treasures from the Africa-Museum*. Tervuren, Belgium: Royal Museum for Central Africa, 1995.

———. *Masterpieces from Central Africa*. Munich: Prestel, 1996.

Vincent, Jeanne-Françoise. *Femmes africaines en milieu urbain*. Paris: ORSTOM, 1966.

———. "Le mouvement Croix-Koma, une nouvelle forme de lutte contre la sorcellerie en pays Kongo." *CEA* 24, 6, no. 4 (1966): 527–63.

Voulgré, Joseph. *Le Congo Français: Le Loango et la vallée du Kouilou*. Paris: Librairie Africaine et Coloniale, 1897.

Wagret, Jean-Michel. *Histoire et sociologie politiques de la République du Congo (Brazzaville)*. Paris: Librairie Générale de Droit de Jurisprudence, 1963.

Walker, Cherryl. "Conceptualising Motherhood in Twentieth Century South Africa." *JSAS* 21, no. 3 (1995): 417–37.

Weinrich, Sister Mary Aquina. "An Aspect of the Development of the Religious Life in Rhodesia." In *Themes in the History of Central Africa*, ed. Ranger and Weller, 218–37.

Wells, Julia. "Why Women Rebel: A Comparative Study of South African Women's Resistance in Bloemfontein (1913) and Johannesburg (1958)." *JSAS* 10, no. 1 (1983): 55–70.

Werbner, Richard, and Terence Ranger, eds. *Postcolonial Identities in Africa*. London: Zed Books, 1996.

White, Luise. *The Comforts of Home: Prostitution in Colonial Nairobi*. Chicago: University of Chicago Press, 1990.

———. "Separating the Men from the Boys: Constructs of Gender, Sexuality and Tension in Central Kenya, 1939–1959." *IJAHS* 23, no. 1 (1990): 1–25.

White, Owen. *Children of the French Empire: Miscegenation and Colonial Society in French West Africa, 1895–1960*. Oxford: Clarendon Press, 1999.

Widman, Ragnar. *The Niombo Cult among the Babwende*. Stockholm: Etnografiska Museet, 1967.

Williams, Sylvia H. "A Yombe Maternity: A Case Study." In *Speeches Given by Sylvia H. Williams, 1935–1966*. Washington, D.C.: Smithsonian Institution, 1996.

Witte, Jehan de. *Un explorateur et un apôtre du Congo-Français: Monseigneur Augouard*. Paris: Emile-Paul Frères, 1924.

Witwicki, Robert. *Marie et l'évangélisation du Congo*. 3 vols. Brazzaville: Centre Chaminade, 1995.

Wright, Marcia. *Strategies of Slaves and Women: Life-Stories from East/Central Africa*. New York: Lillian Barber Press, 1993.

Yates, Barbara A. "Colonialism, Education, and Work: Sex Differentiation in Colonial Zaire." In *Women and Work in Africa*, ed. Bay, 127–52.

Yengo, Patrice. *Identité et démocratie en Afrique et ailleurs*. Paris: L'Harmattan, 1997.

———. *La guerre civile du Congo-Brazzaville, 1993–2002: "chacun aura sa part."* Paris: Karthala, 2005.

———. "Un recours endémique à la violence." *Afrique contemporaine* 186 (April–June, 1998): 33–45.

Zimmerman, Emile. *Mémoire d'un Congolais, 1896–1941*. Madingou: Imprimerie de la Mission, 1941.

Index

Phyllis M. Martin is Professor Emeritus of History at Indiana University. She is editor (with Patrick O'Meara) of *Africa,* editor (with David Birmingham) of *History of Central Africa* (three volumes), and author of *The External Trade of the Loango Coast, 1576–1870* and *Leisure and Society in Colonial Brazzaville.*